The Complete Fashion Sourcebook

John Peacock

The Complete Fashion Sourcebook

with over 2,000 duotone and black-and-white line illustrations

For Henrietta Webb, Janet Powell, Ray Holman, Marion James, Sandy Richards, Catherine Lamb and Jenny Shircore

First published in 2005 in paperback in the United States of America by
Thames & Hudson Inc., 500 Fifth Avenue, New York, New York 10110

thamesandhudsonusa.com

Fashion Sourcebooks previously published as single volumes: *The 1920s*, 1997; *The 1930s*, 1997; *The 1940s*, 1998; *The 1950s*, 1997; *The 1960s*, 1998; *The 1970s*, 1997; *The 1980s*, 1998.

Library of Congress Catalog Card Number 2005923409

ISBN-13: 978-0-500-28572-5
ISBN-10: 0-500-28572-1

Printed and bound in Singapore by Star Standard Industries (Pte) Ltd

Contents

Preface

This collection of drawings shows the radical, and often exhilarating, changes in fashion styles throughout the modern period. From the emancipated 1920s to the status-conscious 1980s, fashions have modified in line with changing times and mores, affected by social conventions, shifts in economic prosperity and advances in techniques of mechanization. Men's fashion has moved more slowly than women's, and is often concerned with nuances of style, but the changes perceptible in women's fashion have been astonishingly wide-ranging.

This Sourcebook is divided into seven parts, each representing a decade. Each decade contains sections on Day Wear, Evening Wear, Sports and Leisure Wear, Underwear and Negligee, Wedding Wear and Accessories, providing a rounded insight into modern developments and trends.

Charts at the back of the book reveal at a glance the evolution of the fashionable silhouette throughout the decades. Brief biographies and histories of the most important international designers and couture houses are also included. Finally, a select bibliography is provided to assist those who may wish to take their studies further.

The 1920s

Introduction • The 1920s

The fashionable woman of the 1920s wanted to look youthful, like an androgynous schoolboy or a pubescent schoolgirl, flat-chested and hipless; at the same time she wanted independence and freedom. These factors forced changes in fashion. Even a casual browse through the pages of this Sourcebook will reveal just how slowly such changes took place year by year between 1920 and 1929, and just how subtle they were. Yet the result was radical. The corseted woman of the previous decade, with her hobble skirts and huge hats, looks as if she has come from another world when compared to the 'modern' woman of the second half of the 1920s. The 'designed' proportions of what was considered to be the perfect, fashionable 1920s female body evolved from the elaborately trimmed dress with its high waist position and ankle-length skirt, at the beginning of the period, to the simple, sparsely decorated, shapeless tube with a hip-level 'waistline' and a skirt barely covering the knees, at the decade's end.

At the same time new fabrics became available, such as kasha, a soft and extremely supple flannel made from a mixture of wool and goat hair; 'art' silk, an easily washed artificial material made from rayon; flamingo, a silk and wool mix with the fashionable crêpe look; satin doubleface, with satin on one side and moiré on the other; and wool, silk and cotton jersey, a fine, machine-knitted fabric previously used only for underwear. Coloured and patterned, this last fabric became a firm favourite of Coco Chanel, and all these innovative materials stimulated thinking about new ways of exploiting their particular qualities and characters. Early use of bias-cutting can clearly be seen in the later pages of this section of the Sourcebook.

As far as men's fashions were concerned, developments in style, colour and cut during the 1920s were painfully slow. In consequence, they require fewer illustrations – the minor differences which do occur in the basic trends have been shown, on average, with one example for each page.

In the main, the fashions I have illustrated are such as would have been worn by the middle or upper-middle classes and by people, who, while not being 'dedicated followers of fashion', would have had a keen interest in the latest styles.

The sources from which I have drawn – chiefly from Great Britain, North America and France – include contemporary magazines, journals and catalogues; museum collections; original photographs, and my own costume collection.

This section of the Sourcebook is divided into ten parts, each of which includes four subdivisions covering Day Wear, Evening Wear (alternately, on two occasions, Wedding Wear), Sports and Leisure Wear, and a section on either Underwear or Accessories. Following the main illustrations are ten pages of schematic drawings accompanied by detailed notes about each example, giving particulars of colour, fabric, cut and trimming, as well as other useful information.

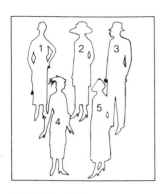
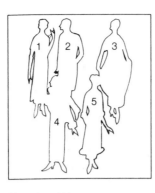
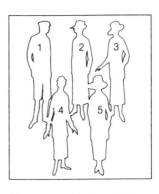

1920 Day Wear

1 Mid-calf-length beige wool dress, high waist marked with brown wool belt, matching binding on scooped neckline, hems of long dolman sleeves, shaped yoke seam, edges of hip-level patch pockets and fringing on floating panels. Silk stockings. Brown leather shoes with buckle trim, pointed toes, louis heels. **2** Pale blue two-piece suit: long edge-to-edge high-waisted jacket, buttoned belt, small collar, wide lapels and front edges bound with light brown silk to match flaps on large patch pockets, button trim from wrist to elbow on tight inset sleeves; narrow mid-calf-length skirt. Hip-length cream silk blouse with low square neckline and sham front-button opening. Hat with large crown and wide brim covered with cream silk, trimmed with brown silk threaded through buckle. Leather button boots with suede uppers, pointed toes, louis heels. **3** Dark blue wool two-piece suit: double-breasted fitted jacket, wide lapels, angled flap pockets, cuffed sleeves; narrow ankle-length trousers with turn-ups. Striped collar-attached shirt. Striped silk tie. Black trilby with wide band. Leather gloves. **4** High-waisted pale green crêpe-de-chine dress, square neckline trimmed with green lace and velvet ribbon to match trim on belt and hems of three-tier skirt, inset sleeves with button trim from wrist to elbow. Green hat with narrow brim, green and cream feather trim. Green leather shoes with cross-over straps, pointed toes, louis heels. **5** Mid-calf-length light brown waterproofed cotton raincoat, fly fastening from under high buckled belt, large collar and wide lapels, vertical welt pockets, inset sleeves with deep armholes, buckle-and-strap trim. Hat with upturned brim, fabric flower trim. Leather shoes with high tongues and buckle trim, pointed toes, louis heels.

Evening Wear

1 Ankle-length violet silk dress with wide scooped neckline, lilac silk-chiffon overdress, high waist marked with wide band of fine silver lace, matching hems of short dolman sleeves and bordering hem of wrapover skirt. Long grey kid gloves. Long bead necklace. Silver leather shoes, rosette trim, pointed toes, louis heels. **2** Double-breasted black wool tailcoat, worn open, small collar, wide silk lapels, matching self-fabric buttons, narrow trousers with no turn-ups. Single-breasted white piqué waistcoat with shawl collar. White shirt with wing collar. White bow-tie. White leather gloves. Black patent-leather pumps, petersham ribbon bow trim. **3** Ankle-length yellow and gold patterned silk-velvet dress, low neckline, high waist position and hemline trimmed with ruched self-fabric; pale yellow silk-chiffon overdress, long dolman sleeves with frilled hems, full skirt with uneven hemline. Gold satin shoes, bow trim, pointed toes, louis heels. **4** Ankle-length double-breasted printed silk-velvet coat, single wrapover fastening, shawl collar faced with satin and trimmed with fox fur which matches cuffs of wide dolman sleeves. Kid gloves. Fine leather shoes trimmed with silver and jet buckles. **5** Ankle-length black crêpe-de-chine dress with narrow shoulder straps; black silk-chiffon overdress, low scooped neckline, high waist position marked with pleated self-fabric belt, trimmed with bunch of silk violets, elbow-length inset sleeves trimmed with curled ostrich feathers to match hem of gathered mid-calf-length skirt. Black satin shoes trimmed with tiny jet buckles, pointed toes, louis heels.

Sports and Leisure Wear

1 Golf. Three-piece brown and cream checked wool suit: fitted single-breasted jacket, flap pockets, single breast pocket, wide lapels; collarless single-breasted waistcoat; knee-length plus-fours. Collar-attached shirt. Wool tweed tie. Brown wool tweed cap. Leather gloves. Long wool socks with turned-down patterned cuffs. Brown leather brogues with fringed tongues. **2** Country wear. Two-piece green and black wool-tweed suit: long single-breasted jacket with pleated side panels, wide lapels, black velvet collar, matching sleeve cuffs, half-belt and self-fabric buttons; ankle-length skirt with pleated side panels. Brown felt hat, large crown with deep band, wide brim turned up at back. Lace-up shoes, pointed toes, stacked heels. **3** Tennis. Long knitted-silk blouse, wide pleated belt, pointed peter-pan collar, shirt sleeves with wide cuffs, single breast patch pocket, fancy stitching to match hems. Mid-calf-length pleated wool skirt. Straw hat with large crown and wide flat brim. Lace-up white canvas shoes. **4** Golf. Three-piece grey wool-tweed suit: long jacket with mock double-breasted fastening, high waist-belt, hip-level pockets, tight inset sleeves with deep cuffs; collarless single-breasted waistcoat; narrow mid-calf-length skirt, hand-stitched edges and detail. Soft wool hat with gathered crown and narrow upturned brim trimmed with braid. Two-tone leather shoes, fringed tongues, pointed toes, flat heels. **5** Sports wear. Hip-length single-breasted wool-tweed jacket, cuffed raglan sleeves, narrow shawl collar, tie-belt and large patch pockets. Straight mid-calf-length beige wool skirt. Collar-attached shirt. Wool-tweed tie. Hat with large crown and wide brim, large bow trim. Leather shoes with bar straps.

Underwear and Negligee

1 Hip-length embroidered pink cotton-satin corset, light boning and top-stitching, front hook-and-bar fastening, back lacing, lace and ribbon trimming, four elasticated suspenders. Fine white cotton chemise with scalloped edges and openwork embroidery, double ribbon shoulder straps. Pale blue velvet house slippers, pointed toes, louis heels. **2** Fine cotton combination chemise and drawers, front opening top to high waist position, fastening with self-fabric buttons, pintuck and lace decoration, double ribbon shoulder straps, drawers gathered from high waist position to knee-level forming frill, pintuck and lace trim. Velvet house shoes trimmed with silk pom-pons. **3** Wrapover knee-length red wool dressing gown, wide quilted red silk shawl collar with corded edge matching deep cuffs of inset sleeves and cuffs of large hip-level patch pockets, cord tie-belt with tasselled ends. Red and grey striped cotton pyjamas. Red leather step-in house slippers. **4** Blue silk nightdress, low square neckline edged with cream lace and coffee-coloured silk ribbon to match hems of wide cap sleeves and inset band above hemline, high waist marked with ribbon belt. Pale blue satin house slippers with rosette trim. **5** Wrapover ankle-length peach-coloured satin dressing gown, deep shawl collar with self-frilled edge and trimmed with re-embroidered lace border which matches deep cuffs of inset sleeves and large hip-level patch pockets, high waist position marked with self-fabric tie-belt with tasselled ends. Embroidered satin mules, pointed toes, low heels.

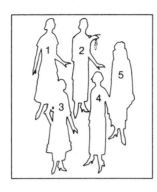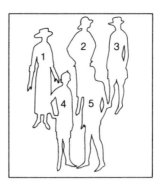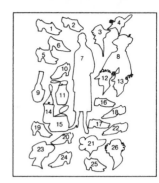

1921 Day Wear

1 Single-breasted mid-calf-length fur coat, fastening with three outsized buttons, large collar over elbow-length cape, inset sleeves with deep cuffs, concealed pockets. Straw hat with wide brim and large crown, satin band and bow trim. Leather shoes, flower rosette trim, pointed toes, louis heels. **2** Double-breasted checked wool-tweed overcoat, inset buttoned belt, wide lapels, narrow inset sleeves, hip-level patch-and-flap pockets, top-stitched edges and detail. Narrow trousers with turn-ups. Brown felt trilby with high crown, brim turned up at back and sides. Leather gloves. Leather lace-up shoes, pointed toecaps. **3** Mid-calf-length double-breasted dark red linen coat, fastening with two outsized plastic buttons which match trim on flared cuffs of inset sleeves; pleated side skirt panel matches sleeve cuffs; side bodice above low waistline trimmed with narrow braid to match sleeves; narrow roll collar. Fox-fur stole. Dark red velvet hat, feather trim. Leather gloves. Leather shoes. **4** Two-piece cream linen suit: hip-length single-breasted jacket, fastening with large buttons which match trim on hem of narrow inset sleeves and on decorative side panel seams above hemline, shaped shawl collar; mid-calf-length straight skirt. Collarless single-breasted striped linen waistcoat. Brown straw hat, large brim swept up on one side, ribbon trim. Long-handled parasol. Brown leather shoes trimmed with round buckles. **5** Pale blue silk dress, low round neckline, mid-calf-length gathered skirt, shorter overdress in self-fabric with open front, strap-and-button fastening, draped self-fabric belt, narrow inset sleeves trimmed at wrist with dark blue lace to match small collar, hem of overskirt and bodice of underdress. Dark blue straw hat trimmed with small plums. Long-handled parasol. Shoes with wide bar strap.

Evening Wear

1 Ankle-length sleeveless yellow silk dress, wide neckline, deep cape collar, embroidered edge repeated on hemline of gathered skirt and tiered side panels, unfitted hip-length bodice, draped self-fabric belt decorated with bunch of silk primroses. Yellow satin shoes trimmed with small round buckles, pointed toes, louis heels. **2** Asymmetric green lace bodice with low V-shaped neckline, asymmetric ankle-length green crêpe-de-chine dress draped from shoulder to opposite hip, jewelled clip, waterfall of self-fabric and green lace to below hemline of straight skirt. Silver kid shoes trimmed with jewelled buckles. **3** Ankle-length grey crêpe-de-chine dress, unfitted hip-length bodice, straight skirt, wide neckline trimmed with grey lace border to match motifs above hemline of mid-calf-length gathered silk-chiffon overskirt, elbow-length inset sleeves with double row of padded and gathered binding which matches three rows on overskirt. Silver kid shoes, large tongues trimmed with tiny silver buckles. **4** Unfitted ankle-length black silk-georgette overdress, wide shaped neckline and head of sleeves embroidered with black glass beads to match border of curved hemline up to hip-level of open sides, low waistline marked by black sequined belt from side to back which matches cuffs of gathered sleeves; black silk-crêpe underdress. Black silk shoes. **5** Hip-length dark red watered-silk cape with high ruched buttoned collar, elbow-length shaped yoke, uneven hemline trimmed with frilled black lace. Ankle-length black silk dress; black lace overdress with scalloped hemline. Black silk shoes trimmed with ribbon flowers, pointed toes, louis heels.

Sports and Leisure Wear

1 Tennis. Hip-length cream cotton top, scooped neckline, collar top-stitched in dark blue to match cuffs of three-quarter-length inset sleeves, front panel seams and shaped hemline, embroidered motif on bodice between collar points, blue stiffened silk belt threaded through panel seams, matching self-fabric buttons. Ankle-length box-pleated cream wool skirt. Natural straw hat, large crown with flat top and striped band, wide flat brim. Cream cotton stockings. Cream canvas lace-up shoes. **2** Golf. Hip-length dark green knitted-wool top, pointed collar, strap opening, long inset sleeves with shaped stitched cuffs matching stitched hemline. Ankle-length green tweed skirt, button opening from waist to hem, knife-pleated panels from side front. Dark brown felt hat with large crown, petersham ribbon band, wide flat brim. Brown leather boots laced to mid-calf, pointed toecaps. **3** Riding. Single-breasted mid-thigh-length brown wool coat with flared skirts, inset buttoned belt, wide lapels, tight inset sleeves with stitched cuffs, four patch pockets with buttoned flaps. Beige riding breeches, laced on side seam. Felt hat, large flared crown, petersham band, wide flat brim. Leather gloves. Short lace-up leather boots. Knee-high leather gaiters, strap-and-buckle fastening. **4** Bathing. Two-piece navy and white striped knitted-cotton bathing costume, hip-length top, low square neckline, plain navy collar which matches cuffs of short inset sleeves, buttoned belt, central bodice panel, self-fabric buttons and cuffs of knee-length drawers. Spotted cotton headscarf. Rubber bathing shoes with crossed straps to mid-calf. **5** Bathing. Two-piece sleeveless blue and white striped knitted-cotton bathing costume, hip-length top, low round neckline and armholes bound in plain white cotton to match hems of top and drawers, buttoned opening on shoulder.

Accessories

1 Leather shoes, turned-down tongues with perforated decoration and fringed ends. **2** White kid shoes, button trim, blue heels and toecaps. **3** Straw hat, large crown trimmed with silk, narrow brim trimmed with silk flowers. **4** Fine straw hat, large crown draped with silk, wide brim trimmed with silk violets. **5** Leather shoes, perforated decoration and top-stitching. **6** Two-tone lace-up leather shoes. **7** Dusty-pink crocheted two-piece: hip-length top, large collar with fancy stitching which matches hems of top and inset sleeves, threaded hip-level belt; pleated skirt. **8** Orange scarf with inset bands of dark green, matching fringe. Straw hat with wide upturned brim edged with dark green ribbon, trimmed with silk flowers. **9** Green silk bag, metal frame and fastening, ribbon handle. **10** Shoes, wide bar straps, perforated decoration, matching pointed toes. **11** Black crêpe bag, metal frame and clasp. **12** Brown wool peaked cap. **13** Grey homburg with black petersham band. **14** Two-tone leather bag, personal initials, metal frame and fastening, rouleau handle. **15** Leather bag with flap front, stud fastening, long strap. **16** Lace-up leather shoes with front seamed panel, no toecaps. **17** Tan leather brogues, perforated decoration, shaped toecaps. **18** Leather sandals, T-strap-and-buckle fastening, no toecaps. **19** Black leather shoes, high tongues trimmed with petersham bows. **20** Cream suede shoes, cut-out pattern, strap-and-button fastening. **21** Hat with tall crown, trimmed ribbon band and loops, bound brim. **22** Two-tone brogues in brown and white leather. **23** Straw hat, large crown and wide brim draped with black lace. **24** Lace-up leather brogues, fringed tongues, stacked heels. **25** Cream satin T-strap shoes with open sides. **26** Straw hat, large crown, small brim, chiffon and silk flower trim.

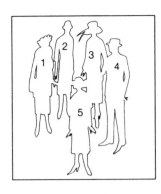
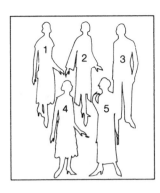
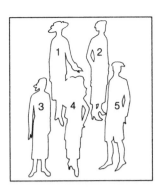
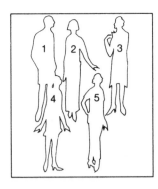

1922 Day Wear

1 Two-piece grey wool suit: long unfitted single-breasted jacket, long narrow collar, wide lapels, single-button fastening at low waist-level, flared skirt with gathered side panels and single box pleats from hip-level side belts, flared sleeves; mid-calf-length skirt with box pleats. Grey silk blouse. Grey fox-fur stole and matching muff. Felt hat with upturned brim, crown decorated with large pink silk roses. Grey leather shoes, buckle trim, pointed toes. 2 Brown and pink striped silk dress, hip-length unfitted bodice, waist marked with chain-belt, round neckline, shaped yoke, three-quarter-length sleeves, mid-calf-length skirt gathered from hipline, decorative use of stripes. Shoes with pointed toes. 3 Blue and cream checked wool dress, hip-level unfitted bodice, V-shaped neckline, three-quarter-length inset sleeves, half yoke, inset band of bias-cut fabric at hip-level, bound pockets and button trim, mid-calf-length gathered skirt. Blue and cream embroidered blouse with full sleeves. Large hat with gathered crown, wide brim trimmed with two feathers. Leather shoes, wide buttoned ankle straps. 4 Two-piece blue-grey wool suit: fitted double-breasted jacket, narrow lapels, patch pockets, button trim; narrow ankle-length trousers with turn-ups. Shirt with buttoned collar. Checked silk tie. Straw boater, dark ribbon band. Blue and white leather shoes, pointed toes. 5 Mid-calf-length single-breasted unfitted fawn wool coat, wide lapels, large cape collar trimmed with brown ribbon-embroidered braid which matches hems of flared sleeves, band at hip-level and large self-fabric buttons. Large brown silk hat, high crown trimmed with wide ribbon band, loops and bows. Leather gloves. Dark flesh-coloured silk stockings. Leather shoes, stitched detail, pointed toes, louis heels.

Evening Wear

1 Mid-calf-length bright pink crêpe-de-chine evening dress, unfitted bodice, wide scooped neckline, short dolman sleeves, low waistline marked with wide black silk-taffeta cummerbund decorated on one side with outsized bow and waterfall with bead-fringed edge; black embroidered-net gathered overskirt with scalloped hem. Black silk shoes, wide ankle straps, buckle trim. 2 Mid-calf-length dark pink crêpe-de-chine dinner dress, unfitted bodice, gathered skirt, underpart of flared sleeves embroidered with bright pink and dark blue glass beads matching neckline and hem of underskirt, deep hipband decorated with self-fabric roses, coat-effect overbodice, upper sleeves and long side panels in plain dark blue crêpe-de-chine. 3 Two-piece black wool suit: single-breasted fitted jacket, wide silk lapels, hip-level piped pockets, breast pocket with silk handkerchief, narrow sleeves with sewn cuffs; narrow trousers, no turn-ups. White cotton starched shirt, wing collar. Black silk bow-tie. Black patent-leather pumps, petersham bow trim. 4 Yellow silk dance frock, hip-length unfitted bodice, low waist marked with black velvet ribbon belt to match edges of scalloped collar, cuffs of short sleeves and gathered tiered skirt. Black satin shoes with double bar straps. 5 Black silk-velvet evening dress, hip-length unfitted bodice, straight ankle-length wrapover skirt, low waist marked with pleated black chiffon belt, large beaded jet motif on side hip which matches clasps on each side of wide neckline and tasselled hem of open waterfall chiffon sleeves. Black silk shoes, pointed toes, louis heels.

Sports and Leisure Wear

1 Country wear. Single-breasted hip-length rust-coloured wool jacket, fastening with two large self-fabric buttons, collar, revers and edges top-stitched to match cuffs of raglan sleeves, stitched cuffs of patch pockets and threaded low-placed belt. Mid-calf-length rust, cream and green checked wool-tweed skirt. Straw boater trimmed with decorative ribbon. Shoes with buckle trim, pointed toes. 2 Sports wear. Long single-breasted beige knitted-wool jacket, fastening with single horn button which matches trim on shaped shawl collar and flaps on patch pockets, inset sleeves with deep cuffs, fringed hem. Mid-calf-length camel-coloured wool skirt, buttoned side vents to knee-level, deep waistband. Striped cotton shirt, plain collar. Knotted silk scarf. Dark red beret with long brown tassel. Leather shoes. 3 Tennis. Fine white cotton blouse, low fastening with two self-fabric buttons which match deep cuffs on raglan sleeves, long shaped roll collar. Mid-calf-length linen skirt, top-stitched front panel with button opening to knee-level, hip-level welt pockets. Hair tied back with scarf. Canvas sports shoes. 4 Holiday wear. Fine white cotton-voile dress, hip-length unfitted bodice gathered into hipband with threaded ribbon belt which matches detail under square neckline, lace collar matching cuffs on three-quarter-length sleeves, mid-calf-length tiered skirt. Hat trimmed with artificial fruit and silk ribbon. Parasol. Leather shoes, buckle trim, pointed toes. 5 Golf. Two-piece light brown wool suit: single-breasted jacket with buttoned belt, narrow sleeves, stitched cuffs, welt pockets; knee-length breeches. Collar-attached shirt. Tweed tie. Checked wool peaked cap. Leather gloves. Knee-length knitted-wool socks. Leather boots. Long buttoned gaiters.

Underwear and Negligee

1 Fine cream wool combination top and drawers, shallow top-stitched stand collar matching button-through strap opening and cuffs of inset shirt sleeves, fly opening from base of strap to crotch. 2 Sleeveless ankle-length peach-coloured crêpe-de-chine nightdress, low scooped neckline edged with narrow lace, shaped yoke decorated with appliqué embroidery, tiny pintucks over bustline, low-placed self-fabric tie-belt. Boudoir cap in matching fabric, turned back brim with fine lace edging, self-fabric flower applied to each corner. Embroidered velvet slippers with scalloped edges, pointed toes. 3 Pale blue satin petticoat, low scooped neckline infilled with pale coffee-coloured lace matching wide shoulder straps and uneven hemline, gathered side panels from hip-level. Blue velvet house shoes, pointed toes, high louis heels. 4 Pink rubber bust flattener with narrow adjustable shoulder straps, flaps button to top-stitched girdle reaching from waist to hip, side-laced opening from hem to high hip-level, four elasticated and adjustable suspenders. Flesh-coloured silk stockings. Velvet house shoes, pointed toes, louis heels. 5 Two-piece pale green silk pyjama suit, hip-length top, short dolman sleeves trimmed with pale cream lace to match low round neckline, central motif and hems of top and ankle-length straight-cut trousers. Green velvet mules trimmed with cream satin, pointed toes, low louis heels.

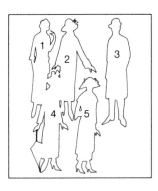 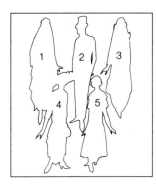 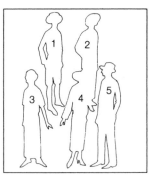 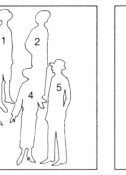

1923 Day Wear

1 Ankle-length grey velvet dress, unfitted bodice to low waistline, open jacket-effect overbodice with long shawl collar, underbodice forming square neckline, smock trim matching line above narrow cuffs of three-quarter-length inset flared sleeves, skirt gathered from hipline, low waistline marked with black velvet sash and outsized black plastic buckle. Black leather shoes, buckle trim.
2 Mid-calf-length grey wool coat, double-breasted wrapover front, fastening with three large carved buttons which match trim on outsized collar, inset sleeves, deep cuffs. Large black varnished straw hat, high crown draped with black chiffon, narrow turned-down brim trimmed with a spray of feathers. Leather shoes with buckle and looped trim, high heels. **3** Knee-length double-breasted dark blue wool overcoat, wide lapels, flap pockets, stitched sleeve cuffs. Narrow ankle-length trousers with turn-ups. Shirt worn with stiff collar and collar pins. Striped silk tie. Black bowler hat. Leather gloves. Lace-up leather shoes, pointed toecaps. Walking stick. **4** Ankle-length sage green wool coat, wrapover front held in place by buckled belt, wide combination collar and revers decorated with fine silk braid which matches side panels of bodice and skirts, long raglan sleeves, half-cuffs fastened with self-fabric buttons. Brimless silk and velvet hat trimmed with silk and velvet ribbon loops and bows. Long-handled umbrella. Leather bar-strap shoes. **5** Ankle-length pale turquoise afternoon dress, low waist marked with two buttoned lace belts which match edging on deep collar, elbow-length flared sleeves, hem of overskirt and underbodice. Straw hat with upswept brim, large crown trimmed with grey, pink and turquoise silk flowers. Bar-strap shoes.

Wedding Wear

1 Ice blue silk-crêpe dress, unfitted bodice gathered into low waist position, wide belt embroidered with self-coloured glass beads matching trim on wide square neckline, at elbow-level on wide flared cuffs of tight inset sleeves and on scalloped hemline of gathered skirt, mid-calf-length at front forming short train at back. Tiara of wax flowers and leaves, long silk-tulle veil. Satin shoes with cross-over straps, pointed toes. **2** Single-breasted black wool tailcoat fastening with single button, wide lapels. Single-breasted collarless grey wool waistcoat. Grey wool trousers. White shirt, wing collar. Grey tie. Black top hat. Black shoes with buttoned spats. **3** Pale pink silk-taffeta dress, unfitted bodice to low waist, wide scooped neckline with self-fabric ruched detail matching large rosettes on mid-calf-length gathered overskirt, short inset sleeves, ankle-length self-fabric underskirt. Tiara of silk and wax flowers, matching posy on one shoulder and centres of rosettes on skirt, long silk-tulle veil. Long white kid gloves. White kid shoes with wide bar straps, pointed toes, louis heels. **4** Ankle-length cream silk dress, wide neckline with satin insert detail matching three-quarter-length wrapover sleeves, overskirt, bias-cut floating panel at back and decoration on unfitted bodice; low waist marked with narrow belt. Large straw hat trimmed with silk flowers. Elbow-length gloves. Kid shoes with buckle trim, pointed toes, louis heels. **5** Ankle-length cream silk dress, wide neckline edged with gathered lace frill to match elbow-length sleeves, unfitted bodice to low waist marked with wide self-fabric sash, gathered skirt decorated with horseshoes of flowers, scalloped hem. Cream silk-organdie cloche hat trimmed with flowers. Cream kid shoes.

Sports and Leisure Wear

1 Bicycling. Two-piece grey wool suit: double-breasted hip-length jacket, low-placed buttoned belt, inset sleeves with stitched cuffs, four pleated patch pockets with buttoned flaps; knee breeches, buttoned straps at knee-level. Collar-attached shirt. Felt hat, large crown, upturned brim. Long knitted-wool socks with patterned cuffs. Lace-up leather shoes. **2** Golf. Two-piece green wool-tweed suit: long edge-to-edge collarless jacket, low waist marked with buckled tailored belt, sloping welt pockets, narrow shoulder yoke, inset sleeves; ankle-length skirt with inverted box pleats. Long single-breasted collarless red wool waistcoat. Cream silk blouse, large collar, deep cuffs. Two-tone leather shoes. **3** Tennis. Ankle-length dress, unfitted hip-length white linen bodice, scooped neckline, inset elbow-length sleeves, low waist marked with self-fabric sash, gathered shaping from half yoke, flared blue linen skirt. Natural straw cloche hat trimmed with wide white ribbon band and bow. White canvas sports shoes. **4** Holiday wear. Mid-calf-length pale peach cotton-voile dress, unfitted bodice decorated with self-coloured embroidery above low waistline to match hems of flared inset sleeves, scooped neckline with narrow collar, buckled belt. Natural straw hat, tall crown, wide brim turned back and trimmed with silk flower. Leather shoes, pointed toes, louis heels. **5** Holiday wear. Single-breasted gold, blue and cream striped linen jacket with wide lapels and patch pockets. Collarless single-breasted waistcoat with welt pockets. Narrow ankle-length trousers with turn-ups. Collar-attached shirt. Spotted silk tie. Straw boater with striped band and bow. Two-tone navy and white leather lace-up shoes, pointed toes.

Accessories

1 Silver chainmail bag, engraved frame, clasp fastening, long chain handle, silver bead trim.
2 Beige leather shoes with suede lace-effect trim, pointed toes, louis heels. **3** Dark green leather shoes with perforated decoration.
4 Pale green silk bag, self-fabric-covered metal frame, clasp fastening, long self-fabric rouleau handle. **5** Silver chainmail bag, engraved frame, clasp fastening, plaited handle, tassel trim.
6 Grey felt hat, upturned brim edged and trimmed with pleated petersham braid. Grey fox-fur stole. **7** Hat with tall silk-organdie crown trimmed with wide silk ribbon, wired lace brim.
8 Ruched purple velvet hat with padded brim, self-coloured satin ribbon trim. **9** Top-stitched yellow straw hat, upturned brim, large crown trimmed with silk flowers at back. **10** Felt hat with unstructured outsized brim, trimmed with silk roses.
11 Lace-up tan leather shoes with perforated decoration.
12 Light brown felt trilby, tall crown trimmed with wide dark brown band and bow, curled brim. Collar-attached shirt. Striped tie. **13** Black bowler with curled brim. **14** Cream kid leather shoes, cross-over buttoned straps, pointed toes, louis heels. **15** Navy blue and white lace-up shoes, perforated decoration, pointed toes. **16** Navy blue and white kid shoes with buttoned bar straps, pointed toes, louis heels. **17** Cream lace-up leather shoes with dark green decorative inserts. **18** Black satin shoes with buttoned bar straps, pointed toes, red louis heels. **19** Black leather shoes with wide buttoned ankle straps, pointed toes, louis heels.

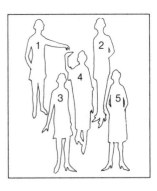

1924 Day Wear

1 Mid-calf-length cream linen dress, unfitted bodice and straight skirt, scooped neckline, brown linen collar matching cuffs of long inset sleeves and inserted front panel, self-fabric buttons from neck to hip-level, low waist marked with narrow buckled tailored belt. Natural straw cloche hat trimmed with wax fruit. Brown leather shoes with wide bar straps. **2** Three-piece natural linen suit: edge-to-edge jacket fastened with self-fabric belt and clasp on low waistline, draped scarf collar, tasselled trim, collar embroidered with pale green silk thread to match hems of flared inset sleeves; mid-calf-length straight skirt. Blouse with straight neckline. Long fur stole. Green felt hat, upturned brim trimmed with feathers. Leather shoes. **3** Hip-length dark blue velvet jacket, double-breasted wrapover front, loop and waterfall side decoration threaded through self-colour beaded braid clasp, matching trim on large collar and hems of inset flared sleeves. Straight mid-calf-length skirt. Black straw cloche hat draped with black silk-chiffon, trimmed with pleated petersham ribbon rosette. Leather gloves. Leather shoes. **4** Single-breasted light brown wool-tweed jacket, narrow lapels, flap pockets. Narrow ankle-length brown flannel trousers with turn-ups. Collar-attached shirt. Wool tie. Fawn felt trilby, trimmed with brown petersham band. Lace-up brown leather shoes. Walking stick. **5** Knee-length burnt-orange velvet coat, unfitted bodice fastened on shoulder and on wide hipband with large decorative buttons, red fox-fur collar matching cuffs of long inset sleeves, hemline, large muff and trim on brim of large dark brown felt hat. Dark brown mid-calf-length dress. Brown leather shoes, pointed toes, high louis heels.

Evening Wear

1 Mid-calf-length black chiffon dress with unfitted bodice and straight skirt cut in one piece, embroidered all over with black glass and crystal beads in leaf patterns, low V-shaped neckline edged with rows of black glass beads to match covered panel seams which extend to below hemline, open plain black chiffon sleeves. Black shoes with wide bar straps. **2** Pale cream crêpe-de-chine dress, straight hip-length unfitted bodice, straight neckline with bust-level beige lace collar falling to hip-level at back, scalloped hemline matching mid-calf-length overskirt, plain crêpe-de-chine loops and waterfalls on side hips. Outsized ostrich-feather fan. Cream silk shoes with tiny rosette trim, pointed toes. **3** Pale pink silk-crêpe sleeveless dress, low scooped neckline, straight unfitted bodice embroidered with beads from side hips and curving up to centre-front to below bust-level, flared and slightly gathered skirt. Satin shoes with double bar straps, pointed toes, high louis heels. **4** Ankle-length pink, red and orange patterned silk-velvet sleeveless dinner dress, wide boat-shaped neckline, asymmetric gold silk overbodice falling in folds from clasp on one shoulder to hipline, floating bias-cut back panel trimmed with feathers to match banded hip and hem detail of open-sided skirt. Feather fan. Fine kid shoes, wide buttoned bar straps with perforated decoration. **5** Lilac silk evening dress, wide boat-shaped neckline, shaped yoke with embroidered and beaded decoration matching bias-cut waterfall sleeves and scalloped hip yoke, bodice gathered into low waistline, gathered bias-cut skirt with handkerchief points and beaded edge. Silk shoes with buckle trim, pointed toes.

Sports and Leisure Wear

1 Holiday wear. Mid-calf-length yellow and blue checked cotton dress, unfitted bodice and straight skirt cut in one piece, square neckline bound with plain blue cotton matching uneven hem of three-quarter-length inset sleeves, side front opening and self-fabric buttons in sets of four, pleated voile trim on opening from neck to waist and repeated on hem of sleeves. Yellow straw cloche hat with white voile trim. Leather shoes with cross-over bar straps. **2** Golf. Double-breasted broad grey and green striped cotton blouse fastening with single self-fabric button, wide revers, narrow yoke, inset shirt sleeves. Straight green tweed skirt, buttoned hipband, hip-level pockets, mock double-breasted button fastening above hemline. Unstructured cotton-velvet hat, sectioned crown, wide brim. Leather shoes with bar straps, low heels. **3** Tennis. Cream double-breasted long collarless tunic, fastening on one side with three self-fabric buttons, boat-shaped neckline, wide binding to above hemline, inset three-quarter-length sleeves, buttoned cuffs, tailored belt. Mid-calf-length cream pleated skirt. Natural straw cloche hat, wide ribbon band. **4** Riding. Single-breasted tan cotton-cord jacket, buttoned belt, box pleats each side front from shaped yoke to hem, large patch pockets with flaps. Light brown knee-breeches. Collar-attached shirt. Wool tie. Long leather boots, laced to knee, strap-and-buckle fastening. **5** Country wear. Mid-calf-length dusty-pink lightweight cotton coat-dress, wrapover front with single-button fastening, long inset sleeves, pink and blue patterned shawl collar matching narrow threaded belt and flared skirt from hip-level. Straw hat, wide brim trimmed with flowers. Leather shoes, cross-over straps, pointed toes.

Underwear and Negligee

1 Fitted flesh-coloured cotton bust flattener, top-stitching, elasticated gusset over side hips, wide shoulder straps, back opening. Flesh-coloured cotton and rubber girdle, elasticated side panels, hook-and-bar front opening, laced adjustment, four adjustable suspenders. Silk stockings. Velvet mules trimmed with satin ribbon bows, louis heels. **2** Two-piece peach silk pyjamas, single-breasted hip-length jacket, loop-and-button fastening, edges embroidered with blanket stitch to match large collar, cuffs of inset sleeves, hip-level welt pockets and turn-ups of ankle-length trousers. Velvet mules trimmed with silk pom-pons. **3** Cotton bust flattener, stitched inserts, adjustable shoulder straps. Cotton girdle, stitched shaped front panel, light boning, four adjustable suspenders. Flesh-coloured silk stockings. House shoes, pointed toes, louis heels. **4** Single-breasted mid-calf-length pale blue and pink crêpe-de-chine housecoat, press-stud fastening concealed under rouleau flower at base of V-shaped neckline, plain pink crêpe-de-chine collar matching cuffs of batwing sleeves and threaded tie-belt with rouleau flower trim. Satin house shoes, pointed toes, louis heels. **5** White cotton petticoat, trimmed on bustline with embroidered and satin ribbon insertions to match hemline, wide shoulder straps and hip-level detail. Velvet mules, pointed toes, louis heels.

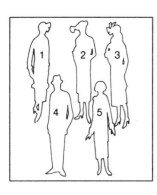  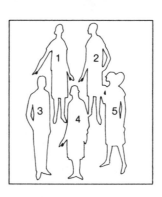 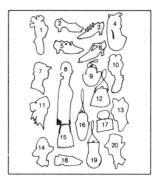

1925 Day Wear

1 Two-piece pale grey wool suit: long jacket, wrapover front fastening with two large self-fabric buttons, wide lapels, large pintucked collar edged with fur to match cuffs of long inset sleeves and hip-length side panels; straight skirt to below knee. Grey felt cloche hat trimmed with pale blue silk ribbon threaded through large buckle. Brown leather shoes, buckle trim. **2** Two-tone navy and cream linen dress, wide boat-shaped neckline, top-stitched edge, self-fabric strap and self-fabric button trim, inset sleeves, flared cuffs, top-stitched detail, unfitted bodice and overskirt effect trimmed with contrasting colour and edged with braid, matching straight skirt. Felt hat, wide upturned brim trimmed with feather pom-pon. Leather shoes, large round buckle trim. **3** Brown wool tweed double-breasted coat, concealed fastening under long roll collar to hip-level buckle trim, waterfall to hem, narrow inset sleeves, fur trim, matching collar. Beige felt cloche hat trimmed with silk ribbon. Beige leather gloves. Leather shoes with bar straps. **4** Double-breasted navy-blue wool jacket, wide lapels, flap pockets, silk handkerchief in breast pocket. Narrow ankle-length grey flannel trousers with turn-ups. Collar-attached shirt. Bow-tie. Pale grey felt trilby. Two-tone lace-up shoes. **5** Hip-length single-breasted dark green leather jacket, fastening with two large plastic buttons, wide lapels and combination collar, top-stitched trim matching cuffs of inset sleeves, buckled belt cut as part of pockets. Leather flower worn on lapel. Checked wool skirt to below knee. Collar-attached shirt. Striped tie. Brimless leather hat, top-stitched trim. Two-tone lace-up leather shoes.

Evening Wear

1 Asymmetric ankle-length gold silk-satin sleeveless overdress, draped from one shoulder to opposite side hip, fixed by bead clasp, open sides, waterfall to hem, sleeveless gold lace underdress, straight neckline, floating panels, scalloped edges to below bustline at front and to hip-level at back. Ostrich-feather fan. Gold kid shoes, pointed toes, high louis heels. **2** Mint green silk-georgette dress embroidered all over with transparent glass beads, sleeveless draped wrapover bodice to hip-level forming low V-shaped neckline, infilled with flesh-coloured silk, narrow hip-level scalloped peplum matching hem of straight skirt. Tiara worn low on forehead. Satin shoes with wide bar straps, pointed toes, louis heels. **3** White silk-net dress embroidered all over with silver glass beads and sequins, straight neckline, narrow beaded shoulder straps, unfitted bodice slightly bloused on hipline, feather flower with jewelled centre on side hip, chiffon waterfall to below knee. Silver kid shoes, pointed toes, louis heels. **4** Mid-calf-length pink silk-taffeta dance dress, sleeveless unfitted bodice, wide V-shaped neckline outlined with rows of lace ribbon, skirt gathered under narrow belt, bow trim and long tails, upturned peplum with lace edge, matching hemline, side panniers formed with garlands of self-fabric roses. Pink silk shoes. **5** Mid-calf-length lilac silk-chiffon dance dress, fitted bodice with horizontal ruching, straight neckline, wide shoulder straps covered with rows of beaded motifs which match ostrich-feather-trimmed hemline of full gathered skirt. Silver kid shoes, pointed toes, louis heels.

Sports and Leisure Wear

1 Tennis. White cotton dress, unfitted bodice with two vertical pleats running from each shoulder under hip-level belt to hem of flared skirt, wide neckline, double peter-pan collar, keyhole opening, short sleeves with narrow cuffs. Draped white cotton turban. White canvas shoes, double bar straps, pointed toes, low heels. **2** Tennis. Unfitted white linen bodice, V-shaped neckline, collar edge trimmed with blue linen to match cuffs of short dolman sleeves, hem of bodice and inset band at waist-level; hip-level tailored belt, flared skirt with centre-front inverted box pleat. Elastic-sided canvas shoes, pointed toes, low heels. **3** Tennis. White knitted-cotton sweater, low V-shaped neckline edged with bands of yellow to match hem and cuffs of inset sleeves. Narrow ankle-length white flannel trousers with turn-ups. White collar-attached shirt, worn open. White canvas lace-up shoes, pointed toecaps. **4** Tennis. Crocheted white cotton top, square neckline edged in blue and yellow to match short inset sleeves, hip-level patch pockets, hemline and edge of inset cape; fine rouleau belt on low waistline. White linen skirt, large box pleat, button trim. White headband. Leather lace-up shoes. **5** Tennis. Hip-length white cotton top, low round neckline, pointed collar, sham shirt front, short cuffed dolman sleeves, piped pockets set into shaped hip yoke. Knotted spotted silk scarf. White linen skirt to below knee, slightly flared, box and inverted box pleats. Wide headband. White canvas shoes with buttoned bar straps, pointed toes, low heels.

Accessories

1 Felt cloche hat, narrow brim, close crown trimmed with silk ribbons. **2** Black leather shoes trimmed with red, red leather heels. **3** Leather shoes with buttoned triple bar straps. **4** Felt cloche hat, notched up-turned brim, petersham ribbon trim, chiffon veil. **5** Black satin shoes, fine cross-over buttoned straps, open sides. **6** Buttoned T-strap shoes, pointed toes, louis heels. **7** Fitted velvet cap with ruched crown, small plain silk peak and narrow brim turned up at back, silk flower trim. **8** Brimless silk cloche, embroidered ribbon and flower motif matching fringed scarf. **9** Ruched velvet evening bag, embroidered central panel, clasp fastening, long ribbon handle. **10** Brimless cloche hat trimmed with petersham ribbon and silk roses. **11** Brimless cloche hat draped and trimmed with silk-organdie bow. **12** Small fan-shaped leather bag, initialled inset panel, metal frame, clasp fastening, long handle. **13** Top-stitched green felt cloche hat, small front brim, crown trimmed with silk butterfly. **14** Linen straw sunhat, domed crown, wide band, narrow brim. **15** Pink crêpe bag made from pleated leaf-shaped pieces, metal frame, clasp fastening, ribbon handle. **16** Silver satin evening bag, silver frame, clasp fastening, long rouleau handle. **17** Small brocade evening bag, flap with stud fastening, self-fabric metal handle. **18** Two-tone lace-up leather shoes. **19** Embroidered velvet evening bag, silver frame, clasp fastening, ribbon handle. **20** Grey felt trilby, tall crown, black ribbon band, wide brim.

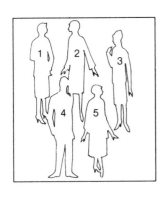   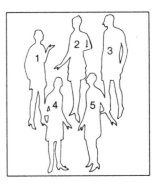

1926 Day Wear

1 Two-piece lilac wool-crêpe suit: long single-breasted collarless jacket, buttoned strap opening from high round neckline to contrasting colour hip-level belt matching cuffs of inset shirt sleeves, patterned lilac and royal blue wool-crêpe shoulder yoke matching straight below-knee-length skirt. Felt cloche hat with upturned top-stitched split brim. Leather shoes with narrow bar straps. 2 Three-piece cream wool suit: hip-length jacket worn open, self-fabric button trim above hem matching trim on split cuffs of semi-set-in sleeves and buttoned stand collar; collarless blouse with long sleeves; straight skirt to below knee, pleated front panel. Felt cloche hat trimmed with pleated ribbon. 3 Unfitted cream wool coatdress, low waistline marked with brown wool tailored belt matching front strap opening, self-fabric buttons, edge of peter-pan collar, cuffs, all edges and decorative panel seams; cream and brown patterned wool front panel, matching cuffs. Cream felt hat with wide petersham band. Two-tone leather shoes, wide bar straps, pointed toecaps, louis heels. 4 Three-piece brown and black checked wool suit: single-breasted jacket, three-button fastening, narrow lapels, flap pockets; single-breasted waistcoat with shawl collar, welt pockets; narrow trousers, no turn-ups. Coloured shirt, white collar. Yellow and red spotted silk tie. Elastic-sided leather boots. 5 Plain light grey unfitted coat, double-breasted fastening, pleated side panels from hip-level, grey and blue checked half-belt matching cuffs of narrow sleeves, wide revers, large collar and lining of wrist-length shoulder cape. Ruched velvet cloche hat, upturned brim. Black leather shoes, wide bar straps, pointed toes, louis heels.

Evening Wear

1 Coffee-coloured crêpe-de-chine sleeveless dress, low V-shaped neckline with flesh-coloured infill outlined with single row of self-fabric rouleau motifs, the same motifs in row above hemline of flared skirt on edge of brown lace side panels which match pointed side panels in unfitted bodice. Gold and brown brocade shoes. 2 Sleeveless evening dress, orange, yellow and brown patterned silk-velvet bodice, low scooped neckline, deep scalloped hemline, threaded orange velvet sash, gold satin gathered skirt and underbodice. Gold kid shoes with top-stitched detail, pointed toes, louis heels. 3 Two-piece black wool suit: edge-to-edge single-breasted jacket fastening with linked buttons, narrow inset sleeves, piped pockets, white silk handkerchief in breast pocket, silk lapels matching stripes on outside leg of narrow trousers, no turn-ups. Collarless single-breasted waistcoat. White starched shirt, wing collar. Black silk bow-tie. 4 Pale orange silk-georgette dress, wide neckline, unfitted bodice gathered above wide draped self-fabric sash edged with beads matching outsized sham buckle, flared skirt to below knee, long sleeves with circular cuffs from elbow-level, scalloped hems. Orange silk petticoat with rouleau straps. Silk shoes dyed to match dress. 5 Shiny turquoise silk-velvet ball gown, straight bodice, V-shaped insertion of flesh-coloured silk, narrow shoulder straps, ankle-length skirt gathered from hip-level over hooped underskirt, three ruched tiers decorated with jewelled straps on centre front. Gold brocade T-strap shoes, pointed toes.

Sports and Leisure Wear

1 Tennis. Collarless cream silk dress, cap sleeves, strap opening with pearl buttons, narrow revers, unfitted bodice decorated with two vertical channel seams running from shoulder to hip-level, button trim, low waistline marked with green and cream ribbon belt, pearl buckle, straight skirt to below knee, pleated side panels. Bar-strap shoes. 2 Country wear. Two-piece lovat green wool-tweed suit: hip-length double-breasted jacket, wide lapels, flap pockets, breast pocket with silk handkerchief; straight skirt to below knee, box pleat. Collar-attached shirt. Tie. Trilby-style hat, high crown, narrow brim. Leather gloves. Leather brogues with tongues. 3 Golf. Lightweight ochre-yellow wool dress, unfitted bodice slightly bloused over hip-level seam, decorative front panel, button trim, pointed collar, keyhole opening, inset shirt sleeves, decorative seam above buttoned cuffs, skirt with graded box pleats, button trim. Brimless cloche hat, stitched inset bands, button trim. Lace-up leather shoes, pointed toecaps. 4 Golf. Multi-coloured knitted-wool sweater with all-over pattern, V-shaped neckline, patch pockets, inset sleeves with ribbed cuffs, matching hem. Checked wool knee-breeches. Collar-attached shirt. Tweed tie. Wool-tweed peaked cap. Knee-length knitted-wool socks. Lace-up leather brogues. 5 Bathing. Two-piece blue and white striped knitted-cotton bathing costume, hip-length sleeveless unfitted top, low scooped neckline infilled with self-fabric cross-over straps, repeated in plain fabric on front at hip-level to match hemline of top and short drawers. Rubber cap trimmed with pleated rubber flower rosette. Rubber shoes.

Underwear

1 Cream cotton combination bust flattener and corset, straight neckline, adjustable shoulder straps, stitched front firming panels, elasticated gussets from side front waist to hip-level, side hook-and-bar fastening, four adjustable suspenders. Crêpe-de-chine petticoat edged with lace. Flesh-coloured stockings. Velvet mules, satin ribbon bow trim. 2 Embroidered pale pink artificial-silk brassiere, shaped with underarm darts and gathers from central ruched panel, self-fabric frilled edging, satin ribbon shoulder straps, back fastening. Knickers in matching fabric with embroidery repeated on side hip above three tiers of frilled lace, elasticated waistband. Embroidered silk house shoes trimmed with satin. 3 Sleeveless white cotton vest, low neckline with top-stitched edge, matching armholes. Mid-thigh-length white knitted-cotton underdrawers, wide waistband, buttoned fly opening to shaped yoke seam, wide legs, machined hems. Step-in red leather house slippers. 4 Pale blue artificial-silk combination chemise and knickers, straight neckline trimmed with applied cream ribbon lace edged with satin ribbon ending in tied bow on centre front, wide knicker legs trimmed to match, decorative bib seam on front bodice, gathers on side hip, ribbon shoulder straps. Blue satin slippers trimmed with silk pom-pons. 5 Pale green artificial-silk combination chemise and knickers, hip-length unfitted bodice, trimmed on straight neckline with open embroidery and scallops of fine lace, matching hemline, wide ribbon shoulder straps, knickers gathered on hipline and into elasticated channel on hem. Flesh-coloured silk stockings. Velvet house shoes.

   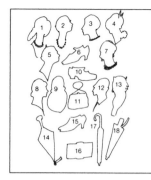

1927 Day Wear

1 Three-piece grey and brown striped suit: single-breasted jacket with two-button fastening, narrow lapels, flap pockets; collarless single-breasted waistcoat; narrow trousers, no turn-ups. White collar-attached shirt. Plain silk tie. Brown bowler hat. Leather gloves. Lace-up leather shoes. Walking stick.
2 Pink and cream checked wool dress, bound square neckline with sham keyhole opening, shirt sleeves, low waistline marked with self-fabric belt, knee-length flared skirt with shaped yoke, posy of leather flowers worn on one shoulder. Cream felt cloche hat with high crown. Leather shoes. **3** Three-piece coffee linen suit: hip-length collarless jacket, front edges and hem bound in pale blue which matches hems of inset sleeves, decorative straps, self-fabric button, stand collar and trim on blouse and hip-level inset band of knee-length flared skirt. Top-stitched straw cloche hat, high crown, wide petersham ribbon trim. Leather shoes, wide shaped bar straps, openwork detail, pointed toes.
4 Multi-coloured artificial-silk dress, boat-shaped neckline, self-fabric bound edge, inset sleeves gathered into tied cuffs, straight unfitted bodice to hipline, self-fabric sash, bow and waterfall, four-tier accordion-pleated knee-length skirt. Leather shoes, pointed toes, louis heels.
5 Navy blue silk-georgette dress, wide neckline, inset sleeves gathered into rouleau bands, unfitted bodice, panel seams with inset waterfall frills lined with bright pink silk to match overskirt effect on straight knee-length skirt, low waistline marked with narrow self-fabric buckled belt. Large fine straw hat, high crown, wide brim. Bar-strap shoes.

Evening Wear

1 Beige crêpe-de-chine dinner dress, hip-length unfitted bloused bodice, low V-shaped neckline infilled with coffee-coloured lace, embroidered collar with scalloped edge matching detail on hems of long flared inset sleeves and hem of gathered knee-length skirt. Bar-strap satin shoes. **2** Bright pink silk-georgette dress, boat-shaped neckline edged with glass beads, matching armholes, hem of hip-length bloused bodice embroidered with pearls and pink and gold beads to match scalloped hip yoke of knee-length gathered skirt, large pink silk rose worn on one shoulder. Gold kid shoes, jewelled buckles, pointed toes. **3** Black silk-crêpe dinner dress, sleeveless hip-length bloused bodice with wide neckline, straight knee-length skirt gathered into beaded jet buckle on side hip, waterfall points to mid-calf. Black satin shoes trimmed with small round buckles, pointed toes. **4** Hip-length sleeveless wrapover silver sequined bodice forming low V-shaped neckline, infilled with pink silk-satin which matches four-tier gathered skirt, three pink silk flowers worn on one shoulder, at centre of low waistline and above hem on one side of second tier of skirt. Silver kid bar-strap shoes.
5 Knee-length salmon pink georgette dress worn over petticoat with wide shoulder straps, sleeveless low scooped neckline, unfitted bodice, swathed self-fabric hip basque trimmed with spray of velvet flowers which matches spray on one shoulder, two-tier pleated skirt with uneven hemline. Gold brocade shoes with cross-over straps. **6** Knee-length green silk dress, cap sleeves, embroidered floating panel from round neckline to low hipline, matching wide hip-level belt, straight knee-level skirt with pleated side panels. Satin shoes dyed to match dress.

Sports and Leisure Wear

1 Holiday wear. Knee-length fine cotton dress, plain pink unfitted bodice to uneven hip seam, V-shaped neckline, pink and white spotted collar, matching bow trim, sewn cuffs of tight inset sleeves, side hip-belts with bow trims and flared skirt. Pink cloche hat, high crown, narrow brim. Leather shoes, bar strap with cut-out detail, pointed toes. Multi-coloured pleated-paper parasol.
2 Golf. Fine wool dress, unfitted plain grey bodice, V-shaped neckline edged with wide band of grey, blue and yellow check to match cuffs of inset sleeves and knee-length pleated skirt, low waistline marked with narrow black leather buckled belt. Grey felt cloche hat trimmed with petersham ribbon. Leather shoes with wide bar straps. **3** Single-breasted bottle green and yellow striped linen jacket, three-button fastening, patch pockets. Cream flannel trousers with turn-ups. Cream collar-attached shirt, worn open. V-neck cream knitted-wool sweater. Canvas lace-up shoes, no toecaps. **4** Tennis. Hip-length unfitted white cotton top, V-shaped neckline edged with self-fabric buttoned band and bound with contrasting colour to match bound armholes and self-fabric buttons, embroidered motif at base of neckline and on small patch pockets. Knee-length box-pleated white linen skirt with shaped yoke. Leather shoes with keyhole openings. **5** Golf. Short single-breasted brown leather jacket, narrow lapels, top-stitched brown velvet collar matching buttoned cuffs of long raglan sleeves and buttoned waistband, sloping welt pockets. Checked wool trousers with turn-ups. Collar-attached shirt. Patterned tie. Brown leather brogues.

Accessories

1 Grey felt hat, unstructured crown, wide brim turned up all round, trimmed with long red feather. **2** Cream felt cloche hat, close-fitting crown, trimmed self-fabric knot with fringed ends, button trim. **3** Draped silk turban, jewelled brooch trim.
4 Unstructured green felt cloche hat, brim turned up at front and back, feather trim. **5** Brimless cloche hat made from silk ribbon, silk flower trim. **6** Gold and black brocade evening shoes, gold kid straps and trim, open sides, plain black satin heels. **7** Red, orange, yellow and black striped silk turban trimmed with black velvet and jewelled brooch.
8 Felt cloche hat with close-fitting crown, draped and padded silk brim. **9** Brimless top-stitched fabric cloche hat, draped chiffon through self-fabric loop.
10 Two-tone leather shoes, buttoned double-bar straps, pointed toes, stacked heels.
11 Kid leather bag, metal frame, clasp fastening, long handle.
12 Grey felt cloche hat, high unstructured crown, wide petersham band, brim turned up at back. **13** Red velvet cloche hat, asymmetric brim turned up on one side, trimmed with bunch of feathers. **14** Short blue and white striped cotton umbrella, wooden handle, carrying strap on tip. **15** Lace-up green snakeskin shoes, pointed toes, high straight heels. **16** Small cream leather clutch bag, wraparound self-strap-and-loop fastening, top-stitched trim.
17 Short black silk rolled umbrella, curled bamboo handle. **18** Multi-coloured hand-painted silk parasol, short painted wooden handle, long carrying strap.

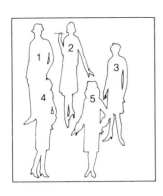  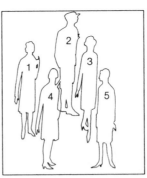 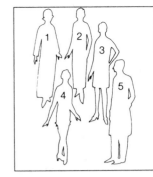

1928 Day Wear

1 Double-breasted, knee-length fitted light-brown checked wool-tweed overcoat, wide lapels, flap pockets, silk handkerchief worn in breast pocket. Wool trousers with turn-ups. Collar-attached shirt. Plain tie. Felt trilby, wide petersham band, brim turned up on one side. Leather shoes.
2 Knee-length tan-coloured crêpe dress, unfitted bodice, curved seam from natural side waist to centre-front point on low waistline matching seam from side hipline of flared skirt, vertical panel seams in front bodice, top-stitched tan-coloured satin collar matching band on bottom edge of low square neckline, hems of long inset sleeves and buckled belt. Leather shoes.
3 Knee-length fine black wool dress, asymmetric neckline bound with wide band of red satin to match waterfall and cuffs of long inset sleeves, bodice and skirt joined with hip-level zig-zag seam, knife pleats in side panel of skirt. Leather shoes, pointed toes, high heels. **4** Knee-length pale green wool coat, wrapover front, fastening with three large plastic buttons at hip-level on wide strap, shawl collar trimmed with fur to match large cuffs of narrow inset sleeves, knife pleats from side hip-level band. Brimless orange felt cloche hat trimmed with bands of cream leather. Cream leather gloves and shoes.
5 Knee-length horizontally banded red-squirrel-fur coat, wrapover front, fastening with single loop and button at hip-level, narrow sleeves with deep cuffs, large fox-fur collar. Rust-coloured felt cloche hat, wide front brim turned up, fitted crown draped with cream silk. Cream leather gloves. Brown leather shoes, small buckle trim, pointed toes.

Wedding Wear

1 Knee-length pink crêpe-de-chine sleeveless wedding dress, unfitted bodice with round neckline, flared skirt, ankle-length pink and gold lace overskirt with scalloped hem, pink velvet padded and ruched belt with large stylized self-fabric stitched bow, long free ends. Headdress of pink velvet roses, ankle-length pink silk-tulle veil. Pink satin shoes with two narrow bar straps, pointed toes. **2** Cream silk-crêpe wedding dress, low neckline edged with tiny pearls, inset sleeves flared from elbow to wrist, deep scallops edged with beads, unfitted bodice to hip-level belt embroidered with pearls and crystal beads matching floating panels of overskirt, knee-length at front to mid-calf-length at back, straight knee-length underskirt. Tiara of pearls, wax flowers and silk ribbon matching spray on shoulder, ankle-length silk-chiffon veil. Satin shoes.
3 Single-breasted dark grey frockcoat, wide lapels, self-fabric buttons. Double-breasted waistcoat with wide shawl collar. Narrow dark grey trousers, no turn-ups. White shirt worn with stiff stand collar. Striped tie. Grey top hat. White gloves. Black shoes worn with spats.
4 White crêpe wedding dress, low neckline edged with bead embroidery to match hems of tight inset sleeves, scalloped low waistline and hemline of flared knee-length skirt. Pearl bead and silk ribbon headdress, long silk veil with beaded hemline. Satin shoes. **5** Pink crêpe-de-chine bridesmaid's dress, low neckline, long inset sleeves, knee-length skirt, split three-tier pink lace overskirt, hemline dips from mid-calf-length at front to ankle-length at back, hip-level gold cord belt with tassel ends. Close-fitting pink lace cap with frilled edge, silk flower trim. Satin shoes.

Sports and Leisure Wear

1 Golf. Collarless beige knitted-wool dress, V-shaped neckline, lapels bound and edged with brown and green knitted wool which matches buttoned cuffs of tight inset sleeves, hip-level buckled belt and hemline of knee-length skirt, zig-zag seam from centre-front on natural waistline to low side hipline, double inverted side box pleats. Leather bar-strap shoes. **2** Golf. Two-piece brown tweed suit: single-breasted jacket, three-button fastening, large pleated patch pockets with buttoned flaps; knee breeches with buttoned cuffs. Collar-attached shirt. Wool tie. Brown tweed peaked cap. Hand-knitted, knee-length socks. Two-tone shoes with fringed tongues.
3 Country wear. Dark green flannel knee-length collarless coatdress, V-shaped neckline, buttoned infill, unfitted diagonally seamed bodice matching hip area of knife-pleated skirt and hems of fitted inset sleeves. Brown and beige felt hat, sectioned crown, brim turned up. Two-tone leather shoes, double bar straps, pointed toecaps, low heels. **4** Holiday wear. Knee-length sleeveless cotton dress, V-shaped neckline, plain white scalloped collar, yellow and white spotted cotton bodice trimmed from base of neckline to scalloped hip seam with white cotton self-fabric buttons, plain white cotton gathered skirt edged with scalloped band of spotted cotton. Brimless yellow and white cloche hat. Leather clutch bag. Leather shoes, buttoned bar straps.
5 Golf. Three-piece dusty-blue knitted-wool suit: collarless edge-to-edge jacket, edges bound in chocolate brown which matches cuffs of inset sleeves, patch pocket trim and buckled belt of self-fabric hip-length blouse; round neckline, self-binding, button fastening, keyhole opening; knee-length pleated skirt, chocolate brown band above hemline. Felt cloche, front brim turned up, petersham band, buckle trim. Leather bar-strap shoes.

Underwear and Negligee

1 Pale blue crêpe-de-chine ankle-length nightdress, wide ribbon shoulder straps, straight neckline edged with coffee-coloured lace which matches hem of self-fabric hip-length edge-to-edge jacket and hems of inset sleeves. Coffee-coloured lace boudoir cap, frilled edge. Velvet slippers trimmed with looped ribbon. **2** Two-piece green silk pyjama suit: hip-length unfitted top, double-breasted sham shirt front, collar and revers, shirt sleeves, double-buttoned cuffs; narrow ankle-length trousers with turn-ups. Satin house shoes.
3 Cream cotton brassiere, elasticated panel between seamed cups, elasticated side panels, back fastening. Cream cotton corset, stitched double-fabric front and side panels, elasticated panels over hips, four adjustable suspenders. Cotton waist-slip with scalloped hem. Velvet mules, feather trim, pointed toes, low heels. **4** Pale turquoise crêpe-de-chine combination chemise and knickers patterned with pink flowers, straight neckline edged with cream lace, self-fabric rouleau shoulder straps, knicker legs trimmed with double lace frill. Flesh-coloured silk stockings. Elasticated silk garters. Satin house shoes. **5** Knee-length double-breasted light blue wool dressing gown, dark blue satin roll collar piped in white to match trim on patch pockets and cuffs of inset sleeves, dark blue satin self-fabric buttons, self-fabric tie-belt. Blue and white striped silk pyjamas, shirt collar, ankle-length trousers. Step-in red leather house slippers, petersham ribbon trim.

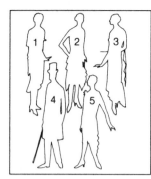

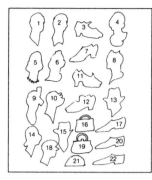

1929 Day Wear

1 Double-breasted navy-blue wool jacket, wide lapels, flap pockets. Light grey flannel straight-cut trousers, turn-ups. White cotton collar-attached shirt. Plain silk tie. White canvas shoes, pointed toecaps. **2** Two-piece wool-tweed suit: hip-level jacket with wrapover front to low-placed self-fabric buckled belt, unfitted bodice, decorative panels above hip-level pleated patch pockets with buttoned flaps, narrow lapels, fur collar matching cuffs of inset sleeves; straight skirt, inverted box pleat. Felt cloche, fitted crown, flared brim. Two-tone leather shoes, pointed toes, high heels. **3** Multi-coloured spotted cotton dress, V-shaped neckline, lace edge matching flared cuffs of inset sleeves and hems of four-tier knee-length skirt, plain cotton bow with long ends at base of neckline. Felt cloche, fitted crown, front brim turned up and edged with contrasting colour. Leather shoes, cross-over straps, pointed toes. **4** Grey wool-crêpe dress, narrow inset sleeves, sewn cuffs, knee-length skirt, pleated panel from low hip-level, short curved side panel, inset band, unfitted bloused bodice, low neckline infilled with white silk blouse-effect, V-shaped neckline, pointed collar, infill of flesh-coloured silk. Shoes with ribbon laces, pointed toes, high heels. **5** Dark red artificial-silk dress patterned with spots of light and dark blue, V-shaped neckline, narrow inset sleeves, frilled cuffs matching low curved waist seam, unfitted bodice, curved V-shaped panel seams from under arm to centre-front on natural waistline, repeated and inverted at low hip-level and above pleats on hem of straight skirt. Cloche hat, fitted crown, asymmetric split brim, self-fabric trim. Leather shoes, pointed toes, high heels.

Evening Wear

1 Sleeveless gold mesh dress embroidered all over with gold sequins, low V-shaped neckline, semi-fitted bodice to curved seam, low on side hip up to centre-front on low waistline, bias-cut floating panel from right shoulder, lined with gold tissue to match scalloped uneven hemline of flared skirt. Gold kid shoes, fine bar straps, open sides, pointed toes. **2** Sleeveless black lace dress, low scooped neckline, unfitted bloused bodice, knee-length flared skirt, wide asymmetric peach-coloured silk sash, looped low on side hip, waterfall to ankle, peach-coloured silk slip. Ostrich-feather fan. Black brocade shoes, satin trim. **3** Sleeveless cream silk-crêpe dress patterned with sprigs of embroidery, low scooped neckline, bloused bodice to low waistline, bias-cut self-fabric floating panels from each shoulder to mid-calf-length at back, straight knee-length skirt at front, curved panel seams across front hip down to side hem, gathered fishtail train from mid-calf on side to ground at back. Silk bar-strap shoes, open sides, pointed toes, high heels. **4** Knee-length fitted black wool overcoat, high front fly opening, wide satin-faced lapels, flap pockets. Black wool trousers, no turn-ups. Wing collar. White bow-tie. White silk scarf. White gloves. Black silk top hat. Black shoes. Walking stick. **5** Sleeveless midnight blue silk-velvet dress, asymmetric V-shaped neckline, hip-length bodice ruched into left side pointed inset panel from low hip-line to bustline, knee-length gathered skirt, gathered waterfall panel on left hip to mid-calf-length, feather flower on right shoulder. Cream silk shoes trimmed with gold embroidery, open sides, pointed toes, high heels.

Sports and Leisure Wear

1 Bathing. Blue and white striped knitted-cotton vest, low-cut armholes, low scooped neckline. Navy blue knitted-cotton drawers, wide waistband, button fastening, fly opening, short legs. **2** Holiday wear. Multi-coloured floral printed artificial-silk dress, V-shaped neckline, bias-cut waterfall frill from left shoulder, narrow inset sleeves, hip-length bloused bodice, diagonal panel seams, knee-length flared skirt, low curved yoke seam, low waistline marked with petersham ribbon belt. Felt cloche, fitted crown, band in contrasting colour, wide brim turned down. Matching leather clutch bag and bar-strap shoes. **3** Country wear. Light brown wool-crêpe dress, waterfall frill from base of V-shaped neckline, bloused bodice pintucked from shaped yoke seam to low waistline to match panel from elbow to above wrist in dolman sleeves, deep hip yoke, knee-length accordion-pleated skirt. Top-stitched felt hat, fitted crown, band in contrasting colour, brim turned down. Leather shoes with flat heels. **4** Bathing. Pink and blue striped knitted-cotton bathing costume, straight neckline edged with knitted braid to match shoulder straps, hemline buckled belt and panel seams. Draped rubber turban, buckle trim. Rubber shoes with bar straps. **5** Golf. Beige tweed shirt, pointed top-stitched collar, matching shoulder yoke, front button-strap opening, sleeve cuffs and single pleated patch-and-flap pocket. Brown and cream checked wool knee-breeches, waistband with self-fabric-threaded buckled belt, side hip button opening matching cuffs at knee-level, vertical piped pockets. Beige felt hat, tall crown, wide petersham band, brim turned down. Knee-high hand-knitted socks. Two-tone lace-up shoes, no toecaps, flat heels.

Accessories

1 Brimless black satin cloche, shaped band, sectioned crown. **2** Felt cloche, fitted crown, asymmetric top-stitched split brim. **3** Brown and cream two-tone leather shoes, buttoned bar straps, pointed toes, stacked heels. **4** Brimless felt cloche with earflaps, embroidered flower trim. **5** Pink felt cloche, fitted crown, self-fabric buckled band, unstructured brim turned down. **6** Brimless grey felt cloche, fitted crown, wide band wrapping over at front, fan-shaped detail. **7** Navy-blue and white leather lace-up shoes, perforated decoration, stacked heels. **8** White felt cloche, fitted crown, wide brim at front, split on one side, lined with black silk, trimmed with white ribbon bow. **9** Felt cloche, silk band, outsized bow trim. **10** Brown felt cloche, crown and brim with top-stitched detail, bow trim. **11** Leather shoes, bow trim. **12** Leather shoes, wide bar straps, openwork detail, stacked heels. **13** Light grey felt trilby, tall crown, black petersham band, wide brim. **14** Pale green felt cloche, fitted crown draped with yellow and white spotted silk scarf. **15** Grey homburg, tall crown, black petersham band matching trim on edge of brim. **16** Multi-coloured striped knitted-cotton bag, wooden frame and handle. **17** Dark brown leather brogues, perforated decoration. **18** Light brown wool-tweed peaked cap. **19** Stamped leather bag, metal frame, clasp fastening, ring handle. **20** Brown leather brogues, perforated decoration, pointed toecaps, stacked heels. **21** Sunburst patchwork leather clutch bag, metal frame, clasp fastening. **22** Dark blue leather lace-up shoes, no toecaps.

The 1930s

Introduction · The 1930s

The holiday mood of the hectic and emancipated 1920s, with its dramatic rejection of womanly curves and feminine flounces, faded with the dawn of the 1930s, a decade plagued by worldwide economic depression.

The fashionable clothes of the previous period, which had been drawn with bold outlines, no waist, abbreviated hemlines and a denial of feminine curves, gave way to a longer, leaner and more figure-hugging silhouette which defined the waist, accentuated the shoulders and narrowed the hips. The fashionable thirties woman emerged mature, understated, cautious and, above all, sophisticated. Her wardrobe contained specialist outfits for every occasion: day, afternoon, sport, spectator sport, informal evening, formal evening, dinner, theatre and more.

Until the middle of the decade, women's fashion moved comparatively slowly. By 1935 the look which had emerged was epitomized by the suit, either crisply tailored or more softly structured. A sleek, fitted jacket, with square, padded shoulders and a tiny waist in its proper place, was teamed with a skirt or dress in matching fabric. This outfit was considered the ultimate in elegance and chic.

The introduction of washable, easy-care luxury fabrics, such as silk, crêpe-de-chine and satin, revolutionized garments of all kinds, from nightdresses to underwear to day dresses and blouses. In addition, the development of man-made fabrics, such as rayon, viscose rayon and tricot, and the improved methods of manufacturing and mass-production techniques meant that well-made and well-cut clothes became available to a wider range of women.

From 1930 evening dresses were a fashion unto themselves. Long or ankle-length, often with a short train, they were moulded onto the body like wet cloth by means of bias-cutting. As much flesh as possible was revealed: for example, halter necklines left the shoulders and most of the back exposed. As the decade progressed, evening dresses became increasingly more extravagant and varied in style, ranging from sleek and figure-hugging crêpes and silk satins, to ruffled diaphanous silk-organdie dresses with puffed sleeves, to multi-layered embroidered net crinolines with tightly fitted, boned, strapless bodices.

Fur – both of the expensive and the cheap varieties – was worn extensively throughout the 1930s in the form of coats, capes, stoles, wraps, accessories and trimmings. The most popular furs were sable, mink, chinchilla, Persian lamb and silver fox, all worn both for day and evening.

As far as men's fashions were concerned, developments in style, colour and cut were extremely slow and, in consequence, they require fewer illustrations.

The minor differences which do occur in the basic trends have been shown, on average, with one example for each page.

In the main, the fashions I have illustrated are such as would have been worn by the middle or upper-middle classes and by people who, while not being 'dedicated followers of fashion', would have had a keen interest in the latest styles.

The sources from which I have drawn – chiefly from Great Britain, North America and France – include contemporary magazines, journals and catalogues, museum collections, original photographs, and my own costume collection.

This section of the Sourcebook is divided into ten parts, each of which includes four subdivisions covering Day Wear, Evening Wear (alternately, on two occasions, Wedding Wear), Sports and Leisure Wear, and a section on either Underwear or Accessories. Following the main illustrations are ten pages of schematic drawings accompanied by detailed notes about each example, giving particulars of colour, fabric, cut and trimming, as well as other useful information.

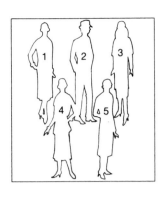

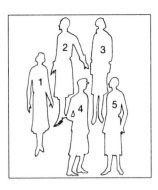
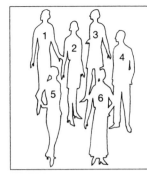

1930 Day Wear

1 Fine cream silk dress spotted in pale orange, low round neckline, brown satin roll collar, ends tied into bow, matching cuffs of long fitted inset sleeves and narrow buckled belt, semi-fitted bodice, top-stitched bolero effect, repeated in hip-level seaming of bias-cut mid-calf-length skirt. Brown leather shoes, bow trim, pointed toes, high heels. **2** Three-piece light-brown wool suit: single-breasted jacket, two-button fastening, flap pockets; single-breasted collarless waistcoat; straight-cut trousers with turn-ups. White cotton collar-attached shirt. Brown and black spotted silk tie. Light-brown trilby. Brown lace-up shoes.
3 Brown and beige wool-tweed two-piece suit: single-breasted knee-length coat, long roll collar, wide fur trim at neck, short shoulder cape, long inset sleeves trimmed with brown velvet L-shaped cuffs, button detail, line repeated as side panels in skirts and incorporates pockets; straight skirt. Fitted brown velvet brimless hat, gathered and buttoned on one side. Brown gloves. Brown leather shoes, elasticated front panels. **4** Dark-red wool-crepe dress, semi-fitted bodice, low neckline, roll collar held in place by self-fabric strap buttoned onto short shoulder cape and at waist above bow-trimmed belt, trim repeated on frilled cuffs of long fitted inset sleeves, bias-cut skirt, curved side panel seams with circular-cut inset short floating panels on side hips. Black leather shoes.
5 Mid-blue, dark-blue and grey flecked wool-jersey dress, asymmetric neckline trimmed with navy-blue top-stitched satin matching threaded tie detail under point of neckline, trim above wrists of inset sleeves, narrow belt and covered buckle, asymmetric hip yoke, flared skirt, pleated side panel. Fitted brimless hat, scalloped edges, matching dress fabric. Navy-blue leather shoes, buckle trim.

Evening Wear

1 Leaf-brown silk-chiffon dinner dress, low boat-shaped neckline, semi-fitted sleeveless bodice, brown velvet ribbon belt with jeweled buckle, bias-cut skirt, deep asymmetric hip yoke, two tiers of circular frills following line through to hem, brown crepe-de-chine underslip, semi-fitted bodice, narrow shoulder straps, bias-cut skirt. Brown satin shoes, pointed toes, high heels. **2** Burnt-orange velvet-embossed georgette evening dress, low scooped neckline, short circular-cut sleeves, bias-cut skirt to knee-level, scalloped seam, orange silk fishtail circular hem, matching belt with jeweled buckle, orange chiffon scarf. Silk shoes, bead trim, pointed toes.
3 Three-piece black wool evening suit: jacket with linked-button fastening, wide lapels faced with satin, piped pockets; low-cut single-breasted waistcoat; straight-cut trousers, satin ribbon trim on outside seams, no turn-ups. White shirt worn with wing collar and black satin bow-tie. Black patent-leather shoes.
4 Black silk-chiffon evening dress, low V-shaped neckline, matching line of inserted lace panel in sleeveless, semi-fitted bodice and in side panels of bias-cut ankle-length skirt, large black velvet roses on one shoulder, dress worn over black silk slip of same shape. Black velvet clutch purse. Black silk shoes.
5 Multicoloured net evening dress, wide boat-shaped neckline, narrow cape collar with frilled edge matching two rows of frills above hem of bias-cut skirt, semi-fitted sleeveless bodice, narrow self-fabric belt, jeweled buckle, scalloped hip-level yoke seam. Small silver clutch purse; matching shoes, pointed toes, high heels.

Sports and Leisure Wear

1 Tennis. Sleeveless semi-fitted white cotton blouse, V-shaped neckline, mock collar and revers trimmed with navy-blue ribbon, matching long knotted tie. Flared white linen skirt, narrow waistband, wide unpressed box-pleats either side centre front, top-stitched to above knee-level. White silk stockings. White leather bar-strap shoes.
2 Skating. Fawn wool-stockinette single-breasted jacket, fastening from hip-level to neck with self-fabric-covered buttons, long fitted inset sleeves, piped pockets above self-fabric buttoned belt. Canary-yellow wool-stockinette scarf, blanket-stitched edges; matching gauntlet gloves and brimless hat. Dark-green wool-stockinette bias-cut skirt to below knee-level. Long beige leather laced skating boots and blades. **3** Country wear. Mottled brown, beige and green wool-jersey three-piece suit: long sweater, V-shaped neckline and mock buttoned strap opening to waist-level edged with dark green crepe-de-chine, matching hip-level pockets, trim on sleeves, pockets, edges of edge-to-edge jacket, scarf and band on edge of beret; flared skirt, top-stitched centre-front inverted box-pleat. Two-tone lace-up leather shoes. **4** Golf. Light-brown and tan checked wool three-piece suit: single-breasted jacket, three-button fastening, flap pockets; collarless single-breasted waistcoat; knee-length plus-fours. Collar-attached shirt. Striped wool tie. Long fawn wool socks. Brown leather lace-up brogues. **5** Golf. Cream machine-knitted wool sweater, V-shaped neckline edged in dark green, matching inset bands, wide centre-front buttoned band, cuffs of inset sleeves and hem. Dark-green accordion-pleated wool skirt. Dark-green wool shirt. Tan wool tie. Dark-green wool brimless hat, tan trim. Tan leather gloves; matching shoes.

Underwear and Negligee

1 Pale-peach artificial-silk chemise top, edged with darker peach binding and appliqué leaves, matching ribbon shoulder straps. Peach brocade corset, deep boned and stitched waistband, ribbed elastic side inserts over hips, boned side-front control darts, centre-front hook-and-bar fastening to mid-hip, laced to hem, four adjustable suspenders. Flesh-coloured silk stockings. **2** Yellow artificial-silk chemise top, edged and trimmed with pale green rouleau, matching shoulder straps; knickers in matching fabric and trim, shaped hip yoke, side-button fastening, long legs, narrow cuffs, inside leg button fastening. **3** Black silk-georgette slip, low brassiere top trimmed with fine black lace, matching hem and hems of knicker legs, black satin ribbon shoulder straps. **4** Green, cream and yellow striped cotton pyjamas: single-breasted jacket, four-button fastening to under shirt collar, single breast patch pocket, long inset sleeves, stitched cuffs; straight-cut trousers. Black leather step-in slippers. **5** Pink cotton corselette, wide shaped boned waistband and fitted upper bodice covered in pink lace, satin ribbon shoulder straps, lightly boned front panels, top-stitched seams, elasticated side-hip panels, four adjustable suspenders, side hook-and-bar fastening. Flesh-coloured silk stockings. **6** Sunrise-pink crepe-de-chine nightdress patterned with cream and pale-green flowers, sleeveless semi-fitted bodice, low V-shaped neckline, two bands of crossed écru lace to give bolero effect, ankle-length bias-cut skirt, self-fabric tie-belt. Pale-pink velvet mules, scalloped edges, pointed toes, medium heels.

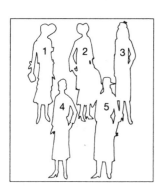 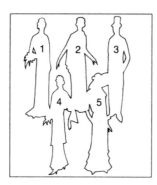 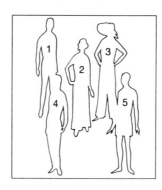 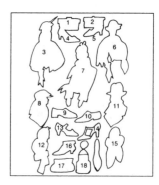

1931 Day Wear

1 Navy-blue wool-georgette dress patterned with large dark-pink flowers, semi-fitted bodice, V-shaped neckline formed by asymmetric wrapover front, edged with circular frill, large bow trim on one side above bust, matching trim above wrists on fitted inset sleeves, self-fabric belt, bias-cut mid-calf-length skirt, low asymmetric hip yoke, three tiers of circular frills. Semi-transparent top-stitched pink silk hat. Navy-blue leather clutch bag; matching shoes. **2** Powder-blue wool-crepe two-piece: edge-to-edge jacket, scalloped hem, matching long flared inset sleeves; dress with semi-fitted bodice, low scooped neckline, white cotton piqué wrapover infill, scalloped edges, self-fabric belt and covered oval buckle, two-tier skirt, scalloped hems. Natural straw hat, pale-blue ribbon band, peach suede flowers. Navy-blue leather clutch bag; matching shoes. Fox-fur stole. **3** Fitted natural-sable hip-length jacket, single fur-covered button-and-loop fastening, high shawl collar, inset sleeves eased into deep cuffs, pelts used vertically, horizontally and diagonally. Cream wool skirt, box-pleats and inverted box-pleats. Tan suede beret. Tan leather shoes. **4** Navy-blue and white wool-crepe dress, low V-shaped neckline faced in white, matching pointed yoke, upper part and pointed cuffs of semi-set-in sleeves, navy-blue covered button detail, pointed scalloped panel above hem of bias-cut skirt, semi-fitted bodice, narrow belt, lower part of sleeves and upper part of skirt all in navy-blue. Navy-blue brimless wool beret. Navy-blue leather shoes. **5** Double-breasted wrapover camel-hair overcoat, wide buckled belt, wide lapels, large collar, inset sleeves, deep cuffs, hip-level welt pockets, top-stitched edges and detail. Straight-cut trousers, turn-ups. Brown trilby. Checked wool scarf. Brown leather gloves and shoes.

Wedding Wear

1 Off-white satin wedding dress, wide scooped neckline edged with pearls, matching hems of fitted full-length inset sleeves, semi-fitted bodice, self-fabric belt, bow trim, long bias-cut skirt gathered from low hip yoke and knee-level seams, short back train. Mid-calf-length silk-tulle veil gathered from self-fabric cap edged with pearls and trimmed with satin roses over each ear. **2** Pale-green satin bridesmaid's dress, sleeveless semi-fitted bodice, decorative curved seam from under arm to centre front, repeated as hip yoke in full-length bias-cut skirt, self-fabric pleated belt, V-shaped neckline, attached self-fabric bias-cut knee-length cape. Tiara of looped ribbon and wax flowers. **3** Morning suit: single-breasted dark-grey wool tailcoat, single-button fastening, double-breasted lapels; single-breasted pale-grey wool collarless waistcoat; black and grey striped trousers, no turn-ups. Light grey top hat. Black shoes worn with grey spats. **4** Oyster crepe-de-chine two-piece wedding outfit: collarless edge-to-edge bolero jacket, inset sleeves, flared cuffs from diagonal seam below elbows; sleeveless dress, semi-fitted bodice, low neckline, self-fabric belt, brooch trim, knee-length overskirt, bias-cut flare from under shaped yoke seam which matches details of ankle-length underskirt. Tiara of silk and wax flowers, full-length silk-tulle veil. Oyster satin shoes, high heels. **5** Turquoise-blue silk-chiffon bridesmaid's dress, semi-fitted bodice, low round neckline, short circular cap sleeves, turquoise and pink chiffon twisted into belt with two-tone bow trim, full-length bias-cut skirt, circular frills at knee, mid-calf and ankle-level. Large pink straw hat, shallow crown, narrow turquoise ribbon band, pink rose trim, wide wired brim. Long pink gloves. Turquoise satin shoes.

Sports and Leisure Wear

1 Swimming. Dark-blue knitted-cotton sleeveless vest, low scooped neckline, open sides, bands of green and red stripes across chest. Fitted green cotton-jersey shorts, self-fabric belt threaded through loops on waistband, metal clip buckle. **2** Beach wear. Sleeveless white cotton blouse, armholes bound in red, matching low V-shaped neckline, scalloped edge of front opening and covered buttons. Red linen trousers, fitted over hips, wide legs, scalloped hems. Brimless white straw hat, wide red ribbon band. **3** Beach wear. Yellow and green spotted linen halter-neck blouse. Yellow linen trousers, fitted over hips, decorative buttoned waistband, side fastening, wide legs flared at hem, two small hip-level triangular-shaped patch pockets in fabric to match blouse. Yellow varnished-straw hat, small crown, yellow and green spotted scarf, outsize brim. **4** Bathing. Navy-blue, pale-blue and fawn flecked wool-jersey costume, armholes and low scooped neckline bound in navy-blue to match buckled belt and inset band on outside seam of fitted legs. Pale-blue rubber bathing cap edged in navy-blue, matching buckled chinstrap. **5** Beach wear. White cotton-jersey vest, low scooped neckline, self-binding, matching armholes, inset red stripe across chest. Red, white and blue striped cotton-canvas shorts, deep waistband, threaded self-fabric buckled belt, wide legs, fly fastening.

Accessories

1 Dark-brown leather clutch bag, orange plastic catch, V-shaped top-stitched tab. **2** Pale-grey leather clutch bag, clasp fastening. **3** Grey moleskin elbow-length shoulder cape combined with sleeveless waistcoat, shawl collar, single-button fastening. Mustard-yellow felt beret, feather trim. Pale-grey suede gauntlet gloves, leather trim. **4** Navy-blue and cream two-tone leather shoes, high heels, almond toes. **5** Cream canvas shoes, tan leather toecaps, matching high heels, laced bar straps and trim. **6** Silver fox-fur stole. Primrose-yellow felt hat, uneven brim, shallow crown, narrow self-fabric band and bow trim. Yellow leather gloves, scalloped frill, bow trim. **7** Long sable stole. Light-brown brimless beret, cream satin-covered button, leaf and rouleau loop trim. **8** Brown and cream checked wool-tweed peaked cap. **9** Brown leather brogues, perforated decoration. **10** Brown and white two-tone leather shoes. **11** Grey felt trilby, tall crown, deep dark-grey petersham ribbon band and bow trim, wide brim. **12** Lilac felt hat, asymmetric top-stitched brim, matching self-fabric bow trim. Grey squirrel scarf, uneven ends threaded through self bow trim. **13** Gold kid evening shoes, brocade fronts and covered heels. **14** Silver kid T-strap dance shoes, sandal fronts, open sides, high heels. **15** South American skunk scarf. Close-fitting brimless feather hat in shades of green. **16** Black leather lace-up ankle-boots, cuffs, low heels. **17** Brown velvet evening bag, shiny brown plastic frame and clasp. **18** Gold kid evening bag, gold metal frame, clasp fastening and long chain handle.

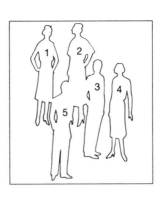
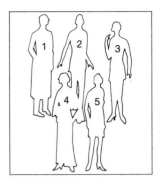

1932 Day Wear

1 Wine-red heavy silk dress, V-shaped neckline meeting point of curved seam running from high waistline at side, matching three seamed panels to hip-level, shaping gathers from shoulder and under bust, long sleeves, full to elbow-level, fitted to wrist, button trim, bias-cut skirt. Dark-red and cream leather shoes, toecaps, high heels. **2** Double-breasted rust coarse-wool-tweed coat, split outsized collar, left side threaded through right forming bow-effect, held by polished-wood button, matching high diagonal three-button fastening at bust level, diagonal elbow-level button trim on long inset sleeves and large round buckle on waist-belt, side hip-level pockets. Small bottle-green felt hat, pointed crown, feather and brooch trim. Bottle-green leather clutch bag, gloves and shoes. **3** Cherry-red ribbed-wool dress, semi-fitted underbodice, horizontal and diagonal rib, double-breasted bolero-effect top, vertical rib matching skirt, large white cotton-piqué lapels, long inset sleeves, horizontal rib, matching narrow belt with round red plastic buckle and curved hip yoke. Red lacquered-straw hat, small pointed crown, white ribbon trim. White cotton gauntlet gloves, red blanket-stitched edges. Fox-fur stole. Red and white leather shoes, toecaps, high heels. **4** Light-brown herringbone weatherproofed wool-tweed coat, double-breasted, two-button fastening, long pointed collar, shaped lapels, button trim, matching detail on long inset sleeves and hip-level pockets. Light-brown knitted-wool beret, brooch trim. Light-brown leather gloves. Brown leather clutch bag; matching shoes. **5** Double-breasted navy-blue wool blazer, wide lapels, flap pockets. Pale-grey flannel trousers, medium-wide legs, turn-ups. White collar-attached shirt. Red and blue striped silk tie. Blue and cream leather lace-up shoes.

Evening Wear

1 Black velvet dinner dress, wide V-shaped neckline, short cape sleeves, padded shoulderline, fitted bodice with asymmetric seaming and gathered shaping, draped and looped self-fabric side-hip detail, long pointed ends, full-length bias-cut flared skirt. Black satin strap sandals. **2** Sleeveless lavender silk-jersey evening dress, low wide V-shaped neckline, curved seam under bust, gathered shaping, bodice gently ruched to hipline, full-length bias-cut flared skirt, asymmetric seam from low side hip to knee level on opposite side, single unpressed knife-pleat and knee-length waterfall on one side. Silver kid strap sandals. **3** Pink silk-organdie dinner dress, asymmetric neckline decorated with self-fabric loops and pointed ends on one side, top-stitched tucks between neckline and short puff sleeves, self-fabric belt, small round self-fabric-covered buckle, full-length bias-cut flared skirt, zig-zag scalloped hip yoke. **4** Heavy black satin-crepe evening dress, wide white piqué shoulder straps, matching large bow trim on side of shaped neckline, bias-cut fitted bodice and full-length flared skirt, pointed seaming under bust, side panel seams pointing to centre front from waist to knee level. **5** Formal dinner dress, beige lace semi-fitted bodice, low-cut back, wide curved V-shaped neckline, attached short shoulder cape, waist-length at back, full-length bias-cut flared skirt in heavy dull-beige silk-crepe.

Sports and Leisure Wear

1 Golf. Hand-knitted bottle-green wool crew-neck sweater and matching collarless cardigan, single-breasted, three-button fastening in deep waist rib, patch pockets, inset sleeves with turned-back cuffs. Green, yellow and brown flecked wool-tweed flared skirt, wide box-pleat buttoned on each side from waist to hip-level, knife-pleat under box-pleat from below button detail to hem. Brimless dark-yellow wool sectioned beret, stalk in centre. Brown and yellow leather shoes, low stacked heels. **2** Holiday wear. Beige cotton dress patterned with brown circles, semi-fitted bodice, cowl neckline, elbow-length circular-cut cape sleeves, draped cummerbund, bias-cut mid-calf-length skirt, asymmetric seaming. Small brimless brown felt hat, cream petersham ribbon bow trim. Beige leather shoes. **3** Tennis. Machine-knitted white cotton shirt, short inset sleeves, buttoned strap opening from chest-level to under collar. White linen trousers, pleats under deep waistband, self-fabric buckled belt, side-hip pockets, wide legs, turn-ups. White leather lace-up shoes. **4** Tennis. Sleeveless white linen dress, semi-fitted bodice, separate apron front, buttoned at bust level, wide stiffened self-fabric belt, asymmetric white plastic buckle, flared panelled mid-calf-length skirt. White leather lace-up shoes, thick medium-high heels. **5** Golf. Hand-knitted maroon wool collarless cardigan, single-breasted, fastening with five leather buttons, inset sleeves, turned-back cuffs, patch pockets above deep welt. Grey and brown flecked wool trousers, side-hip pockets, wide legs, turn-ups. Light-grey wool collar-attached shirt. Striped wool-tweed tie. Two-tone leather lace-up shoes.

Underwear and Negligee

1 Mid-calf-length mustard-yellow quilted-silk dressing gown, wrapover front, black satin roll collar edges piped with yellow silk to match deep cuffs of inset sleeves, tops of hip-level patch pockets and tie-belt with tassel ends. Pale-grey silk pyjamas. Black leather step-in slippers. **2** Pale-peach satin combination camisole and knickers, brassiere top, scalloped edges matching hems of wide legs, button fastening in crotch, narrow self-fabric rouleau shoulder straps. **3** Cream cotton-satin brassiere, fitted cups, adjustable fitting strap from back fastening, narrow adjustable shoulder straps. Lightweight white rubber girdle, high waist, light boning, double front panel, laced side opening, four adjustable suspenders. Pleated pink artificial-silk slip. Dark-flesh silk stockings. **4** Pale-green crepe-de-chine two-piece pyjama suit: short bolero jacket, scalloped edges bound in self-fabric and trimmed with one tiny self-fabric-covered button in each point, full-length sleeves flared from elbow, trimmed with dark-green chiffon and black lace; combination bias-cut top and wide flared trousers, low shaped neckline and seam under bust trimmed to match sleeve hems, wide trousers fall from pointed hip seam and have scalloped hems to match bolero. Pale-green velvet mules trimmed with satin. **5** Pink satin and elastic combination brassiere and girdle, fitted brassiere covered with pink lace, narrow adjustable shoulder straps, hip-length body, elasticated side panels and centre-front gusset, four cotton and elastic adjustable suspenders. Short silk slip. Satin house shoes.

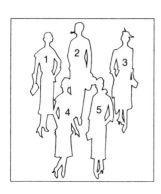

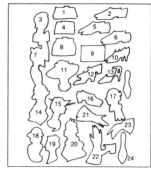

1933 Day Wear

1 Lido-green wool dress, cape collar, scalloped edge bound in black to match half-cuffs of long tight sleeves, belt and covered buckle; semi-fitted bodice, panels extend into flared skirt, brass button trim on diagonal hip seams, matching collar and cuffs. Black felt hat, narrow upturned split brim, self-fabric trim. Black leather clutch bag; matching shoes. 2 Brown and grey checked wool-tweed single-breasted jacket, three-button fastening, patch pockets, inverted box-pleat decoration. Fawn wool trousers, wide legs, turn-ups. Cream collar-attached shirt. Brown wool tie. Fawn trilby. Brown shoes. 3 Slate-blue wool-crepe dress, diagonal fastening to under burnt-orange top-stitched satin collar which matches buttons, belt, round buckle and cuffs set at three-quarter-length on long inset sleeves, gathered heads and padded shoulders, diagonal seam from side waist to opposite side hip, two inverted box-pleats at matching angle on side front of flared skirt. Slate-blue brimless pillbox hat, blue feather trim. Tan leather clutch bag, gloves and shoes. Grey fox fur. 4 Yellow crepe-de-chine dress patterned in brown and dark-red, fitted bodice, round neckline, curved off-the-shoulder yoke edged with narrow frill, repeated in three tiers under low curved hip seam, flared skirt, waist-level slotted belt tied at back, long tight sleeves. Small dark-red felt hat, narrow upturned brim, button trim. Brown leather shoes. 5 Double-breasted wine wool coat, two-button fastening at waist level, inset bias-cut decoration between two vertical panel seams, matching decoration on hip-level pockets, sleeve hems and above trim, inset sleeves with buttoned point extension from elbow. Black felt hat, narrow brim, button trim. Wine and cream striped silk scarf. Black leather clutch bag and shoes.

Evening Wear

1 Black wool two-piece evening suit: double-breasted jacket, wide lapels faced with satin, matching covered buttons, hip-level piped pockets, breast pocket, white silk handkerchief; wide trousers, no turn-ups. White silk shirt worn with wing collar. Black satin bow-tie. Black patent-leather shoes. 2 Pale-gold satin evening dress, low V-shaped neckline and shaped seam under bust to waist-level form upper bodice and shoulder straps, bias-cut bodice and flared skirt with asymmetric seaming. 3 Fine turquoise silk-velvet dance dress, scooped neckline, three-tier self-fabric frilled short cap sleeves, matching frill inserted in shaped seam under bust and four tiers of frills above hem of flared skirt, bias-cut bodice and skirt with shaped seams at hip and knee level. 4 Yellow crepe-de-chine sleeveless dance dress, low wide V-shaped neckline edged with three rows of circular-cut frills of white silk-organdie, black velvet ribbon bow with long ends on centre front, matching cummerbund, semi-fitted bodice, panel seams, repeated in wide flared skirt, circular-cut godets inserted at knee-level of each seam. 5 Dinner outfit: deep-gold satin collarless jacket, wrapover front, tied at back with long waterfall ends, short circular-cut semi-inset sleeves, padded shoulders; black silk-velvet dress, bias-cut fitted bodice and full-length flared skirt, panel seams curving from side-waist to off-centre hip ending in wide flared box-pleat.

Sports and Leisure Wear

1 Country wear. Three-piece brown and beige checked wool suit: single-breasted jacket, two-button fastening, wide lapels, flap pockets; collarless single-breasted waistcoat; wide trousers, turn-ups. White collar-attached shirt. Spotted silk tie. Beige trilby. Brown leather shoes. 2 Racing or garden-party wear. Pink lace two-piece: unlined bolero, scalloped hem, matching elbow-length circular-cut oversleeves, full-length tight undersleeves, button fastening at wrist, long narrow scarf collar; sleeveless dress worn over full-length pink silk petticoat, V-shaped neckline, bodice ruched either side narrow central panel, self-fabric belt, clasp fastening, ankle-length bias-cut flared skirt, scalloped seam at hip-level. Pink straw hat, shallow crown, wide brim. Cream kid shoes. 3 Golf. Three-piece light-brown hand-knitted wool suit: edge-to-edge collarless jacket, buttoned belt, shaped hem, dark-brown cable-knit trim of long inset sleeves, shaped hem and V-shaped neckline of sleeveless sweater and above hemline of flared skirt. Dark-brown hand-knitted wool hat, rolled brim, stalk trim. Brown and cream leather lace-up shoes, flat heels. 4 Country wear. Two-piece beige and brown flecked wool-tweed suit: single-breasted jacket, two-button fastening, wide lapels, long inset sleeves, padded shoulders, panel seams from shoulders to top of flap pockets; flared panelled skirt. Cream silk blouse, top-stitched stand collar, matching strap opening. Tan felt hat, petersham trim. Tan leather gauntlet gloves and clutch bag. Brown leather lace-up shoes. 5 Tennis. White cotton dress, square neckline, small collar, asymmetric button opening from hip-level through inset waistband to neckline, slightly flared skirt, three knife-pleats on left side. White canvas lace-up shoes, low heels.

Accessories

1 Brown leather clutch bag, decorative stitching, clasp fastening. 2 Brown leather lace-up shoes, piped seams. 3 Red and blue spotted silk beret. Matching scarf tied into large bow. 4 Bottle-green leather clutch bag, tan and cream leather applied trim. 5 Brown leather lace-up shoes, buckled overstrap, perforated trim. 6 Brown and cream leather lace-up shoes. 7 Dusty-pink felt beret, top-stitched pink satin band, self-fabric trim. 8 Blue and beige leather clutch bag, top-stitched trim. 9 Black leather envelope clutch bag, top-stitched flap. 10 Fawn suede lace-up shoes, tan leather heels and trim. 11 Fine pale-yellow straw hat, wide wired brim, shallow crown, satin roses trim. 12 Bottle-green and cream leather shoes, low thick heels. 13 Black satin dance shoes, ankle straps, cut-away sides and front detail, high slender heels. 14 Brown straw hat, tall crown, wide satin band and bow trim, narrow top-stitched brim. 15 Green felt trilby, black petersham band, feather trim. 16 Lace-up tan leather shoes, perforated decoration, low thick heels. 17 Hand-knitted slate-blue beret, bow trim. Matching scarf, double-scalloped hem. 18 Powder-blue felt hat, shallow crown, self-colour petersham band and bow trim, navy-blue and white striped ribbon band, curled brim. Buttoned fur collar. 19 Black straw pillbox hat, black and white ribbon bow trim on back. 20 Small grey felt hat with turned-up brim, grey ribbon trim. 21 Pink and blue felt gauntlet gloves. 22 Brown leather gauntlet gloves, elasticated at wrist, mock side-button fastening. 23 Hand-knitted cream cotton gauntlet gloves, inset wristband, scalloped edges. 24 Brown and cream leather bar-strap shoes, low stacked heels.

1934 Day Wear

1 Cream and green flecked linen-tweed coat-dress, bloused bodice, front opening from waist to under collar and revers, cream silk infill, long inset sleeves, sewn cuffs, panel seams from padded shoulders to waist, double-breasted button trim, seams continued to hem of flared skirt, self-fabric belt, diamond-shaped brown plastic buckle. Cream felt trilby. Brown leather clutch bag; matching shoes. **2** Double-breasted fawn and donkey-brown herringbone wool-tweed coat, large collar and wide lapels, long inset sleeves with cuffs, padded shoulders, tailored self-fabric buckled belt, narrow skirt, hip-level welt pockets. Brown felt hat, brown and fawn petersham ribbon trim. Orange silk scarf. Fawn suede shoes. **3** Green, red and cream diagonally striped cotton dress, bloused bodice, V-shaped neckline, large self-fabric bow trim, short inset sleeves with cuffs, padded shoulders, flared skirt, green suede belt, large buckle. Green straw hat, wide brim, shallow crown, red and cream petersham ribbon trim. Green leather clutch bag and gauntlet gloves. Brown and cream leather shoes. **4** Three-piece fawn and light-brown striped wool suit: single-breasted jacket, three-button fastening, wide lapels, flap pockets; collarless single-breasted waistcoat; wide trousers, turn-ups. Fawn striped white cotton collar-attached shirt. Brown, red and black patterned silk tie. Fawn felt trilby. Brown leather lace-up shoes. **5** Silver-grey wool-crepe two-piece suit: bloused top, short peplum, V-shaped neckline edged with top-stitched black satin, matching buckled belt, inset sleeves flared and gathered at elbow-level, fitted to wrist, top-stitched black satin cuffs, padded shoulders, black and white leather scarf-effect with flared ends buttoned to bodice; bias-cut flared skirt. Black hat. Black and white leather shoes.

Evening Wear

1 Black lace evening dress worn over shell-pink shift of same shape, sleeveless bloused bodice, low scooped neckline draped with bias-cut shell-pink silk-velvet scarf, held on each shoulder by pearl-edged brooch, armholes draped in same fashion, matching velvet belt ruched into pearl-edged buckle, bias-cut skirt, curved V-shaped seam from side hip to centre-front seam, slight train. Wide pink plastic wrist-bangle. **2** Pale-gold silk-satin sleeveless evening dress, boat-shaped neckline draped with self-fabric scarf, ends fall to knee-level at back, hems trimmed with velvet leaves in golds, browns and oranges, matching hem of full-length bias-cut flared skirt, bodice and skirt cut in one piece, asymmetric seaming across body from right shoulder to hem. **3** Moss-green silk-satin sleeveless evening dress, cowl draped from halter-neck, back fastening, fitted bias-cut bodice to four rows of horizontal panels on hipline, curve on side hip and flare into wide panels at hem forming slight train. **4** Black silk-velvet sleeveless evening dress, curved seam under bust from side to centre front, low V-shaped neckline, infilled with bright-red and pink silk roses, matching spray on curved seam at knee-level above deep circular-cut gathered frill, bias-cut fitted bodice and narrow skirt cut in one piece. Large paste wrist-bangle. **5** Jade-green silk-satin sleeveless evening dress, low V-shaped neckline, trimmed on point with large pleated white silk-organdie bow, bias-cut fitted bodice and skirt, intricate seaming under bust, on front bodice and on side hips through to hem, slight train.

Sports and Leisure Wear

1 Holiday wear. Blue, yellow and cream striped cotton jacket, single-breasted two-button fastening, wide lapels, flap pockets. Cream flannel trousers, wide legs, turn-ups, leather belt. Machine-knitted white cotton shirt, short buttoned strap opening to under collar, worn open. Brown leather lace-up shoes. **2** Holiday wear. Pale-blue linen two-piece: fitted blouse top, mock wrapover buttoned fastening, wide shoulder straps, button trim, V-shaped armholes; flared skirt, centre-front box-pleat, hip-level patch pockets, wide waistband, button trim. Blue and yellow checked cotton blouse, short puff sleeves, narrow cuffs, knotted bow trim, matching bow-tie under tiny peter-pan collar. Yellow straw hat, wide brim, shallow crown. Blue and white leather shoes. **3** Holiday wear. White cotton dress patterned in coffee, high round neckline, bound edge, pleated jabot matching short sleeves set into curved yoke seam and hem of straight skirt, bloused bodice, white leather belt buckled over right hip. Brown cotton beret. White cotton gauntlet gloves. Brown leather clutch bag, white trim. Brown leather shoes. **4** Golf. Yellow, brown, beige and orange hand-knitted wool sweater, wide neckline, scarf collar, ends tied at front, long inset sleeves, plain brown turned-back ribbed cuffs, matching deep waistband, above waist to hip-level. Brown and beige wool-tweed flared panelled skirt. Brown knitted-wool beret. Brown leather lace-up shoes, flat heels. **5** Golf. Hand-knitted maroon wool sweater, V-shaped neckline, long inset sleeves, turned-back cuffs. Beige and fawn flecked wool-tweed breeches, legs gathered above knees, side hip pockets. Beige wool collar-attached shirt. Striped wool tie. Beige checked wool-tweed cap. Maroon, cream and fawn checked wool stockings. Brown leather lace-up shoes.

Underwear and Negligee

1 Pale-blue artificial-silk nightdress, bloused bodice trimmed with coffee lace, repeated in V-shaped hip panel and band above hem, tied self-fabric rouleau belt with bow, matching neck edge and shoulder straps. Blue satin mules trimmed with loops of self-fabric rouleau, medium heels. **2** White machine-knitted cotton collarless vest, short sleeves, bound hems to match V-shaped neckline and front opening, rubber buttons. Short white machine-knitted drawers, elasticated waistband, single-button fastening, fly-front opening, V-shaped hip yoke, wide legs, machine-stitched hems. **3** Full-length pale-green crepe-de-chine slip, brassiere top trimmed with fine cream lace and silk ribbon, matching shoulder straps, inverted V-shaped seam from side-waist to centre-front under bust and triangular panels decorating hem of full skirt. **4** Sky-blue combination bodice and pyjama trousers, patterned in bright pink, sleeveless wrapover top, fastening on side left hip, edges piped in pink, matching armholes and ribbon belt threaded from side-front to tied bow at back, wide flared trousers. Blue satin slippers. **5** Cream artificial-silk dressing gown, patterned in orange, brown and yellow spots and circles, sleeveless wrapover bodice, elbow-length circular-cut cape collar, edged with orange, brown and yellow ribbons, matching side-front edge, hip-level tied bow and long ends and top of single hip-level patch pocket. Yellow satin house shoes, brown and beige feather pompon trim, high heels.

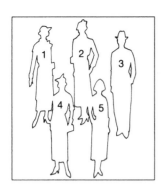
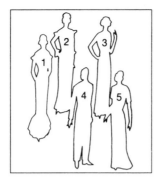
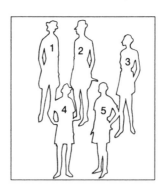
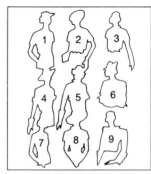

1935 Day Wear

1 Charcoal, black and pale-grey flecked wool-tweed coat-dress with horizontal rib, wrapover semi-fitted bodice, low V-shaped neckline, black suede vest infill, matching wide buttoned belt with arrow-shaped end, short shoulder cape under scarf collar tied into large bow, long inset sleeves, padded shoulders, white piqué cuffs, narrow knee-length skirt, mid-calf-length underskirt, wide box-pleat. Black straw hat, light-grey ribbon trim. Black leather clutch bag; matching shoes, bow trim, high heels.
2 Single-breasted dark-blue, grey and black wool-tweed coat, long inset sleeves, black Persian lamb 'cuffs' from wrist to above elbow and point to below padded shoulders, matching large collar, narrow skirts, hip-level piped pockets. Varnished black straw hat, asymmetric brim, self-straw trim. Black leather clutch bag and gloves. Black and white leather shoes. **3** Two-piece grey flannel suit: double-breasted jacket, wide lapels, piped pockets; wide trousers, turn-ups. Grey and white striped cotton collar-attached shirt. Red and grey striped silk tie. Grey trilby. Black leather shoes. **4** White linen two-piece suit: fitted hip-length jacket, fastening on left side with large navy-blue plastic buttons from hem to bust, square neckline, shallow collar, inset elbow-length cuffed sleeves, padded shoulders, navy-blue suede belt, asymmetric white plastic buckle; narrow panelled skirt, inverted box-pleats from knee-level. Navy-blue silk scarf with white spots; matching brimless hat. White cotton gauntlet gloves. Navy-blue leather clutch bag. Navy-blue and white leather shoes. **5** Fawn wool dress, semi-fitted bodice, padded shoulders, round neckline, bias-cut jabot fastened in four places with red plastic buttons, matching hems of raglan sleeves, belt and side-hip panel seams of flared skirt. Fawn felt hat. Beige suede shoes, red leather trim.

Evening Wear

1 White silk-organdie sleeveless evening dress spotted in black, wide neckline and combined yoke, deep gathered self-fabric frill edged with black silk ribbon and black lace, bias-cut fitted bodice and narrow skirt, wide gathered frill above ankle-length at front and mid-calf-length at back, trimmed to match yoke frill, black velvet ribbon belt knotted on right side. **2** Two-piece dark-plum velvet theatre/dinner suit: waist-length single-breasted jacket, four-button fastening, panelled semi-fitted bodice, circular black net hip yoke attached at waist under self-fabric belt, matching collar on wide neckline and cuffs of long tight inset sleeves; full-length bias-cut panelled flared skirt. Brimless pillbox hat covered with tiny black organdie flowers.
3 Bronze silk-satin formal evening dress, bias-cut bodice and full-length flared skirt cut in one piece, central seam front and back, wide extended shoulder straps draped and tied above V-shaped neckline, low back.
4 Black wool formal two-piece evening suit: double-breasted tailcoat, worn open, wide satin lapels, matching covered buttons; wide trousers, black satin ribbon trim on outside seams, no turn-ups. Double-breasted white piqué waistcoat, wide shawl collar. White starched-front shirt worn with wing collar and white bow-tie. Black patent-leather shoes.
5 Sleeveless black lace theatre/dinner dress worn over peach silk-crepe dress cut on same lines, V-shaped neckline, panelled bodice, full-length bias-cut panelled skirt, slight train. Waist-length black velvet jacket, bias-cut waterfall collar, ends tied and knotted on centre-front waist, circular-cut elbow-length sleeves, padded shoulders.

Sports and Leisure Wear

1 Riding. Hip-length moss-green, fawn and tan flecked wool-tweed fitted jacket, single-breasted fastening, panel seams, wide lapels, tight inset sleeves, button trim, diagonal welt pockets below waist. Fawn twill jodhpurs, turn-ups, stitched panel on inside leg at knee level. Fawn wool sweater. Green, tan and cream striped silk scarf worn at neck. Moss-green felt hat worn at an angle, curled brim. Brown leather gloves; matching lace-up ankle-boots. **2** Riding. Dark-green wool single-breasted jacket, three-button fastening, wide lapels, inset sleeves, stitched cuffs, button trim, patch pockets with inverted box-pleats. Light-brown twill jodhpurs, full to above knees, buttoned over knees, worn tucked into long brown leather boots. Cream wool collar-attached shirt. Pale-green, grey and tan checked wool tie. Brown trilby. Brown leather gloves. **3** Beach wear. Yellow cotton two-piece: orange and green large spot pattern, short top, halter-neck gathered onto white cotton rope, tied at front into large bow; flared shorts cut without waistband, wide legs, central crease. Yellow and white checked cotton shoes, self-fabric rouleau bow fastening, flat heels. 4 Tennis. Cream machine-knitted cotton, ribbed design, open collar, narrow shoulder yoke continued into short dolman sleeves, bodice bloused into waistband. Short white linen culottes, knife-pleats from waist to low hip-level. White cotton ankle-socks. White canvas lace-up sports shoes. **5** Beach wear. Pink, navy-blue and white checked cotton combination blouse and shorts, strap opening from hip-level to under pointed revers, large white plastic buttons, matching trim on breast patch pockets and large buckle on belt, short sleeves, padded shoulders, shorts with wide leg. Navy-blue leather shoes, strap-and-bow fastening, flat heels.

Blouses and Accessories

1 Hip-length blue linen collarless blouse, left side fastening, square neckline, large navy-blue plastic buttons, short inset sleeves, top-stitched satin binding, matching belt and patch pocket, padded shoulders. Navy-blue felt hat, split brim, top-stitched satin trim.
2 Brown and beige striped taffeta collarless blouse, round neckline, bias-cut facing, top-stitched detail, matching short inset sleeves and side panels in bodice, narrow waistband, plastic bow trim. Brown felt hat worn at an angle, cream petersham bow trim. Brown leather clutch bag; matching gloves. **3** Pale-blue silk-crepe blouse, pattern of pink flowers, scarf collar tied into large bow, short dolman sleeves, padded shoulders. Navy-blue suede belt, round buckle. **4** Hip-length dark-brown linen blouse, large cream linen collar matching cuffs of short raglan-style sleeves, centre-front zip fastening, button trim, top-stitched self-fabric belt. Beige felt hat, brown ribbon trim. Beige leather gauntlet gloves, bow trim. **5** White frilled organdie jabot, bow trim, wing collar. Navy-blue linen jacket, wide lapels. Navy-blue felt hat. Navy-blue leather gauntlet gloves. **6** Cream artificial-silk blouse, strap fastening, shirt collar, shoulder yoke, short inset sleeves, padded shoulders, small breast patch pocket. Brown lacquered-straw hat, fancy crown. **7** Hip-length cream crepe-de-chine collarless blouse, shaped seam under bust, cream crepe-de-chine raglan sleeves patterned with outsized bright-pink spots. **8** Oatmeal silk blouse, short raglan-style sleeves, pink, yellow and pale-blue checked taffeta pleated jabot. Wide pink leather belt, round buckle. Cream straw hat, pink ribbon trim. **9** Red and white spotted silk blouse, long inset sleeves trimmed from wrist to elbow with pleated white organdie, matching collar and front opening to bust-level.

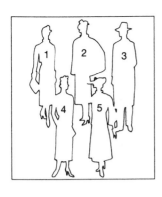
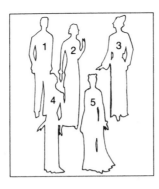

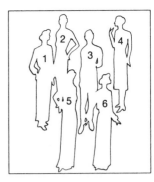

1936 Day Wear

1 Pale-blue and cream linen two-piece suit: semi-fitted top, double-breasted fastening between two small bust-level patch pockets and under narrow roll collar, long inset sleeves, padded shoulders, dark-blue linen belt fastening under bow trim; flared skirt, box-pleats sewn to low hip-level. Light-brown silk scarf worn in V-shaped neckline. Dark-blue brimless hat. Cream gauntlet gloves. Navy-blue leather clutch bag; matching shoes, stacked heels. **2** Hip-length green wool cape, front edges bound in brown leather, padded shoulders, matching flared skirt. Beige wool collarless single-breasted jacket, fastened with self-fabric covered buttons in two sets of three, single patch pocket above brown leather buckled belt and two below. Brown felt hat, asymmetric truncated crown. Beige leather gauntlets. Brown leather bar-strap shoes. **3** Fawn rainproofed wool overcoat, fly fastening under wide lapels, raglan sleeves, button trim, flap pockets. Striped wool trousers, wide legs, turn-ups. Brown felt trilby. Brown leather gloves and lace-up shoes. **4** Bottle-green wool collarless coat-dress, single-breasted fastening with large black buttons, high neckline, matching belt buckle, long cuffed sleeves, gathers from shoulder yoke/epaulettes, flared skirt, wide knife-pleats sewn to low hip. Black felt pillbox hat with green silk roses. Black clutch bag. Black and white leather shoes. **5** Pale-yellow lightweight wool coat-dress, single-breasted fastening with large buttons from tie-belt to under matching scarf collar, dropped and padded shoulderline, three-quarter-length panelled sleeves, narrow cuffs, seams of panelled bodice continued into flared skirt from waist to hem. Dark-ochre felt hat, wide brim split to form peak at front, self-trim. Cream gauntlet gloves. Brown leather shoes.

Evening Wear

1 Cream synthetic-and-wool mixture dinner jacket, single-breasted, single-button fastening, wide lapels faced with silk, flap pockets. Black mohair trousers, wide legs, silk braid trim on outside seam, no turn-ups. Black silk pleated cummerbund, matching bow-tie. White piqué collar-attached shirt. Black leather shoes. **2** Rust silk-crepe evening dress, semi-fitted bodice, low draped décolletage, self-fabric padded and twisted shoulder straps, narrow belt, clasp fastening, bustle attached to back of belt, bias-cut skirt, slight train at back. **3** Dull-mulberry crepe dinner dress, single-breasted bloused bodice, three-button fastening to under bust, hook-and-bar fastening under collar, button trim, padded shoulders, dropped sleeve head, long wide inset sleeves, wide self-fabric belt, button fastening, hip-level narrow circular skirt, curved central split to above ankles, hip-level triangular flap pockets set at an angle. Hat in matching fabric, pointed crown, twisted padded brim. Black satin shoes, crossed straps. **4** Red silk-velvet dinner/theatre dress, bloused bodice, low V-shaped neckline, deep armholes edged with wide band of stiffened gold tissue, matching set of covered buttons on either side centre-front seam, padded shoulders, draped skirt, pleated floating panel from waist to ground at front, short train at back. **5** Dull-moss-green crepe evening dress, ruched bodice, narrow shoulder straps hidden under pleated pale-grey silk chiffon, trails to ground at back, brooch trim on neck edge, panelled skirt flared from knee-level with circular-cut inset godets.

Sports and Leisure Wear

1 Country wear. Ochre, beige and tan checked wool-tweed two-piece suit: single-breasted fitted jacket, three-button fastening from waist to under wide lapels, full-length fitted inset sleeves, padded shoulders, patch-and-flap pockets; narrow skirt, centre-front split from hem to below knee. Cream crepe blouse. Tan felt hat, feather trim. Light-brown leather envelope clutch bag, matching gloves. Brown and tan leather lace-up shoes, high-stacked heels. **2** Ski wear. Two-piece bottle-green wool suit: hip-length double-breasted belted jacket, fastening from hem to under stand collar, inset sleeves, large hip-level patch-and-flap pockets; wide trousers gathered into buttoned cuffs on ankle. Cream silk scarf at neck. Knitted rust wool hat, pompon trim. Knitted cream wool gauntlet mittens. Dark-green leather lace-up boots. **3** Holiday wear. Grey and cream striped linen two-piece suit: single-breasted jacket, single-button fastening, wide lapels, flap pockets; wide trousers, turn-ups. Cream cotton collar-attached shirt. Green, tan and grey striped silk tie. Natural straw boater, green ribbon band. Tan leather gloves and lace-up shoes. **4** Country wear. Green, brown and red checked wool single-breasted overcoat, raglan sleeves, large collar, wide lapels, flap pockets. Plus-fours in matching fabric. Green and red spotted silk scarf. Brown wool-tweed peaked cap. Brown leather gloves and lace-up shoes. **5** Holiday wear. Pale yellow artificial-silk dress patterned in brown, round neckline, top-stitched facing, matching panel seams and hip-level patch pockets, short flared raglan sleeves, padded shoulders, bloused bodice, cord lacing decoration each side centre-front from neck to bustline, flared skirt, panel seams end in pleats, white leather belt. Beige straw hat. White gloves and shoes.

Underwear and Negligee

1 White artificial-silk two-piece pyjama suit: hip-length top, unfitted and gathered from shoulder yoke seam, tie-belt, buttoned strap fastening from bust-level to under peter-pan collar, long inset sleeves gathered into narrow cuffs, appliqué flowers and leaf motifs in pinks, blues and greens decorate upper part of bodice; matching wide hems of flared trousers. Pink leather moccasins. **2** Peach satin brassiere, fitted cups covered in peach lace, adjustable shoulder straps, back fastening. Cream perforated latex girdle, elasticated front gusset and waistband, four adjustable and detachable suspenders. Pale-flesh silk stockings. **3** Salmon-pink light-weight knitted-wool unit-suit: sleeveless vest with V-shaped neckline, front strap fastening, rubber buttons; knickers with short pant legs. Brown wool carpet slippers. **4** Pale-turquoise silk slip, neck edge trimmed with coffee lace matching hemline of flared skirt, shaped side panels from underarm, self-fabric rouleau shoulder straps. Turquoise velvet mules. **5** Pale-blue silk nightdress, draped neckline, armholes shaped into neck, trimmed with cream lace, shaped seam under bust, ground-length bias-cut flared skirt. **6** Salmon-pink artificial-silk negligee, high round neckline gathered in by self-colour ribbon, matching tie at waist-level, full-length bishop-style inset sleeves gathered into padded shoulders and into ruched elasticated bands at wrist-level, ground-length full skirt and bodice cut in one piece.

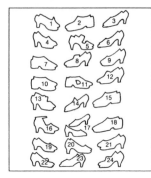

1937 Day Wear

1 Three-piece light-grey and charcoal striped wool suit: single-breasted jacket, three-button fastening, wide lapels, flap pockets; collarless single-breasted waistcoat; wide trousers with turn-ups. Fawn and white striped cotton collar-attached shirt. Grey, brown and tan striped silk tie. Grey trilby. Black leather gloves and shoes. **2** Short brown linen collarless bolero-style jacket, edge-to-edge, long inset sleeves, padded shoulders, mock-flap pockets. Cream linen dress, top-stitched, buttoned step opening from bust to under round neckline, flared skirt, inverted box-pleat from above knee-level to hemline, brown leather belt, large gilt buckle. Brown felt hat, cream silk drapery. Cream gauntlet gloves. Brown leather bag. Brown and cream leather shoes. **3** Fawn and rust checked wool collarless double-breasted coat, large buttons under high neckline and on waistline, small mock-flap pockets on bust and hip-level, long inset sleeves, padded shoulders, flared skirt. Rust silk scarf. Brown felt hat, narrow curled brim. Brown leather bag, gloves and shoes. **4** Navy-blue linen collarless coat, edge-to-edge, loop-and-button fastening on waist, fitted panelled bodice and flared skirt cut in one piece, full-length inset sleeves, padded shoulders, navy-blue suede flower. Collarless white linen dress patterned with red birds. Navy-blue lacquered-straw hat, shallow crown trimmed with white ribbon bow, wide brim. White cotton gauntlet gloves. Navy-blue leather bag. Navy-blue and white leather shoes. **5** Dark-red lightweight wool dress, bloused bodice, shaped seam under bust, ruched either side central seam, wing collar, full-length inset sleeves, padded shoulders, two-tier flared skirts, wide black suede belt knotted into bow on centre front. Black suede shoes, bow trim.

Wedding Wear

1 Cream silk-crepe two-piece: wrapover jacket, long shawl collar, draped tied belt, long waterfall ends, inset sleeves, full from padded shoulders, gathered at elbow-level, tight and ruched from elbow to wrist-level, pointed hem, button fastening from wrist to elbow; full-length dress, cowl neckline, panelled flared skirt, slight train. Brimless hat, covered in cream silk, edged with pearls; short cream net veil. **2** Bias-cut oyster satin wedding dress, high round neckline edged with two rows of pearl-edged embroidered net, matching trim on gathered puff oversleeves and pearl-edged hem of tight undersleeves, fitted bodice, seam from centre-front under bust to bust point to side seams above waist, fitted skirt, short train. Ground-length Edwardian lace veil, scalloped edges; heart-shaped headdress of wax flowers and pearls. **3** White silk-crepe wedding dress, draped neckline between raglan seams of white silk-chiffon sleeves, flared to wrists and below, bias-cut bodice and skirt cut in one piece, short train. White pleated silk fan-shaped headdress; long silk-tulle veil, embroidered edges. **4** Turquoise satin bridesmaid's dress, pattern of pink, white, pale-blue and pale-green flowers and leaves, padded shoulders, short inset puff sleeves gathered into narrow bands, semi-fitted bodice, centre-front seam ruched from bust-level to under V-shaped neckline, velvet ribbon belt, round buckle, flared skirt. Turquoise straw hat, rouleau band and bow in dress fabric. **5** Pale-pink silk-taffeta wedding dress, high round neckline, small mandarin collar, padded shoulders, short puffed oversleeves, tight undersleeves ruched from wrist to elbow, decorative pearl-button trim, matching centre-front seam from under neckline to low hip-level flared skirt. Pale-pink silk-organdie headdress, pearl trim; long pink silk-tulle veil.

Sports and Leisure Wear

1 Country wear. Two-piece brown and black flecked wool-tweed suit: single-breasted jacket, three-button fastening, narrow lapels, flap pockets, knee-length plus-fours. Hand-knitted brown wool sweater. Cream collar-attached shirt. Brown wool-tweed tie. Brown wool-tweed peaked cap. Long beige wool socks. Brown and tan leather lace-up shoes. **2** Country wear. Bottle-green, cream and rust checked wool seven-eighths-length coat, single-breasted, single-button fastening, wide lapels, padded shoulders, inset sleeves, buttoned cuffs, patch pockets. Bottle-green wool skirt, centre-front knife-pleat. Cream wool scarf. Bottle-green felt hat, small crown, rust ribbon band. Brown leather shoes. **3** Tennis. White cotton dress, bloused bodice, stepped button fastening under round neckline, vertical epaulettes, padded shoulders, puff sleeves, wide self-fabric buckled belt, flared skirt, small hip-level patch pockets set at an angle, facing knife-pleats from pocket points. White cotton ankle-socks. White sports shoes. **4** Country wear. Double-breasted tan wool coat, wide lapels, outsized collar, padded shoulders, long sleeves, button trim, self-fabric buckled belt, hip-level patch-and-flap pockets, flared skirts. Cream and green patterned silk scarf. Brown felt hat, shallow rounded crown, self-felt trim. Brown leather gloves and shoes. **5** Holiday wear. Pale-blue artificial-silk two-piece suit patterned in white and fawn circles: short fitted single-breasted jacket, three self-fabric-covered buttons under wide lapels, padded shoulders, puff sleeves, waist-level mock-flap pockets; flared skirt, pintucked panels from hip yoke. Beige lacquered-straw hat, small crown, flat top, wide brim, yellow and white felt flower trim. White gloves. Light-brown leather bag and shoes.

Footwear

1 Brown suede shoes, high vamps, open sides, leather heels. **2** Dark-green leather lace-up shoes, no toecaps, decorative top-stitching. **3** Cream leather shoes, donkey-brown leather trim on toes, matching high heels. **4** Navy-blue leather shoes, high vamps, button-and-strap trim, high heels. **5** Black satin dance shoes, red linings, wide bar straps, covered button fastening, high heels. **6** White kid shoes, navy-blue trim, matching high heels. **7** Cream leather lace-up brogues, brown toecaps and trim, perforated detail. **8** Wine suede shoes, self-suede looped trim, high heels. **9** White canvas shoes, navy-blue leather toecaps and trim, matching high heels. **10** Black leather shoes, high strap-and-buckle fastening. **11** Tan leather sandals, open sides, matching detail on front, strap-and-buckle fastening. **12** Donkey-brown leather shoes, high vamps, ribbon lace-up fastening, high heels. **13** Black suede evening shoes, gold kid linings, black satin bar straps, high slender heels. **14** Bottle-green calf-leather shoes, high tongues, self-leather buckles, high heels. **15** Black leather lace-up shoes, top-stitched trim. **16** Silver kid evening sandals, open sides, matching details on front, ankle straps, high slender heels. **17** Navy-blue leather shoes, wide white leather inserted trim, high heels. **18** Brown lace-up country brogues, perforated detail. **19** Cream kid shoes, black patent-leather toecaps and high heels. **20** Black leather shoes, stitched detail, high heels. **21** Brown suede shoes, tan leather shaped toecaps, high heels. **22** Olive-green leather shoes, self-leather roll trim, high slender heels. **23** Black leather shoes, stitched detail, high heels. **24** Ginger-brown leather shoes, high tongues, self-leather covered buckles, high stacked heels.

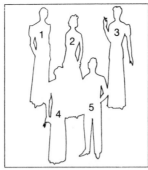
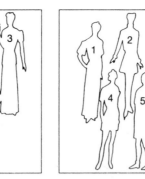
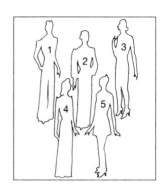

1938 Day Wear

1 Lightweight navy-blue wool dress, high round neckline trimmed with white cotton piqué tabs, navy-blue and white spotted silk scarf set into diagonal panel seams, long inset sleeves, padded shoulders, self-fabric belt, plastic buckle, flared skirt, seamed side panels, end front-facing knife pleats. Navy-blue suede shoes, chain trim.
2 Navy-blue wool two-piece suit: double-breasted fitted jacket, two-button fastening under wide lapels, flap pockets; straight-cut trousers, turn-ups. White collar-attached shirt. Striped silk tie. Navy-blue trilby, black ribbon band. Black leather shoes.
3 Pale-green linen mixture two-piece suit: edge-to-edge collarless cardigan jacket, long sleeves, padded shoulders, hip-level patch pockets, self-fabric buckled belt; straight skirt, wide front panel. Brown silk blouse, bow-tie neckline. White straw hat, small crown, asymmetric brim, brown ribbon trim. White gloves. Brown leather handbag; matching leather shoes, diagonal bar straps, high heels. **4** Pale-blue washable-silk dress, button fastening from hem to under tiny collar, top-stitched panel seams from padded shoulders to above knee-level end in inverted box-pleats, top-stitching repeated on hems of puff sleeves, on narrow belt, on hip-level pockets and on covered buttons. Brown lacquered-straw hat, tiny flat-topped crown, white ribbon trim, wide stiff brim. Large brown leather handbag, matching shoes, high tongues, openwork, high heels. **5** Dark-beige wool single-breasted coat, two-button fastening, hip-length shaped front panel in leopard-patterned cloth, incorporating pockets, large collar, padded shoulders, long inset sleeves, flared skirts. Tan felt hat, flat circular brim, upturned edge, small crown, narrow self-fabric strap at back. Cream leather shoes, tan leather toecaps and bow trim.

Evening Wear

1 Evening coat in multicoloured brocade on gold background, single-breasted fastening with small gilt flower-shaped buttons from above knee-level to under outsized lapels, fitted bodice, padded shoulders, short puff sleeves, ground-length flared panelled skirts. Long white kid gloves. Small gold sequined bag. Gold kid strap sandals. **2** Deep-wine taffeta evening dress, fitted bodice shirred on centre-front seam from curved hip seam to low neckline, wide shoulder straps, self-fabric ground-length underskirt gathered from hip, spotted net overskirt, frilled self-fabric trim at knee-level and on hem. **3** Two-piece dinner ensemble: hip-length oyster silk-satin blouse, collar and rever-shaped seams from padded shoulders to side hem, V-shaped neckline faced to below bust, tassel trim, horizontal pintucked yoke matching upper part of short puff sleeves, side-hip panels from waist to hem and half-belt with vertical pintucks; ground-length black velvet skirt.
4 Multicoloured printed silk-crepe dinner dress on black background, fitted bodice, curved seams from side waist to under square keyhole below high round neckline, padded shoulders, short puff sleeves, wide self-fabric tie-belt, ground-length flared skirt. Elbow-length black silk gloves. **5** Two-piece black wool evening suit: single-breasted fitted jacket, linked-button fastening under wide lapels, bound pockets; straight-cut trousers, braid trim on outside seams, no turn-ups. White cotton piqué shirt worn with wing collar. Black satin bow-tie. Black patent-leather shoes.

Sports and Leisure Wear

1 Beach wear. Ankle-length pale-green towelling beach coat, multicoloured outsized flower print, single-breasted fastening from mid-calf level to under long pointed green satin top-stitched collar which matches cuffs of elbow-length puffed sleeves, buttoned belt and covered buttons; fitted bodice, padded shoulders, hip-level pockets in side seams of flared skirts. Green leather strap sandals, peep-toes, platform soles. **2** Skating. Dark-green machine-knitted sweater, ribbed polo collar matching cuffs of long inset sleeves, padded shoulders. Thigh-length navy-blue wool gored skirt, narrow waistband, button fastening. Long navy-blue leather boots.
3 Holiday wear. Three-piece cruising suit in heavyweight navy-blue silk: collarless edge-to-edge thigh-length jacket, long flared sleeves, padded shoulders, hip-level patch pockets trimmed with natural and sandstone silk; matching single-breasted blouse, fastening from waist to under pointed collar; ankle-length wide flared trousers, central creases and turn-ups, waistband decorated with three buttons. Navy-blue canvas sandals, peep-toes, wooden platform soles and short thick heels. **4** Tennis. Single-breasted collarless white linen blouse, short inset sleeves, curved half-yoke from under arm to mid-shoulder, small breast pockets, decorative blue silk handkerchief in left pocket. Tailored white linen flared shorts, central top-stitched seams end in inverted box-pleats, top-stitched belt and buckle. White ankle-socks and sports shoes. **5** Tennis. White machine-knitted cotton shirt, pointed collar, short buttoned-strap opening, short sleeves. Tailored white linen shorts, zipped fly, buttoned waistband, pleats and central creases, slanted side pockets, no turn-ups. White ankle-socks and sports shoes.

Underwear and Negligee

1 Two-piece pale-blue washable-satin pyjama suit: fitted top trimmed with three diagonal pink satin ribbons on each side from side seams to under pleated peter-pan collar, matching trim on elbow-length puffed sleeves and bow trim over keyhole opening; ground-length flared trousers, fitted over hips, narrow waistband. Pale-blue peep-toe slippers. **2** Green spotted cream silk dressing gown, wrapover front, bloused bodice, padded shoulders, full-length bishop-style sleeves, deep cuffs, skirts fitted over hips, flared to ground-length, hip-level patch pockets, outsized revers faced with white spotted green silk, matching lining of wide tie-belt. **3** Vest and knicker set in machine-knitted peach silk: hip-length vest top, lace-edged neckline, narrow satin ribbon shoulder straps, deep rib from under bust to hip, elasticated waist rib; long fitted knickers, wide rib at hem, elasticated waistband. Peach velvet mules, high heels. **4** Pale-green washable-silk nightdress, bloused bodice pintucked under arms and across front bustline, edged at neck with self-fabric ruched frills, matching pintucked shoulder straps, narrow self-fabric tie-belt, ground-length flared skirt. **5** Black satin cami-knickers, trimmed on neck edge and diagonally over bust with inset flat rouleau embroidery, matching shoulder straps, fitted bodice, shaped seam under bust, knickers fitted over hips, wide flare to hem, fine lace edging. Black velvet mules, black satin rosettes and trim, high heels.

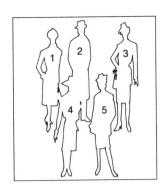

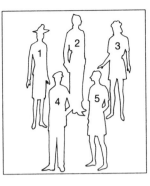

1939 Day Wear

1 Edge-to-edge light-brown wool-tweed coat, held at waist by buckled self-fabric belt and at bust-level with a hook and bar, narrow fur collar matching cuffs of long inset sleeves, trim on shaped yoke seam and hip-level seams incorporating pockets, flared skirts. Wine felt hat, self-colour ribbon trim. Brown leather handbag and gloves; matching shoes. **2** Single-breasted fawn, grey and tan checked wool-tweed overcoat, three-button fastening under wide lapels, cuffed raglan sleeves, vertical hip-level welt pockets, top-stitched edges and detail. Grey wool trousers. Tan wool scarf. Collar-attached shirt. Tweed tie. Grey felt trilby. Brown leather gloves and shoes. **3** Two-piece rust, cream and fawn flecked wool-tweed suit: hip-length edge-to-edge jacket, held at waist by wide rust leather tie-belt and with hook and bar under leopard-skin collar, matching panels under bust to hemline, cut away over side hips, padded shoulders, long inset sleeves; flared skirt. Brimless fawn felt hat, rust silk trim. Black leather handbag and gloves, matching sling-back shoes, peep-toes, high heels. **4** Silk dress, slightly bloused collarless bodice, patterned blue, lilac and pink on navy-blue background, gathers between half-yoke seams above bust and shaped seam above waist, elbow-length puff sleeves, plain navy-blue silk flared panelled skirt, self-fabric belt. Blue straw hat, pink ribbon trim. Pink gloves. Navy-blue leather shoes, cross straps, peep-toes. **5** Hip-length fawn wool unfitted jacket, single-breasted fastening from bust-level to under stand collar, curved half-shoulder yoke joined to vertical side-panel seams, hip-level welt pockets, long cuffed sleeves. Light-brown wool skirt. Fawn felt hat, navy-blue ribbon trim. Fawn leather gloves. Fawn and navy-blue leather shoes, perforated decoration.

Evening Wear

1 Pearl-grey evening dress, finely pleated fitted bodice, low neckline, narrow self-fabric rouleau shoulder straps, deep waist inset of pearl-grey satin, ground-length sunray-pleated skirt; dress worn over a slip of primrose-yellow silk. Grey satin muff decorated with Iceland poppies in tea-rose-pink and soft-orange. **2** Royal-blue silk-crepe evening dress, strapless boned bodice shirred in three vertical lines, three-tier skirt, knee-length top skirt, longer at back, draped from side hip to side hip, mid-calf-length middle tier, longer at back, ground-length third tier. Royal-blue satin strap sandals, peep-toes, thin platform soles. **3** White silk-chiffon evening dress, hand-painted design of large garlands of anemones in tones of pink, mauve, pale-blue and apple-green, high waist seam under bust, wide self-fabric shoulder straps, fitted panelled bodice and ground-length flared skirt cut in one piece with no waist seam. Long apple-green silk gloves. **4** Dinner ensemble: collarless fitted jacket, wide horizontal stripes of black, red, silver and gold sequins, edge of V-shaped neckline and front edges bound in black satin, gold and black glass buttons, long tight sleeves, pleated heads, padded shoulders. Ground-length black velvet flared skirt. Black satin shoes, peep-toes. **5** Cream rayon-organdie evening dress patterned with pale-sea-green fern leaves, hip-length fitted bodice, sweetheart neckline, short puff sleeves, worn over strapless boned underbodice in plain cream rayon, matching ground-length skirts, each gathered into scalloped hip seam. Pink and pale-green silk flower hair decoration. Pale-sea-green purse.

Sports and Leisure Wear

1 Golf. Two-piece brown, fawn and green checked wool-tweed suit: fitted edge-to-edge jacket, linked-button fastening under notched shawl collar in plain brown wool-tweed, matching stitched cuffs of long inset sleeves, hip-level flap pockets and side panels of skirt, front panel wide box-pleat. Collarless single-breasted flannel waistcoat. Cream silk scarf in neck. Fawn felt hat, truncated crown, wide brim. Brown and cream leather lace-up shoes. **2** Winter sports. Two-piece wine-red waterproofed wool-gaberdine suit: single-breasted jacket fastening from hip-level to under wide lapels, six welt pockets with button trim, black patent-leather buckled belt, long inset sleeves; full trousers gathered into cuffs at ankle level. Black knitted-wool scarf and pixie hood. Lambswool gauntlet mittens. Black boots. **3** Boating. Yellow linen blouse, button fastening from waist to under open collar, short sleeves, stitched cuffs, yoke seam above bust, two inset mock-pointed flap pockets. Navy-blue linen flared shorts, side-hip pockets, button trim, matching waistband. White ankle-socks. Lace-up navy-blue canvas shoes with rope soles. **4** Golf. Single-breasted brown and beige flecked wool-tweed jacket, three-button fastening, wide lapels, large patch pockets. Light-brown flannel trousers, straight-cut legs, turn-ups. Green knitted-wool sweater, V-shaped neckline. Cream cotton shirt. Rust wool tie. Light-brown wool-tweed peaked cap. Brown and beige leather shoes. **5** Boating. Blue, white and green striped cotton shirt, pointed collar worn open, short sleeves, stitched cuffs, large chest-level patch pockets with buttoned flaps. Navy-blue linen shorts, wide legs, no turn-ups. Navy-blue canvas step-in shoes, rope soles.

Accessories

1 Beige felt beret, top-stitched detail. Brown velvet scarf. **2** Grey felt hat, pleated brim, fur trim. **3** Navy-blue leather shoes, high vamps, ribbon laces, top-stitched detail, high heels. **4** Brimless black felt hat, top-stitched edges and detail, pink and grey pleated organdie fans at back. **5** Green felt hat, tall crown, gold satin ribbon trim. **6** Bottle-green and white leather shoes, top-stitched detail, ribbon laces, high heels. **7** Black and white leather shoes, ribbon laces. **8** Wine-red suede shoes, wide bar straps, black pleated-leather bow trim, medium heels. **9** Cream linen hat, top-stitched asymmetric crown, wide brim. **10** Small grey felt hat, tiny crown, upswept narrow brim, green feather trim. **11** Navy-blue and grey bar-strap shoes, ribbon laces, high heels. **12** Blue felt hat, pleated crown, self-felt bow trim. **13** Deep-purple felt hat, shallow crown, flat top, upswept brim, fine veil. **14** Mustard-yellow felt hat, wide upswept brim, black petersham ribbon trim. Fur scarf. **15** Brown leather shoes, pleated fan-shaped tongues, high heels. **16** Natural leather strap sandals, leather thong fastening, low wooden heels and platform soles. **17** Brown leather bag, ruched detail, rouleau handles and trim. **18** Dark-green leather bag, long handle, zip fastening. **19** Navy-blue leather bag, metal frame, rouleau handles, zip fastening. **20** Pale-pink straw hat, wide brim, shallow crown, pink and white petersham ribbon trim. **21** Cream leather sling-back shoes, peep-toes, top-stitched detail, high heels, platform soles. **22** Brown leather bag, metal frame, short handle, gilt monogram. **23** Apple-green leather strap sandals, open sides, peep-toes, low thick heels. **24** Grey leather shoes, elasticated sides, perforated detail, medium heels. **25** Tiny brown straw top hat, ribbon trim. **26** Leather sandals, peep-toes, wooden platform soles.

The 1940s

Introduction • The 1940s

Women's fashion in the 1940s divides into two separate parts: from 1940 to 1946, and from early 1947 to the end of the decade. The first part was dominated by the Second World War. Dress, echoing military uniforms, was consciously and almost wholly utilitarian. In the United Kingdom, rationing came into effect in the summer of 1941 and the following year saw the introduction of the Utility Clothing Scheme which restricted among other things the amount of cloth that could be used in garments, the maximum length and width of a skirt, and the number of pleats, buttons and trimmings. These limitations gave rise to simple designs that were well cut, well proportioned and stylish, usually in the form of jackets or dresses with square, padded shoulders and straight, knee-length skirts. In the United States similar restrictions were imposed, though for a shorter time than in the United Kingdom. American designers, also constrained by rationing, began to use alternative fabrics in new and inventive ways. In both the US and the UK, the experience gained in the speedy mass-production of uniforms, and in economical cutting and use of cloth, led to more scientific and better mechanized methods of large-scale production in the clothing trade.

Wartime shortages were often a spur to creativity. Though women who were involved in war work were likely to wear almost anything, fashionable or not, so long as it was functional and fitted the occasion, attempts were made to brighten up the utilitarian look with frivolous little hats which were often concocted from raffia, ribbon, curtain fabric or even paper and men's silk neckties. Old straw and felt hats were expertly remodelled and trimmed with feathers or homemade silk flowers. Brightly coloured, boldly patterned silk headscarves, bound around the head in the form of a turban, were immensely popular.

Paris, traditionally the world's most powerful force in fashion, lost much of its influence due to wartime isolation. But in 1947 it came back with a bang. On 12 February of that year the French couturier Christian Dior launched his 'Corolle line', instantly nicknamed 'The New Look' – the most famous and controversial collection any designer has ever produced. The New Look was not in fact new – a number of Parisian designers had shown similar lines in the years immediately preceding the war – but it was ultra-feminine and grandly extravagant, and arriving as it did so soon after the war, when some rationing and restrictions were still in force, it caused a sensation. The old pre-1947 lines were demolished at a stroke. Luxurious and romantic, the Corolle line was lavish in its use of fabric, trim and detail. Day dresses had mid-calf-length billowing skirts, narrow waists, lightly padded hips and bosoms, narrow rounded shoulders and every hard edge softened. Even the smart tailored suit with its long jacket was moulded over a padded lining and teamed with a pencil-slim skirt which was only twelve inches from the ground. The look was finished with a new fashion accessory: a slender rolled umbrella with a long, elegant handle.

The New Look called for new physical features: rounded shoulderlines meant the discarding of the bulky shoulder pads that had previously been worn with every garment; rounded bosoms and tiny waists required new-style underwear and corsets; the fuller, wider skirts needed layers of flounced and stiffened petticoats.

Men's fashions during the 1940s were relatively stationary and somewhat dull, dominated as they were by military uniform. In consequence they require fewer illustrations than women's. The types of clothes worn by men during this period as well as the basic trends have been shown, on average, with one example per page.

In the main, the fashions I have used are such as would have been worn by men and women of the middle or upper-middle classes and by people who, while not necessarily being 'dedicated followers of fashion', would have had a keen interest in the latest styles.

The sources from which I have drawn – chiefly from Great Britain, North America and France – include contemporary magazines, catalogues and journals; museum collections; original dated photographs, and my own costume collection.

This section of the Sourcebook is divided into ten parts, each of which includes four subdivisions covering Day Wear, Evening Wear (alternately on two occasions, Wedding Wear), Sports and Leisure Wear, and a section on either Underwear or Accessories. Following the main illustrations are ten pages of schematic drawings accompanied by detailed notes about each example, giving particulars of colour, fabric, cut and trimming, as well as accessories and other useful information.

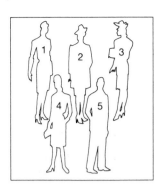

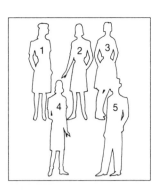

1940 Day Wear

1 Mustard-yellow wool dress, V-shaped neckline to above high top-stitched yoke seam, gathered shaping from shoulders and neck point, centre-front seam from under yoke to hem of knee-length flared skirt, seam top-stitched from yoke to above hip-level, gathered shaping at each side, inset waistband, side fastening, elbow-length sleeves, padded shoulders. Brimless brown felt hat, silk cord trim. Brown suede gloves. Fur muff. Brown suede shoes, self-fabric roll trim, high heels. **2** Three-quarter-length fawn imitation-fur collarless coat, single-breasted fastening from above waist to under V-shaped neckline, large brown plastic buttons, hip-level welt pockets, full-length sleeves, padded shoulders. Brown wool skirt. Fawn felt hat, tiny crown, flat top, brown ribbon trim, curled brim. Brown leather gloves; matching shoes. **3** Blue-grey wool two-piece jumper suit: fly fastening from hem to under high collar, self-fabric buckled belt, long inset sleeves, padded shoulders, angled chest-level piped pockets; knee-length skirt, pleated front panel. Grey felt hat, black ribbon band, red feather trim. Black leather bag; matching gloves and shoes, high lace-up vamps, high heels. **4** Pink wool-crepe dress, bloused bodice, high round neckline, gathered shaping from curved yoke seams, matching hip panels and pockets in knee-length flared skirt, three-quarter-length sleeves, narrow cuffs, padded shoulders, narrow self-fabric buckled belt. Pale-grey felt hat, blue velvet ribbon trim. Pink suede gloves. Grey wool clutch bag, blue plastic clasp top. Blue leather shoes, bow trim, high heels. **5** Two-piece dark-grey wool suit: single-breasted jacket, three-button fastening, flap pockets; straight-cut trousers, turn-ups. Blue and white striped cotton shirt, plain white collar. Blue and grey striped silk tie. Black leather lace-up shoes.

Evening Wear

1 Two-piece black wool evening suit: double-breasted jacket, wide lapels faced with black silk, hip-level piped pockets, breast pocket, white silk handkerchief; straight-cut trousers, no turn-ups. White cotton shirt. Black silk bow-tie. Black patent-leather lace-up shoes. **2** Deep-blue fine wool-crepe evening dress, low V-shaped neckline, ruched shaped side panel of self-fabric from hip-level to under deep scooped armholes, slender bodice and skirt cut in flared panels, no waist seam. Silver kid strap sandals. **3** Black silk-jersey dinner dress, full-length inset sleeves, narrow shoulder yoke, padded shoulders, fitted bodice, ankle-length flared skirt, narrow belt, clasp fastening, shaped neckline, pleated front panels of bodice and skirt in yellow-gold tissue; matching turban hat with large bow trim on one side. Black suede shoes, peep toes. **4** Full-length silk-taffeta evening dress, fitted bust-length top in royal-blue, wide square neckline, brooch trim at each point, short inset sleeves, padded shoulders, matching band of royal-blue on hem of pale-violet skirt, gathered from hip seam, skirt matches lower fitted bodice from under bustline to hip-level. **5** Fine black wool dinner dress, bloused bodice, V-shaped neckline, gathered shaping from asymmetric inset band above bust, black sequined embroidered motif, three-quarter-length inset sleeves, ruched detail above hems, full-length skirt, gathered front panel from hip-level seam. Black and grey fox-fur stole. Black satin strap sandals.

Sports and Leisure Wear

1 Holiday wear. Dress in white linen patterned in red, bloused bodice from above wide shaped inset band, collar and wide lapels, short puff sleeves, padded shoulders, knee-length gathered skirt. Small white straw hat, shallow crown, red ribbon trim; hat worn with red open-mesh cotton snood. White canvas shoes, peep toes. **2** Tennis. Knee-length white linen dress, fly fastening from under collar to hip-level, tuck to hem of flared skirt, bloused bodice, welt pockets at chest-level, short sleeves, padded shoulders, self-fabric belt, large hip-level patch pockets, flaps from under belt. White leather shoes, bow trim, wedge heels. **3** Beach wear. Blue and white striped cotton sundress, wide plain white cotton shoulder straps matching bindings of shaped neckline and centre-front button-fastening through to hem and trim on angled hip-level shaped patch pockets, knee-length skirt gathered from waist. Blue canvas sling-back shoes, peep toes, high wedge heels. **4** Tennis. White cotton two-piece jumper suit: hip-length collarless top, self-fabric buckled belt, high round neckline, two small patch pockets with buttoned flaps, one on bustline, the other above, short inset sleeves, padded shoulders; knee-length box-pleated skirt. White cotton ankle socks. White canvas slip-on shoes. **5** Holiday wear. Single-breasted beige linen-tweed jacket, three-button fastening, patch pockets, narrow lapels. Straight-cut light-brown flannel trousers with turn-ups. Cream cotton collar-attached shirt. Blue and brown cotton tie. Natural straw trilby, high crown, blue petersham ribbon band, narrow brim turned up at back. Light-tan leather lace-up shoes.

Underwear and Negligee

1 Maroon-red wool dressing gown, front panels of fitted bodice and full-length flared skirt cut in one piece without waist seam, button-through fastening from under wide sweetheart neckline to mid-calf-level, self-fabric covered buttons, half-belt set into side panel seams, tied at back, full-length fitted sleeves, padded shoulders. **2** Pink cotton unstructured brassiere, cups shaped with darts, ribbon shoulder straps, back fastening. Pink cotton-satin knickers, wide legs, scalloped hems, side-hip button fastening. **3** Pale-green satin slip, darted bust shaping in V-shaped panels, neck edge trimmed with fine lace pleating, satin ribbon shoulder straps, knee-length flared skirt. Green velvet mules, green satin bow trim, high heels. **4** Sage-green cotton dressing gown finely checked in grey, wrapover front and shawl collar piped in plain grey cotton matching turned-back cuffs of full-length inset sleeves, edges of tie-belt and stitched cuffs on patch pockets. Green and white striped cotton pyjamas. Black leather house slippers. **5** Red and black striped taffeta housecoat, collarless wrapover front, narrow shoulder yoke, full-length inset sleeves gathered into narrow cuffs, padded shoulders, wide waist sash, large bow tied on side hip, wide full-length skirt cut in flared panels. **6** Pale-blue silk nightdress, low square neckline edged with pale-coffee lace to match trim on short cap sleeves and hem of full-length flared skirt, skirt and bodice cut in wide panels, no waist seam.

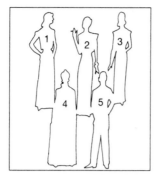
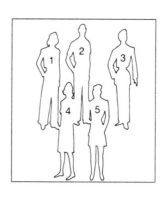
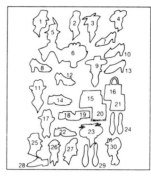

1941 Day Wear

1 Charcoal-grey wool two-piece suit: long single-breasted fitted jacket, three-button fastening, turned-up collar and lapels, seams of top-stitched panels continue into knee-length skirt, hip-level patch pocket, inverted box-pleat, black ribbon bow trim matching small breast pocket, fitted inset sleeves, padded shoulders. Brimless draped black silk hat, pink silk carnation trim. Black leather clutch bag; matching shoes. **2** Powder-blue linen dress, bloused bodice above navy-blue leather buckled belt, matching buttons on mock double-breasted fastening, top-stitched darts on right side of fabric continue as hip yoke in knee-length flared skirt, white cotton-piqué roll collar matching cuffs of short sleeves, padded shoulders. Navy-blue felt hat, small crown, swept-up bonnet brim. Navy-blue leather clutch bag. White cotton gloves. Navy-blue leather shoes. **3** Yellow crepe dress patterned with grey and white flowers, bloused bodice, self-fabric buckled belt, elbow-length sleeves, padded shoulders, gathered shaping between high round neckline and curved half-yoke seams, cut repeated under bustline and on hipline of knee-length skirt, gathered side panels. Small white straw hat, yellow flower trim. White leather clutch bag. White gloves. Black and white leather shoes. **4** Tan and beige patterned wool-jersey edge-to-edge coat, full-length fitted sleeves, padded shoulders, hip-level welt pockets, wide ribbed grey wool-jersey lapels matching buckled belt and collarless dress. Beige felt hat. Long beige leather gloves. Tan leather shoes. **5** Grey wool three-piece suit: single-breasted jacket, three-button fastening, wide lapels, piped pockets; single-breasted collarless waistcoat; straight-cut trousers, turn-ups. White cotton collar-attached shirt. Striped silk tie. Grey felt trilby. Black leather lace-up shoes.

Evening Wear

1 Fine grey wool-crepe dinner dress, bloused bodice, button fastening from above waist-level to under low V-shaped neckline, self-fabric covered buttons, small beaded patch pockets at bust-level, short inset sleeves, padded shoulders, floor-length flared skirt gathers at front from decorative pinafore panel, self-fabric belt tied into bow. Silver kid strap sandals. **2** Dinner ensemble: bright-pink silk-taffeta blouse, wide padded shoulders, shaped epaulette extensions, self-fabric covered button trim, roll collar; full-length black silk-crepe skirt, draped around high waist and over hips, front panel of unpressed pleats. Black satin shoes. **3** Blue, pink and silver flower-patterned fine silk-brocade evening dress, fitted and ruched bodice from low neckline to hip-level, shaped epaulette shoulder straps, floor-length flared skirt. Silver kid shoes, peep toes. **4** Floor-length red velvet evening cape, wide padded shoulders, embroidered and beaded stand collar matching large patch pockets at hip-level. Floor-length black taffeta evening dress. Elbow-length black silk gloves. Black satin strap sandals. **5** Two-piece black wool evening suit: single-breasted fitted jacket, linked-button fastening, wide lapels faced in black satin, hip-level piped pockets, breast pocket with folded white silk handkerchief; straight-cut trousers, no turn-ups, satin ribbon on outside seams. White cotton shirt worn with wing collar. Black satin bow-tie. Black patent-leather lace-up shoes.

Sports and Leisure Wear

1 Casual wear. Short-cropped double-breasted ruby-red wool-tweed jacket, wide lapels, long inset sleeves, padded shoulders. Pale-grey wool-flannel trousers, high waist, wide legs, turn-ups. Oxblood-red leather lace-up shoes, flat heels. **2** Tennis. White cotton shirt, buttoned-strap fastening to under attached long pointed collar worn open, two matching chest-level patch pockets with buttoned flaps, short sleeves, stitched cuffs. White flannel trousers, straight-cut legs, turn-ups, pleats under wide waistband, self-fabric buckled belt, hip-level pockets set into side seams. White leather lace-up shoes. **3** Golf. Single-breasted dark-green wool jacket, single self-fabric covered button under small shawl collar and above wide round stitched neckline seam, one matching button on inset waistband, two below to high hip-level and one on each cuff of long full sleeves, padded shoulders, thigh-length flared skirts. Rust-brown wool trousers, wide legs, turn-ups. Tan leather step-in shoes, fringed tongues, flat heels. **4** Tennis. White cotton dress, wide mock-lapels from centre-front seam, small collar, short sleeves, narrow cuffs, padded shoulders, wide tuck from outside edge of hip-level pockets to hemline of flared knee-length skirt, self-fabric belt, metal clasp fastening. White canvas lace-up shoes, flat heels. **5** Tennis. White linen all-in-one playsuit, single-breasted button fastening from waistline through deep inset waistband to under narrow lapels, small collar, short inset sleeves, stitched cuffs, padded shoulders, short divided skirt, knife-pleat each side centre-front. White canvas lace-up sports shoes, rubber soles and toecaps, flat heels.

Accessories

1 Blue felt hat, front trimmed with checked silk ribbon, narrow brim. **2** Silk turban embroidered with gold sequins. **3** Beret, self-fabric half-bow trim. **4** Cream straw hat, tiny crown, ribbon-and-bow trim, wide flat brim. **5** Red felt hat, small crown, flat top, draped silk band, feather trim, small brim. Silk taffeta scarf. **6** Pink straw hat, silk flower trim. **7** Leather shoes, wide crossed strap fronts, peep toes, high heels. **8** Navy-blue and white leather shoes, perforated detail. **9** White straw hat, tiny crown, flat top, navy-blue ribbon trim split at front, wide brim. **10** Dark-red suede shoes, high tongues, scalloped edges, bow trim. **11** Grey trilby, black band, curled brim. **12** Tan leather shoes, high vamps, stitched detail, high heels. **13** Suede shoes, self-binding and rouleau bow trim, peep toes, high heels. **14** Leather shoes, high tongues, strap-and-buckle fastening, no toecaps. **15** Blue suede monogrammed clutch bag, clasp fastening. **16** Green leather handbag, double rouleau handles, clasp fastening. **17** Fawn trilby, high crown, wide ribbon band, bow trim, wide brim. **18** Tan leather sandals, open sides and front detail, strap-and-buckle fastening. **19** Evening bag, metal frame, clasp fastening. **20** Leather clutch bag, zip fastening in side, fringed leather trim. **21** Brown leather clutch bag, hand top-stitched flap and band. **22** Leather lace-up shoes, no toecaps. **23** Straw hat, wide brim, self-straw bow trim. **24** Red leather shoes, high tongues, bow trim. **25** Trilby, flat top, brim turned up at back. **26** Wool-tweed golf cap, side sweep to crown, narrow peak. **27** Tiara of pink, white and blue silk flowers. **28** Leather step-in shoes, high tongues, no toecaps. **29** Blue velvet house slippers, self-fabric bow trim. **30** Black velvet hat, trimmed with multicoloured silk flowers.

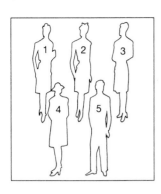

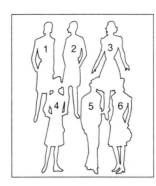
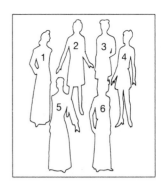

1942 Day Wear

1 Wine-red wool two-piece suit: hip-length edge-to-edge jacket, fastening with loops and buttons in four sets of four from above hemline to under narrow stand collar, self-fabric buckled belt, two inset bands of bias-cut self-fabric from under arms to centre-front at bust-level, full-length tight inset sleeves, padded shoulders; bias-cut knee-length flared skirt. Red silk turban. Black leather envelope clutch bag; matching shoes, lace-up detail, high heels.
2 Two-piece wool jumper suit: long single-breasted turquoise jacket, large hip-level patch-and-flap pockets, upper bodice tucked from above self-fabric tie-belt to under high yoke seam, shirt collar in fawn, matching lapel facings, yoke, full-length sleeves under padded shoulders and knee-length box-pleated skirt. Brown leather shoes.
3 Cherry-red wool dress, semi-fitted bodice above self-fabric belt with covered buckle, knee-length flared panelled skirt, black wool yoke with scalloped top-stitched edges continues over padded shoulders above long sleeves, scalloped pockets set vertically at hip-level into panel seams. Black leather shoes, turned-down tongues, high heels.
4 Knee-length green and blue herringbone wool-tweed coat, single-breasted fastening from waist-level to under wide lapels, large collar, flared from under arm to hem, long raglan sleeves, padded shoulders, hip-level welt pockets, top-stitched edges, raised and top-stitched seams. Blue and green patterned silk scarf. Navy-blue felt hat, small crown, turned-down brim. Navy-blue leather shoes, round toes, high heels. **5** Two-piece blue and grey striped wool suit: double-breasted unfitted jacket, wide lapels, patch pockets, stitched cuffs; wide trousers, turn-ups. White cotton collar-attached shirt. Blue and silver-grey patterned silk tie. Black leather lace-up shoes.

Wedding Wear

1 White silk wedding dress, fitted bodice and full-length skirt cut in flared panels, no waist seam, short train, shaped panels gathered from padded shoulders to under bust each side of V-shaped neckline, tight wrist-length inset sleeves. Pleated white silk-organdie headdress, floor-length silk-tulle veil.
2 Morning suit: single-breasted dark-grey wool morning coat, single-button fastening above waist seam, wide lapels, flower in buttonhole; single-breasted collarless waistcoat in matching fabric; straight-cut black and grey striped wool trousers, no turn-ups. White cotton shirt worn with wing collar. Grey striped silk tie, pearl stud. Dark-grey top hat. Pale-grey suede gloves. Black leather shoes; grey felt spats.
3 Dusty-pink rayon-satin bridesmaid dress, fitted bias-cut bodice from shaped hip seam to matching seam under bust, upper bodice shaped by gathers from padded shoulders to bustline, short inset sleeves, narrow stitched cuffs, spray of fresh flowers worn on one side shoulder, full-length flared skirt. Headdress of tiny pink wax flowers. **4** White silk wedding dress, top-stitched V-shaped neckline matching cuffs of tight full-length inset sleeves, padded shoulders, side bodice fitted from hip-level, gathered bust shaping, central bodice and ground-length skirt cut without waist seam, side skirt gathered from hip seams, short train. Headdress of gathered white satin ribbons, ground-length silk-tulle veil.
5 Oyster rayon-satin wedding dress, round neckline, three-strand pearl necklace, seam under bust, pointed at centre-front, gathered shaping, tight full-length inset sleeves, padded shoulders, lower bodice and ground-length skirt cut without waist seam, diagonal side and hip seams, short train. Headdress of tiny wax flowers, ground-length silk-tulle veil.

Sports and Leisure Wear

1 Tennis. White linen dress, button fastening, small collar, buttoned belt, short inset sleeves, stitched cuffs, piped pockets at bust-level, two decorative panels, one from padded shoulders, one from waist continuing to hip-level in flared skirt, concealed pockets in outer panels, wide unpressed box-pleats. White leather shoes. **2** Tennis. White cotton collar-attached shirt, pointed collar, short inset sleeves, stitched cuffs, patch pocket. White linen pleated shorts, turn-ups, elasticated cotton belt, clasp fastening. White cotton ankle socks. White canvas sports shoes. **3** Holiday wear. Pale-blue cotton blouse, small collar, threaded ribbon fastening matching trim on cuffs of short puff sleeves, padded shoulders. Sleeveless single-breasted checked cotton fitted waistcoat, low scooped neckline, pointed hemline. Knee-length pale-blue cotton gathered skirt, bias-cut band above hemline to match waistcoat. White leather shoes, crossed straps, low wedge heels. **4** Holiday wear. Dark-blue cotton flared pinafore skirt, waistband extended to form shaped bib, wide shoulder straps, self-fabric buckled belt, hip-level patch pockets, mock-buttoned flaps. Red and blue spotted cotton blouse, notched shawl collar, button fastening, elbow-length sleeves, padded shoulders. Red straw hat. Red canvas shoes, peep toes, wedge heels. **5** Country wear. Brown and tan wool-tweed single-breasted jacket, flap pockets, single ticket pocket. Light-brown wool trousers, straight-cut, turn-ups. Brown wool sweater. Patterned silk scarf. Brown trilby. Brown leather shoes. **6** Country wear. Brown and grey tweed dress, small collar, button fastening, padded shoulders, short inset sleeves, stitched cuffs, patch pockets, buttoned belt and flaps, flared skirt, centre-front box-pleat. Brown felt hat. Brown suede gloves; matching shoes.

Underwear and Negligee

1 Hand-quilted black silk-satin dressing gown patterned with multicoloured posies of flowers, wrapover front, wide notched shawl collar, edges piped in plain black satin through to hem of flared skirts, padded shoulders, full-length wide inset sleeves, self-fabric tie-belt, large hip-level patch pockets. **2** Pale-peach-pink rayon slip, fitted bodice and bra top, neckline bordered with pale-cream nylon lace matching hemline of flared skirt, narrow satin ribbon shoulder straps. Satin house slippers. **3** Pink silk camisole, fitted bra top, appliqué of cream lace flowers. Knickers in matching fabric, shaped hip yoke, side-button fastening, flared legs, lace flower appliqué on sides. **4** Peach-pink silk-satin camisole patterned with self-colour sprays of flowers, straight neckline edged with pale-coffee lace, fine self-fabric rouleau shoulder straps tied on shoulders. Knickers in matching fabric, flared legs and side pleats edged with lace. Coffee velvet mules, low thick heels. **5** Single-breasted cream wool housecoat, fastening with black wool-covered buttons from knee-level to under rounded shawl collar which narrows to back of neck, fitted bodice and ground-length flared skirts cut in one piece, no waist seam, padded shoulders, black and white striped wool full-length inset bishop-style sleeves gathered into buttoned cuffs.
6 Cream rayon-satin sleeveless nightdress, bloused bodice over drawstring waist, narrow ribbon tie, low V-shaped neckline edged with fine dark-cream nylon lace matching deep armholes, under-bust seaming, seamed decoration over bust and trim on hemline of flared skirt.

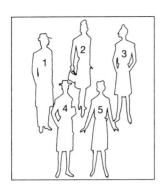

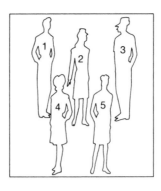

1943 Day Wear

1 Knee-length charcoal-grey wool double-breasted overcoat, wide lapels, diagonal hip-level piped pockets, single breast pocket. Grey flannel trousers, turn-ups. Blue cotton collar-attached shirt. Plain blue wool tie. Dark-grey trilby. Black leather lace-up shoes. 2 Three-piece blue and grey striped wool suit: hip-length semi-fitted edge-to-edge jacket, self-fabric buttoned belt, wide curved lapels, padded shoulders, fitted full-length inset sleeves, collarless top, loop-and-button fastening under white cotton-piqué bow-tie; knee-length flared skirt, two sets of knife-pleats facing centre-front. Navy-blue straw hat, flared topless crown set onto narrow band, brooch trim. Navy-blue leather gauntlet gloves; matching handbag and shoes. 3 Collarless linen dress, red and cream spotted bodice, button fastening under large bow tie, padded shoulders, short inset sleeves, self-fabric buckled belt, pointed half-yoke and floating patch pockets with side openings, plain cream linen knee-length flared skirt. Red leather lace-up shoes, wooden soles and heels. 4 Light-brown and green flecked wool-tweed coat, wrapover front, tie-belt, wide lapels and large collar, gathered shaping under shoulder yoke, padded shoulders, wide full-length inset sleeves, panel seam from yoke to hemline, triangular patch pockets set at an angle at hip-level, button trim, top-stitched edges and detail. Bottle-green silk scarf; matching straw hat. Green leather clutch bag, flap-and-button fastening; matching shoes, low wedge heels, thick soles, wide bar straps. 5 Yellow linen dress, semi-fitted bodice buttoned under collar and revers, padded shoulders, short brown linen inset sleeves matching inset band across bustline with yellow linen rosette trim, self-fabric tie-belt, knee-length flared and panelled skirt. Brown leather shoes.

Evening Wear

1 Mustard-yellow wool-crepe dinner dress, hip-length fitted bodice, centre-front seam ruched from above inset hip-level frill to under high grown-on collar, padded shoulders, full-length fitted sleeves, slightly flared ankle-length skirt. Large yellow silk flower hair decoration. Black fox-fur stole. Black suede shoes, gold kid trim, peep toes. 2 Midnight-blue rayon-crepe dinner dress, collarless cross-over draped bodice from narrow shoulder yoke to under bust seam, padded shoulders, full-length fitted sleeves, narrow ruched inset panel from wrist to above elbow-level, self-fabric tie-belt, ground-length flared skirt, front panel gathered from curved hip yoke. Silver-grey draped silk turban. Silver kid shoes. 3 Ruby-red silk dinner dress, semi-fitted bodice, low V-shaped neckline, bound edges end in bow at point, short inset sleeves, gathered shaping from padded shoulders through self-fabric loops over bust, cut-away triangular panel on each side neck edge to loop, self-fabric tailored belt, ankle-length skirt, unpressed pleats over side hips. Gold kid shoes. 4 Black satin dinner dress, low V-shaped neckline, padded shoulders, full-length inset sleeves, gathered shaping from under bust seam, knotted self-fabric tie on centre-front point of seam, ground-length skirt, gathered front panel from shaped hip seam. Black satin shoes. 5 Emerald-green silk dinner dress, fitted bodice, self-fabric covered button trim on centre-front from shaped hip seam to under sweetheart neckline, gathered shaping from seam over bust, padded shoulders, short inset sleeves, ground-length flared skirt patterned with wreaths of multicoloured flowers. Green and gold satin shoes, peep toes.

Sports and Leisure Wear

1 Casual wear. Brown knitted-wool sweater, high round neckline, rib matching hems of long inset sleeves, padded shoulders. Rust wool straight-cut trousers, pleats from wide waistband, side-button fastening, hip-level pockets set into side seams, wide turn-ups. Brown leather lace-up shoes. 2 Country wear. Light-green, fawn and brown wool-tweed two-piece suit: fitted hip-length single-breasted jacket, three-button fastening from waist-level to under narrow lapels, half-yoke, panel seams and shaped patch pockets with button trim, top-stitched to match edges, padded shoulders, full-length inset sleeves; knee-length box-pleated skirt. Tiny brown felt trilby-style hat. Leather gloves. Dark-green leather lace-up shoes, low wedge heels. 3 Golf. Machine-knitted yellow wool shirt, short inset sleeves, stitched cuffs, short buttoned strap fastening to under collar. Light-brown wool straight-cut trousers, pleats from waistband, side hip pockets, turn-ups, brown leather belt. Fawn felt trilby. Brown leather lace-up shoes. 4 Holiday wear. Pale-green cotton dress, semi-fitted bodice, knee-length flared skirt, self-fabric belt and covered buckle, two diagonal welt pockets over bust and hipline trimmed with green and white striped cotton to match notched collar and cuffed shirt-style sleeves, padded shoulders. White straw hat, turned-back brim. White canvas sling-back shoes, peep toes, high wedge heels. 5 Holiday wear. Cream linen dress spotted in red, pink and blue, button-through from above hemline to under collar, padded shoulders, elbow-length inset sleeves, shaped tucked shoulder yoke matches vertical hip-level pockets set above knife-pleats in knee-length flared skirt, self-fabric tie-belt. Red leather shoes, trimmed in blue, elasticated side panels, flat heels.

Accessories

1 Yellow felt spats, fur trim, leather rouleau bow fastening. 2 Tiny blue felt hat, blue silk-jersey veil. 3 Bottle-green leather handbag, threaded strap fastening, two rouleau handles. 4 Black leather handbag, clasp fastening, rouleau handles. 5 Tan leather shoes, high tongues, bow trim, high heels. 6 Pink brimless felt hat, folded crown set onto narrow band. 7 Brown felt hat, tiny crown, flat top, petersham band, wide brim, lip edge. 8 Light-brown suede lace-up shoes, perforated decoration. 9 Navy-blue leather lace-up shoes, thin platform soles, wedge heels. 10 Cream suede lace-up shoes, high heels. 11 Mustard-yellow velvet crownless hat, wide brim gathered into drawstring, self-fabric rouleau bow at back. 12 White straw hat, wide navy-blue ribbon band and bow trim on top of tiny flat crown, matching headband under turned-up brim. 13 Light-tan leather shoes, fringed tongues, metal stud trim, low thick heels. 14 Green leather shoes, tongues looped through bar straps, high wooden wedge heels. 15 Blue leather shoes, elastic inserts, thin platform soles, low wedge heels. 16 Brown leather lace-up shoes, square toes, wooden wedge heels. 17 Brimless cream felt hat, double looped crown forming bow effect. 18 Brimless evening hat, small crown covered with loops of gold organdie ribbon. 19 Ruby-red suede shoes, leather rosette trim, matching high heels. 20 Grey leather bar-strap shoes, thin platform soles, high wedge heels. 21 Black leather shoes, self-leather bow trim, high heels. 22 Navy-blue leather sling-back shoes, peep toes, high heels. 23 Brown leather clutch bag, press-stud fastening. 24 Brown leather handbag, clasp fastening, rouleau handles. 25 Natural leather handbag, flap between two handles. 26 Red leather shoes, blue trim, high heels.

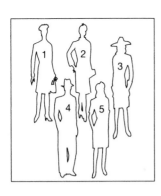
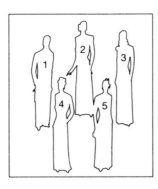
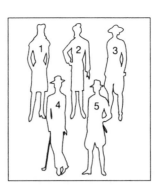

1944 Day Wear

1 Silver-grey wool-crepe two-piece suit: fitted single-breasted jacket, button fastening, narrow roll collar, three-quarter-length inset sleeves, ruched shaping from short vertical seams each side centre-front, hip-length cut-away skirts; narrow knee-length skirt, unpressed pleat on centre-front. Pleated pink organdie hat, self-fabric flower trim. Black leather gloves and outsized handbag. Black and white leather shoes. 2 Turquoise wool single-breasted coat, two-button fastening, grown-on stand collar, padded shoulders, wide full-length inset sleeves, fitted bodice, side panel seams to waist-level, diagonal flap pockets set on hipline, knee-length flared skirts. Tiny bottle-green felt hat covered in grey silk-tulle, pink silk rose trim. Dark-grey leather gloves; matching clutch bag. Grey and white leather shoes. 3 Dusty-pink rayon-crepe dress, padded shoulders, tight inset sleeves, bodice and narrow knee-length skirt cut without waist seam, ruched shaping on bust and hipline from both sides of narrow central panel running from under V-shaped neckline to low hip-level. Navy-blue straw hat. Long navy-blue cotton gloves. Navy-blue and white leather shoes. 4 Three-piece dark-blue wool suit: single-breasted jacket, high two-button fastening, flap pockets, wide lapels; collarless single-breasted waistcoat; straight-cut trousers, pleats from waist, turn-ups. White cotton collar-attached shirt. Blue spotted silk tie. Dark-blue felt trilby. Black leather lace-up shoes. 5 Grey cotton dress checked in bright-green, three-button fastening, self-fabric tie-belt, wide lapels, small detachable white cotton lapels matching cuffs on short inset sleeves, padded shoulders, mock-flap pockets above bustline, knee-length flared skirt, shallow knife-pleats widely spaced at each side centre-front. Green leather shoes, peep toes.

Evening Wear

1 Double-breasted black wool tailcoat worn open, wide lapels faced in black silk. Straight-cut trousers, pleats from waist, no turn-ups. White double-breasted cotton-piqué waistcoat, low neckline, wide shawl collar. White cotton shirt worn with wing collar. White cotton-piqué bow-tie. Black fine kid-leather lace-up shoes. 2 Lilac-grey matt-silk-crepe evening dress, semi-fitted bodice, low wide sweetheart neckline, short cap sleeves gathered over padded shoulders, ruched shaping over bustline, narrow self-fabric belt, floor-length flared skirt. 3 Mustard-yellow silk-velvet dinner dress, low V-shaped neckline edged with mustard-yellow satin collar, padded shoulders, tight full-length inset sleeves, self-fabric belt and covered buckle, fitted bodice, darts under bust continued as panel seams in floor-length flared skirt, pleated shaping under bust and over hips, small posy of silk flowers worn on one shoulder. Black satin strap sandals. 4 Grey silk-chiffon evening dress, fitted bodice, ruched from centre-front seam under low shaped neckline to hip-level, narrow self-fabric rouleau shoulder straps, floor-length skirt draped over hips, gathered front panel from centre-front hipline to hem, deep-purple silk underdress. Purple kid-leather shoes, peep toes. 5 Pale-blue wool-crepe two-piece dinner suit: hip-length fitted jacket, centre-front loop and self-fabric covered button fastening from waist to under V-shaped neckline, ruched shaping from seams over bustline matching shaping from vertical seams at waist-level, padded shoulders, tight full-length inset sleeves, floor-length flared skirt. Blue velvet hair decoration; matching clutch purse. Blue leather strap sandals.

Sports and Leisure Wear

1 Holiday wear. Pink linen dress patterned with small circles of deep-blue, fastening with blue plastic triangular-shaped buttons from under collar to above knee-level, semi-fitted bodice, gathers from shoulder yoke, short cap sleeves under shoulder pads, self-fabric buttoned belt, knee-length flared skirt, pockets set into panel seams at hip-level. Blue leather lace-up shoes, low thick heels. 2 Golf. Hip-length olive-green suede top, button fastening from waist-level to under yoke seam, welt pockets on hipline, pale-green linen shirt-style collar matching long cuffed sleeves and knee-length skirt with centre-front inverted box-pleat. Dark-green leather lace-up shoes, square toes. 3 Riding. Single-breasted brown and tan wool-tweed waisted jacket, two-button fastening, wide lapels, flap pockets, flared skirts. Light-brown wool jodhpurs, turn-ups. Cream cotton collar-attached shirt. Tan wool tie. Light-brown felt hat, shallow crown, wide brim. Tan leather gloves. Tan leather elastic-sided ankle-boots. 4 Golf. Brown, fawn and rust flecked wool-tweed single-breasted jacket, three-button fastening, wide lapels, flap pockets. Fawn wool trousers, turn-ups. Light-brown wool sweater. Cream cotton collar-attached shirt. Brown wool tie. Dark-green felt trilby, shallow crown, straight brim. Brown leather lace-up shoes. 5 Riding. Mid-brown wool single-breasted jacket, three-button fastening, wide lapels, flap pockets. Yellow wool collarless single-breasted waistcoat. Dark-cream wool jodhpurs. Cream cotton collar-attached shirt. Dark-green wool tie. Light-brown felt trilby, shallow crown, brown petersham band, straight brim. Knee-high dark-brown leather boots.

Underwear and Negligee

1 Pink hip-length cotton corset, moulded and seamed cups, adjustable shoulder straps, elasticated side panels on waist and hips matching centre-front gusset above hemline, top-stitched panel seams, four adjustable suspenders, back fastening. Flesh-coloured nylon stockings. Cream leather mules, high wedge heels, feather trim. 2 Blue rayon-satin slip, self-fabric rouleau shoulder straps, low neckline edged with blue rayon lace, shaped seam above natural waist position, knee-length flared skirt. Blue satin slippers, peep toes. 3 Knee-length pale-grey wool dressing gown, wrapover front, long dark-blue roll collar edged with blue and grey twisted silk cord through to hem on front edges which matches trim on patch pockets, trim above stitched shaped cuffs of long inset sleeves and tasselled cord belt. Blue and white striped cotton pyjamas. Black leather step-in slippers. 4 Sleeveless pale-turquoise rayon-satin nightdress, pink, pale-blue and green pattern of flowers and leaves, low neckline, frill of white cotton broderie anglaise under plain rayon-satin binding, bow trim on centre-front matching hemline of ankle-length flared skirt, shaped seam above natural waistline. Turquoise satin slippers, peep toes. 5 Light-brown cotton knee-length dressing gown, dark-tan overcheck, wrapover front, plain dark-brown cotton tie-belt matching wide roll collar, welt pockets and turned-back cuffs of long inset sleeves. Brown and cream striped pyjamas. Brown leather step-in slippers.

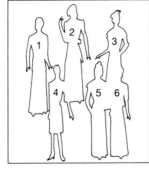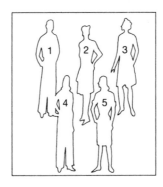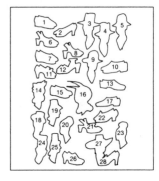

1945 Day Wear

1 Brown fake-fur hip-length unfitted jacket, single-breasted fastening with three large brown plastic buttons, wide lapels, padded shoulders, full-length inset sleeves, bound pockets set diagonally on hipline. Brown wool knee-length skirt. Brown felt brimless hat, orange silk flower trim. Light-brown leather gloves; matching clutch bag. Brown leather shoes, self-leather cross-over tabs. 2 Double-breasted camel-hair overcoat, long lapels, diagonal welt pockets on hipline, knee-length skirts. Brown wool trousers, turn-ups. White cotton collar-attached shirt. Brown silk tie matching handkerchief in breast pocket of overcoat. Dark-brown trilby. Brown leather gloves and lace-up shoes. 3 Dusty-pink wool-crepe two-piece jumper suit: hip-length collarless top, short inset sleeves, padded shoulders, top-stitched tucks under half-yoke seams above bustline matching tucks above self-fabric belt and decoration on hip-level patch pockets; knee-length flared skirt. Brown velvet ribbon-bow hair decoration. Brown leather shoes, square toes. 4 Pale-blue linen hip-length single-breasted jacket, button fastening, wide lapels, elbow-length inset sleeves, padded shoulders, two-tier frilled overskirt set wide of centre-front and under self-fabric belt and covered buckle. Navy-blue linen flared skirt. Navy-blue straw crownless hat. Navy-blue leather gloves; matching handbag. Navy-blue and white leather shoes. 5 Collarless charcoal-grey fine wool-crepe dress, front-button fastening from inset waistband to under wide lapels, full-length bishop-style inset sleeves, padded shoulders, knee-length gathered skirt, pockets set into panel seams at hip-level. Layered circles of white organdie form hat, trimmed with two large grey silk flowers. Black leather shoes trimmed with rolls of self-leather, round toes, high heels.

Evening Wear

1 Two-piece dinner suit: navy-blue hip-length top patterned with pale-blue and gold flowers, sweetheart neckline, self-fabric tailored belt and covered buckle, plain pale-blue silk elbow-length inset sleeves; matching ankle-length flared skirt, top-stitched hem, edges and detail. Gold kid strap sandals. 2 White silk-crepe evening dress patterned with bright-green flowers and leaves, low sweetheart neckline, padded shoulders, inset puff sleeves, bodice cut without waist seam from under bust seam to hem of floor-length flared skirt, panel seams each side centre-front from under bust to hem, gathered shaping under bust and over hips, self-fabric belt set into panel seams above natural waist, tied at back. 3 Cream silk-satin evening dress, low square neckline, padded shoulders, short cap sleeves, shaped tucks over bust to top seam of hip-length inset band of brown silk-satin which matches binding on hem of ground-length flared skirt and large bow hair decoration. Long brown satin gloves. 4 Black crepe cocktail dress, semi-fitted bodice ruched from V-shaped neckline to under bust and over hipline of split skirts, padded shoulders, elbow-length inset sleeves, self-fabric tailored belt and covered buckle, knee-length straight skirt. Black suede shoes. 5 Two-piece evening ensemble: hip-length pink crepe asymmetric wrapover top, waterfall frill on side hip, padded shoulders, short cap sleeves; ankle-length black crepe wrapover skirt patterned with silver and pink bows, inset self-fabric waterfall frill on side hip from waist to knee-level. Pink and white flower hair decoration. Silver kid strap sandals. 6 Black fine wool dinner dress, floor-length flared panelled skirt from high waistline, white bloused bodice, mock threaded tie with bow trim under cowl neckline, padded neckline, elbow-length inset sleeves.

Sports and Leisure Wear

1 Casual wear. Red and black flecked handknitted wool jacket, zip fastening from wide waist-level rib to under narrow ribbed stand collar which matches cuffs of long inset sleeves and four welt pockets. Dark-grey straight-cut trousers, pleats from waist, hip-level pockets set into side seams, turn-ups. Red and yellow patterned silk cravat. Black leather lace-up shoes. 2 Holiday wear. White beach dress patterned with orange and brown spots, cut-away armholes, fitted bodice, mock-wrapover front under low sweetheart neckline, self-fabric tailored belt and covered buckle, knee-length flared skirt. Green canvas sling-back shoes, peep toes, wedge heels. 3 Cycling. Cream and light-brown linen-tweed two-piece suit: single-breasted button fastening from below waist-level to under high collarless neckline, hip-length fitted bodice, padded shoulders, short inset sleeves, welt pockets over bust-level, silk handkerchief in one; knee-length flared culottes, pockets set into side seams on hipline, hand-stitched edges. Brown leather lace-up shoes, flat heels. 4 Casual wear. Olive-green linen two-piece trouser suit: edge-to-edge collarless short bolero jacket, padded shoulders, short inset sleeves, hand-stitched edges matching large hip-level patch pockets on straight-cut high-waisted trousers, self-fabric buttoned braces, turn-ups. Sleeveless yellow cotton blouse, low neckline. Dark-olive-green leather lace-up shoes, flat heels. 5 Tennis. White cotton dress, front-button fastening from above knee-length hem to under collar and revers, padded shoulders, short inset sleeves, wide split cuffs, semi-fitted bodice and flared skirt cut without waist seam, vertical pockets set into sides of decorative hip-level patches. White leather shoes, cross-straps, cut-away sides, flat heels.

Accessories

1 White leather lace-up shoes, brown leather wedge heels and platform soles. 2 Dark-red leather shoes, perforated decoration, stacked heels. 3 Navy-blue felt trilby, black ribbon trim, wide brim. 4 Brown felt trilby, high crown, straight brim. 5 Green felt trilby, wide band, turned-down brim. 6 White leather sling-back shoes, peep toes, navy-blue leather heels and platform soles. 7 Cream leather shoes, peep toes, wedge heels. 8 Red leather sling-back shoes, peep toes, platform soles. 9 Light-grey felt trilby, high crown, navy-blue ribbon trim. 10 Brown leather lace-up shoes, stacked heels. 11 Olive-green leather bar-strap shoes, high heels. 12 Cream leather shoes, ankle straps, buckle fastening, cut-away sides, black leather toecaps and high heels. 13 Black leather lace-up shoes. 14 Brimless hat covered with tiny silk flowers, satin bow trim. 15 Green suede elastic-sided shoes, wedge heels, thin platform soles. 16 Brown felt hat, trim of two orange feathers. 17 Brown leather lace-up shoes, perforated decoration, stacked heels. 18 Green felt hat, tiny crown, flat top, red ribbon-and-bow trim matching edge of brim. 19 Navy-blue felt hat, high crown, flat top, self-felt band-and-bow trim over wide peak. 20 Draped grey silk-jersey brimless hat. 21 Tan leather sling-back shoes, bar straps, platform soles, stud trim, high heels. 22 Dark-grey suede shoes, leather heels. 23 Draped black wool turban with top-knot. 24 Brimless fawn wool-tweed hat, draped through loop on centre-front. 25 Bottle-green felt hat, tiny crown, flat top, turned-up brim, fringed edge. 26 Brown leather lace-up shoes, top-stitched detail, high heels. 27 White straw hat, tall crown, flat top, wide split red silk ribbon matching edge of wide brim. 28 Tan leather shoes, self-leather curled tongues, top-stitched detail, high heels.

  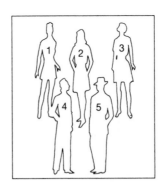 

1946 Day Wear

1 Bottle-green wool dress, fitted bodice, three-quarter-length inset sleeves, padded shoulders, knee-length gathered skirt, hip-level welt pockets, self-fabric covered button trim, shoulder-wide white cotton-piqué bertha collar, hand-stitched edges. Black leather shoes, high heels. **2** Pale-grey wool double-breasted coat, wide lapels, bracelet-length inset sleeves, padded shoulders, front panels of bodice and skirts cut without waist seam, upper side panel seamed above waist-level, lower side panel seamed on hipline, vertical pockets set into seams at hip-level. Red silk scarf. Red wool beret with stalk. Grey leather gloves; matching sling-back shoes, high heels.
3 Cream, pale-green and apricot flecked linen-tweed dress, fitted bodice from top-stitched hip seam which matches finish on high round neckline, short inset sleeves, padded shoulders, narrow knee-length skirt. Bottle-green linen turban. Beige leather gloves; matching shoes, peep toes. **4** Grey wool double-breasted knee-length overcoat, wide lapels, large collar, inset sleeves, buttoned strap at wrist-level, self-fabric belt, leather buckle, large patch-and-flap pockets, top-stitched edges and detail. Dark-grey wool trousers, turn-ups. Navy-blue and red spotted silk scarf. Dark-blue felt trilby. Black leather gloves and shoes. **5** Two-piece cherry-red wool suit: collarless single-breasted long jacket, button fastening from hip-level to under high neckline, three-quarter-length inset sleeves, black buckled leather belt; narrow knee-length skirt. Small black straw hat trimmed with red, black and grey silk flowers. Black leather gloves; matching large handbag and plain high-heeled shoes.

Wedding Wear

1 Frost-white silk-crepe wedding dress, bloused bodice above narrow self-fabric belt, top-stitched scalloped yoke matching finish of high round neckline, long fitted inset sleeves, long point over hand, padded shoulders, ground-length flared skirt with train. Headdress of wax flowers, long silk-tulle veil. **2** White silk-taffeta wedding dress, fitted bodice, V-shaped point on front, off-the-shoulder cape collar under high round neckline, long fitted inset sleeves, point over hand, padded shoulders, ground-length gathered skirt. Earphone headdress of real flowers, matching small bouquet, two-tier silk-tulle veil. **3** Ivory-white crepe wedding dress, low V-shaped neckline, long fitted sleeves, padded shoulders, upper bodice draped from seam under bust, lower bodice draped and swathed from central knot to hip-level, ground-length flared skirt. Long ivory-white silk-tulle veil from silk flower headdress.
4 Cream crepe wedding dress, fitted bodice, V-shaped point on centre-front, high neckline split to rounded yoke seam, gathered shaping under seam, long fitted inset sleeves, point over hand, padded shoulders, ground-length flared skirt, panel of unpressed pleats at front, long train. Headdress of silk lilies, long silk-tulle veil. **5** Cream silk-taffeta wedding dress, fitted bodice from hipline seam, low square neckline with rounded edges, long fitted inset sleeves, self-fabric covered buttons above wrists, padded shoulders, ground-length flared skirt, gathered side panels, short train. Headdress of silk flowers, long silk-tulle veil.

Sports and Leisure Wear

1 Holiday wear. One-piece cream linen beach suit patterned in red: fitted bra top, wide shoulder straps, triangular bib, point on centre of low neckline and attached to wide waist of tailored shorts, flared legs with turn-ups, hand-stitched edges and detail. **2** Cycling. Apricot handknitted wool sweater, sunray pattern from under wide banded high round neckline, short inset sleeves, padded shoulders. Brown wool above-knee-length flared culottes, wide waistband, double row of buttons above wide box-pleats each side centre-front. Brown leather lace-up shoes, low wedge heels, thin platform soles. **3** Tennis. White cotton blouse, buttoned-strap fastening, narrow lapels, long pointed collar, shaped yoke seam, short inset sleeves, stitched cuffs. Above-knee-length flared white linen culottes, grown-on waistband, four-button fastening above central creases, hip-level welt pockets. White leather lace-up shoes, flat heels. **4** Golf/casual wear. Hip-length petrol-blue wool jacket, zip fastening from above self-fabric buttoned belt to under wide lapels, decorative panel seams curve over bust and hipline, pockets set into seams at hip-level, full-length inset sleeves gathered into cuffs, top-stitched edges and detail. Straight-cut dark-grey wool-flannel trousers with turn-ups. Draped green wool-jersey turban. Black leather shoes, strap-and-buckle fastening, flat heels. **5** Golf. Single-breasted black, brown and rust checked wool-tweed jacket, wide lapels, shoulder yoke, self-fabric belt, leather buckle, large hip-level patch pockets, side openings. Straight-cut brown wool-flannel trousers with turn-ups. White cotton collar-attached shirt. Rust-brown wool tie. Dark-brown felt trilby, wide brim turned up on one side. Brown and cream leather lace-up shoes, toecaps, stacked heels.

Underwear and Negligee

1 Peach cotton-satin bra covered in self-colour cotton lace, seamed cups, narrow ribbon adjustable shoulder straps, back fastening. Cream cotton hip girdle patterned with peach satin flowers, top-stitched seamed control panels, elasticated front gussets and side panels, four elasticated suspenders. Flesh-coloured nylon stockings.
2 All-in-one pink cotton bra and girdle, raised self-colour lace pattern, seamed cups, adjustable shoulder straps, top-stitched control panels, elasticated front gusset and side panels, top-stitched edges, lace trim, four adjustable ribbon suspenders. Flesh-coloured nylon stockings. Pink velvet mules, satin ribbon trim, high heels. **3** Pale-blue silk ankle-length nightdress, shaped seam above waist-level, low V-shaped neckline, coffee lace trim and border. Matching short bolero, high round neckline, self-fabric bow tie, short inset puff sleeves. Pale-blue quilted satin slippers, feather trim.
4 Pale-green silk camiknickers patterned with self-colour satin spots, low neckline, shaping above curved half seam under bust, side panel seams, centre-front seam, flared legs, top-stitched hems, self-fabric rouleau shoulder straps. **5** Lilac-grey silk-jersey housecoat, zip fastening from shaped waist seam through ruched inset cummerbund to under low V-shaped neckline, draped shaping from padded shoulders to under bust seam, long sleeves gathered into armholes and into ruched cuffs, ground-length bias-cut skirts.

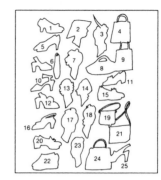

1947 Day Wear

1 Silver-grey wool dress, fitted bodice, high round neckline, centre split to bust-level, three-quarter-length inset sleeves, no shoulder pads, self-fabric belt and covered buckle, hip yoke, mid-calf-length straight skirt, gathered front panel. Charcoal-grey felt beret. Black leather gloves; matching shoes, ankle straps, high heels. **2** Crimson wool jumper suit: fitted bodice, long dolman sleeves, white cotton cuffs matching collar, tucked shoulder yoke with centre-front notch, self-fabric belt and covered buckle, narrow hip basque worn over small pads; mid-calf-length panelled skirt. Dark-brown felt hat, padded brim. Dark-brown leather shoes, peep toes. **3** Petrol-blue wool coat, double-breasted fastening from waist to under wide lapels, high collar, long inset sleeves, rounded shoulderline, no pads, set of two welt pockets on hipline, button trim, full mid-calf-length skirts, small bust and hip pads. Black felt hat, bright-green and blue feather trim. Black gloves. Black leather shoes, shaped sides, high heels. **4** Black and grey flecked wool-tweed two-piece suit: hip-length single-breasted fitted jacket, narrow lapels, small collar, long inset sleeves, rounded shoulderline, no pads, angled welt pockets, button trim; straight mid-calf-length skirt, single knife-pleat on centre-front. Brimless black straw hat, silk flower trim. Black leather gloves. Grey umbrella, long black handle. Black leather shoes. **5** Dark-mustard-yellow taffeta dress, fitted bodice, self-fabric covered button fastening from low hip seam to under small stand collar, long inset sleeves, rounded shoulderline, no pads, mid-calf-length skirt gathered from shaped hip seam, small hip and bust pads. Lacquered black straw hat, tiny crown, wide brim turned down. Black leather shoes, ankle straps, cut-away sides, peep toes, high heels.

Evening Wear

1 Black silk-taffeta evening dress, fitted bodice, small waist, low neckline, narrow self-fabric rouleau shoulder straps, decorative off-the-shoulder frilled cape, ground-length flared skirt from low hip seam, set of unpressed pleats on side. **2** Black silk-chiffon evening dress, fitted bodice draped from small waist to under bust, strapless upper bodice, draped stole over one shoulder trimmed with two outsized pink silk peonies, ground-length pleated skirt, black silk under-bodice and underskirt follow the same shape. Long black silk gloves. **3** Ice-blue silk-taffeta evening dress, fitted boned strapless bodice, low neckline decorated with dark-blue, pink and crystal beads matching hem of ice-blue silk-chiffon overskirt, ground-length taffeta underskirt, both skirts gathered from waist. Long ice-blue satin gloves. **4** Dusty-pink silk-satin evening dress, fitted bodice, low neckline banded in self-fabric to match wide shoulder and off-the-shoulder straps, infilled with pale-coffee lace matching bra-shaped upper bodice and narrow frilled cape, ground-length flared panelled skirt. **5** Taffeta dinner dress, fitted shirt-style bodice in black, button fastening from above self-fabric belt and covered buckle, pointed collar worn turned up at back of neck, short inset sleeves, split cuffs, coral-pink skirt, mid-calf-length at front, dipping to ground at back, pleated black lace overskirt following same shape. Black satin gloves; matching strap sandals, ankle straps, open sides, high heels.

Sports and Leisure Wear

1 Golf. Collarless handknitted cardigan, brown V-shaped front panel incorporating narrow shoulder yoke matching full-length inset sleeves, ribbed cuffs, main body in light-fawn, button fastening from deep rib to under high round neckline. Below-knee-length flared skirt checked in autumn colours, large single patch pocket on side of left hip. Brown wool peaked cap. Brown leather lace-up shoes. **2** Golf. Dark-green waterproofed-cotton two-piece suit: short bloused jacket, zip fastening from wide waistband to under knitted collar, shoulder yoke, large patch-and-flap pockets, long inset sleeves, buttoned cuffs, top-stitched edges and detail; straight-cut trousers, pleated from waist, turn-ups. Peaked cap in matching fabric. Brown leather step-in shoes. **3** Country wear. Beige wool-tweed edge-to-edge sleeveless jacket, single loop-and-button fastening under small collar, held at waist by wide brown leather buckled belt, large patch pockets attached to hems of hip-length rounded skirts. Sage-green wool dress, shirt-style sleeves, below-knee-length flared skirt, central inverted box-pleat, side button fastening. Brown felt brimless hat. Brown leather lace-up shoes, thick heels. **4** Casual wear. Straight-cut rust wool trousers and sideless top, long keyhole opening under small collar, pleats from under inset waistband, no turn-ups. Light-brown wool handknitted sweater, long inset sleeves, deep ribbed hems. Cream, rust and green patterned silk scarf. Brown leather lace-up shoes. **5** Tennis. White cotton blouse and skirt: unfitted top, low square neckline, wide self-fabric binding matching edges of cap sleeves; short flared skirt, large box-pleat at front under buttoned waistband. White cotton peaked cap. White cotton ankle socks. White canvas lace-up shoes.

Accessories

1 Navy-blue leather shoes, rolled tongue trim. **2** Crownless pink straw hat, wide brim, two large hat pins. **3** Grey felt hat, black feather trim. **4** Black leather handbag, two rouleau handles. **5** Beige leather shoes, top-stitched detail, platform soles, high heels. **6** Red leather sling-back shoes, openwork detail, peep toes. **7** Beige felt hat, self-colour satin bow trim matching binding on wide brim. **8** Bottle-green leather handbag, wooden handle. **9** Navy-blue leather handbag, flap with decorative clasp fastening, top-stitched edges, long rouleau handles. **10** Black suede shoes, ankle straps, open sides, peep toes, platform soles, high heels. **11** Brown leather shoes, high tongues, strap-and-buckle trim, square toes, low heels. **12** Gold kid strap sandals, high heels. **13** Mustard-yellow felt hat, trimmed with green velvet leaves and yellow berries. **14** Brimless maroon felt hat, self-fabric bow trim on back. **15** Red leather shoes, high pointed tongues matching backs, rouleau bow trim, thin platform soles, high wedge heels. **16** Black satin strap sandals, medium heels. **17** Navy-blue felt hat, wide navy-blue and white striped silk ribbon trim matching binding on edge of wide turned-up brim. **18** Brimless red straw hat, black pom-pon trim on top. **19** Tan leather bag, flap-and-clasp fastening, long handle. **20** Olive-green leather shoes, high tongues, self-leather bow trim, top-stitched edges. **21** Tan canvas shoulderbag, flap with leather strap-and-stud fastening matching long handle. **22** Pale-grey leather shoes, top-stitched navy-blue leather strap trim, keyhole opening under rouleau bow, peep toes, wedge heels. **23** Wine-red brimless felt hat, feather pom-pon trim. **24** Crocodile handbag, clasp fastening. **25** Crocodile sling-back shoes, high tongues, draped trim, high heels.

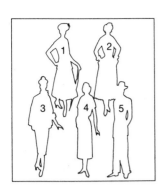

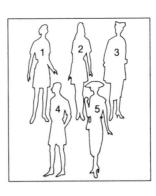

1948 Day Wear

1 Dull-grey silk dress, three-quarter-length dolman sleeves cut in one with fitted bodice, high neckline slashed and rounded off at front, narrow self-fabric belt and covered buckle, mid-calf-length flared skirt, deep tuck over padded hips. Brimless black felt hat, domed crown, self-felt trim on one side. Long black leather gloves. Plain black leather shoes, high heels. Black silk rolled umbrella, long handle. **2** Lilac and grey striped wool dress, fitted bodice, shaped yoke trimmed with three buttons to match trim above white cotton cuffs of long inset sleeves and large hip-level patch pockets, narrow self-fabric belt and covered buckle, mid-calf-length accordion-pleated skirt. Plain black leather shoes. **3** Deep-blue wool edge-to-edge hip-length flared jacket, wide three-quarter-length dolman sleeves, deep turned-back cuffs, small stand collar. Mid-calf-length straight-cut black wool skirt. Brimless black felt hat, deep-blue feather pom-pon trim. Long black leather gloves. Plain black leather shoes, high heels. **4** Rust-brown linen dress, short dolman sleeves, fitted bodice, asymmetric fastening under small collar, leather buttons, diagonal seaming over bustline matching hip-level detail, pocket concealed in upper seam, self-fabric belt and covered buckle, mid-calf-length flared skirt. Plain brown leather shoes, high heels. **5** Double-breasted navy-blue wool jacket, long wide lapels, patch pockets, silk handkerchief in breast pocket. Light-grey flannel straight-cut trousers, turn-ups. White cotton collar-attached shirt. Blue and grey striped silk tie. Grey felt trilby, narrow self-colour ribbon band, wide brim worn turned up at back. Black leather lace-up shoes, no toecaps.

Evening Wear

1 Black silk-taffeta evening dress, wide boat-shaped neckline, fitted bodice from hip-level to under bust, upper bodice with gathered shaping under bust, black shiny sequin trim matching three-quarter-length inset sleeves and two wide bands set into ground-length gathered skirt. **2** Ice-blue satin evening dress, delicately patterned with pin-head spots of black and gold, fitted bodice between off-the-shoulder band of ruched self-fabric and matching band on hipline, ground-length gathered skirt from hip-level. Silver kid strap sandals. **3** Formal dinner dress, white silk-chiffon upper bodice, gathered shaping from seam under bust, low V-shaped off-the-shoulder neckline, three-quarter-length sleeves gathered from shoulder and into narrow cuffs, fitted lower bodice of white silk-taffeta patterned with pale-blue, silver and pink flowers matching ground-length flared skirt. **4** Navy-blue satin evening dress, fitted boned strapless bodice, low shaped neckline edged with bias-cut 'collar' in silver satin with navy-blue velvet spot pattern, ground-length skirt gathered from V-pointed waist seam. Navy-blue satin shoes. **5** Pale-silver-grey silk-taffeta evening gown, fitted ruched bodice, wide off-the-shoulder collar ruched to one side, tightly-fitted elbow-length sleeves, ground-length flared skirt, centre-front unpressed inverted box-pleat. Silver kid shoes, peep toes.

Sports and Leisure Wear

1 Tennis. Short white linen dress, semi-fitted bodice above inset waistband, button fastening from under long pointed collar to hip-level above two box-pleats, short dolman sleeves and yoke cut in one piece, triangular-shaped mock-flap pockets set into yoke seam matching flaps on hip-level patch pockets, piped pockets above with button trim. White cotton ankle socks. White canvas lace-up sports shoes. **2** Leisure wear. Green and yellow striped cotton sleeveless playsuit, square neckline, gathered shaping from under yoke seam to inset waistband, button fastening from under deep armhole to hip-level on one side, wide stitched turn-ups. Yellow cotton blouse, pointed collar, short dolman sleeves, stitched cuffs. Leather sandals. **3** Country wear. Short flared edge-to-edge brown and tan flecked wool-tweed coat, wide three-quarter-length dolman sleeves, deep turned-back cuffs, long shawl collar, large hip-level patch-and-flap pockets. Brown wool sweater; matching skirt. Brimless brown felt hat, self-felt bow trim. Brown leather gloves and shoes. **4** Tennis. White cotton collar-attached shirt, buttoned-strap opening, short inset sleeves, stitched cuffs, single breast patch pocket. Tailored white linen shorts, deep waistband, side hip pockets, no turn-ups. White cotton socks. White canvas lace-up shoes. **5** Holiday wear. White cotton dress patterned with blue and orange irregular spots, front button fastening from above hemline of narrow mid-calf-length skirt to under high neckline, short cap sleeves, fitted bodice, narrow self-fabric belt and covered buckle, bias-cut waterfall frill bound in blue cotton falling from waist-level to above hemline under button fastening. Dark-blue nylon-gauze hat, shallow crown, wide turned-down brim. Blue leather handbag; matching shoes, peep toes.

Underwear and Negligee

1 White silk all-in-one pyjama suit, green, pink and blue flower pattern, fitted lower bodice from waist to under bust, sleeveless upper bodice, gathered shaping under bust, low V-shaped wrapover neckline, ankle-length wide flared trousers. Green satin slippers, flat heels. **2** Pink cotton bra, seamed cups, self-colour lace trim, narrow ribbon shoulder straps, back fastening. Pink cotton front-fastening corset, stitched panel seams, elasticated side panels, four adjustable suspenders. Flesh-coloured nylon stockings. **3** White cotton corset incorporating bra, seamed cups, appliqué lace trim matching front panel of corset, elasticated cotton side panels, narrow ribbon shoulder straps, four adjustable suspenders. Flesh-coloured nylon stockings. **4** White cotton housecoat spotted in pale-blue, fitted bodice, V-shaped neckline and edge of zip fastening trimmed with self-fabric frill to match cuffs of shirt-style sleeves, ground-length skirt gathered from shaped hip yoke. **5** Quilted cream silk-satin dressing gown, multicoloured pattern of flowers, wrapover front fastening on one side with plain cream silk ribbon bow which matches wide lapels, small collar and bound hems of full-length flared sleeves, knee-length flared panelled skirts. Collarless cream satin pyjamas, self-fabric covered buttons, wide flared trousers. Cream satin slippers, multicoloured silk pom-pon trim. **6** Red wool double-breasted housecoat, black buttons, large shoulder-wide cape collar, black wool edging matching front edge, shaped cuffs on long inset sleeves and hip-level patch pockets, ground-length flared skirts.

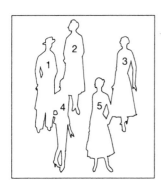 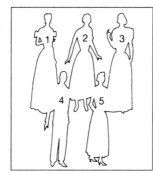 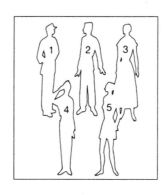 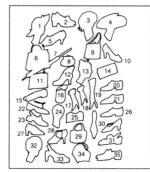

1949 Day Wear

1 Light-brown waterproofed-cotton raincoat, single-breasted fastening, wide lapels, large collar worn turned up, raglan sleeves, self-fabric belt, leather buckle, diagonal hip-level welt pockets, top-stitched edges and detail. Brown wool trousers with turn-ups. Blue and white striped cotton collar-attached shirt. Blue and brown spotted silk tie. Brown trilby. Brown leather gloves and lace-up shoes. **2** Light-grey/blue wool-tweed double-breasted unfitted coat flecked in navy-blue, large buttons, wide lapels, large collar, raglan sleeves, split turned-back cuffs, hip-level welt pockets, top-stitched edges and detail. Navy-blue felt hat, wide ribbon band, narrow brim, fine veil. Navy-blue leather shoes.
3 Yellow and grey flecked linen-tweed dress, button fastening from above hemline of flared panelled skirt to under narrow shawl collar, fitted bodice, shaped seam under bust, gathered shaping, elbow-length dolman sleeves, self-fabric belt and covered buckle. Dark-grey suede shoes, peep toes, high heels. **4** Two-piece grey wool suit: single-breasted fitted jacket, flared skirts over padded hips, self-fabric belt and covered buckle, half-yoke seam above bust-level, inset cuffs of silver-grey silk with fine black spots matching lapels, collar and turned-back cuffs of three-quarter-length dolman sleeves; mid-calf-length straight skirt. Brimless black felt hat, grey and black feather trim. Black leather gloves; matching plain shoes.
5 Dark-red wool single-breasted coat, fitted bodice and full skirts cut in flared panels without waist seam, button fastening from padded hipline to under wide rounded lapels, top-stitched edges, full-length inset sleeves from dropped shoulderline. Mid-grey felt hat, narrow turned-back brim, self-felt trim. Light-grey silk scarf. Grey gloves. Black leather handbag; matching shoes.

Evening Wear

1 Turquoise and silver silk-brocade evening dress, fitted boned strapless bodice, ground-length flared skirt, unpressed knife-pleats each side centre-front, low neckline trimmed with tucked cuff of plain deep-turquoise silk-satin matching wide cummerbund and large bow trim on off-the-shoulder strap. Above-elbow-length deep-turquoise satin gloves.
2 Silver-grey satin evening dress, fitted boned strapless bodice, self-fabric overbodice split to waist on centre-front, ankle-length skirt gathered from waist. Silver kid shoes, wrapover detail, peep toes. **3** Dark-green and black printed silk-taffeta evening dress, draped fitted bodice incorporating wide off-the-shoulder cape collar to elbow-level, ground-length flared skirt worn over petticoats. Elbow-length black satin gloves; matching shoes. **4** Two-piece black wool evening suit: double-breasted jacket, wide lapels faced with black satin matching button fastening and trim on inset sleeves, piped pockets; straight-cut trousers, no turn-ups. White silk collar-attached shirt. Black satin bow-tie. Black patent-leather lace-up shoes.
5 Burgundy-red silk evening dress, sleeveless fitted bodice, low sweetheart neckline, ruched shaping over bust, horizontal tucks above waist seam, gold embroidery and bead trim on wide shoulder straps, ankle-length flared skirt. Above-elbow-length black satin gloves; matching plain shoes, medium-high heels.

Sports and Leisure Wear

1 Ski wear. Dark-green weatherproof cotton jacket, zip fastening from above hem of hip-length skirts to under pointed collar, raglan sleeves, buttoned cuffs, hip-level welt pockets, chest-level zipped pockets, inset waistband with button-and-strap adjustment at side. Black weatherproof cotton trousers gathered at ankle-level and tucked into black leather ski-boots. Black wool neck-scarf. Green cotton peaked cap.
2 Ski wear. Blue weatherproof corded-cotton jacket, zip fastening from above hems of hip-level skirts to under chin of hood, drawstring fastening matching waist, shaping from under yoke seam, long inset sleeves gathered into cuffs, large hip-level patch-and-flap pockets. Dark-blue weatherproof cotton trousers, gathered at ankle-level and worn tucked into black leather ski-boots. Red leather mittens. **3** Holiday wear. Pale-blue cotton dress, all-over pattern of yellow spots, button fastening from hip-level to under narrow shawl collar, short semi-raglan sleeves, turned-back cuffs, self-fabric belt and covered buckle, hip-level patch pockets, flared skirt. Dark-blue leather strap sandals. **4** Winter sports wear. Bottle-green corded-wool waist-length jacket, double-breasted fastening, matching waistband, wide lapels, full-length raglan sleeves gathered into cuffs. Black wool trousers, pleats from waist, legs narrow to hems, stirrups under feet. Orange wool neck-scarf; matching brimless hat, black pom-pon trim. Large sunglasses. Black leather ski-boots. **5** Holiday wear. Red and white patterned cotton two-piece beach suit: strapless bra top, neckline cuffed in plain navy-blue cotton knotted on centre-front; matching buttoned waistband of short skirt, narrow knife-pleats from hip yoke.

Accessories

1 Black straw hat, pink rose trim. **2** Brown leather shoes, high tongues, strap-and-buckle trim, thick heels. **3** Brimless grey felt hat, self-felt flower trim. **4** Navy-blue straw hat, wide brim, cut detail. **5** Cream quilted leather shoes. **6** Brown leather handbag, rouleau handles, brass trim. **7** Red nylon umbrella, long red plastic handle. **8** Black silk evening bag, pearl bead trim. **9** Grey leather handbag, wide strap handle. **10** Grey suede shoes, perforated leaf design. **11** Green leather handbag, rouleau handles, brass clasp and trim. **12** Brown leather ankle-boots, laces, high heels. **13** Pink wool-jersey hat, rouleau trim. **14** Navy-blue leather bag, brass clasp and trim. **15** Red leather shoes, bow trim, flat heels. **16** Brown silk evening bag, long handle, gold clasp. **17** White nylon gloves, pleated cuffs. **18** Grey suede gloves, scalloped cuffs. **19** Black satin gloves, embroidered-flower trim. **20** Brown leather golf shoes, fringed tongues. **21** Brown leather sandals, strap-and-buckle fastening, crepe soles. **22** Yellow leather pumps, blue lacing and ankle straps. **23** Green leather strap sandals. **24** Brimless straw hat, uneven edge, top-stitching. **25** Black satin evening bag, bead trim. **26** Tan leather lace-up shoes, stitched trim. **27** Black suede shoes, open sides, cross straps, peep toes, thick heels. **28** Black satin T-strap shoes, nylon-mesh strap fronts, high heels. **29** Beige leather drum-shaped handbag, thick handle, brass fittings. **30** Black satin shoes, open sides, rouleau strap trim, high heels. **31** Grey suede sling-back shoes, high wedge heels, top-stitched bar straps. **32** Brimless yellow wool beret. **33** Cream leather sling-back shoes, peep toes, high heels, platform soles. **34** Brown leather bag, wide strap handle, top-stitched detail, brass trim. **35** Black leather step-in shoes.

The 1950s

Introduction · The 1950s

On 12 February 1947 Christian Dior launched his 'Corolle' line, the first collection from his recently opened fashion house. Instantly nicknamed the 'New Look', it brought a luxury, femininity and grace to postwar fashion, and had a dramatic, transforming effect on the female silhouette. The 'New Look' would almost completely dominate the greater part of the next decade.

This section of the Sourcebook shows the development of women's fashion from the comparatively early days of the 'New Look', when the square shoulders and masculine details of the 1940s still lingered, through the ultra-feminine and luxurious styles of the mid-1950s – clothes with gently softened shoulderlines, tiny corseted waists, roundly padded hips and long, swirling skirts only eleven inches above the ground – up to the straight, semi-fitted, knee-length 'sack' dress of the decade's end, which heralded Mary Quant's 'shifts' of the 1960s.

The glamour of films and film stars also had a profound effect on the 1950s woman, who wanted her every outfit to be suffused with elegance, sophistication and sex appeal. Figure-hugging sweaters as worn by Marilyn Monroe and Jane Russell, Brigitte Bardot's pink and white cotton gingham wedding dress, and the gamine look of Audrey Hepburn were all deeply influential.

During this period many new and easy-care fabrics were introduced, including Terylene, a man-made material which was crease-resistant but which could be permanently pleated; Orlon, a wool-like fabric, usually machine-knitted; crease-resistant Banlon and Acrilan; and Poplin, a strong, hard-wearing mix of man-made fibres and cotton. All these fabrics encouraged new fashions: the slender 'pencil' skirt, which lasted throughout the period, varying only in length and trim; the 'wash-and-wear' sweater; the permanently pleated skirt and the 'drip-dry' shirt.

During the Second World War men's fashion had been relatively stationary and somewhat dull, dominated as it was by military uniform. Before the 1950s it had fallen into three main categories: elegant bespoke tailoring, cheap imitations of the latter and work clothes. The introduction of ready-to-wear, the development of mass-production techniques and the new man-made fabrics gave it new life, bringing to the man-in-the-street smart suits and sports jackets, and stylish trousers with permanent creases. Nevertheless, the development of men's fashion in this period remained slow and in consequence it requires fewer illustrations than women's – the differences which do occur in the basic trends have been shown, on average, with one example for each page.

In the main, the fashions I have used are such as would have been worn by men and women of the middle or upper-middle classes and by people who, while not necessarily being 'dedicated followers of fashion', would have had a keen interest in the latest styles.

The sources from which I have drawn – chiefly from Great Britain, North America, Italy and France – include contemporary magazines, catalogues and journals, museum collections, original dated photographs, and my own costume collection.

This section of the Sourcebook is divided into ten parts, each of which includes four subdivisions covering Day Wear, Evening Wear (alternately, on two occasions, Wedding Wear), Sports and Leisure Wear, and a section on either Underwear or Accessories. Following the main illustrations are ten pages of schematic drawings accompanied by detailed notes about each example, giving particulars of colour, fabric, cut and trimming, as well as accessories and other useful information.

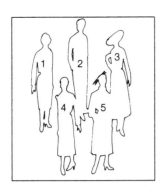
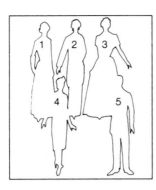

1950 Day Wear

1 Two-piece brown wool-crêpe suit: single-breasted hip-length jacket with shaped hemline, pink cotton collar which matches half-cuffs of long raglan sleeves and covered buttons, self-fabric belt with metal buckle, bloused bodice, diagonal seams which follow line of raglan sleeves and piped pockets; straight mid-calf-length skirt. Brown felt hat, curled half-brim at front, pink ribbon trim. Pink leather gloves. Flesh-coloured nylon stockings. Brown leather shoes, round toes, high thick heels. **2** Single-breasted blue wool jacket, three-button fastening, patch pockets with welt and central pleat, inset sleeves, button trim. Straight-cut grey flannel trousers, turn-ups. White collar-attached shirt. Blue wool tie. Black leather lace-up shoes, no toecaps. **3** Green and cream checked wool dress, bias-cut collar with fringed edge which matches cuffs of three-quarter-length dolman sleeves, fitted bodice with concealed front opening, green leather belt with metal buckle, flared skirt, centre-front inverted box pleat, two bias-cut shaped box pleats with button trim. Cream straw hat, wide brim. Cream leather gloves. Nylon stockings. Brown leather shoes. **4** Pale blue linen dress, bloused bodice, self-fabric buttons from under asymmetric white linen collar to waistline, self-fabric bow trim, navy-blue leather belt, metal buckle, flared skirt, unpressed box pleat, diagonal welt pockets. Pale grey brimless felt hat. Nylon stockings. Navy-blue leather shoes, peep toes, high heels. **5** Mid-calf-length beige wool coat, concealed opening, full inset sleeves tapered into button cuffs which match wrapover collar and diagonal hip-level pockets, wide self-fabric belt and buckle, flared skirt with side pleats. Small brimless brown felt hat, feather trim. Nylon stockings. Brown leather shoes, cut-away sides, round toes, high heels.

Evening Wear

1 Formal evening gown, fitted maroon silk-velvet bodice, low V-shaped neckline trimmed at point with black silk and velvet cabbage roses, drop shoulderline, wide cap sleeves, V-shaped pointed waist seam, ground-length cream corded-silk flared skirt with centre-front unpressed inverted box pleat. Above-elbow-length black silk gloves. Black jet drop earrings. Black satin strap sandals. **2** Knee-length wrapover collarless fur coat, curved front edges, hem dips to back, wide inset sleeves narrowing to wrists. Straight ankle-length black satin skirt. Black and silver drop earrings and matching necklace. Black satin shoes. **3** White tulle evening dress patterned with black flock spots, strapless fitted bodice draped over bustline, draped stole collar, full-length gathered skirt over white silk-taffeta under-skirt. Clip-on earrings and matching necklace. **4** Mid-calf-length cream satin cocktail dress embroidered with multicoloured sprays of flowers, strapless boned bodice draped over to single decorative shoulder strap, fitted straight skirt with asymmetric drapery to side hip. Drop earrings. Bead necklace. Black satin shoes, peep toes, shaped front and open sides trimmed with gold kid, ankle straps, high heels. **5** Two-piece black wool evening suit: double-breasted jacket, wide satin-faced shawl collar which matches covered button fastening and trim on cuffless inset sleeves, padded shoulders, hip-level welt pockets, breast pocket; straight-cut trousers, no turn-ups, satin stripe on outside seam. White cotton collar-attached shirt. Black satin bow-tie. Black patent-leather lace-up shoes, round toes, no toecaps.

Sports and Leisure Wear

1 Holiday wear. Pink cotton beach-dress, fitted bodice, button opening from low neckline to waistline, narrow shoulder straps, decorative triangular flaps over bustline which match triangular hip-level flap pockets and wide buckled belt, mid-calf-length panelled skirt. Green leather strap mules with flat heels. **2** Holiday wear. Pale green cotton bikini bra-top, knotted at centre front, narrow self-fabric rouleau halter straps, back fastening. Pale green linen tailored shorts, wide waistband, turn-ups, green and white striped canvas belt with metal buckle. Pink leather pumps, bow trim, flat heels. **3** Golf. Hip-length olive-green wool top, self-fabric button fastening from under small collar to point of V-shaped inset top-stitched yoke, drop shoulderline, inset shirt-style sleeves gathered into buttoned cuffs. Wide leather belt with metal buckle. Mid-calf-length olive-green, rust and cream checked wool box-pleat skirt. Olive-green brimless beret. Lace-up leather brogues, flat heels. **4** Ski wear. Two-piece weatherproof maroon cotton ski-suit: hooded hip-length top, centre-front zip fastening in bloused bodice, wide leather belt with round metal buckle, flared skirts with diagonal piped pockets; straight-cut trousers gathered on ankles, low piped pockets. Leather gauntlet mittens. Goggles. Lace-up leather ski-boots, extra strap-and-buckle fastening. **5** Walking. Hand-knitted cream wool sweater, high V-shaped neckline with ribbed edge which matches hem and cuffs of inset sleeves. Grey collar-attached wool shirt. Red and yellow spotted scarf. Narrow heavy wool knee breeches, fly fastening, strap-and-buckle fastening on knee. Knee-length hand-knitted cream wool socks. Brown leather lace-up brogues.

Underwear and Negligee

1 Sleeveless white machine-knitted cotton singlet, machine-stitched detail around low scooped neckline and armholes. White machine-knitted cotton drawers, elasticated waistband, fly front, machined hems. Red leather slippers, round toes, flat heels. **2** Cotton and lace brassiere, wired cups, light boning, elasticated panels and hem, back fastening, adjustable shoulder straps. Elasticated cotton girdle, high fitted waist, stitched front panel, embroidered motif, light boning, side zip fastening, four adjustable suspenders. Flesh-coloured nylon stockings. Pink velvet mules, white feather trim, round toes, low heels. **3** Hip-length strapless combination brassiere and girdle, wired cups trimmed with lace, light boning, elasticated front panel, stitched side panels, elasticated gussets, light boning, side zip fastening, four adjustable/removable suspenders. Flesh-coloured nylon stockings. Black ballet pumps. **4** Mid-calf-length pink nylon petticoat, fitted bodice, bra cups trimmed with lace to match gathered frill on hem of panelled skirt, self-fabric rouleau shoulder straps, side zip fastening. Pink satin ballet pumps, ribbon trim, round toes, flat heels. **5** Collarless wrapover cream nylon dressing gown, bodice gathered from shoulder yoke to waistline, full-length gathered skirts, wide self-fabric belt tied into large bow on one side, gathered elbow-length cream nylon lace sleeves. Cream satin slippers.

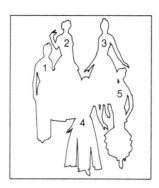

1951 Day Wear

1 Hip-length green and grey vertically striped flannel jacket, black astrakhan collar, two breast-level shaped flap pockets horizontally striped to match hip-level patch-and-flap pockets, connecting box pleats and shaped cuffs of long inset sleeves. Straight grey flannel skirt. Dark green felt hat, upswept brim, self-fabric bow trim. Black leather handbag and gloves. Dark green rolled umbrella, bamboo handle. Black leather shoes, mock lace-up front, high heels.
2 Blue and grey checked cloth two-piece suit: hip-length single-breasted top, shaped bias-cut pleated front panel, button fastening to under white piqué collar, grey ribbon bow tie, inset shirt sleeves, bias-cut buttoned cuffs matching waist-belt; straight skirt. Black leather shoes, bar straps. **3** Beige linen dress, buttoned strap fastening from under wing collar to knee-level ending in knife pleat, bloused bodice, narrow rouleau belt, inset sleeves, buttoned cuffs, straight skirt, double top-stitched yoke, piped pockets. Brown leather sling-back shoes, high heels.
4 Knee-length single-breasted khaki cotton weatherproof raincoat, wide lapels, raglan sleeves, diagonal hip-level welt pockets, self-fabric belt, leather buckle, horn buttons, top-stitched edges and detail. Straight-cut trousers, turn-ups. Striped collar-attached shirt. Checked tie. Brown felt trilby. Leather gloves. Brown leather lace-up shoes. **5** Fitted mid-calf-length yellow, blue and grey checked cloth coat, drop shoulderline and panel seams join to form hip-level buttoned flap pockets, piped pockets in bias-cut side panels, button fastening from waist to under collar, tight sleeves, flared skirts. Grey felt hat, feather trim. Leather gloves and handbag. Long umbrella. Navy suede shoes, scalloped edges, perforated decoration.

Evening Wear

1 Navy-blue crêpe evening dress, asymmetric draped overbodice, fitted boned strapless underbodice embroidered all over with stylized flower motifs in multicoloured glass beads, overdress with self-fabric belt, metal buckle, full-length straight skirt gathered at waist, unpressed knife pleat at front and back on one side. Long navy-blue satin gloves. Glass bead necklace matching clip-on earrings. Navy-blue satin strap sandals. **2** Pale salmon-pink organdie ball gown, fitted boned bodice, beaded and embroidered motif on centre front which matches wide shoulder straps and asymmetric overskirt, full-length gathered striped organdie underskirt worn over layers of fine tulle. **3** Oyster satin cocktail dress, fitted boned strapless bodice, mid-calf-length gored skirt, self-fabric belt with self-fabric oval buckle. Black velvet short spencer jacket, low scooped neckline with shawl collar forming bow tie fastening, elbow-length inset sleeves with cuffs. Double row of pearls matching cluster clip-on earrings. Black satin shoes. **4** White crêpe evening dress embroidered all over with yellow and black flower motifs, draped fitted boned bodice, wide shoulder straps form short draped sleeves, full-length straight skirt gathered at waist, two floating side panels gathered at waist lined with yellow silk. Elbow-length white silk gloves. Drop earrings and matching necklace. Satin shoes. **5** Black lace and silk-taffeta evening dress, fitted boned strapless bodice edged with scallops of lace which match hem above wide gathered double frills of taffeta, dips from mid-calf-length at front to ground at back. Full-length purple satin gloves. Matching set of jewelry: clip-on earrings, necklace, bracelet. Black satin shoes, peep toes, high heels.

Sports and Leisure Wear

1 Golf. Waist-length beige wool jacket, front zip fastening from base of wide waistband to under shirt-style collar, breast-level shaped patch pockets with flaps, single flap pocket with tail trim on one side of waistband, inset sleeves gathered into buttoned cuffs, top-stitched edges and detail. Mid-calf-length beige, yellow and brown checked wool box-pleated skirt. Beige felt beret with stalk. Beige wool stockings. Brown lace-up leather shoes.
2 Holiday wear. Blue and yellow striped cotton beach dress, fitted bodice with seamed bra top, V-shaped waist seam, halter straps tied at back, thigh-length skirt with wide box pleat. Natural straw hat, small crown, outsized brim, ribbon and pom-pon trim. Large beach bag which matches dress. Blue canvas sling-back shoes trimmed in white, low wedge heels. **3** Country wear. Brown and green checked wool shirt, bias-cut peter-pan collar which matches breast-level pleated patch-and-flap pockets, shoulder yoke, buttoned cuffs of inset sleeves and fringed necktie. Light brown wool straight-cut trousers with turn-ups, diagonal hip-level pockets, side fastening. Wide leather belt with metal buckle. Brown knitted wool hat, wide turned back rib with matching pom-pon. Lace-up leather shoes. **4** Tennis. Waist-length hand-knitted white cotton top, shirt-style collar trimmed with ribbing to match strap opening, edge of short sleeves and hemline. Tailored white canvas shorts with turn-ups. Lace-up white canvas sports shoes.
5 Cricket. Hand-knitted white cotton sweater, V-shaped neckline trimmed with green to match stripe above cuffs of inset sleeves and stripe above hemline. White cotton collar-attached shirt, worn open. White flannel trousers with turn-ups. White leather and canvas lace-up shoes.

Accessories

1 Cream straw hat, small crown, wide brim, raffia trim. Clip-on earrings. **2** Brimless spotted silk hat which matches outsized bow-tie. **3** Brimless hat trimmed with mimosa. **4** Pale blue straw hat, small crown, wide brim trimmed with bias-cut frill of white silk-organdie. **5** Brimless beige felt beret with stalk. **6** Yellow straw hat, turned-up brim, trimmed with posy of white flowers at back. **7** Close-fitting mesh veil, trimmed loops of silk ribbon at back. Matching set of jewelry: clip-on earrings, necklace, dress clip. Black astrakhan shoulder wrap threaded through self-fabric belt, long ends. Elbow-length black suede gloves. **8** Felt hat, small brown crown, white petersham band, cream brim. **9** Yellow straw hat, small crown, white petersham band, flared brim. **10** Black bowler hat, curled brim. Striped collar-attached shirt. Spotted silk tie. **11** Dark blue trilby, narrow band. **12** Brown trilby, wide band. Yellow and brown checked silk scarf. **13** Tan and cream leather lace-up shoes. **14** Beige lace-up suede boots, rubber soles. **15** Tan leather step-in shoes. **16** Cream and tan leather shoes, perforated decoration, bow trim, high heels. **17** Navy-blue leather handbag, flap-and-stud fastening, small handle. **18** Brown leather handbag, metal stud fastening, top-stitched detail. **19** Red leather step-in shoes, bow trim, flat heels. **20** Dark brown leather shoes, side keyhole, white bow and trim, high heels. **21** Black leather shoes, perforated decoration, high heels. **22** Black suede shoes, peep toes, strap fronts, open sides, high heels. **23** Green leather sandals, sling-backs, ankle straps, peep toes, low heels. **24** Brown leather and snakeskin sling-back shoes, medium heels. **25** Navy-blue suede shoes, laced keyhole opening, bands of perforated decoration, medium navy-blue leather heels.

 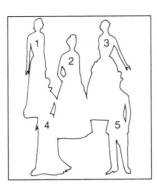 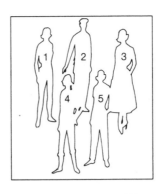 

1952 Day Wear

1 Single-breasted grey wool overcoat, narrow lapels, pointed collar, raglan sleeves, buttoned strap at wrist, hip-level diagonal welt pockets, self-fabric belt, leather-covered buckle, horn buttons, top-stitched edges and detail. Straight-cut dark grey flannel trousers, turn-ups. Blue and white striped cotton collar-attached shirt. Striped silk tie. Grey trilby, narrow band, curled brim. Leather gloves. Black leather lace-up shoes, no toe-caps. **2** Mid-calf-length light blue wool coat, concealed opening, hip-level vertical welt pockets, raglan sleeves gathered into deep cuffs, large grey fox-fur collar. Brimless grey felt hat cut away on one side. Grey leather gloves. Nylon stockings. Grey suede shoes, round toes, high heels. **3** Cream cotton dress patterned with red, wide top-stitched tuck at bust-level to give effect of overbodice which matches double yoke above mid-calf-length gathered skirt, V-shaped neckline, white piqué collar matching cuffs on short dolman sleeves, tailored belt with self-fabric buckle. Flesh-coloured nylon stockings. White leather shoes, high heels. **4** Grey cotton gabardine dress, fitted bodice, three-button fastening from waist to under pink and grey checked cotton collar and revers which match cuffs of three-quarter-length dolman sleeves, tailored belt with round buckle, hip-level shaped patch pockets and inverted box pleat in centre front of mid-calf-length flared skirt. Black leather shoes, ankle straps, round toes, high heels. **5** Black and white checked wool dress, fitted bodice, turned-down wing collar, wrist-length dolman sleeves, red leather belt, narrow mid-calf-length skirt, shaped yoke seam with concealed pockets, tiny red silk posy on one shoulder. Black fine straw hat, wide brim. Black leather gloves, handbag and shoes.

Wedding Wear

1 Oyster satin dress, fitted bodice, draped oyster chiffon cummerbund, low V-shaped neckline and shoulders incrusted with pearl and crystal beads, framed with deep bias-cut satin collar, long tight inset sleeves fastened on wrist with row of loops and tiny pearl buttons, flared gored skirt with long back train. Small headdress trimmed with pearl and crystal beads, waist-length and ground-length silk-tulle veils. **2** Cream wild-silk strapless dress, ruched over bust, tight fitted panelled boned bodice and wide flared skirt cut in one piece without waist seam; short bolero, shallow grown-on collar and rounded edges bound with self-fabric, long tight dolman sleeves, point over hand, pearl button fastening. Headdress of wax flowers, waist-length double silk-tulle veil. **3** White silk-chiffon dress, draped boned bodice, removable white lace bolero with scalloped edges and long tight sleeves, gathered skirt. Headdress of fresh flowers to match bouquet, long chiffon veil. **4** Pink silk-satin dress with self-colour all-over pattern, fitted bodice, ruching over bust, wing collar, long tight inset sleeves, draped hip yoke split at front forming back train, flared panelled skirt. Fabric tiara trimmed with pearls, waist-length silk-tulle veil. **5** Dark grey wool tailcoat, single-button fastening, flower worn in buttonhole on lapel, breast pocket with handkerchief. Collarless single-breasted pale grey waistcoat. Grey and black striped wool straight-cut trousers, no turn-ups. White shirt, wing collar. Grey striped cravat and pin. Grey top hat. Grey gloves. Black leather lace-up shoes, no toecaps.

Sports and Leisure Wear

1 Holiday wear. Sleeveless yellow and white striped top, fitted bodice, button fastening to under revers and pointed collar, bound cut-away armholes. Bias-cut tailored shorts, side button fastening, large patch pocket on one side, sewn turn-ups, wide black elasticated cotton belt with metal clasp fastening. Yellow and white fabric headband. Yellow and white striped towelling strap sandals, sling-backs, cork soles. **2** Country wear. Dark green and brown tweed double-breasted sports jacket, three-button fastening, inset sleeves, button trim, three angled flap pockets, breast pocket. Straight-cut trousers, no turn-ups. Cream cotton collar-attached shirt. Striped wool tie. Beige felt cap with small peak. Leather lace-up shoes, no toecaps. **3** Holiday wear. Pale blue and cream checked sleeveless dress, slightly bloused bodice, curved yoke seam edged with plain white cotton to match collar and bow tie, covered buttons, tailored belt, covered buckle and edges of large hip-level pocket flaps, gathered mid-calf-length skirt, bias-cut side panels, bias-cut shoulder yoke. White cotton headband. Pale blue canvas shoes, peep toes, ruched decoration, sling-backs, high heels. **4** Beach wear. Hand-knitted pale green cotton sleeveless waist-length top, wide off-the-shoulder collar with fringed edge. Mid-calf-length fitted green linen trousers with turn-ups, hip-level welt pockets. Orange silk headscarf. Cream canvas shoes, rope soles. **5** Golf. Green wool blouse, small collar and buttoned strap opening edged with braid to match hems of dolman sleeves. Straight-cut tan wool trousers, deep waistband, rust leather belt, hip-level welt pockets, turn-ups. Brown leather shoes, buttoned strap, flat heels.

Underwear and Negligee

1 Pale pink cotton brassiere, seamed and darted cups, elasticated side panels, back fastening, adjustable shoulder straps. Pale pink cotton corselette, high waist, light boning, elasticated control panels, side hook fastening, adjustable suspenders. Flesh-coloured nylon stockings. Satin house shoes. **2** Two-piece green and white spotted silk pyjama suit: sleeveless top, wide yoke edged with plain white frill trimmed with fine lace to match hem of gathered top, bound neckline and rouleau bow tie fastening match yoke edge and fastening; trousers gathered from wide waistband into buttoned cuffs on ankles, side hip fastening. Flat satin pumps. **3** Pale peach silk nightdress patterned with self-coloured sprays of flowers, bodice ruched and smocked from waistline to under bust, bra-style top edged with lace, wide shoulder straps, bow trim, full-length gathered skirt, hem decorated with gathered frill edged with lace. Satin ballet pumps. **4** White cotton brassiere, stitched and wired cups, elasticated side panels, back fastening, adjustable shoulder straps. Mid-calf-length pleated white nylon waist-slip, deep waistband with light boning, side fastening. Shoes with round toes, high heels. **5** Two-piece blue and red striped cotton pyjama suit: hip-length single-breasted shirt-style jacket, pearl four-button fastening, small lapels, pointed collar, wide shoulder yoke, long inset sleeves, sewn cuffs, three shaped patch pockets, self-fabric tie-belt; long shorts with stitched cuffs. Red and black leather step-in house slippers.

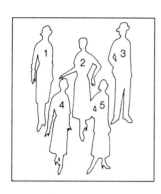  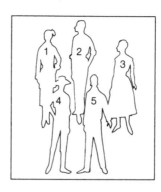 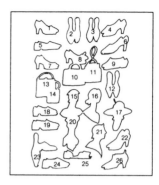

1953 Day Wear

1 Grey flannel dress, fitted bodice, neckline scooped to below bustline, infilled with white piqué blouse, button fastening, large pointed collar, cuffs show under three-quarter-length cuffed dolman sleeves of dress, narrow fitted skirt, diagonal hip-level welt pockets, wide grey suede belt with self-fabric buckle. Brimless draped white silk hat. Grey suede gloves. Black leather shoes with round toes. **2** Pale blue linen dress, slightly bloused panelled bodice, short dolman sleeves, bust-level step opening, three self-fabric buttons, shirt collar, mid-calf-length knife-pleated skirt from fitted hip yoke, wide navy-blue leather belt, metal buckle. Navy-blue leather shoes, round toes, high heels. **3** Dark grey wool three-piece suit: double-breasted jacket, narrow lapels, small collar, fitted sleeves, three-button trim; collarless single-breasted waistcoat, welt pockets, pointed hem; straight-cut trousers, no turn-ups. Collar-attached shirt. Plain silk tie. Dark blue trilby, black band. Black leather lace-up shoes, toecaps. **4** Collarless cream silk dress, elbow-length semi-inset sleeves, fitted bodice, centre-front concealed opening between buttoned notches at neck and waistline, mid-calf-length flared skirt, side panel seams form hip-level pockets. Brown leather shoes, scalloped front detail, round toes, high heels. **5** Two-piece red wool suit: unfitted single-breasted hip-length jacket, five-button fastening to under shirt collar, side panel seams end at diagonal welt pockets, wide inset sleeves, drop shoulderline, narrow cuffs; mid-calf-length flared gored skirt. Small brimless black felt hat. Black silk neckscarf. Black leather shoes.

Evening Wear

1 Mid-calf-length black lace cocktail dress, black silk-taffeta strapless underbodice and flared underskirt, fitted lace bodice, high round neckline trimmed with black velvet ribbon band to match bow tie and narrow belt, drop shoulderline forms short cap sleeves, flared skirt follows line of underskirt worn over stiffened petticoats. Black velvet shoes, shaped fronts above round toes, high heels. **2** Black corded-silk cocktail dress, sleeveless oyster satin bodice, wrapover forms low V-shaped neckline, pleated cummerbund to under bust, fitted mid-calf-length skirt. Elbow-length black silk gloves. Black satin shoes, round toes, high heels. **3** Pale pink satin ball gown, panelled bodice and full-length flared skirt cut in one piece without waist seam, wide off-the-shoulder V-shaped neckline framed with large stole collar, trimmed at centre front with self-fabric bow and posy of silk violets. Above-elbow-length pink suede gloves. Matching costume jewelry set: pearl clip-on earrings, necklace, bracelet. **4** Full-length black velvet evening dress, sleeveless fitted bodice, wrapover effect to one side, self-fabric bow trim, low scooped neckline, straight skirt gathered from low curved waist seam, unpressed knife pleat from side front. Above-elbow-length black silk gloves. Clip-on earrings. Bead necklace. Black satin strap sandals. **5** Red silk cocktail dress, slightly bloused bodice, wide off-the-shoulder neckline forming short sleeves, gathers over bust, black velvet ribbon belt and bow, mid-calf-length gathered skirt from fitted hip yoke worn over stiffened petticoats. Gold hoop earrings. Gold and black bracelet. Black satin shoes, round toes, high heels.

Sports and Leisure Wear

1 Country wear. Long wrapover light brown sheepskin jacket, cream wool shawl collar matching cuffs of long inset sleeves, wide self-fabric belt, leather covered buckle, side panel seams, hip-level diagonal welt pockets, top-stitched edges and detail. Brown knitted-wool sweater. Mid-calf-length brown and yellow checked wool skirt. Brimless beige knitted-wool hat, wired edge, trimmed at back with self-fabric tassel. Brown leather shoes, strap-and-buckle fastening, flat heels. **2** Golf. Dark brown wool shirt, large box-pleat patch pockets with buttoned flaps, sleeves worn rolled to elbow, shoulder yoke, pointed collar worn open, top-stitched detail. Plain cream silk cravat. Straight-cut beige cavalry-twill trousers, side hip pockets, turn-ups, brown leather belt. Brown leather shoes. **3** Holiday wear. Red denim pinafore dress, wide shoulder straps decorated with blue ricrac braid to match edges of neck and outsized patch-and-buttoned flap pockets, gathered skirt, wide red suede belt. White and red spotted cotton blouse, stand collar, strap opening, cap sleeves. Red leather sandals. **4** Holiday wear. White cotton blouse, shirt collar worn open, three-quarter-length sleeves gathered into buttoned cuffs. Short sleeveless blue cotton bolero decorated with appliqué motifs. Mid-calf-length striped fitted tight trousers, hip-level pockets in side panel, wide waistband. Large blue straw hat, red ribbon trim. Red leather mules. **5** Golf. Black and cinnamon checked brushed-wool hip-length jacket, double-breasted front panel, large collar, inset sleeves, stitched cuffs, decorative top-stitching. Dark grey jersey-wool tight trousers, wide turn-ups. Leather shoes, strap-and-buckle fastening, flat heels.

Accessories

1 Silver kid evening shoes, ankle straps, peep toes, perforated decoration, high heels. **2** Pale blue leather sling-back shoes, peep toes, perforated decoration. **3** Tan leather shoes, strap-and-button trim. **4** Brown suede shoes, leather trim, high heels. **5** Leather sling-back shoes, peep toes, flat heels. **6** Leather shoes, bar strap and buckle, perforated decoration. **8** Navy-blue leather shoes, self-bow trim, top-stitched detail. **7** Black leather shoes, top-stitched detail, high heels. **9** Cream leather shoes, top-stitched strap, navy-blue platform soles and low wedge heels. **10** Leather handbag, double leather handles, clasp fastening. **11** Cream leather handbag, tan suede top and handle. **12** Red leather shoes, ruched fronts, button trim, peep toes. **13** Leather handbag, double rouleau handles, clasp fastening. **14** Black grosgrain evening bag, rouleau handles, clasp fastening. **15** Brimless straw hat trimmed with velvet leaves and plastic berries. **16** Cream felt hat, curled brim, red petersham ribbon trim. **17** Two-tone felt hat, small red crown, white silk trim, wide white brim, red rose trim. **18** Brown leather shoes, strap-and-buckle fastening, top-stitched detail. **19** Brown leather golf shoes, strap-and-buckle fastening, fringed tongues, perforated decoration. **20** Brimless yellow straw hat, white pom-pon trim. **21** Brushed-felt hat, fluted brim, self-fabric rouleau band and bow. **22** Black suede ankle-boots, lined and trimmed with fur, high heels. **23** Leather brogues, perforated decoration. **24** Leather shoes, top-stitched detail, toecaps. **25** Embroidered cloth shoes, open sides, peep toes, flat heels. **26** Elastic-sided black suede ankle-boots, lined and trimmed with fur, leather soles, high heels.

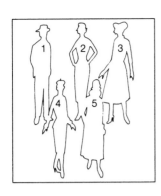

1954 Day Wear

1 Three-piece striped blue cloth suit: single-breasted jacket, three-button fastening, narrow lapels; collarless single-breasted waistcoat, welt pockets; straight-cut trousers, narrow hems, turn-ups. Red and white striped collar-attached shirt. Blue silk tie. Black trilby. Black shoes. **2** Wrapover black cotton piqué dress, fitted bodice, wide V-shaped neckline, cap sleeves, shiny black and white buttons, mid-calf-length straight skirt, black patent-leather belt. Small black straw hat, white trim. Elbow-length black cotton gloves. Black leather shoes, peep toes, patent-leather trim, high heels. **3** Red wool button-through dress, fitted bodice to under bust, dolman top with stand collar and elbow-length sleeves, red leather covered buttons from collar to above hemline, flared skirt with panels of knife pleats. Cream straw hat, wide bonnet brim, tall crown draped with red silk. Red leather shoes, round toes, high heels. **4** Royal-blue and black wool-tweed two-piece suit: single-breasted jacket, shiny black buttons from waistline to under narrow collar, fitted bodice, concealed pockets set into seams on side hip below waistline, mock buttoned flap pockets below rounded shoulderline, dolman sleeves, deep cuffs; straight skirt. Royal-blue felt beret with stalk. Black cotton gloves. Black leather sling-back shoes, round toes, high heels. **5** Navy-blue showerproof cotton raincoat, red and silver buttons from waistline to under rounded revers, peter-pan collar worn turned up, inset sleeves, deep cuffs, large patch pockets with mock flaps, red saddle-stitched edges and detail. Red and white patterned silk scarf. Small navy-blue felt hat, low crown, red petersham trim. Navy-blue leather gloves and shoes.

Evening Wear

1 Full-length unfitted red velvet evening coat, boat-shaped neckline and hip-length armholes edged with wide band of embroidered and beaded decoration, three-button fastening below neckline, unpressed box pleats from neck to hem, short back train. Long black kid leather gloves. Costume jewelry: clip-on drop earrings, matching bracelet. **2** Two-piece black wool evening suit: waisted double-breasted jacket, silk lapels matching covered buttons, piped pockets; straight-cut trousers, narrow hems, no turn-ups. White collar-attached shirt. Narrow black silk bow-tie. Black patent-leather shoes. **3** Black cotton gabardine evening dress, strapless boned bodice, neckline edged with white grosgrain flap matching band and large bow at above knee-level on full panelled skirt which is worn over stiffened petticoats. Long black kid leather gloves. Bead necklace. Clip-on earrings. **4** Silver and white cotton-piqué evening dress, hip-length fitted boned bodice, low scooped neckline to below bust infilled with ruched self-fabric, wide shoulder straps cut in one piece with side panels of bodice, full-length narrow skirt, draped over hips, unpressed flared box pleat at back. Matching set of costume jewelry: clip-on earrings, necklace, bracelet. White kid gloves. Shoes with peep toes. **5** Mid-calf-length pink taffeta cocktail dress, fitted boned bodice to under bust, unpressed self-fabric frill standing up over bust, wide skirt cut in flared panels forming V-shape on hipline, self-fabric button trim on side hips. Drop earrings. Long navy-blue silk gloves. Navy-blue satin sling-back strap sandals.

Sports and Leisure Wear

1 Beach wear. One-piece multicolour-spotted white stretch-cotton bathing costume, strapless boned fitted top, stitched and wired cups, panel seams, short gathered drawers from piped V-shaped hip seam. Towelling mules, peep toes, rope soles. **2** Ski wear. Wind and rainproof yellow ribbed cotton-poplin top, elasticated waistline, wide stand collar, inset sleeves with drop shoulderline, single piped pocket at bust-level with zip fastening to match pockets in skirt. Narrow black jersey trousers, stitched creases. Brimless black knitted-wool hat, wide turned-back rib. Hand-knitted black and yellow wool mittens. Fur-lined and trimmed ski-boots. **3** Tennis. Hand-knitted white cotton sweater, V-shaped neckline, cuffed raglan sleeves. White cotton collar-attached shirt, pointed collar worn open. Tailored white cotton-poplin shorts, diagonal side pockets, no turn-ups. Knitted white ankle socks. White canvas lace-up sports shoes, rubber soles. **4** Holiday wear. White glazed-cotton sundress printed with multicoloured roses, fitted bodice, halter neckline gathered into one-piece fitted cup, mid-calf-length flared panelled skirt, self-fabric tailored belt and self-fabric buckle. Triangular cape in matching fabric edged with black cotton fringe. Flat leather pumps, bow trim. **5** Golf. Hip-length brushed-wool jacket, zip fastening from hem to under large peter-pan collar worn turned up, cuffed raglan sleeves, asymmetric patch pockets, buttoned welt, top-stitched edges and detail. Ankle-length light-brown jersey fitted tight trousers. Light brown wool hat, narrow ribbed brim. Brown leather shoes, fringed tongues, flat heels.

Underwear and Negligee

1 Knee-length gold silk dressing gown patterned with black and brown motifs, wrapover front, shawl collar, three patch pockets, cuffed inset sleeves, self-fabric tie-belt. Black and gold silk pyjamas. Black velvet step-in slippers, satin binding. **2** Cream silk pyjama suit: hip-length single-breasted jacket, shoulder yoke, pink satin pointed peter-pan collar which matches strap fastening, welts of shaped breast-level patch pockets and hems of inset sleeves; wide ankle-length trousers. Pink fake-fur mules, cross-over fronts, peep toes. **3** Pale yellow crêpe-de-chine waist-length camisole patterned with sprigs of cream flowers, V-shaped neckline edged with cream lace to match hemline, satin ribbon shoulder straps and bow trim, side fastening. Half-slip in matching fabric gathered from elasticated waistband, lace-edged hem, satin ribbon bow trim. Cream velvet and satin mules, peep toes, high heels. **4** Full-length pale blue cotton-voile nightdress patterned with pink and cream flower sprays, deep cream lace yoke, plain cream cotton-satin peter-pan collar which matches rouleau pipings and bindings, bow tie of keyhole opening and tie-belt, bloused bodice, gathered skirt. Cream satin pumps, bow trim. **5** Waist-length fine white cotton camisole patterned with pale pink, fitted bra top, narrow shoulder straps, side fastening. Knickers in matching fabric, ruched and elasticated waistband, flared legs edged with pleated frill. Pink satin mules, pink feather trim, high heels.

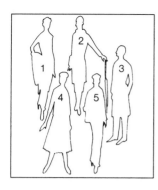

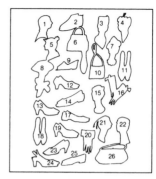

1955 Day Wear

1 Collarless off-white silk-tweed dress, long fitted bodice, short cap sleeves, two mock flap pockets set into hip seam, fitted tapered skirt. Brimless red felt hat trimmed with silk leaves and berries. Large clip-on earrings. Brooch worn below shoulderline. Elbow-length red suede gloves. Long wild mink stole. Red suede shoes, round toes, high heels.
2 Two-piece red wool suit: long fitted double-breasted jacket fastening with metal buttons from hip-level to under black fur collar, matching fur muff worn on one sleeve, hip-level vertical welt pockets; narrow skirt. Brimless black velvet hat. Long umbrella. Black leather shoes. **3** Knee-length single-breasted raincoat, vertical welt pockets in upper body, patch-and-flap pockets in skirts, inset sleeves, half straps, button trim, self-fabric buckled belt, multi-lines of top-stitching on hem, top-stitched edges and detail. Narrow trousers, no turn-ups. Step-in shoes. **4** Charcoal-grey flannel two-piece suit: hip-length unfitted jacket, single-breasted fastening from hipband to under stiff white cotton collar, large grey and white striped silk bow, three-quarter-length sleeves cut in one piece with panelled bodice, half strap, button trim; sunray-pleated skirt. Brimless black felt hat. Short white cotton gloves. Black leather shoes.
5 Two-piece green linen suit: edge-to-edge flared jacket, wide lapels buttoned over large square collar, three-quarter-length cuffed sleeves, button trim, vertical welt pockets; fitted dress, wrapover buttoned collar, fitted tapered skirt. Brimless black felt hat, brooch trim. Black fabric gloves. Black leather shoes, peep toes, high heels.

Evening Wear

1 Brick-red silk-taffeta strapless ball gown, asymmetric draped shoulder cape, long fitted boned bodice, draped hip yoke forming long sash to one side, full-length skirt gathered from hipline worn over stiffened petticoats. Long black silk gloves. **2** White embossed-silk evening dress, wide shoulder straps, straight neckline with wide V-shaped cut in centre front, fitted bodice, seam under bust, no waist seam, flared skirt with large pale pink satin bow between each side panel seam at knee-level. Costume jewelry: large drop earrings, black and white stones set in silver; matching necklace. Long black silk gloves. White satin shoes. **3** Gold lurex brocade blouse, off-the-shoulder neckline framed with deep collar and large knotted tie, fitted hip-level bodice with panel seams, open seams at hip-level, tight elbow-length sleeves. Floor-length black duchess-satin wide flared skirt. Black satin shoes. **4** Pale sky-blue duchess-satin cocktail dress, fitted boned bodice, shaped seam under bust, narrow rouleau shoulder straps end in tiny self-fabric bows, mid-calf-length flared skirt, wide front panel with two hip-level concealed pockets. Long cream satin gloves. Pale sky-blue satin shoes, round toes trimmed with self-fabric rosebuds, high heels. **5** Cream silk cocktail dress, hip-length fitted bodice embroidered with rows of rhinestones to match undercollar and short sleeves, off-the-shoulder neckline edged with narrow collar which matches hip-level cuff above gathered mid-calf-length skirt worn over stiffened petticoats. Pearl stud earrings with matching bracelets. Cream satin shoes, round toes, high heels.

Sports and Leisure Wear

1 Football. Black, orange, grey and white horizontally striped machine-knitted shirt, long inset sleeves, ribbed cuffs, white cotton collar with three-button strap opening. Baggy white cotton shorts, fly opening, side hip pockets. Striped knitted-wool socks matching colours in shirt. Brown leather ankle-boots, hard toecaps, pegged soles. **2** Beach wear. Patterned elasticated-cotton bathing costume, hip-length fitted bodice, plain white elasticated-cotton halter straps which fasten at back and match narrow cuff on straight neckline and band at hip-level above short flared skirt. Brimless green raffia hat with pointed crown. Clip-on plastic flower-shaped earrings. Green canvas sling-back shoes, white trim, flat heels. **3** Holiday wear. White glazed-cotton dress patterned with sprays of lilac flowers, fitted collarless bodice and full flared skirt cut in one piece, V-shaped neckline forms mock wrapover bodice and button fastening ending in deep unpressed box pleat in centre front of skirt, short cap sleeves. Lilac straw hat, shallow crown, wide brim. White plastic hoop earrings. Short transparent white nylon gloves. White canvas shoes, open lapel-effect fronts, lilac button trim. **4** Tennis. White cotton blouse, self-fabric buttons, rounded grown-on collar, short cap sleeves. Short flared white cotton-poplin skirt, grown-on waistband, threaded buckle fastening, side hip pockets incorporated into short curved side panel seams, top-stitched detail. White cotton ankle socks. White canvas sports shoes. **5** Country wear. Hip-level hand-knitted brick-red wool sweater, outsized cowl collar, drop head inset sleeves, ribbed hems. Knee-length black wool tight knee breeches with turn-ups. Knee socks, diamond-shaped pattern. Black leather pumps, bow trim, flat heels.

Accessories

1 Green ribbed knitted-wool ski-hood. **2** Brown leather ankle-boots, dark brown knitted-wool scalloped yokes, thick soles, small heels. **3** Brimless hat draped in black silk, flat top, brooch trim. **4** Bright pink silk rose worn as evening hat. **5** Hand-knitted royal-blue wool peaked ski-cap, deep cuff side and back, pom-pon trim. **6** Grey leather handbag, side-to-side zip fastening over top, strap-and-brass clasp over fastening at centre. **7** Black velvet hat, pointed crown, fur brim. **8** Crownless navy-blue rough straw hat. **9** Gold brocade evening mules, high wedge heels. **10** Brown leather shoulder bag, flap-and-clip fastening, long handle. **11** Grey leather shoes, asymmetric half straps, central seam, top-stitching. **12** Red leather shoes, narrow self-strap, perforated decoration, low heels. **13** Tan suede shoes, tan leather piping, medium heels. **14** Cream leather shoes, top-stitched detail, brown leather button trim, flat heels. **15** Small pink felt hat, narrow upturned brim. **16** Short pink cloth gloves, satin ribbon and bow trim. **17** Yellow canvas shoes, self-fabric central strap with black fringe, black button trim, flat heels. **18** Navy-blue lace evening shoes, satin trim, peep toes. **19** Black suede shoes, hand top-stitching, low sides, high heels. **20** Short red leather gloves, cuffs trimmed with tiny black buttons and braid. **21** Brimless hand-knitted cream wool hat, flat top, tassel trim. **22** Small grey silk evening hat, draped crown, wired velvet leaves on each side. **23** Brown leather shoes, crossed strap fronts, open sides, perforated decoration, high heels. **24** Light brown sling-back half-sandals, shaped fronts, peep toes, medium heels. **25** White canvas shoes spotted in green, low sides, button trim, flat heels. **26** Large brown leather handbag, shaped sides, top-stitching, single strap, clip fastening.

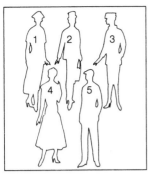
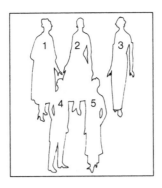

1956 Day Wear

1 Two-piece lilac linen suit: hip-length double-breasted jacket, button fastening from waistline to under bust, rounded grown-on collar and upper shoulder panel of short dolman sleeves cut in one piece, sewn half cuffs and narrow front panel to bust-level, fitted bodice and jacket skirt cut without waist seam, cut-away front; narrow skirt. Deep lilac straw hat, sloping brim, tiny crown. Purple suede gloves. Matching purple suede outsized handbag with double handles. Matching purple suede shoes with high heels. 2 Two-piece cream wool suit: unfitted single-breasted collarless jacket, fastening with four outsized buttons, long raglan sleeves, side hip-level self-fabric trim; narrow skirt. Large cream leather handbag, rouleau handle. Matching cream leather shoes, round toes, button trim, high heels. 3 Two-piece green and brown tweed suit: hip-length unfitted jacket, single-breasted fastening to under fur collar, two welt pockets above bustline, inset three-quarter-length two-piece sleeves, button trim, self-fabric tie-belt on low waistline; narrow skirt. Brimless brown velvet hat, self-fabric bow trim on back. Three-quarter-length brown leather gloves. Matching brown leather shoes. 4 Pea-green cotton dress, low neckline, black glazed-cotton scarf tied under large self-fabric collar, elbow-length inset sleeves, bodice fitted from hipline to under bust, gathered top, full skirt. Black leather shoes, shaped fronts, high heels. 5 Tan wool-tweed single-breasted sports jacket, two-button fastening, flap pockets, breast pocket. Light brown cavalry-twill straight-cut trousers with turn-ups. Collar-attached cream cotton shirt. Green wool tie. Brown wool fitted cap, small peak. Light brown suede lace-up shoes.

Evening Wear

1 Wrapover red velvet evening coat, flared from shoulder to wide mid-calf-length hem, shawl collar, inset three-quarter-length sleeves gathered into deep fitted cuffs, hip-level bound pockets. Small hat, beaded red silk pointed crown, padded roll brim matching coat fabric. Costume jewelry: clip-on bead earrings, matching necklace. Black satin gloves. Black satin shoes. 2 Black satin cocktail dress, low wide neckline, tight three-quarter-length inset sleeves, upper bodice ruched and gathered to central self-fabric bar forming bow-effect, fitted lower bodice and bell-shaped skirt cut in flared panels without waist seam. Large bead earrings, matching pendant necklace. Black satin shoes, peep toes. 3 Black crêpe evening dress, fitted bodice, wide shoulder straps, narrow flat rouleau self-fabric belt, bow tie on centre front of waist, straight ankle-length panelled skirt gathered on side waist. Long black silk gloves. Matching black silk shoes, pointed toes. 4 Edge-to-edge black wool tailcoat, two linked-button fastenings, silk lapels. Collarless single-breasted white piqué waistcoat. Straight-cut trousers, black satin ribbon stripe on outside seam, no turn-ups. Collar-attached white cotton shirt, large bow-tie matching handkerchief in breast pocket. Black patent-leather lace-up shoes. 5 Strapless cream silk evening gown, high waist marked with self-fabric flat rouleau bow, mid-calf-length flared overskirt, split on centre front, straight ankle-length underskirt. Costume jewelry: large earrings, necklace. Long cream silk gloves. Cream satin shoes, pointed toes.

Sports and Leisure Wear

1 Golf. Hip-length beige machine-knitted wool collarless jacket, zip fastening from wide ribbed welt to under V-shaped neckline, bloused body with brown washable-suede side panels from shoulders to sloping welt pockets, cuffed inset sleeves. Beige cavalry-twill straight-cut trousers, narrow hems, no turn-ups. Collar-attached cream brushed-cotton shirt. Brown wool tie. Light brown wool-tweed peaked cap. Brown leather lace-up shoes. 2 Golf. Hip-length dark green suede sleeveless jerkin top, V-shaped neckline, hip-level self-fabric tie-belt, large hip-level patch-and-flap pockets. Collarless machine-knitted beige wool sweater, long cuffed inset sleeves. Brown wool trousers, narrow hems. Brown leather shoes, flat heels. 3 Beach wear. Multicoloured diamond-patterned glazed cotton blouse, low wide neckline, mock-button fastening on bustline, short kimono sleeves. Knee-length trousers in matching fabric, wide waistband, side fastening. 4 Country wear. Light brown machine-knitted wool cardigan-jacket, wide button fastening from wide ribbed welt to under V-shaped neckline, small ribbed collar matching cuffs of long inset sleeves. Cream and beige checked silk neckscarf. Green, beige and brown checked wool-tweed flared panelled skirt. Beige wool stockings. Brown leather lace-up shoes. 5 Holiday wear. Yellow cotton-poplin dress, low sweetheart neckline, ruched bra-top which matches shoulder straps with frilled edges, white piping and rouleau bow trim, hip-length fitted pintucked bodice trimmed with white buttons, full gathered yellow poplin skirt patterned with garlands of green and white flowers. Yellow canvas mules, platform soles, low wedge heels.

Underwear and Negligee

1 Full-length red brushed-cotton dressing gown, wide curved cross-over yoke edged with red nylon pleating to match trim on cuffs of three-quarter-length sleeves and tops of large hip-level patch pockets, two-button diagonal fastening on yoke edge, self-fabric belt fastening in large bow on side waist, flared skirt. 2 White nylon brassiere, stitched undercups, elasticated panels side and back, lace trim, adjustable shoulder straps, back fastening. White nylon girdle, front control panel, elasticated waistband and side panels, four adjustable suspenders, lace trim. Flesh-coloured nylon stockings. Shoes with peep toes, medium heels. 3 White nylon slip, hip-length fitted bodice, narrow ribbon shoulder straps, lace trim which matches hem of three-tier gathered skirt. Satin shoes, medium stiletto heels. 4 Two-piece green and white cotton pyjama suit: unfitted jacket gathered from rounded off-the-shoulder yoke seam, single-breasted three-button fastening to under shawl collar, three-quarter-length full inset sleeves gathered into contrasting colour cuffs which match yoke and flaps of hip-level patch pockets; green knee-length trousers, contrasting colour hems. Green velvet house slippers, flat heels. 5 Pale blue nylon sleeveless nightdress, V-shaped neckline, pleated collar which matches front bodice panel from yoke seam to wide inset waistband and front and back panels of full-length skirt, armholes edged with ruched nylon to match edges of collar and neckline. Satin slippers with cross-over straps and peep toes.

   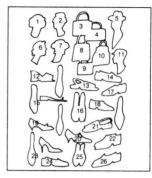

1957 Day Wear

1 Olive-green wool-tweed two-piece suit: knee-length single-breasted unfitted jacket, three large buttons from hip-level to under narrow revers, large collar, long raglan sleeves, hip-level flap pockets; straight skirt. Patterned silk scarf at neck. Brimless orange velvet hat, large crown gathered into wide band. Short brown leather gloves; matching outsized handbag; matching shoes, narrow bar straps, pointed toes. **2** Pale grey lightweight wool dress, button-through fitted bodice, small wing collar, red nylon-chiffon bow tie, three-quarter-length inset sleeves, narrow cuffs, button trim, wide stiffened self-fabric belt, metal buckle, unpressed pleats from waist of bell-shaped skirt, stiffened petticoats. **3** Two-piece cream wool-jersey suit: single-breasted semi-fitted jacket, wide rounded revers, front opening and hem bound in red to match covered buttons, two welt pockets above bustline, piped low waist-level pockets set into curved side panel seams, inset sleeves; straight skirt. Draped red wool-jersey turban. Cream cotton gloves. Red leather envelope purse; matching bar-strap shoes, pointed toes, high stiletto heels. **4** Bright pink wool unfitted double-breasted coat, large buttons from hip-level to under large collar, wide inset sleeves, deep split cuffs, pockets set into side seams at hip-level. Brimless black felt hat, brooch trim. Short black leather gloves; matching bar-strap shoes, pointed toes, stiletto heels. **5** Navy-blue linen dress, large self-fabric collar, white cotton piqué over-collar, three-quarter-length sleeves, buttoned cuffs, fitted bodice, self-fabric wide stiffened belt, straight skirt, unpressed pleats from waist. Brimless navy-blue straw hat, white straw leaf trim. White cotton gloves. Navy-blue leather bar-strap shoes, pointed toes, high stiletto heels.

Evening Wear

1 Short white cotton cocktail dress, fitted hip-length bodice, straight neckline edged with white cotton broderie anglaise embroidered in black to match gathered three-tier bell-shaped skirt worn over stiffened petticoats, black velvet ribbon shoulder straps and bow trim on centre-front neckline. White leather bar-strap shoes, pointed toes, stiletto heels. **2** Full-length fine Irish linen ball gown, pale pink fitted boned strapless bodice, edged with self-fabric pleating, deep pink gathered skirt, wide olive-green pleated belt threaded through large self-fabric buckle. **3** White silk evening dress patterned with life-size pink and red roses and rosebuds with long leafed stalks, sleeveless semi-fitted bodice, straight neckline, full-length straight skirt, centre-back kick pleat, wide plain white silk stiffened belt, large self-fabric bow trim. Long white silk gloves. Matching white silk shoes with pointed toes. **4** Short cocktail dress in synthetic taffeta, multicoloured pattern, wide off-the-shoulder wrapover neckline which stands away over shoulder and at back, fitted bodice, front panel from waist to under bust ruched to match short side hip panels in gathered bell-shaped skirt worn over stiffened petticoats, three-quarter-length inset sleeves. Short satin gloves. Matching satin shoes, pointed toes, stiletto heels. **5** Deep pink duchess-satin ball gown, fitted bodice, large stand-away off-the-shoulder wrapover collar, large black velvet rose trim at centre front, full-length bell-shaped skirt, unpressed pleats at side front and back waist. Long silk gloves.

Sports and Leisure Wear

1 Country wear. Single-breasted green and beige wool-tweed jacket, three-button fastening, narrow lapels, three patch pockets. Light brown wool trousers with turn-ups. Beige brushed-cotton collar-attached shirt. Tan wool tie. Beige wool-tweed peaked cap. Brown leather lace-up shoes, no toecaps. **2** Tennis. White synthetic-linen sleeveless blouse, button fastening from waist to under narrow stand collar, curved side panel seams. Short flared skirt in matching fabric, side panel seams form scalloped hemline, top-stitched detail, narrow waistband, threaded tailored self-fabric buckled belt. White cotton ankle socks. White canvas lace-up sports shoes. **3** Beach wear. Strapless elasticated navy-blue nylon and cotton panelled bathing costume, hip-length fitted boned bodice incorporating briefs, white piping over bustline matches rouleau bow on centre front. Orange straw hat trimmed with self-colour raffia, pointed crown, wide brim. **4** Holiday wear. Red and white horizontally striped cotton dress, sleeveless fitted bodice, shallow bias-cut yoke incorporating square neckline, sunray-pleated skirt, horizontal stripes increasing in width to hemline. Red straw hat, tall crown, flat top, self-straw band and bow trim, wide straight brim. Outsized red raffia bag, painted wooden handle, flap-and-stud fastening. Red plastic and rubber mules, straps between toes. **5** Leisure wear. Hip-length blue, green and white striped knitted-cotton sleeveless tunic-top, off-the-shoulder collar, wide blue leather belt with large buckle. Mid-calf-length dark blue cotton tight trousers. Dark blue leather shoes, pointed toes, bow trim, flat heels.

Accessories

1 Grey velvet beret, full crown gathered into padded rouleau band. **2** Black felt hat, small crown, turned-down brim, white feather trim. **3** Large black leather handbag, double rouleau handles, clasp fastening. **4** Yellow leather handbag, double handles, top-stitched flap matching seams and edges, brass fittings. **5** Dark green brushed-wool trilby, plaited band, feather trim. **6** Brimless beige felt hat, white silk band and bow trim. **7** Brown felt hat, small crown, large two-tier fur brim. **8** Large beige leather handbag, sides and flap trimmed in tan leather to match rouleau handle, brass fittings. **9** Blue leather envelope-shaped handbag, small rouleau handle, brass fittings. **10** Large cream leather handbag, strap-and-buckle fastening, wooden handles. **11** Brown wool-tweed peaked cap. **12** Mules, striped canvas crossed straps, high wedge cork heels. **13** Light brown leather sandals, crêpe soles. **14** Tan leather step-in shoes, self-leather bow and trim. **15** Mules, studded instep strap, raised stud worn between two toes, low wedge cork heels. **16** Red leather lace-up shoes, self-leather laces with tassel trim, square toes. **17** Black leather elastic-sided step-in shoes, seamed fronts. **18** Black leather lace-up shoes, pointed toes. **19** Pale blue pearlized leather shoes, low buckled bar strap, pointed toes, medium stiletto heels. **20** Black leather T-strap shoes, pointed toes, high stiletto heels. **21** Dark brown leather sandals, crêpe soles. **22** Beige suede lace-up shoes, synthetic soles. **23** Red leather shoes, low-cut shaped fronts, pointed toes, high stiletto heels. **24** Blue leather lace-up shoes, flat heels, crêpe soles. **25** Beige pearlized leather shoes, double bar straps, pointed toes. **26** Navy-blue leather step-in shoes, self-leather trim, flat heels.

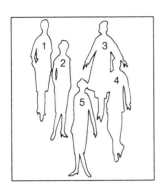 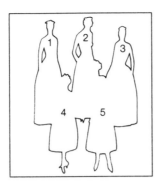 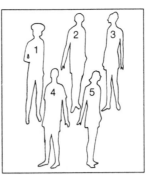 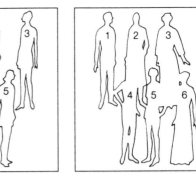

1958 Day Wear

1 Oatmeal silk-tweed two-piece suit: semi-fitted single-breasted jacket fastening with two large buttons, U-shaped neckline with tied roll collar, three-quarter-length magyar sleeves, bust-level mock flap pockets, front panel seams split above hemline; straight skirt to just below knee-level. Draped burnt-orange silk-jersey turban, self-fabric bow trim. Cream suede gloves. Tan leather shoes, buckle trim, pointed toes, medium stiletto heels. **2** Pale blue lightweight wool collarless sack dress, wide self-fabric belt threaded through large buckle under bust, mock strap fastening from hemline to neckline under button trim, short cap sleeves. Cream cotton gloves. Blue pearlized leather T-strap shoes, pointed toes, high stiletto heels. **3** Olive-green, violet and black loosely woven wool-tweed seven-eighths-length single-breasted coat fastening with three outsized buttons from hip-level to under large stand-away collar, wide full-length sleeves with deep armholes, wide self-fabric cross-over buttoned belt from high waist position with fringed ends, hip-level bound pockets. Straight skirt in matching fabric. Olive-green felt beret, wide band. Deep violet leather gloves. Matching deep violet leather bar-strap shoes, pointed toes. **4** Single-breasted grey, black and brown striped wool-tweed jacket, two-button fastening, narrow lapels, flap pockets. Black wool-mixture narrow trousers, no turn-ups. Black knitted-cotton collar-attached shirt. Rust suede tie. Beige suede lace-up ankle-boots. **5** Grey flannel sleeveless sack dress, gathers from under buttoned band at neckline which matches band on narrow hemline, low hip-level mock flap pockets. Black leather shoes, pointed toes, low stiletto heels.

Wedding Wear

1 Ivory silk wedding gown, fitted bodice, self-fabric bow trim on centre front from waist to under bust, low scooped neckline, tight inset sleeves, bell-shaped wrapover overskirt cut away at front to show bell-shaped underskirt, both with unpressed pleats from waist. Ivory velvet bow headdress, waist-length silk-tulle veil. **2** Oyster silk dress, fitted bodice and full-length bell-shaped skirt cut in flared shaped panels without waist seam, high waist marked by wide satin band and bow, shaped seam following line of band over bust, satin-covered buttons from bustline to under high round neckline which match buttons on wrists of tight inset sleeves, points over hands. Headdress of silk flowers and leaves, short veil. **3** White lace wedding gown, fitted bodice, scalloped hems of long tight sleeves match centre front of full-length skirt and edge of low scooped neckline which continues under bust to form bolero effect. Headdress edged with pearls, trimmed with silk flowers, short veil. **4** Short cream satin wedding dress, fitted bodice, off-the-shoulder neckline, draped upperbodice and short sleeves link with self-fabric bows, bell-shaped skirt with unpressed pleats from waist worn over stiffened petticoats. Headdress of silk flowers and loops of ribbon, short veil. Cream satin gloves, bow trim. Matching cream satin shoes, bow trim, pointed toes, low stiletto heels. **5** Short pale pink silk dress, fitted bodice, deep inset waistband, straight neckline, long inset sleeves, bell-shaped skirt with unpressed pleats from waist worn over stiffened petticoats. Headdress of silk flowers, waist-length silk-tulle veil. Satin shoes, pointed toes.

Sports and Leisure Wear

1 Holiday wear. Hip-length unfitted sleeveless cream cotton blouse, low square neckline, narrow hipband, self-fabric bow trim. Fitted navy-blue linen shorts. Cream straw hat, wide turned-up brim bound with navy-blue petersham ribbon. Navy-blue leather mules, wide straps over instep, narrow strap between two toes, flat heels. **2** Tennis. Thigh-length white cotton-mixture sleeveless sack dress, gathers from high yoke seam, pointed collar, bound armholes which match keyhole opening and rouleau bow trim fastening, hip-level flap pockets. White cotton ankle socks. White canvas lace-up sports shoes. **3** Tennis. Thigh-length white linen-mixture dress, hip-length semi-fitted sleeveless bodice, self-fabric button fastening from wide hip-belt to under boat-shaped neckline, shaped panel side seams form knife pleats in flared skirt. White ankle socks. White canvas lace-up sports shoes. **4** Holiday wear. Two-piece pea-green cotton beach suit: single-breasted shirt jacket, button fastening from hip-level to under pointed collar, short inset sleeves, stitched cuffs which match three patch pockets and hems of thigh-length shorts, elasticated waistband, fly opening. Brown leather strap sandals. **5** Tennis. Thigh-length white linen dress, low V-shaped neckline, collar with scalloped edge which matches hem of flared skirt, semi-fitted bodice and skirt cut in flared panels without waist seam, bound armholes. White stretch-fabric headband. White cotton ankle socks. White canvas lace-up sports shoes.

Underwear and Negligee

1 White string-mesh sleeveless singlet, low round neckline, deep scooped armholes. White string-mesh briefs, elasticated waistband, high-cut legs, white knitted-cotton double front panel, side opening. **2** Red, black and yellow checked brushed-cotton travel gown, wrapover front, wide roll collar, full-length cuffed inset sleeves, patch pockets, self-fabric tie-belt. Pale yellow cotton pyjamas. Red leather slippers. **3** Powder-blue brushed-wool full-length housecoat, wrapover front, large single-button fastening under high round neckline, wide three-quarter-length magyar sleeves, hip-level patch pockets, high waistline marked with wide ruched pale blue satin belt and matching covered buckle. **4** White nylon-satin corselette, moulded bra, lace trim matching small control panel under bust, elasticated panels over side hips which match small shaped panels either side of centre front above hem, adjustable shoulder straps, four adjustable suspenders. Flesh-coloured nylon stockings. **5** Pale salmon-pink nylon satin bra, moulded cups, lace trim, adjustable shoulder straps, back fastening. Pale salmon-pink nylon satin lightweight pull-on girdle, deep waistband with curved dip at centre front, elasticated front panel, double top-stitched support, four adjustable suspenders. Flesh-coloured nylon stockings. **6** Pale turquoise nylon nightdress, ruched self-fabric panels under and over bust bound on either side with pale pink nylon to match bow trim and double shoulder straps, curved neckline with lace trim, full-length double layer skirt gathered from high waistline under bust.

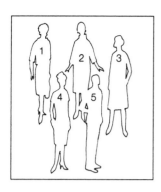

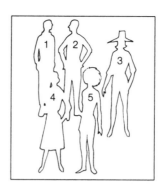

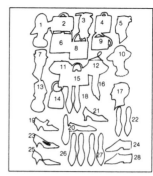

1959 Day Wear

1 Camel-coloured lightweight wool two-piece suit: single-breasted semi-fitted jacket, three outsized buttons, wide neckline, stand-away collar, three-quarter-length magyar sleeves and front panels of jacket cut in one piece, mock flap pockets above side hem; below-knee-level narrow skirt, tucks from waistband. Brimless fur hat. Brown leather gloves. Matching large brown leather handbag, beige trim. Matching brown leather shoes, button trim, pointed toes, high stiletto heels. **2** Brown and black wool-tweed single-breasted coat, fastening with outsized buttons from hip-level to bow trim under high stand collar, three-quarter-length wide dolman sleeves, vertical hip-level welt pockets, hem below knee-level. Brimless burnt-orange felt hat, self-fabric band and button trim. Black gloves. Black patent-leather shoes, ruched bar trim, pointed toes. **3** Two-piece machine-knitted suit patterned with large cream, brown and pale green squares: hip-length sleeveless unfitted top, ribbed V-shaped neckline matching hem; box-pleated skirt. Two-tone brown and cream leather shoes, pointed stitched toecaps. **4** White synthetic-jersey dress patterned with black flowers, high waistline marked with plain white belt threaded through and over with drapery from side hip-level of narrow skirt, low boat-shaped neckline, short inset sleeves. Black brimless pillbox hat. Short white gloves. Black patent-leather Y-strap shoes, pointed toes, high stiletto heels. **5** Two-piece black and grey checked lightweight wool suit: single-breasted jacket, three-button fastening, narrow lapels, flap pockets; straight-cut trousers, narrow hems, no turn-ups. White collar-attached shirt. Blue silk tie and pocket handkerchief. Black leather step-in elastic-sided shoes.

Evening Wear

1 Silk-taffeta short evening dress, all-over design of yellow, cream and ochre stylized roses, fitted and boned strapless bodice joined to bell-shaped skirt by intricate cross-over seaming at waist-level. Long ochre silk stole, fringed hems. Gold kid Y-strap shoes, pointed toes. **2** Pink, silver and smoky-grey patterned brocade theatre coat, edge-to-edge, fastening under self-fabric bow on centre front of wide stand-away collar, coat flared from shoulder to hemline, three-quarter-length flared inset sleeves. Pillbox hat in matching fabric. Long pink suede gloves. Pink silk shoes, pointed toes, high stiletto heels. **3** Single-breasted white linen tuxedo jacket, shawl collar faced with white silk to match single covered button fastening, hip-level piped pockets, inset sleeves, single-button trim. Black linen trousers, narrow hems, no turn-ups, outside seams trimmed with satin ribbon. White collar-attached shirt. Black satin under-collar continental bow-tie. Black lace-up patent-leather shoes, no toecaps. **4** Pale dusty-pink lace short evening dress, fitted overbodice, deep V-shaped neckline, flared sleeves with scalloped hems which match hem of bell-shaped skirt, sleeveless silver-grey satin underdress, low square neckline, bell-shaped skirt to below knee-length worn over stiffened petticoat, wide stiffened-satin cummerbund. Silver kid shoes, pointed toes, medium stiletto heels. **5** Strapless cream duchess-satin ball gown, fitted boned bodice and full-length bell-shaped skirt cut without waist seam, neckline edged with ruched silk-chiffon, beaded and embroidered uneven scalloped seam under bust, repeated on edges of cream velvet inset panel in skirt between hip-level at front and above hemline at back. Long cream silk gloves.

Sports and Leisure Wear

1 Ski wear. Knitted red wool sweater, Fair Isle design in black and white across upper chest and upper arm of inset sleeves, shallow ribbed roll collar which matches sleeve cuffs and hem. Black knitted-wool polo-neck sweater. Black stretch-cloth trousers. Black leather ski-boots. Red wool mittens lined in fur. **2** Ski wear. Pale fawn elasticated cloth all-in-one overall suit, zip fastening from crotch to bust-level under collar and revers, elbow-length cuffed sleeves, top-stitched shoulder dart, decorative buttoned flap, narrow trousers, stitched creases. Bright orange knitted-wool sweater, high round neckline, three-quarter-length sleeves. Balaclava-style hood in bright orange knitted wool. White leather ski-boots. **3** Beach wear. White swiss-cotton two-piece beach suit: shirt blouse, three-quarter-length sleeves gathered into cuffs, bodice printed with three rows of graded brown spots in sets of three on each side of button opening; decoration repeated on fitted shorts, plain white cotton tie-belt. White straw hat, tall crown, wide white cotton band printed with brown spots, wide brim. **4** Holiday wear. Rayon blouse and skirt in bright multicoloured garden print: sleeveless blouse, straight neckline, drawstring waist; gathered knee-length skirt, plain red tie-belt. Green leather T-strap shoes, pointed toes. **5** Beach wear. Cream linen sunsuit spotted in red, fitted bodice and shorts cut in one piece, side panel seams curve at hip-level to form piped pockets, curved seam over bustline follows shape of neckline, narrow rouleau shoulder straps with matching bow trim. Large natural straw hat, large brim edge trimmed with strands of self-straw.

Accessories

1 Brown brushed-felt hat, large brim, tall crown draped with deep gold chiffon. **2** Brown leather bag, inset leather handles. **3** Brimless grey satin hat, large self-fabric bow trim. **4** Black leather bag, flap with stud fastening, brass trim. **5** Black silk pillbox hat, self-fabric bow trim at back, short black silk-tulle veil. **6** Black leather bag, clasp fastening, long handle. **7** Cherry-red velvet brimless draped hat. **8** Tan leather bag, side zip pocket, top-stitched trim. **9** Green leather and brown canvas shoulder bag, long adjustable strap, strap-and-buckle fastening. **10** Brown felt hat, tall crown, wide fur brim. **11** Gold beaded clutch bag. **12** Brown velvet evening bag gathered into gold beaded frame, gold chain handle. **13** Dark green felt brimless hat, piped trim. **14** Fawn leather unstructured bag, round bamboo handle. **15** Oblong beige hessian bag, brown leather trim which matches rouleau handle, brass fittings. **16** Cream kid gloves, threaded strap trim. **17** Small yellow cloth cap, top-stitched peak. **18** White matt-leather T-strap shoes, perforated decoration, pointed toes. **19** Cream and tan leather bar-strap shoes, pointed toe-caps, high stiletto heels. **20** Navy-blue leather shoes, red binding and bow trim, pointed toes. **21** Dark blue suede shoes, dark blue leather bow trim which matches louis heels. **22** Black leather shoes, fabric asymmetric button trim, pointed toes. **23** Navy-blue leather shoes, open sides, pointed toes, high stiletto heels. **24** Black leather elastic-sided shoes, seamed fronts. **25** Black suede shoes, cut-away sides, pointed toes, high stiletto heels. **26** Sage-green patent-leather shoes, pointed toes, buckled trim. **27** Red patent-leather shoes, key-hole with self-leather bow trim, pointed toecaps. **28** Brown suede step-in elastic-sided shoes, no toecaps.

The 1960s

Introduction · The 1960s

The New Look of 1947 which dominated the 1950s was a backward glance at a more 'feminine' time. The 1960s woman, on the other hand, looked firmly ahead. She demanded equal rights and equal pay. She rejected the shackles of voluminous, hampering skirts and the restrictions of corseted waists and high stiletto heels. She wanted to be free, to look young and to have fun.

The way to achieve this young look was obvious: straighten the curves and shorten the skirts. It was a style reminiscent of the 1920s. Skirts began the decade at knee-level and rose steadily, until in 1965 they emerged as the 'mini'. Eventually they shot up above the stocking top, leaving a gap which made the transition to tights inevitable. 'Maxi' skirts made a brief appearance towards the end of the decade, often seen as the skirts of a top coat worn over a 'mini'. And throughout the decade trousers and trouser suits steadily increased in popularity. Styles for evening wear became less rigid – it was not unusual to see both long and short evening dresses at the same function.

The fashion revolution that brought about these developments started in the streets of London, with talented designers like Mary Quant and Barbara Hulanicki. In the United States, James Galanos and Rudi Gernreich were also reaching a young audience. In France, too, some Parisian couturiers – among them Yves Saint Laurent, Pierre Cardin, André Courrèges and Emanuel Ungaro – responded to these new attitudes. In this decade, every one of these creative talents, as well as fashion's leaders and stylesetters, were young. They were lively, highly individual, inventive, gimmicky and greatly concerned with the creation of 'image'.

The main outlets for the new young fashions were small boutiques, selling clothes that were not quite 'one-offs', but were made by individual outworkers producing small quantities in a limited range of colours and sizes. Quant and Hulanicki (of Biba fame) were in the vanguard, but other British and French couturiers began to turn to boutiques and ready-to-wear during the 1960s.

Until the 1960s men's clothes had generally consisted of a traditional three-piece suit of a subtle colour for town wear or a smart tweed sports jacket and toning flannel trousers for country or casual wear (little or no differentiation was made between summer and winter). The details changed almost imperceptibly from season to season or decade to decade. These relatively static styles became less and less acceptable to the 1960s man, who was living in a world in which everything seemed to be changing fast and in which pop groups like the Beatles and the Rolling Stones, photographers like David Bailey and Anthony Armstrong-Jones, and actors like Michael Caine and Jean-Paul Belmondo exerted a strong sartorial influence.

Boutiques for men sprang up in London's Soho – those in Carnaby Street being the most famous – and Savile Row tailors found that their hegemony was being challenged. Male dress, like female dress, became less class-bound. It also underwent a certain feminization. Men grew their hair long, donned pretty, printed shirts worn open at the neck, discarded neckties, and took to wearing polo-neck sweaters and skintight trousers. By the end of the sixties they were at home in silk, satin and chiffon, as well as frills, bows and lace.

Easy-care synthetic fabrics such as Crimplene, Dacron and Terylene were much used during the 1960s. These materials were crease-resistant, could be permanently pleated, were easy to wash and needed little or no ironing. Synthetic yarns also took dyes easily, giving rise to colours that were clear and bright, reflecting the mood of the period.

Leather-look plastic was also popular and was used for a wide variety of accessories for women, including shoes, knee-high boots, shoulder bags, wrist-length gloves and 'butcher's boy' peaked caps. Plastics were also employed for a range of garments, from brightly coloured mini skirts to see-through raincoats and umbrellas.

In the main, the fashions I have illustrated are such as would have been worn by the middle or upper-middle classes and by people who, while not being 'dedicated followers of fashion', would have had a keen interest in the latest styles.

The sources from which I have drawn – chiefly from Great Britain, North America, France, Italy and Germany – include contemporary magazines, catalogues and journals, original dated photographs, museum collections, and my own costume collection.

This section of the Sourcebook is divided into ten parts, each of which includes four subdivisions covering Day Wear, Evening Wear (alternately, on two occasions, Wedding Wear), Sports and Leisure Wear, and a section on either Underwear and Negligee or Accessories. Following the main illustrations are ten pages of schematic drawings accompanied by detailed notes about each example, giving particulars of colour, cut and trimming, as well as other useful information.

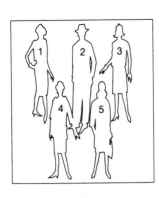

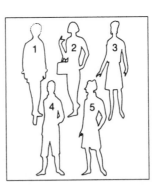
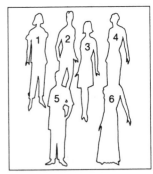

1960 Day Wear

1 Mint-green linen sleeveless dress, bloused bodice above inset waistband, strap opening, large single self-covered button trim, small revers, wide stand-away collar, cut-away armholes, narrow knee-length skirt. Brimless coffee straw hat, self-straw bow trim. Dark-coffee fabric gloves; matching leather shoes, pointed toes, self-leather trim, high stiletto heels. **2** Light-grey flannel two-piece suit: single-breasted jacket, three-button fastening, narrow lapels, flap pockets; straight-cut trousers, no turn-ups. White cotton collar-attached shirt. Red and blue striped silk tie. Grey trilby, wide navy-blue band. Black leather step-in shoes. **3** Cream wool two-piece sleeveless jumper suit: hip-length bloused top, wide round neckline and cut-away armholes bound with navy-blue wool to match flap pockets and hem of knee-length flared skirt. Brimless navy-blue felt hat trimmed with stalk worn on back of head. Short navy-blue leather gloves; matching shoes, pointed toes, self-leather flower trim, high stiletto heels. **4** Beige and tan flecked linen-tweed two-piece suit: long single-breasted jacket fastening with three large burnt-orange leather buttons which match hip-level tie-belt, wide neckline, stand-away collar, three-quarter-length inset sleeves; narrow knee-length skirt. Orange and brown banded straw hat, turned-back brim. Brown leather gloves; matching shoes, pointed toes, fine bar straps, stiletto heels. **5** Brown and black checked double-breasted wool coat, fastening from hip-level inset band to under high black fur collar with large shiny black plastic buttons, three-quarter-length inset sleeves; matching knee-length skirt. Brimless black felt hat, embroidered motif on front. Black suede gloves. Large black patent-leather handbag. Black patent-leather and suede shoes, pointed toes.

Evening Wear

1 Two-piece black wool evening suit: single-breasted jacket, single-button fastening, piped pockets, long roll collar faced with black silk; straight-cut trousers, no turn-ups. Single-breasted red silk waistcoat, scooped collarless neckline; bow-tie in matching fabric. White silk collar-attached shirt, tucked front. Black leather elastic-sided ankle-boots. **2** Silver-grey silk evening ensemble: knee-length sleeveless top, high round neckline edged with silver and crystal beads, semi-fitted bodice and flared skirt cut without waist seam, skirt split on side seams from hem to hip-level; matching tight ankle-length trousers. Silver-grey leather sling-back shoes, spike heels and pointed toecaps in darker silver. **3** Rose-pink, grey and silver patterned silk-satin evening dress, bloused bodice from low waist marked by narrow rose-pink satin belt with bow trim matching wide-set shoulder straps and trim, narrow ankle-length skirt. Full-length pink satin gloves. Silver kid shoes, pointed toes, button trim. **4** Cream silk evening dress, narrow rouleau shoulder straps, vertical pintucks from low neckline of semi-fitted bodice to mid-calf-level of flared skirt, no waist seam, skirt hem finished with wide gathered frill to ground. Elbow-length chocolate-brown fabric gloves; matching shoes. **5** Bottle-green satin evening dress, horizontal panels beaded and embroidered in black, fitted bodice, wide boat-shaped neckline, elbow-length inset sleeves, ankle-length bell-shaped skirt, black satin belt tied into bow on centre-front. Elbow-length black satin gloves; matching shoes.

Sports and Leisure Wear

1 Ski wear. Long pale-blue weatherproof cotton ski-jacket, fur-lined, centre-front zip fastening from band on hem to under fur-lined and trimmed hood, adjustable button straps on sides of hem, long raglan sleeves, two waist-level diagonally-placed piped pockets with zip fastenings, top-stitched edges and detail. Dark-blue stretch-nylon ski-pants tucked into black leather lace-up ankle-boots. Dark-blue leather mittens lined and trimmed with fur. **2** Beach wear. All-in-one cotton jumpsuit with printed patchwork pattern in greens and yellows, concealed centre-front zip fastening to under high round neckline, shaped cut-away armholes, bodice and trousers cut without waist seam, narrow legs, small split on each seam above hem. Outsized beach bag in matching fabric. **3** Holiday wear. Natural colour linen dress, wide shoulder straps buttoned onto straight neckline of hip-length bloused bodice, knee-length flared skirt. Beige canvas shoes, green leather trim, pointed toes. **4** Country wear. Olive-green knitted-wool sweater, wide V-shaped neckline, long inset sleeves, turned-back ribbed cuffs. Dark-cream brushed-cotton collar-attached shirt, collar worn open. Olive-green and red spotted silk cravat. Dark-brown cotton cord breeches, side pockets, narrow legs. Handknitted rust-brown stockings. Dark-brown leather lace-up brogues. **5** Country wear. Tan knitted-wool sweater, outsized ribbed polo collar, three-quarter-length sleeves set into large square armholes, ribbed hems. Knee-length tan, green and cream checked wool culottes, side hip pockets. Tan knitted-wool tights. Brown leather lace-up ankle-boots, pointed toes, flat heels.

Underwear and Negligee

1 Fine pale-yellow cotton pyjamas patterned with multicoloured posies of flowers: hip-length top, high round neckline, edges of peter-pan collar bound in plain yellow cotton, rouleau bow trim matching piped off-the-shoulder yoke seam and hems of puff sleeves, hem curved up to side seams, bow trim matching hems of narrow mid-calf-length trousers. Yellow velvet slippers, pointed toes, flower trim, flat heels. **2** Peach-pink brassiere, boned support between fitted cups, lace trim and edging, elasticated side panels, back fastening, adjustable shoulder straps. Peach-pink elasticated cotton girdle, double fabric front panel, lace-effect side front panels, adjustable suspenders. Flesh-coloured nylon stockings. **3** Combined cream cotton strapless brassiere and hip-length girdle, shaped and fitted cups, lace trim and edging, wired supports, back fastening, adjustable suspenders. Primrose-yellow nylon waist slip, nylon lace edging. Cream satin slippers. **4** White cotton brassiere, elasticated panel between seamed cups, narrow halter straps, back fastening. White stretch-nylon pantie-girdle, wide waistband, shaped front panel, long legs, zigzag stitched detail. **5** White cotton pyjama suit spotted with dark-green: wrapover collarless jacket, edges bound in dark-green to match tie-belt, elbow-length kimono sleeves; straight-cut trousers. **6** Pale-coffee nylon nightdress, shaped shoulder straps and upper part of bodice cut in one and edged with cream nylon lace matching hem of floor-length skirt, gathered from shaped waist seam. Coffee slippers with pointed toes.

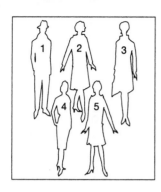 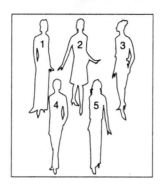  

1961 Day Wear

1 Short camel-coloured wool car coat, double-breasted fastening with leather buttons, wide lapels, large collar, hip-level patch-and-flap pockets, top-stitched edges and detail. Dark-brown knitted-wool polo-neck sweater. Tapered beige wool trousers, no turn-ups. Beige brushed-felt trilby. Elastic-sided brown leather ankle-boots. **2** Sage-green, lilac and grey wool-tweed two-piece suit: hip-length unfitted jacket, double-breasted fastening, narrow lapels, stand-away collar, vertical welt pockets set into side panel seams at hip-level, full-length inset sleeves; knee-length box-pleated skirt. Sage-green patent-leather shoes, pointed toes, bow trim, high stiletto heels. **3** Cream and pink flecked wool-tweed coat, flared knee-length skirts from high waist position, double-breasted fastening with large cream wood buttons from mid-thigh to under stand collar, full-length inset sleeves, top stitched edges and detail. Deep-pink brimless felt hat. Black leather gloves; matching outsized handbag and shoes with pointed toes. **4** Smoke-blue slubbed-linen dress, semi-bloused bodice above wide inset waistband, dark-blue leather double-breasted button trim from waist to low hip-level, wide square neckline, short inset sleeves, straight knee-length skirt, pockets in side panel seams. Cream leather shoes, navy-blue leather pointed toecaps and high stiletto heels. **5** Light-grey flannel dress, hip-length semi-fitted bodice, wide boat-shaped neckline trimmed in dark-grey to match hip-belt, cuffs of elbow-length inset sleeves and lining of pleats in knee-length flared skirt; neckline and hip-belt have matching buckle detail. Black leather shoes, pointed toes, medium-high stiletto heels.

Evening Wear

1 Fine silk-satin evening dress patterned with outsized flowers in greens and blues on pearl-grey background, boned fitted bodice, cross-over draped panels form small train from waist-level at back, narrow self-fabric rouleau shoulder straps, straight ankle-length skirt, split on one side from hem to knee-level. Full-length emerald-green satin gloves; matching shoes with pointed toes. **2** Pale-dusty-pink silk-taffeta cocktail dress, semi-fitted bodice cut in one piece with knee-length flared skirt, square neckline, wide shoulder straps, outsized self-fabric bow on centre-front at hip-level, centre of bow trimmed with self-fabric roses and leaves. Silver kid sling-back shoes, pointed toes, high stiletto heels. **3** Navy-blue silk cocktail dress, bloused bodice pleated from wide round neckline, pleats lined with rose-pink satin matching cowl at back, wide self-fabric pleated cummerbund, large bow decoration on one side, brooch trim, straight knee-length skirt. Elbow-length navy-blue satin gloves; matching shoes, pointed toes, fine straps, high stiletto heels. **4** Two-piece black wool evening suit: double-breasted jacket, wide lapels faced in black satin matching covered buttons, piped pockets; tapered trousers, outside seams trimmed with satin braid, no turn-ups. Black kid-leather lace-up shoes. **5** Green-grey lightweight wool-crepe evening dress, sleeveless bloused bodice from hip-level, high round neckline edged with detachable feather collar, straight ankle-length skirt, split from hem to knee-level on one side, lined with green satin. Green satin shoes, pointed toes, crossed bar straps.

Sports and Leisure Wear

1 Winter sports wear. Orange and brown heavyweight wool-tweed poncho, pointed hemline edged with dark-orange wool tasselled fringe, drawstring hood, dark-orange wool pom-pon trim. Tight brown heavyweight stretch-nylon ski-pants worn tucked into lace-up brown leather après-ski ankle-boots, pointed toes, flat heels. **2** Swimwear. Royal-blue sailcloth swimming shorts, wide legs split on outside seams above hem, elasticated waistband. **3** Swimwear. Powder-blue acetate and cotton mixture stretch-fabric swimsuit, pleated reinforced central panel, self-fabric bow trim under shaped and boned cups, narrow shoulder straps, short skirt, built-in briefs. **4** Beachwear. Hip-length white knitted-cotton T-shirt, short cap sleeves edged in navy-blue to match deep V-shaped neckline, bow trim, infill and fitted shorts with high-cut legs. Navy-blue leather thong mules. **5** Tennis. Cream and white striped cotton dress, vertical stripes used on hip-length semi-fitted bodice, cut-away armholes, straight neckline, centre-front nick above seam running through to hem of knee-length bias-cut skirt, hip-level bow-tied belt, horizontal stripes. White cotton ankle socks. White canvas lace-up sports shoes.

Accessories

1 Olive-green leather handbag, thick rouleau handle, clasp fastening. **2** Green leather shoes, pointed toes, button trim, stiletto heels. **3** Fine cream straw cloche hat, wide orange band, bow trim. **4** Tan leather sandals, strap-and-buckle fastening, crepe soles. **5** Cream leather lace-up shoes, top-stitched brown leather fronts. **6** Navy-blue leather shoes, pointed toes, bow trim, stiletto heels. **7** Brimless fur hat, pom-pon trim. **8** Black leather step-in shoes, strap detail. **9** Black leather shoes, strap-and-buckle fastening. **10** Cream leather shoes, black leather trim, stiletto heels. **11** Elastic-sided black leather boots, pointed toes, stacked heels. **12** Elastic-sided black leather ankle-boots, pointed toes, low stacked heels. **13** Red leather pumps, navy-blue bow and trim, flat heels. **14** Beige suede lace-up ankle-boots, crepe soles. **15** Grey patent-leather shoes, square toes, buttoned-strap trim. **16** Red leather shoes, pointed toes, threaded-bow trim. **17** White leather shoes, black toecaps and bow trim. **18** Bottle-green straw cloche hat, wide pink band, white flower trim. **19** Lilac satin gloves, ruched sides, button trim. **20** Tan leather gauntlet gloves, bow trim. **21** Red-and-white patterned hat, black band and rosette trim. **22** Brown leather handbag, flap, stud fastening, thick handle. **23** Crocheted cotton hat. **24** Sage-green canvas bag, tan leather buckled straps, long handle. **25** Black evening bag, sequin trim. **26** Brown leather handbag, clasp fastening, double handles. **27** Brown leather shoes, pointed toes, narrow bar straps. **28** Black leather shoes, wrapover strap, button trim. **29** Black leather shoes, black suede frill. **30** Navy-blue leather shoes, narrow diagonal straps, button trim. **31** Tan leather handbag, mock-flap with straps, thick handle. **32** Black cotton gloves, ruched pleat, button trim.

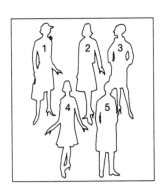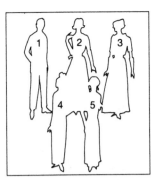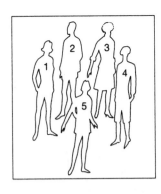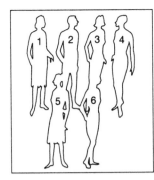

1962 Day Wear

1 Pink wool-tweed two-piece suit: semi-fitted waist-length jacket, single-breasted fastening with four buttons, high round neckline, padded binding and rouleau bow tie, bracelet-length inset sleeves, turned-back cuffs; knee-length flared skirt, wide centre-front box-pleat. Beige felt hat, split brim turned up at back forming peak at front. Brown leather gloves; matching handbag and shoes, pointed toes, stiletto heels. 2 Black and pink checked wool-tweed two-piece suit: short edge-to-edge box-shaped jacket, stand collar bound in black to match hems of long inset sleeves, buttoned patch pockets and front edges; knee-length flared skirt. Semi-fitted pink silk blouse, high round neckline, long cuffed sleeves. Black patent-leather T-strap shoes, low heels. 3 Cream and beige bouclé wool-tweed coat, single-breasted fastening with three black leather buttons, three-quarter-length raglan-style sleeves, wide stand collar, hip-level welt pockets, skirts tapered to knee-length hem. Black leather gloves; matching handbag and sling-back shoes, pointed toes, side bow trim, stiletto heels. 4 Sage-green flecked linen-tweed dress, sleeveless hip-length semi-fitted bodice, armholes bound in black to match binding on high round neckline, bow tie and inset band on hipline, knee-length flared skirt, self-fabric inset godet on each side centre-front and back. Black leather shoes, pointed toes, bar-strap and bow trim, stiletto heels. 5 Cream showerproof cotton raincoat, double-breasted fastening, raglan sleeves, strap-and-buckle trim matching shoulder trim, floating yoke, welt pockets, knee-length skirts, buckled belt, top-stitched edges and detail. Tapered brown wool trousers. Cream collar-attached shirt. Narrow brown wool tie. Elastic-sided brown leather ankle-boots.

Evening Wear

1 Navy-blue wool and mohair mixture two-piece evening suit: single-breasted jacket, single-button fastening, long shawl collar faced in navy-blue satin matching split-sleeve cuffs, covered buttons and under-collar bow tie; tapered trousers, no turn-ups. White cotton collar-attached shirt, concealed fastening under box-pleat. Black leather lace-up shoes. 2 Silver-grey satin evening dress, high round neckline, sleeveless semi-fitted bodice embroidered with silver, pink and crystal beads and bead fringing, full-length skirt gathered under pink satin ribbon belt, bow tie on centre-front. Full-length pink satin gloves; matching shoes with pointed toes, fine bow trim. 3 Fine pale-orange silk-chiffon evening dress printed with outsized paisley pattern in pinks, yellows and browns, bloused bodice above gold kid buckled belt, low pointed neckline, small stand-away collar, short inset sleeves, ankle-length gathered skirt; deep-orange silk underdress, strapless and boned bodice, ankle-length flared skirt. Dark-cream fabric gloves. Gold kid shoes, pointed toes, medium-high stiletto heels. 4 Black wool-crepe evening dress, slashed neckline, hip-length semi-fitted bodice, full-length inset sleeves, deep band of bead embroidery at wrist-level matching detail on hipline and above hem on straight ankle-length skirt. Black satin shoes, pointed toes. 5 Rich cream satin evening dress patterned with lilac and blue flowers and gold leaves, strapless boned bodice cut in one with straight ankle-length skirt, neckline edged with pleated plain gold satin, bow trim on one side, matching gold fabric forms wide box-pleat in back of skirt. Cream satin shoes, pointed toes, fine bar-strap and bow trim.

Sports and Leisure Wear

1 Beach wear. Orange, red and green floral cotton bikini: bra top, separated and wired pre-formed cups, halter straps, back fastening; briefs with elasticated waist, high-cut legs. 2 Beach wear. Two-piece beach suit: pale-green cotton shirt, brown and green striped cotton collar matching cuffs of long inset sleeves, trim on two chest-level patch pockets and shorts with elasticated waistband. Light-brown leather sandals, open sides and toes, detachable back straps. 3 Country wear. Sage-green and beige wool-tweed two-piece suit: short single-breasted jacket, three-button stepped fastening from waist-level to under long pointed collar, three-quarter-length inset sleeves, turned-back cuffs, waist-level patch pockets with pleat trim and buttoned flaps; knee-length flared skirt. Sage-green knitted-wool polo-neck sweater. Brimless red fox-fur hat. Dark-cream knitted-wool tights. Long brown leather boots, side-zip fastening, pointed toes, low spike heels. 4 Casual/Spectator sports wear. Waist-length red leather sleeveless tunic, wide boat-shaped neckline, side-zip fastening. White cotton collar-attached shirt, full-length sleeves, deep cuffs, four-button fastening. Knee-length black and white checked wool breeches; matching butcher's boy peaked cap. Red knitted-wool tights. Black leather lace-up shoes, pointed toes, low heels. 5 Tennis. Short white cotton dress, wide round neckline and deep armholes bound in self-fabric, hip-length semi-fitted bodice, box-pleated skirt. Elastic-sided white canvas shoes, low rubber wedge heels.

Underwear and Negligee

1 Pastel-blue nylon knee-length sleeveless nightdress, low square neckline and armholes edged in fine nylon lace, base of yoke edged with scalloped lace to match hem of gathered skirt. 2 White knitted-cotton singlet, low scooped neckline and cut-away armholes; briefs in matching fabric, double-fabric front panel, high-cut legs, elasticated waist. 3 Black lace bra mounted over stiffened flesh-coloured satin, seamed and wired cups, black satin shoulder straps set wide apart continue under cups, fine lace trim, back fastening. Elasticated black satin pantie-girdle, black lace panels over flesh-coloured satin each side centre-front, fine lace trim on waist and around high-cut legs. 4 White cotton bra, deep plunging neckline, seamed cups lined with fine pre-formed foam, elasticated side panels, adjustable shoulder straps, back fastening. Elasticated white cotton girdle, cross-over top-stitched panels front and back, four adjustable and detachable suspenders. 5 Pale-turquoise nylon slip, bra-top edged and trimmed with black nylon lace to match hem of knee-length flared skirt, adjustable shoulder straps. 6 Dull-peach-pink stretch-cotton-satin bra, low-cut neckline, elasticated panel between seamed cups over pre-formed foam, embroidered trim, elasticated shoulder straps, back fastening. Pink stretch-nylon-satin pantihose, double-fabric front panel, embroidered trim, long legs, scalloped hems with bow trim matching detail on waist.

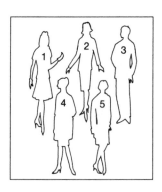  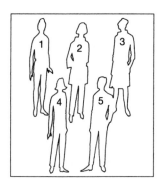 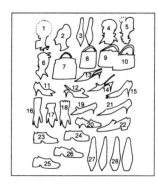

1963 Day Wear

1 Poppy-red linen two-piece suit: hip-length semi-fitted jacket, single-breasted fastening with outsized pearl buttons from above hem to under low round neckline, curved yoke seam, short dolman sleeves; knee-length box-pleated skirt. White silk scarf draped over head and shoulders. Short white cotton gloves. Red leather shoes, fine rouleau straps, pointed toes, high stiletto heels. **2** Powder-blue fine wool-tweed two-piece jumper suit: semi-fitted hip-length top, buttoned flap pockets set into seam above hipline, button fastening under high collar, dropped shoulderline, long inset sleeves, top-stitched edges and detail; knee-length straight skirt. Short coffee leather gloves; matching shoes, chisel toes, high stiletto heels. **3** Rust-brown cotton-corduroy single-breasted jacket, single-button fastening, large patch-and-flap pockets, chest-level flap pocket. Tapered dark-brown wool trousers, no turn-ups. Pale-grey cotton shirt, attached white cotton collar. Grey, brown and red striped knitted-silk tie. Tan leather step-in shoes. **4** Three-quarter-length white wool coat, double-breasted fastening from waist to under stand-away collar, three-quarter-length inset sleeves, hip-level diagonal welt pockets. Knee-length black and white checked wool skirt. Long white fabric gloves. Black leather shoes, pointed toes, high stiletto heels. **5** Grey wool-flannel dress striped in navy-blue and red, semi-fitted bodice and knee-length straight skirt cut without waist seam, self-fabric tie-belt on hipline, strap fastening from above hemline to under narrow revers, long pointed collar, full-length inset sleeves, buttoned cuffs, low hip-level patch pockets, button trim. Red leather shoes, pointed toes, narrow bar straps, stiletto heels.

Evening Wear

1 Formal evening dress, black ribbon-lace fitted bodice, wide scalloped neckline matching short sleeves and hem, full-length oyster-cream satin flared skirt, large self-fabric bow trim on centre-front at hip-level above unpressed knife-pleat. Full-length black satin gloves; matching shoes with pointed toes. **2** Jade-green silk cocktail dress, deep cut-away armholes, low V-shaped neckline, self-fabric bow at base, brooch trim, knee-length skirt flares from seam under bust. Jade-green satin shoes, pointed toes, high stiletto heels. **3** White linen single-breasted tuxedo jacket, single-button fastening, long shawl collar faced with white silk, matching covered buttons, hip-level piped pockets. Tapered black linen trousers, black silk ribbon stripe on outside seams, no turn-ups. White cotton collar-attached shirt, concealed fastening. Black satin bow-tie. Black leather shoes. **4** Evening dress, sleeveless brown silk bloused bodice embroidered all over with transparent shiny sequins, low scooped neckline, cut-away armholes form wide shoulder straps, brown velvet ribbon bow trim on centre-front under bust, floor-length flared skirt. Full-length brown suede gloves; matching shoes, pointed toes, delicate crossed-strap trim. **5** Dusty-pink silk-crepe evening dress, fitted bodice from under bust seam, wide self-fabric shoulder straps tied into flat bows on top of shoulders, narrow ankle-length skirt, gathers under bust seam. Large unlined self-fabric stole edged with bright-pink feathers. Pink satin shoes, pointed toes, high stiletto heels.

Sports and Leisure Wear

1 Beach wear. Lime-green cotton-jersey one-piece bathing costume, bloused bodice from above self-fabric belt, bow trim, shaped neckline, narrow shoulder straps, self-fabric briefs. Burnt-orange draped cotton-towelling hat. Gold kid-leather thong mules, leaf-shaped straps. **2** Casual wear. Red and yellow flecked wool-tweed two-piece jumper suit: long unfitted top, full-length flared inset sleeves, wide neckline, red knitted-wool deep polo-neck collar matching tie-belt and hip-level pockets; trousers tapered to narrow hems. Red leather shoes, blunt toes, tongues, button trim. **3** Golf. Dark-brown leather sleeveless jerkin top, low V-shaped neckline, welt pockets set into hip-level seam, hand top-stitched edges and detail. Red, orange, brown and grey striped knitted-wool sweater, wide neckline, stand-away polo-neck collar, three-quarter-length sleeves. Dark-grey wool flared knee-length skirt, inverted box-pleats each side centre-front. Dark-brown leather peaked cap. Brown leather lace-up shoes, fringed tongues, round toes, flat heels. **4** Casual wear. Pale-yellow knitted-wool cardigan-jacket, single-breasted fastening, self-colour rib matching hems of long inset sleeves and pointed collar, multicoloured embroidered flower sprays under shoulder and above waist. Silver-grey wool-flannel tapered trousers. Bright-yellow ankle socks. Mid-grey suede step-in shoes, fringed strap-and-button trim, square toes, flat heels. **5** Casual wear. Mid-grey, dark-grey and red striped knitted-cotton shirt, loop and button under collar, plain red cotton strap with single-button fastening matches hip-level welt pockets and buttoned cuffs of long inset sleeves. Tapered mid-grey cotton trousers, narrow hems, no turn-ups, side hip pockets. Black leather lace-up shoes, round toes, top-stitched detail.

Accessories

1 Brimless red and brown fur hat. **2** Red wool beret, top-stitched band, gathers at front. **3** Gunmetal-grey leather shoes, pointed toes, bow trim. **4** Red leather peaked cap. **5** Navy-blue wool beret, red wool pom-pon trim. **6** Bottle-green felt pillbox hat, self-fabric bow trim. **7** Sage-green leather handbag, double handles, clasp fastening. **8** Grey leather handbag, flat handle, large flap, stud fastening. **9** Black leather handbag, single handle, clasp fastening, top-stitched trim. **10** Red leather handbag, gilt clasp and trim, threaded double rouleau handles. **11** Black leather shoes, pointed toes, black suede straps, gilt bow trim, stiletto heels. **12** Black patent-leather sling-back shoes, pointed toes, black petersham ribbon bow trim. **13** Navy-blue leather sling-back shoes, pointed toes, red leather straps and trim, stiletto heels. **14** Black leather sling-back shoes, red leather straps and trim. **15** Black patent-leather shoes, open sides, self-bow trim, stiletto heels. **16** Long black leather gloves, button trim. **17** Short grey fabric gloves, turned-down cuffs, gilt stud trim. **18** Pink suede gloves, scalloped edges. **19** Navy-blue leather shoes, open sides, self-bow trim, cream side panels, perforated decoration. **20** Beige suede shoes, round toes, perforated decoration. **21** Dark-green pearlized-leather shoes, pointed toes, open sides. **22** Light-brown leather step-in shoes, strap-and-button trim, low stacked heels. **23** Black leather shoes, strap-and-buckle fastening, square toes. **24** Brown elastic-sided step-in shoes. **25** Black leather elastic-sided step-in shoes. **26** Light-brown leather moccasin-style shoes, self-leather trim. **27** Black leather lace-up shoes, pointed toes. **28** Dark-green leather shoes, round toes, self-leather trim.

  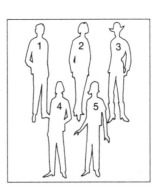 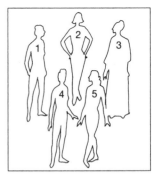

1964 Day Wear

1 Navy-blue rayon dress, semi-fitted bodice and above-knee-length flared skirt cut without waist seam, wide neckline, white rayon peter-pan collar, cut-away armholes. White straw hat, turned-back brim. White nylon tights spotted in navy-blue. Navy-blue leather shoes, pointed toes, low spike heels. 2 Cherry-red linen and rayon mixture two-piece jumper suit: waist-length unfitted top, deep scooped neckline, wide self-fabric binding, buttoned cross-over on centre-front infilled with pale-blue and white patterned fabric, button fastening, collar set onto wide neckline, short self-fabric inset sleeves, machined hems; above-knee-length straight skirt, gathers at waist. Short dark-blue leather gloves; matching clutch bag and shoes, pointed toes, low heels. 3 Grey and white slubbed-silk jacket, single-breasted fastening, narrow lapels, diagonal flap pockets. Fine black wool tapered trousers, no turn-ups. Pale-grey cotton collar-attached shirt, button-down collar points, red knitted-silk tie. Black leather elastic-sided step-in shoes, square toes. 4 Brown cotton-corduroy dress, semi-fitted bodice and above-knee-length skirt cut without waist seam, deep scooped neckline infilled with detachable cream knitted-cotton polo neck matching cuffs on hems of three-quarter-length inset sleeves. Brown leather shoes, almond-shaped toes, keyhole, bow trim, low thick heels. 5 Black wool two-piece suit: edge-to-edge unfitted jacket, lapels faced in pink silk to match lining and hip-length blouse, low V-shaped neckline, self-silk ties, long sleeves with tied cuffs show under full-length inset sleeves of jacket; above-knee-length flared skirt. Black leather bar-strap shoes, square toes, low thick heels.

Wedding Wear

1 Cream silk-dupion wedding dress, sleeveless fitted bodice, scooped neckline, small split above centre-front seam, cut-away armholes, self-fabric belt tied into large bow at front, ground-length flared skirt, three deep tucks above hemline. Cream silk-net veil attached to silk rose headdress. Cream silk shoes, pointed toes. 2 Pale-coffee silk wedding dress, fitted bodice, horizontal tucks from waist to under scalloped edge of off-the-shoulder elbow-length coffee lace collar, tight full-length sleeves, ankle-length bell-shaped skirt, three tucks above hemline. Long pale-coffee net veil, velvet ribbon bow headdress. Coffee satin shoes, almond-shaped toes, low heels. 3 Dark-grey wool tailcoat, single-button fastening. Single-breasted pale-grey wool waistcoat. Grey and black striped wool tapered trousers, no turn-ups. White shirt, wing collar. Grey, white and black striped silk cravat. Light-grey top hat. Grey fabric gloves. Black leather lace-up shoes, square toes. 4 White cotton-organza wedding dress, fitted bodice, deep inset band from waist to under bust trimmed with band of white cotton flower-shaped braid matching slashed neckline, hems of tight full-length inset sleeves and trim at hip-level and knee-level on ground-length gathered skirt, tucks over hem of organza overskirt, bodice and skirt mounted over plain white cotton. White silk water-lily headdress, short white cotton-net veil. White kid shoes, pointed toes. 5 White silk wedding dress, semi-fitted bodice and ankle-length flared skirt cut in one piece without waist seam, round neckline, three-quarter-length flared inset sleeves edged with shaped stiffened bands, matching hemline. Long white silk-tulle veil attached to white silk headband. White kid shoes, pointed toes, stiletto heels.

Sports and Leisure Wear

1 Golf. Grey knitted-wool cardigan-jacket, single-breasted fastening with black leather ball buttons, high round neckline, front edges and hem bound in black leather to match cuffs of inset sleeves and hip-level welt pockets. Tapered grey wool trousers, no turn-ups. Black knitted-wool polo-neck sweater. Black leather shoes, fringed tongues, square toecaps. 2 Country wear. Brown and tan wool-tweed two-piece suit: double-breasted jacket, high fastening under narrow lapels, small collar, side panel seams, hip-level flap pockets, full-length inset sleeves; tapered trousers. Handknitted brown wool polo-neck sweater. Brown leather shoes, keyhole front, bow fastening. 3 Riding. Blue brushed-cotton shirt, small collar and revers, high yoke seam, patch pockets with box-pleat and buttoned flap, full-length inset sleeves, buttoned cuffs. Tight beige cotton trousers, deep waistband, brown leather buckled belt. High brown leather boots, top-stitched trim, square toes, low stacked heels. 4 Tenpin bowling. Dark-yellow handknitted wool collarless cardigan-jacket, single-breasted fastening with grey leather buttons matching piping on high round neckline, front edges, hems and trim on full-length inset sleeves and hip-level patch pockets. Tapered dark-yellow wool trousers. Red knitted-wool polo-neck sweater. Red cotton socks. Red leather step-in shoes, high tongues, strap trim, square toes, flat heels. 5 Holiday wear. Blue and white striped knitted-cotton T-shirt, slashed neckline, short inset sleeves. Red cotton-corduroy tapered trousers, narrow hems, stirrups under feet. Red leather pumps, pointed toes, flat heels.

Underwear and Negligee

1 Flesh-coloured Lycra one-piece footless body suit, low scooped neckline, narrow shoulder straps, low-cut armholes. 2 One-piece white cotton longline girdle and bra patterned with tiny blue and green flowers, narrow shoulder straps cut in one with underwired and seamed cups, fine lace edging matching side panel seams, centre-front zip fastening, four adjustable and detachable suspenders. Flesh-coloured nylon stockings. 3 Pink-cream silk-velvet housecoat, three-quarter-length sleeves and ankle-length skirt gathered from round cream satin shoulder yoke, wide round neckline, deep-pink piping matching edges of short opening, small covered buttons and bound hems of sleeves, skirt and sleeve hems decorated with scattered appliqué of pink and cream satin leaf shapes. 4 Black machine-knitted Courtelle and wool mixture two-piece set patterned with posies of pink flowers: fitted top, low scooped neckline, fine black lace edging matching scooped armholes and elasticated waist and hems of longline knickers. 5 Black nylon-satin bra, low neckline, wide shoulder straps, seamed and underwired cups trimmed and edged with black nylon lace, back fastening. Black Lycra pull-on pantie-girdle, draped cross-over front panels from side-front panel seams, short legs.

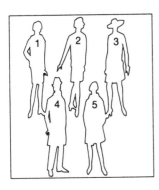

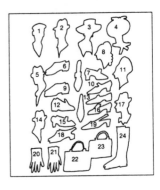

1965 Day Wear

1 Grey and brown wool-tweed two-piece suit: unfitted hip-length jacket, double-breasted wrapover front, strap-and-buckle fastening, wide pointed lapels, stand-away collar, curved top-stitched seam from under arm, matching pockets, full-length inset sleeves, top-stitched edges and detail; straight mini-skirt two or three inches above knee. Black polo-neck sweater. Black tights. Black leather step-in shoes, high tongues, round toes, low heels.
2 Hip-length unfitted cream wool top, high round neckline, full-length inset sleeves, black patent-leather belt on low waistline. Straight black wool mini-skirt. Black patent-leather shoes, almond-shaped toes, low thick heels. **3** Berry-red Terylene and wool mixture tweed dress, hip-length sleeveless bodice, top-stitched bib panel matching wide neckline, deep armholes and hip-level buttoned belt, flared mini-skirt, side-front box-pleats. Red felt hat, small crown, deep ribbon band, wide brim. Short black leather gloves; matching shoes, high vamp, button trim, low thick heels. **4** Grey and black striped wool-tweed double-breasted knee-length overcoat, black fur collar, breast pocket, hip-level welt pockets. Tapered grey wool trousers, no turn-ups. Grey trilby, wide ribbon band, narrow brim. Black leather gloves and lace-up shoes. **5** Egg-yellow wool coat, single-breasted stepped fastening with brass buttons, high collar, full-length inset sleeves, hip-level flap pockets, flared skirts two or three inches above knee. Shiny blue plastic bar-strap shoes, round toes, flat heels.

Evening Wear

1 Black lace evening dress, fitted bodice and ankle-length flared skirt cut without waist seam, low scooped neckline, scalloped edge matching edges of three-quarter-length inset sleeves and hem of skirt; underbodice and underskirt of same shape in black silk. Black satin shoes, pointed toes, stiletto heels. **2** Black silk-chiffon cocktail-evening dress, high neckline, bloused bodice above black satin belt tied into bow at front, matching black satin bindings of three-quarter-length dolman sleeves and hems of two-tier pleated mini-skirt; strapless black silk-crepe underbodice and flared underskirt. Black satin shoes, almond-shaped toes, satin bow and rose trim, low thick heels.
3 White Terylene-crepe evening dress, semi-fitted bodice and flared ankle-length skirt cut without waist seam, slashed neckline, bust-length yoke banded with blue, green and silver sequins to match cuffs of full-length bishop-style inset sleeves and hemline of skirt. Silver kid shoes, round toes.
4 Red silk mini-length semi-fitted theatre coat embroidered all over with large red sequins, single-breasted fastening with large covered buttons which match wide silk binding of front edges, round neckline and hems of three-quarter-length flared inset sleeves. Brimless cap in matching sequined fabric. Red leather sling-back shoes, pointed toes, low thick heels.
5 White and gold brocade evening dress, semi-fitted bodice and straight ankle-length skirt cut without waist seam, skirt split from hemline to knee-level on one side, deep V-shaped neckline, cut-away armholes, low back. Gold kid shoes, almond-shaped toes, self-kid rose on one side, low louis heels.

Sports and Leisure Wear

1 Ski wear. Royal-blue quilted-nylon sleeveless ski jacket, zip fastening from hem to under rounded stand collar, inset waistband with small quilting to match hip-level diagonal welt pockets. Black knitted-wool fine rib polo-neck sweater. Black brushed-nylon ski-pants. Royal-blue leather gauntlets. Black leather ski-boots. **2** Holiday wear. Yellow cotton dress, hip-length sleeveless bloused bodice, inserted graded sunburst bands of bright-red cotton from low round bound neckline, matching flared mini-skirt and hip-level tie-belt. Red leather shoes, almond-shaped toes, decorative side straps, bow trim, low thick heels. **3** Casual wear. Pale turquoise and silver-grey knitted-wool skinny-rib sweater, fitted body ribbed from low round neckline to hem, matching elbow-length sleeves. Dark-turquoise wool mini-skirt, flared shaped panels from V-shaped hip yoke, top-stitched detail, tan leather belt, oval metal buckle. Tan leather bar-strap shoes, side-buckle fastening, almond-shaped toes. **4** Casual wear. Short navy-blue wool coat, double-breasted fastening under wide-set collar, full-length inset sleeves, strap-and-button trim above hem, hip-level diagonal pockets, top-stitched edges. Yellow, navy-blue and cream checked wool tapered trousers. Navy-blue and yellow patterned silk scarf. Navy-blue peaked cap. Navy-blue leather step-in shoes, chain trim, round toes, flat heels. **5** Surfing wear. White knitted-cotton T-shirt, wide neckline edged in bright-green to match hem of shirt and hems of short inset sleeves, bright-green and yellow logo on chest. Bright-green cotton-sailcloth shorts, white-trimmed edges and seams.

Accessories

1 Black leather peaked cap.
2 Natural-straw trilby, twisted ribbon band, narrow brim.
3 Red felt hat, large crown, flat top, wide brim, flat edge.
4 Cream straw hat, wide brim, flat edge, brown ribbon trim, centre-front bow. **5** Brown leather trilby, seamed panel front and back, inset band, narrow brim.
6 Beige suede lace-up shoes, man-made soles. **7** Dark-plum suede shoes, wide bar straps, square toes, low thick heels.
8 Brimless white felt hat, black feather and brooch trim. **9** Dark-green leather sandals, strap-and-buckle fastening, open sides, openwork detail, crepe soles.
10 Cream leather shoes, brown leather bar straps, heels and trim. **11** Brimless grey felt hat.
12 Cream dull-plastic shoes, threaded straps through high tongues, wedge heels. **13** Brown leather step-in shoes, strap-and-button trim, flat heels. **14** Navy-blue felt trilby, narrow curled brim.
15 Black leather bar-strap shoes, button fastening, almond-shaped toes, high thick heels. **16** Black patent-leather shoes, large self-patent buckle trimmed with black grosgrain, medium-thick heel.
17 Sage-green felt trilby, black petersham band and bow, matching trim on narrow curled brim. **18** Bright-green plastic T-strap sling-back sandals, peep toes, low thick heels. **19** Black leather sling-back shoes, white strap and trim, low heels. **20** Tan leather driving gloves, elasticated strap over large keyhole opening.
21 Olive-green leather driving gloves, large and small perforated decoration. **22** Brown leather handbag, metal clasp and trim, thick rouleau handle, top-stitched detail. **23** Navy-blue leather handbag, flap, metal clasp fastening, thick rouleau handle.
24 Dark-brown leather boots, matching narrow buckled strap under top edge of cream leather uppers, flat heels.

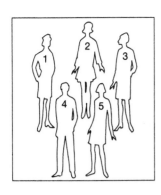
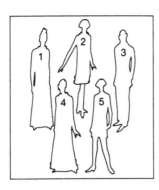

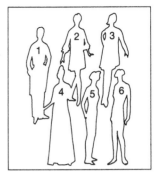

1966 Day Wear

1 Silver plastic raincoat spotted in red, double-breasted fastening, wide pointed lapels and collar, full-length inset sleeves, buckled self-fabric belt and covered buttons, hip-level diagonal welt pockets, flared mini-length skirts. Square pillbox hat in matching fabric. Red leather shoes, round toes, high tongues, low thick heels. **2** Navy-blue and white striped knitted-cotton dress, hip-length unfitted bodice, wide neckline bound in plain red knitted-cotton to match deep cuffs of long inset sleeves and bound hem of gathered mini-skirt. Red cotton-sailcloth butcher's boy peaked cap. Red leather shoes, almond-shaped toes, wide bar straps. **3** Green, cream and tan striped fine wool jumper suit: hip-length unfitted top, single-breasted fastening under small collar, full-length shirt sleeves, deep cuffs, buttoned hipband, top-stitched edges and detail; straight mini-skirt. Dark-cream wool tights. Shiny tan plastic shoes, large buckle trim, square toes, low thick heels. **4** Light-brown wool jacket, high three-button fastening under narrow lapels, small collar, three flap pockets. Dark-brown cotton-jumbo-cord tapered trousers, no turn-ups. White collar-attached shirt, small collar with round edges. Red and brown spotted silk tie. Brown leather elastic-sided ankle-boots, square toes. **5** Grey-pink Crimplene-jersey dress, hip-length unfitted sleeveless bodice, double-breasted jacket-effect with self-fabric covered buttons, matching narrow hip-level belt, large grey-pink textured Crimplene-jersey collar, flared mini-skirt in matching fabric. Grey suede sling-back shoes, high vamps, square toes, flat heels.

Evening Wear

1 Cream Terylene-crepe evening dress, unfitted bodice and full-length flared skirt gathered from under outsized pearl bead trim around high round neckline, no waist seam, cut-away armholes. Cream pearlized-leather shoes, large buckle trim, almond-shaped toes. **2** Yellow silk-crepe mini-length unfitted shift dress, cut-away armholes, high round neckline trimmed with loops of fine yellow silk-velvet ribbon to match two rows around hemline of flared skirt. Yellow satin sling-back shoes, almond-shaped toes, low thick heels. **3** Black mohair and silk evening suit: high three-button single-breasted fastening under narrow satin-faced shawl collar, matching covered buttons, piped pockets; tapered trousers, braid trim on outer side seams, no turn-ups. White silk collar-attached shirt. Narrow black satin bow-tie. Black leather lace-up shoes, almond-shaped toes. **4** Mint-green silk-chiffon evening dress, unfitted bodice and full-length skirt gathered from under cut-away armholes and high round neckline, no waist seam, neckline and armholes decorated with tiny green and silver silk flowers, matching band above hemline of skirt; underdress of mint-green silk follows same lines as chiffon dress. Silver kid shoes, almond-shaped toes. **5** Lilac silk shift dress, unfitted bodice and mini-skirt decorated with bands of royal-blue sequins, full-length inset sleeves embroidered all over with matching sequins, hems bound in lilac satin to match wide square neckline and narrow hemline of skirt. Royal-blue suede shoes, gold kid sling-backs and T-straps, almond-shaped toes, low thick heels.

Sports and Leisure Wear

1 Beach wear. Green, white and red striped cotton draped bra top, low neckline, knot of self-fabric between seamed cups, draped cut-away front, bare midriff, narrow shoulder strap. Long bias-cut striped sash in matching fabric tied on side hip over green cotton hipster trousers, tight over hips and upper legs, flared from knee-level to hemline. **2** Sailing. Fitted white knitted-cotton shirt, pointed collar, keyhole opening, loop-and-button fastening, short inset sleeves, top-stitched hems. Navy-blue cotton sailcloth hipster shorts, fly-front, piped side hip pockets, high-cut legs, wide red leather belt, large metal buckle. White cotton peaked cap, navy-blue ribbon trim. **3** Golf. Beige, brown and orange checked wool two-piece: single-breasted shirt top, pointed collar worn turned up, full-length inset sleeves, buttoned cuffs; flared mini-skirt, centre-front inverted box-pleat, wide waistband, self-fabric belt, metal buckle. Beige knee-high wool socks. Brown leather bar-strap shoes, round toes. **4** Holiday wear. White Crimplene-jersey sleeveless dress, wide round neckline bound in black to match hemline of straight mini-length skirt, pointed edges of cropped hipster skirt and bow trim where points meet on centre-front, bare midriff. Black leather sling-back shoes, almond-shaped toes, low thick heels. **5** Casual wear. Multicoloured spotted Bri-nylon stretch top, high round neckline, full-length inset sleeves, matching tights, wide headband and narrow tie-belt on white plastic 'leather-look' hipster mini-skirt. Long white plastic boots, square toes, flat heels.

Underwear and Negligee

1 Green, blue and grey striped silk dressing gown, wrapover front, self-fabric tie-belt, full-length inset sleeves, turned-back cuffs, large hip-level patch pockets, breast pocket. Blue cotton-poplin pyjamas: single-breasted jacket; ankle-length straight-cut trousers. Navy-blue leather slippers, round toes. **2** Red cotton mini-length nightdress, black satin peter-pan collar, black lace edging to match waterfall jabot, two-tier circular-cut cuffs of elbow-length inset sleeves and hemline trim. **3** Pink cotton mini-length nightdress, pale-blue and white pattern of flowers, skirt and bodice gathered from under wide neckline bound with pink satin ribbon, bow trim, lace edging matching centre-front mock strap-and-button fastening, lace trimmed hemline, cut-away armholes. **4** Pale-blue Crimplene negligee and nightdress: negligee with lace-effect from under bust, elbow-length kimono-style sleeves, all hems and edges bound with blue satin ribbon matching bow trim on centre-front under bust, full-length skirts gathered from high waist position; nightdress with lace-effect fitted bodice, low neckline, high waistline, full-length flared skirt. **5** Black Lycra and lace body suit, narrow shoulder straps, low neckline, half cups, wide lace trim, panelled body, high-cut legs, lace trim, four suspenders. Flesh-coloured nylon stockings. **6** Black Lycra body suit, multicoloured spot pattern, fine shoulder straps, keyhole between seamed cups, long legs.

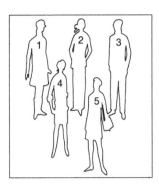
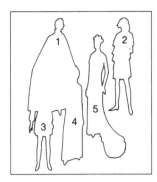
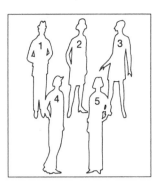
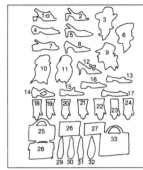

1967 Day Wear

1 Navy-blue wool two-piece suit: hip-length unfitted jacket, double-breasted fastening under wide round neckline, brass buttons, matching epaulets and flap pockets, three-quarter-length inset sleeves, top-stitched edges and detail; flared mini-skirt. Navy-blue wool polo-neck infill. Yellow wool peaked cap. Short navy-blue leather gloves; matching knee-high boots, round toes, flat heels. 2 White cotton two-piece trouser suit with multicoloured pattern of flowers and leaves: long fitted jacket, double-breasted fastening, stand-away collar, pointed lapels, long narrow inset sleeves, welt pockets; flared trousers, turn-ups. Lilac cotton polo-neck sweater. Purple leather bar-strap shoes, round toes, flat heels. 3 Mid-grey wool and Terylene unfitted jacket flecked with black, high four-button single-breasted fastening, narrow lapels, three patch pockets, leather-covered buttons, top-stitched edges and detail. Dark-grey wool and Terylene tapered trousers, permanent creases, no turn-ups. Black wool polo-neck sweater. Black leather elastic-sided ankle-boots. 4 Grey flannel dress, unfitted hip-length bodice, detachable white cotton collar matching cuffs of three-quarter-length inset sleeves, black silk scarf-tie, hip-level wide black leather belt, large metal buckle, straight mini-skirt. Black leather T-strap shoes, almond-shaped toes. 5 Bright-yellow cotton-canvas semi-fitted coat, flared skirt, pointed lapels, long collar, single-breasted fastening with triangular yellow plastic buttons matching trim on triangular flap pockets, long inset sleeves, top-stitched edges and detail. Yellow plastic beret. Knee-high white cotton socks. Navy-blue leather-look plastic shoulder bag, short gloves and step-in shoes.

Wedding Wear

1 White silk wedding dress, semi-fitted bodice and ankle-length straight skirt cut without waist seam, cut-away armholes, ground-length white silk-organdie cape gathered from high round neckline under frilled organdie stand collar, cape scattered with silk flowers matching silk and organdie bonnet. White kid shoes, square toes. 2 White cotton broderie-anglaise wedding dress, straight neckline with scalloped and embroidered edge above high yoke seam matching three-tier gathered three-quarter-length inset sleeves and hemline of flared mini-skirt. White velvet choker. White suede T-strap shoes, almond-shaped toes, low thick heels. 3 White pintucked cotton wedding dress, bloused bodice, pintucked cotton-organza and lace yoke edged with frilled lace continuing over bishop-style sleeves in matching fabric, deep cuffs with frilled hems matching high stand collar, gathered mini-skirt, band of pintucked organza and lace above hemline, white satin belt, bow tie on side waist. Hair decorated with white organza flowers. White satin shoes, bow trim, almond-shaped toes. 4 Pale-turquoise velvet wedding dress, high neckline split on centre-front seam, full-length inset sleeves, high waist position marked by wide pale-turquoise silk belt, bow tie on centre-front, ground-length flared skirt. Pearl tiara; long silk-tulle veil. Pale-turquoise satin shoes. 5 Fine cream wool-crepe wedding dress, high round neckline, short inset sleeves, semi-fitted bodice, no waist seam, ground-length skirt, long back train. Long cream silk-tulle veil attached to headdress of peach-pink roses. Short cream kid gloves; matching shoes.

Sports and Leisure Wear

1 Country wear. Short weatherproof green cotton overcoat, front-zip fastening from above hemline to ends of wide collar, full-length inset sleeves, vertical welt pockets above hip-level patch pockets, buttoned flaps, top-stitched edges and detail. Tapered dark-green wool trousers, narrow hems, no turn-ups. Brown wool polo-neck sweater. Green and brown checked trilby, small crown, self-fabric band, narrow brim. Brown waterproofed suede lace-up ankle-boots. 2 Holiday wear. Sleeveless cotton dress, hip-length plain white unfitted bodice, high round neckline, dark-blue and red striped mini-skirt, low side-hip pockets, slotted self-fabric belt, button trim. Red and white striped hat, high crown, wide turned-up brim. Red leather sling-back shoes, round toes, strap detail, low thick heels. 3 Holiday wear. Mini-length sleeveless rayon shift dress with multicoloured Pop-Art design, high round neckline, bound hemline and cut-away armholes. Purple leather sling-back shoes, round toes, low thick heels. 4 Golf. Brown waist-length knitted-wool collarless cardigan, edges and hem in dark-beige matching welt pockets and deep welts of full-length inset sleeves, large plastic buttons. Burnt-orange wool trousers fitted over hips, flared from knee to hem, side hip pockets. Cream wool shirt, long pointed collar. Orange leather-look plastic peaked cap. Tan and white leather lace-up brogues, flat heels. 5 Holiday wear. Two-piece cotton beach pyjamas patterned in lime-greens, royal-blues and bright-pinks: hip-length unfitted bias-cut top, high round neckline, three-quarter-length inset sleeves, deep turned-back cuffs; wide straight-cut trousers. Green canvas sling-back shoes, round toes, flat heels.

Accessories

1 Cream leather sling-back strap sandals, low heels. 2 Red leather sling-back strap sandals, medium heels. 3 Beige felt hat, high crown, wide brim. 4 Grey shoes, twisted strap fronts, flat heels. 5 Navy-blue sling-back shoes, high heels. 6 White straw hat, wide brim, red ribbon binding. 7 Brown leather sling-back sandals, cross-strap fronts, perforated decoration, wedge heels. 8 Green leather shoes, draped side detail, high heels. 9 White canvas peaked cap, navy-blue and red ribbon trim, brass button detail. 10 Blue and white striped cotton peaked cap. 11 Red wool beret. 12 Red leather shoes, black leather bar strap, ribbon bow trim, high heels. 13 Black patent-leather shoes, velvet bow trim, flat heels. 14 Black leather shoes, cream T-strap and trim. 15 White leather bar-strap shoes, blue trim. 16 White leather shoes, red Pop-Art patterned toe-caps. 17 Brown leather shoes, cream uppers. 18 Cream leather gloves, navy-blue trim. 19 Red and black leather gloves. 20 Beige fabric gloves, black spots. 21 Red leather gloves, navy-blue and white detail. 22 Dark-green leather gloves, purple trim. 23 White cotton gloves, black and white checked cuffs. 24 Grey plastic gloves, black trim. 25 Green and grey checked canvas handbag, flap, clasp fastening, leather handles. 26 Black leather bag, suede trim. 27 Black and white leather envelope-shaped bag. 28 Blue plastic handbag, two outside pockets, buttoned flaps, flap, concealed fastening, flat handle. 29 White leather shoes, square toes, black Pop-Art trim. 30 Green leather shoes, brass-buckle trim. 31 Black leather shoes, square toes, black and white checked buckle trim. 32 Cream leather shoes, brown toe-caps and trim. 33 Tan leather handbag, two outside pockets, flap, clasp fastening, flat handles.

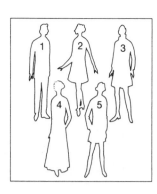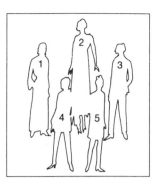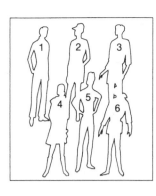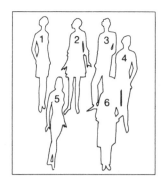

1968 Day Wear

1 Navy-blue wool and Terylene two-piece suit: fitted double-breasted jacket, flap pockets, no breast pocket, sewn cuffs, top-stitched edges and detail; tapered trousers, narrow hems, permanent creases, no turn-ups. Pale-blue cotton collar-attached shirt. Wide silk tie, blue and red stripes, Windsor knot. Black leather shoes, strap-and-buckle fastening. **2** Beige and brown flecked silk-tweed sleeveless dress, high round neckline, wide brown leather waist-level belt slotted through two mock box-pleats running from bust-level yoke seam to hemline of flared mini-length skirt, top-stitched edges and detail. Brown leather sling-back shoes, round toes, bar straps, low thick heels.
3 Pale-grey wool mini-length coat patterned in pale-blues, pinks and greens, strap-and-buckle fastening from waist-level to under stand collar, full-length two-piece inset sleeves, large hip-level patch-and-flap pockets, top-stitched edges and detail. Short pale-grey leather gloves; matching over-knee-length boots, strap-and-buckle trim, inside-leg zip fastening, round toes, low square heels.
4 Red wool maxi-length coat, fitted double-breasted bodice fastening under large collar, full-length inset sleeves, edge-to-edge flared skirts, hip-level welt pockets. Black wool mini-skirt. Brimless black fur hat. Black plastic 'leather-look' over-the-knee boots, mock-lacing on centre-front seam, round toes, low heels. **5** Pink synthetic-silk-crepe dress, hip-length semi-fitted bodice, horizontal tucks, strap-and-button fastening under pointed collar, full-length sleeves gathered into deep cuffs, knife-pleated mini-skirt. Pale-pink nylon tights. Grey and white leather shoes, round toes.

Evening Wear

1 Winter dinner/theatre ensemble: fine white cotton blouse, semi-fitted bodice, ruffled frill either side mock-buttoned strap fastening, self-fabric covered buttons, pintucked stand collar with frilled edge matching cuffs of full-length bishop-style sleeves; ankle-length yellow, red and black checked wool skirt, black leather belt, metal clasp fastening. Black leather shoes, round toes, buckle trim, low thick heels. **2** Gold and bronze synthetic fabric evening dress, floor-length accordion-pleated skirt and fitted bodice, high waist position marked by narrow gold kid belt, wide neckline with trim of gold, bronze and crystal beads which continues over shoulders to hems of full-length inset sleeves. **3** Navy-blue wool and mohair two-piece evening suit: fitted jacket, edge-to-edge linked-button fastening, long shawl collar faced in silk and edged with braid, piped pockets, no breast pocket, two side vents; tapered trousers, narrow hems, no turn-ups, braid trim on outside seams. White cotton collar-attached shirt. Navy-blue silk bow-tie. Navy-blue suede ankle-boots. **4** Pale-grey silk-crepe two-piece evening suit with self-colour satin pattern: unfitted mini-length tunic, full-length inset sleeves gathered into deep cuffs, hip-level welt pockets, chain belt set with black stones, detachable self-fabric scarf; narrow ankle-length trousers. Black velvet mules, almond-shaped toes, eyelet trim, low thick heels.
5 Canary-yellow fine wool-crepe cocktail dress, semi-fitted bodice and flared mini-length skirt cut without waist seam, high round neckline edged with beads matching cut-away V-shaped armholes and hemline. Gold kid shoes, almond-shaped toes, low thick heels.

Sports and Leisure Wear

1 Casual wear. Tan wool fine-knit polo-neck sweater, fitted body, machined welt, low-slung belt, half-ring and chain fastening, full-length inset sleeves, buttoned cuffs. Fitted brown cotton trousers flared from knee-level to hem, no turn-ups. Dark-yellow leather cowboy boots, pointed toes, stacked heels. **2** Tennis. White knitted-cotton T-shirt, high round neckline, short inset sleeves. White cotton-poplin shorts, side hip pockets, deep waistband, self-fabric belt, metal clasp fastening. White cotton peaked cap, wide visor. White ankle socks. White canvas sports shoes. **3** Holiday wear. Pale-blue towelling two-piece beach suit: edge-to-edge collarless jacket banded in blue and white, three-quarter-length inset sleeves, single breast patch pocket, self-fabric tie-belt; fitted shorts, elasticated waistband, mock fly-front. **4** Country wear. Dark-rust-brown edge-to-edge sheepskin coat, cream lambswool collar and lining matching turned-back cuffs of full-length inset sleeves, mini-length flared skirts. Beige knitted-wool polo-neck sweater. Camel-coloured wool fitted shorts, top-stitched creases, brown leather belt. Rust-brown wool tights. Brown leather knee-high boots, round toes, flat heels. **5** Beach wear. Red plastic bikini: small asymmetric bra top, single shoulder strap and armhole bound in silver plastic to match appliqué spot on one side, edges and zipped side pocket of fitted shorts. **6** Beach wear. Blue and white striped cotton unfitted top, boat-shaped neckline, wide three-quarter-length two-piece sleeves, buttoned outside seams, deep white plastic belt matches buttons. Red cotton headscarf.

Underwear and Negligee

1 Salmon-pink nylon combination bra and semi-fitted slip, underwired bra cups, wide adjustable shoulder straps, low neckline edges with self-colour nylon lace matching trim on edge of side front panel seams running from under bust to flared hemline of mini-length skirt. **2** White cotton mini-length collarless edge-to-edge negligee, self-colour satin spot pattern, ribbon fastening on centre-front at bust-level matching ribbon trim on front edges, detail above double broderie-anglaise frill on elbow-length inset sleeves, under neckline of matching nightdress and above two-tier frills of broderie-anglaise trimming on hemlines of nightdress and negligee. **3** Two-piece pale-green knitted-cotton sleepsuit: hip-length top, V-shaped neckline bound in dark-green matching cuffs of full-length inset sleeves, hemline of top and cuffs of ankle-length trousers. **4** White knitted-cotton T-shirt, high round neckline, short inset sleeves. Y-front briefs in matching fabric, elasticated waistband, high-cut legs. **5** Flesh-coloured stretch-nylon all-in-one body stocking, low neckline, narrow shoulder straps, high-cut legs. **6** Synthetic-silk dressing gown, multicoloured pattern on black background, long shawl collar, wrapover front, self-fabric tie-belt, full-length inset sleeves, turned-back cuffs, two large hip-level patch pockets, knee-length skirts. Ankle-length black pyjama trousers. Black leather step-in slippers.

 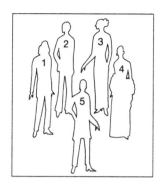 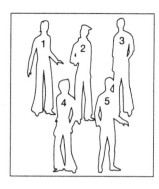 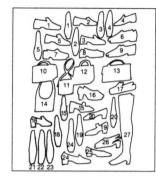

1969 Day Wear

1 Pink Crimplene collarless coatdress, high round neckline, high waist position marked by narrow self-fabric belt, round buckle, concealed fastening under scalloped wrapover front, matching hemline, fitted full-length inset sleeves. Pale-grey felt hat, high crown, black band, wide brim. Black leather gloves and sling-back shoes, square toes, low thick heels. 2 Red wool maxi-length coat, fitted bodice and flared skirts cut without waist seam, top-stitched double-breasted front panel under black fake-fur collar, collar matches cuffs of full-length inset sleeves and brimless hat, hip-length shaped flap pockets, button trim. Ankle-length straight-cut black wool trousers. Black leather boots, round toes, low thick heels. 3 Dark-green wool double-breasted overcoat, large black fur collar matching sleeve cuffs, hip-level shaped flap pockets. Black Terylene and wool flared trousers, no turn-ups. Green flannel collar-attached shirt worn open. Grey, green, orange and black patterned silk scarf. Black leather ankle-boots. 4 Cream, blue-grey and charcoal-grey checked wool-jersey two-piece suit: edge-to-edge waist-length box-shaped jacket, long collar, full-length inset sleeves gathered into cuffs, mock-flap pockets, button trim matching pockets on hipline of flared mini-skirt, centre-front knife-pleat. Cream synthetic-silk blouse, scarf-tie neckline. Knee-high cream cotton stockings. Black leather step-in shoes, square toes, flat heels. 5 Rust-red and grey checked wool semi-fitted dress, vertical inset stripe on centre-front of plain cream wool running from under narrow shaped stand collar to horizontal stripe on hipline, matching stripes above bust and waistline and as cuffs on full-length inset sleeves. Brown leather strap sandals, low thick heels.

Evening Wear

1 Pale-yellow silk-crepe two-piece evening dress, hip-length semi-fitted top, high round neckline embroidered with gold and white beads to match detail either side centre-front seam, edges and hem of skirt, armhole seams, wrist trim of long inset sleeves, low waist tie-belt and hems of ankle-length straight-cut trousers. Yellow satin shoes, square toes, high tongues, gold embroidery trim, low thick heels. 2 Navy-blue velvet fitted jacket, green and red stripe pattern of leaves and flowers, two-button single-breasted fastening, flap pockets. Navy-blue wool and mohair flared trousers, no turn-ups. White collar-attached shirt, ruffled front; navy-blue velvet bow-tie worn under wide-set shirt collar. Black leather lace-up shoes. 3 Fine black wool-crepe ankle-length evening dress, semi-fitted bodice and straight skirt cut without waist seam, skirt split on one side to above knee-level, tight full-length inset sleeves, high round neckline. Short sleeveless bolero jacket, low scooped neckline, black, red and gold bead embroidery. Black satin shoes, almond-shaped toes, high heels. 4 Jade-green satin evening dress, semi-fitted bodice and full-length flared skirt cut without waist seam, high polo collar, halter-style cut-away armholes. Black and jade-green feather boa. Jade-green satin pumps, round toes. 5 Black silk two-piece evening suit: knee-length single-breasted fitted jacket worn open, four-button fastening under high lapels, hip-level welt pockets in flared skirts; narrow ankle-length trousers in matching fabric. Collarless single-breasted gold and black brocade waistcoat. White silk polo-neck shirt. Black satin ankle-boots, round toes, low thick heels.

Sports and Leisure Wear

1 Golf. Grey, forest-green and brown checked wool sleeveless jumpsuit, semi-fitted bodice, single-breasted fastening under V-shaped neckline, bell-bottom trousers, narrow hip-level green leather belt, matching covered buttons. Grey knitted-wool sweater, ribbed polo collar, body and full-length inset sleeves. Brown leather step-in shoes, round toes, flat heels. 2 Golf. Pale-fawn mock-suede waist-length jacket, zip fastening to under brown knitted-wool collar which matches side panels of fitted waistband, full-length inset sleeves, buttoned cuffs, vertical welt pockets under yoke seam. Light-brown wool trousers fitted over hips, flared from knee-level, side hip pockets. Tan knitted-wool polo-neck sweater. Fawn wool-tweed peaked cap. Dark-brown leather ankle-boots. 3 Leisure wear. Unfitted black cotton top, round neckline and loop-and-button fastening edged with rows of gold and black braid matching trim on shoulder seams, elbow-length inset sleeves and hemline, wide black leather belt, large brass buckle. Black cotton bell-bottom trousers, no turn-ups. 4 Country wear. Camel-coloured wool hip-length jacket, sheepskin lining, zip fastening from hemline to under neck of hood, full-length inset sleeves, self-fabric belt, large hip-level patch-and-flap pockets. Brown wool bell-bottom trousers. Brown leather round-toed boots, flat heels. 5 Casual wear. Blue and white spotted cotton-voile shirt, pointed collar worn open. Fitted blue brushed-cotton trousers, curved side-hip pockets, black leather belt, large metal buckle. Red silk neckscarf and multicoloured bead necklace. Knee-high brown leather boots.

Accessories

1 Beige leather step-in shoes, high tongues. 2 Tan leather step-in shoes, high tongues, strap-and-stud trim. 3 Grey leather step-in shoes, high tongues, strap-and-ring trim. 4 Navy-blue leather step-in shoes, strap with tassel-tie trim, square toes. 5 Black velvet step-in evening shoes. 6 Dark-green leather lace-up shoes, ruched detail. 7 Black leather step-in shoes, strap-and-buckle fastening. 8 Black leather lace-up shoes, stitched fronts. 9 Black and white leather lace-up shoes. 10 Olive-green leather bag, black and red inset stripe, brass clasp and trim. 11 Red plastic shoulder bag, zipped top pocket over buckled strap and flap. 12 Cream plastic leather-look bag, top zip fastening, front flap pocket, double self-fabric handles. 13 Beige canvas bag, flap edged in green webbing to match straps and trim, brass fittings, single handle. 14 Yellow plastic bag, long handle, top zip pocket matching front pocket. 15 Navy-blue and cream leather T-strap shoes, perforated decoration. 16 Black leather shoes, high thick heels, round toes, thin platform soles. 17 Brown mock-suede mules, peep toes, cut-out detail, low wedge heels, thin platform soles. 18 Navy-blue leather shoes, high tongues, large square buckle trim, low stacked heels. 19 Brown and black leather bar-strap shoes, low stacked heels. 20 Cream plastic leather-look shoes, button trim, stacked heels. 21 Grey leather shoes, strap-and-button trim. 22 Red leather shoes, trimmed linked rings. 23 Black patent-leather shoes, large round buckle trim 24 Tan leather shoes, fringed tongues, low heels. 25 Pale-grey leather lace-up shoes, low heels. 26 Navy-blue and red leather sling-back shoes, perforated decoration, low heels. 27 Thigh-length black plastic boots, stretch uppers, patent-look shoes.

The 1970s

Introduction • The 1970s

In the 1970s, advances in production technology enabled clothing manufacturers to plan ahead, ensuring a uniformity of style, finish and cost, and making standard off-the-peg garments available everywhere, in all colours and sizes.

Ready-to-wear clothing at the beginning of the 1970s was classic. The look for women was streamlined, well cut, clean and unfussy; the look for men was similar – sleek, long-line jackets with wide lapels, teamed with flared trousers. As the decade progressed, women's clothes retained their classic, well-tailored appearance, though they became more closely fitted to the body, and skirts lengthened. Fashion details included buttoned-down flap pockets, long collars, tight sleeves with deep cuffs and wide, hip-level belts. Women began to wear trousers more often and for more varied occasions. Trouser suits, in a wide variety of fabrics from crushed velvet to linen tweed, became popular. Fabrics with a matt surface were most in vogue: brushed cottons, cotton velvets, wool jersey, and real and imitation suede.

Both bright colours and more subtle and subdued shades were fashionable. Bright colours were worn alone or combined with others: for example, canary yellow was teamed with dark brown and grey; lilac with purple and pink; slate grey, dull turquoise and terracotta were worn with black.

Many of the decade's younger and more unconventional women and men wanted to break away from what was on offer in the high street from well-known manufacturers and designers, and as the 1970s progressed their dress became increasingly individualistic. Though they still wore mass-produced clothing, it was often mixed with clothes from past decades and other cultures. National costumes, slinky day and evening wear from the 1930s (the Biba look), and Carmen Miranda 1940s platform shoes were worn by women alongside ethnic shawls and embroidered shirts from Greece and Turkey, and sequined silks and gold jewelry from India. Nor were men immune to these trends: a not untypical seventies look comprised an eighteenth-century-style frilled shirt, a multicoloured embroidered ethnic waistcoat and velvet trousers tucked into knee-high riding boots. Any one of these elements could also be teamed with off-the-peg garments.

In the main, the fashions I have illustrated here are such as would be worn by the middle or upper-middle classes and by people who would have had a keen interest in the latest styles, while not being 'dedicated followers of fashion'. It therefore follows that I have not included many of the more idiosyncratic outfits described above.

Men's fashions, as always, moved more slowly than women's, though the 1970s witnessed a more obvious change in design detail than previous decades. The suit still dominated, but with subtle changes to jacket fit and shape, length, button fastening and the width of lapels, which grew almost to cover the chest towards the close of the decade. Trousers also changed shape, often made without pockets to obtain the much-desired smooth hipline and with hems flaring to cover platform-soled shoes. Hand-knitted jackets and cardigans in bright colours and bold patterns, with shawl collars and tie belts, were much worn for leisure activities. The ideal shirt at the beginning of the seventies was fitted, pastel coloured and had a long pointed collar, and was teamed with a wide, boldly patterned, brightly coloured 'kipper' tie. By the decade's end it had changed to a baggy, subtly coloured, linen-tweed garment with a tiny collar, worn with a narrow leather tie. These differences and the basic trends in men's fashion have been shown, on average, with one example on each page.

The sources from which I have drawn – chiefly from Great Britain, North America, France, Italy and Germany – include contemporary magazines, catalogues and journals, original dated photographs, museum collections, and my own costume collection.

This section of the Sourcebook is divided into ten parts, each of which includes four subdivisions covering Day Wear, Evening Wear (alternately, on two occasions, Wedding Wear), Sports and Leisure Wear, and a section on either Underwear and Negligee or Accessories. Following the main illustrations are ten pages of schematic drawings accompanied by detailed notes about each example, giving particulars of colour, cut and trimming, as well as other useful information.

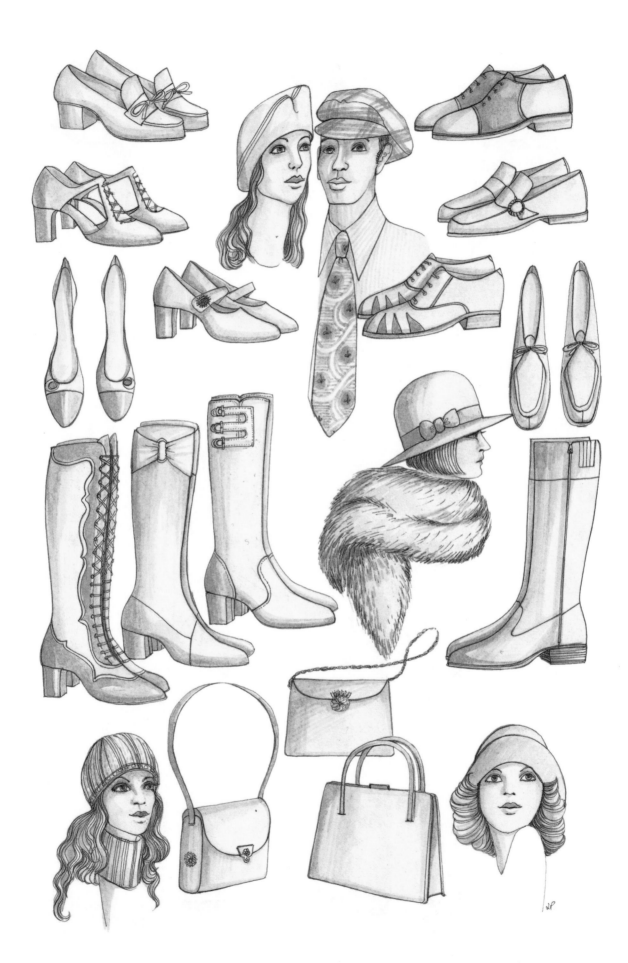

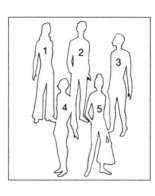
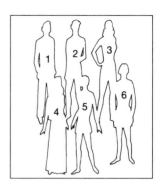

1970 Day Wear

1 Two-piece grey and maroon checked wool suit: hip-length single-breasted jacket, fastening from above hemline to under shirt collar, large black silk bow trim, long inset sleeves, split at wrist-level, button trim, wide black patent-leather belt, large buckle, hip-level flap pockets, button trim; flared mini skirt, wide box-pleats. Black leather gloves. Black patent-leather bar-strap shoes, low thick heels. **2** Two-piece dark-grey and navy-blue flecked wool-tweed suit: single-breasted jacket, high three-button fastening, narrow lapels, shaped flap pockets, top-stitched edges and detail; straight-cut trousers, no turn-ups. Blue cotton collar-attached shirt. Blue and grey striped silk tie. Black leather step-in shoes. **3** Double-breasted cream wool-gabardine midi-length coat, outsized lapels, large collar, bolero cut in one with bodice, long inset sleeves, buttoned strap above wrist, self-fabric belt, round brown plastic buckle, matching buttons, hip-level patch pockets, flared skirts. Cream wool polo-neck sweater. Brown felt fedora, high crown, brown band, wide brim. Brown plastic knee-high boots, fitted legs, thick heels. **4** Unfitted grey flannel dress, buttoned-strap fastening from hip-level to under shirt collar, long inset sleeves gathered into deep cuffs in navy-blue flannel, matching shoulder yoke and small plastic buttons, mini skirt. Knee-length navy-blue leather boots, fitted legs, thick heels. **5** Brown velvet jumpsuit, semi-fitted bodice, buttoned-strap fastening from bust-level to under high round neckline, zip fastening under strap to crotch, long inset sleeves, deep cuffs, trousers fitted over hips, hip-level vertical welt pockets set into central seam on front, flared legs from low hip-level to hem, top-stitched edges and detail. Yellow velvet cap, gathered crown, large peak. Yellow plastic clogs, blunt toes, wooden soles.

Evening Wear

1 Two-piece black mohair and silk evening suit: single-breasted fitted jacket, high two-button fastening, narrow silk-faced lapels, matching covered buttons, fine bound pockets; narrow trousers, no turn-ups. White silk shirt worn with wing collar. Narrow black silk bow-tie. Black patent-leather step-in shoes, blunt toes. **2** Ankle-length semi-fitted black silk-chiffon evening dress, high polo-neck, long inset sleeves, right sleeve and right side front and back of dress beaded and embroidered in yellow, gold and green from shoulder to hem of straight skirt, dress worn over black silk slip. Black satin boots, blunt toes, high heels. **3** Multicoloured paisley-patterned evening pyjamas: strapless hip-length smocked bodice; wide flared trousers gathered from hip-level. Black and yellow glass bead necklace: jabot of glass flowers hanging from fine gold chains. Black satin shoes, large square jeweled buckles, blunt toes. **4** Cocktail ensemble: silver ribbon-embroidered lace hip-length top, low V-shaped neckline, scalloped edges matching hemline and edges of long inset sleeves; multilayered pink and grey silk-chiffon mini-length skirt gathered from hip-level. Silver stretch-Lurex tights. Silver kid sling-back shoes, blunt toes decorated with self-kid flower, low square heels. **5** Purple crushed-velvet cocktail dress, fitted bodice worn open at front and laced from high round neckline to waist-level with black satin laces, cut-away armholes, mini-length skirt gathered from waist. Black stretch-lace tights. Black satin bar-strap shoes, blunt toes, high thick heels.

Sports and Leisure Wear

1 Holiday wear. All-in-one crocheted pink cotton jumpsuit, semi-fitted hip-length bodice, front zip fastening from hip-level to under high round neckline, cut-away armholes, trousers flared from knee-level. Pink leather shoes, top-stitched detail, blunt toes, low thick heels. **2** Beach wear. White knitted-cotton T-shirt, high round neckline trimmed with bands of red and navy-blue to match cuffs of long inset sleeves and hip-level band, manufacturer's logo on side chest. Fitted dark-blue cotton shorts, fly fastening, logo matching one on shirt on side front hem. **3** Swim wear. Swim trunks in multicoloured patterned stretch-nylon, red elasticated-nylon belt threaded through self-fabric loops on hipline, large round clasp fastening. **4** Cycling. Turquoise knitted-wool hip-length sweater, ribbed edge of low round neckline knitted in pale-coffee, matching cut-away armholes, inset band under bust also edged with brown, repeated over ribbed hem, appliqué gold star over left breast. Pale-turquoise synthetic-crepe blouse, long pointed collar, button fastening, long inset sleeves gathered into buttoned cuffs. Dark-turquoise cotton fitted shorts. Flesh-coloured nylon tights. Turquoise, beige and brown knitted-wool beret. Knee-high brown leather fitted boots, blunt toes, flat heels. **5** Beach wear. Fine yellow cotton crocheted bikini: small bra top, cups linked at front by wooden ring covered in matching cotton, back fastening, fine halter-straps fastening at back of neck; tiny briefs in matching fabric. Large yellow and white canvas bag, top-stitched detail. Yellow canvas pumps, round toes, bow trim, flat heels.

Underwear and Negligee

1 Red cotton pyjamas: hip-length single-breasted jacket, four-pearl-button fastening from waist to under shirt collar, long inset sleeves, stitched cuffs piped in white to match edge of front opening, collar and hip-level welt pockets; trousers with elasticated waist, legs slightly flared, no turn-ups. Red leather slippers, flat heels. **2** White knitted-cotton T-shirt, high round neckline with stitched edge matching hems of short inset sleeves. White knitted-cotton underpants, Y-front opening, elasticated waistband. **3** Beige nylon and Lycra bodysuit, moulded and seamed bra top, elasticated and adjustable shoulder straps, panelled body, high-cut legs. **4** Lime-green nylon nightdress, low V-shaped neckline and cut-away armholes edged with fine pale-coffee nylon lace, neckline trimmed above point with tiny self-fabric rouleau bow, ground-length gathered skirt falls from deep inset band of smocking under bust which also provides shaping under bust. Lime-green satin pumps. **5** Combination bodysuit and slip, pale-pink and black stretch-nylon lace bodice, unstructured bra top, elasticated and adjustable shoulder straps, pink nylon mini-length skirt falls from hip seam curved front and back. **6** Pink nylon and Lycra bra, moulded, seamed and darted cups, removable wire supports, pale-coffee nylon lace trim, elasticated and adjustable shoulder straps, back fastening. Pink nylon flared mini-length slip, elasticated waist, scalloped hemline trimmed with wide pale-coffee nylon lace.

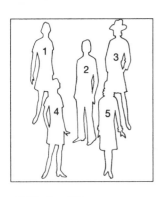

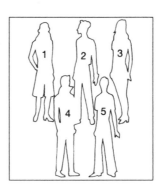
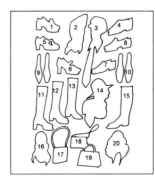

1971 Day Wear

1 Semi-fitted blue-grey wool dress, high round neckline bound in tan to match shaped bindings on short inset sleeves, shaped inset bands of tan and cream above waistline and on shoulders, knee-length flared skirt. Black plastic knee-high fitted boots, round toes.
2 Pale-blue denim single-breasted jacket, two-button fastening, wide lapels, large patch pockets, shaped flaps, top-stitched edges and seams. Dark-pink cotton trousers, flared from above knee-level, no turn-ups. Deep-pink knitted-wool polo-neck sweater. Brown shiny plastic ankle-boots, blunt toes, stacked heels. 3 Dark-grey wool coat, single-breasted buttoned-strap fastening from low hip-level to under large collar and lapels, buttoned shoulder yoke, long cuffed sleeves, self-fabric tie-belt, vertical welt pockets in knee-length flared skirts, top-stitched edges and seams. Blue and brown striped silk scarf. Grey felt hat, tall crown, dark ribbon band, wide brim. Knee-high black leather boots, strap-and-buckle trim, blunt toes. 4 Cream wool dress, semi-fitted black and cream patchwork bodice trimmed with silver studs, high round neckline, short inset sleeves, mini-length flared skirt, centre-front seam split six inches above hemline, black leather belt, silver clasp fastening set with black stone. Black leather shoes, high vamp, round toes, stacked heels. 5 Pale-blue wool coat, semi-fitted bodice, asymmetric fastening, three large horn buttons from waist to under collar of looped wool which matches cuffs of long inset sleeves, vertical welt pockets in knee-length flared skirts, top-stitched edges. Cloche hat in matching fabric. Pale-blue gloves. Dark-blue leather T-strap shoes, round toes.

Evening Wear

1 Black silk-taffeta evening dress, fitted pintucked bodice, black lace yoke and stand collar with matching scalloped edges, elbow-length inset puffed sleeves, frilled cuffs trimmed with ribbon and lace to match hems of two-tier skirt, embroidered and beaded shaped black velvet belt. Black satin shoes, round toes, low thick heels. 2 Tangerine rayon-crepe evening dress, unfitted bodice and ground-length skirt cut in one piece, high waist position marked with gold lamé belt beaded and embroidered in black, full raglan sleeves gathered into edge of low round neckline and into narrow rouleau cuffs. Black satin shoes, round toes, crossed straps. 3 Pale-gold-yellow evening dress, spotted in orange and gold Lurex, high-waisted fitted bodice, fine gold Lurex piping either side of mock-button fastening of self-fabric-covered buttons on centre front, on high waist seam and seam between tight inset upper sleeves and gathered lower sleeves, matching narrow rouleau cuffs, ankle-length flared skirt. Gold kid shoes, round toes, bow trim, low thick heels. 4 Two-piece dark-green silk and mohair evening suit: fitted single-breasted jacket, two-button fastening under low-cut wide satin-covered lapels, deep flap pockets, inset sleeves, single-button trim; flared trousers, braided outer seams, no turn-ups. White silk collar-attached shirt, pintucked either side of fly fastening. Dark-green velvet bow-tie. Black patent-leather elastic-sided boots. 5 Two-piece black wool and silk suit: hip-length fitted single-breasted jacket, single-button fastening under wide satin-faced shawl collar, panel seams from shoulder to hem; wide-flared trousers, no creases or turn-ups. White silk scarf tied in neck of jacket. Black velvet shoes, round toes, high thick heels.

Sports and Leisure Wear

1 Country wear. Short green suede jacket, single-breasted buttoned-strap fastening from above waistband to under pointed shirt collar, side panel seams, patch pockets, inset sleeves, buttoned cuffs, top-stitched edges and seams. Beige, green and white herringbone wool-tweed culottes, flared from hip to knee, pockets set into side seams. Beige wool polo-neck sweater. Brown, green, beige and white knitted-wool hat, padded brim. Knee-high brown leather boots, side zip fastening, thick heels. 2 Ski wear. Yellow nylon suit: waist-length jacket, front zip fastening from above buttoned waistband to under quilted shirt collar, buttoned-down points, quilted side panels with zipped pockets, long inset sleeves, buttoned strap above hem; fitted trousers, front zip opening, matching vertical pockets and side opening, quilted front panels. Knitted red and yellow striped hood. Red and yellow leather gloves. Red leather ski boots. 3 Holiday wear. Blue brushed-cotton fitted hip-length T-shirt, wide round neckline, short inset sleeves, wide leather belt, metal buckle, decorative studs. Fitted shorts to match T-shirt. Beige leather lace-up shoes, thick heels. 4 Ski wear. Red nylon suit: short jacket, fake fur front and back, matching collar, front zip fastening, inset sleeves; quilted trousers, zipped vertical pockets and side openings. Black wool polo-neck sweater. Red nylon hood. Red and black padded leather gloves. Black leather ski boots. 5 Holiday wear. Blue and white broken striped knitted-cotton shirt, zip fastening, pointed collar, flap pockets, short inset sleeves, edges and detail outlined in yellow. White synthetic linen-look trousers, waistband with buckle fastening, fitted over hips, piped pockets, flared from knee, no turn-ups. White leather step-in shoes, top-stitched detail.

Accessories

1 Dark-green leather shoes, high vamp, bow trim, low thick heels. 2 Pink wool beret, top-stitched detail. 3 Large checked wool cap. Striped shirt, long pointed collar. Wide 'kipper' tie, bold pattern. 4 Green and cream lace-up leather shoes, man-made soles and heels. 5 Black leather shoes, cut-away sides, open fronts with decorative lacing, round toes, high thick heels. 6 Pink grosgrain evening shoes, bar-strap, decorative clasp fastening, medium-high thick heels. 7 White leather shoes, red trim and laces, thick man-made soles and stacked heels. 8 White leather step-in shoes, high tongues, buckle trim, man-made soles and heels. 9 Grey leather shoes, black patent-leather toecaps and asymmetric buckle trim, round toes. 10 Beige suede shoes, leather laces, top-stitched seams. 11 Knee-high maroon leather lace-up boots, round toes, thick high heels, cream suede uppers, scalloped seams piped in white. 12 Powder-blue suede knee-high boots, self-suede draped band threaded through silver ring below knee-level, round toes, high thick heels. 13 Long tan leather boots, mock strap-and-buckle fastening at knee-level, high thick heels. 14 Mole-grey felt hat, large crown, black ribbon trim, wide brim. Silver fox-fur scarf. 15 Long brown leather boots, side zip fastening, elasticated inserts at knee-level, thick soles, stacked heels. 16 Stone knitted-wool beret. Matching polo-neck sweater. 17 Dark-red leather shoulder bag, flap with gilt-clasp fastening, matching trim on side panel, long handle. 18 Black silk evening bag, flap with jeweled gilt clasp, long gilt-chain handle. 19 Large black patent-leather handbag, metal frame, clasp fastening, double self-leather rouleau handles. 20 Blue felt hat, large crown, turned-back brim.

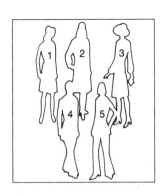
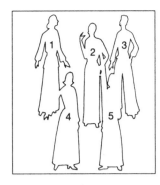
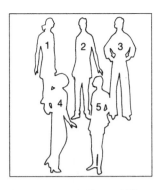
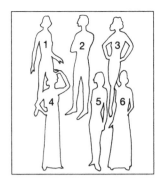

1972 Day Wear

1 Grey and white flecked wool two-piece suit: hip-length single-breasted jacket, small revers, pointed collar, narrow inset sleeves, bust-level mock-flap pockets, hip-level patch pockets with flaps, self-fabric tie-belt, top-stitched edges and detail; knee-length flared skirt. Pale-grey polo-neck sweater. Grey felt hat, twisted black ribbon band. Black leather gloves, matching T-strap shoes, peep toes. **2** Fawn wool coat, buttoned-strap fastening from hem to under large collar, wide batwing sleeves, buttoned cuffs, self-fabric buckled belt, hip-level patch pockets, side opening, mock-flap pockets, button trim, knee-length flared skirts, top-stitched edges and detail. Green and red patterned white silk scarf. White jersey-wool pull-on hat. Knee-high brown suede boots, leather platform soles and thick heels. **3** White cotton dress spotted in black, pointed collar, long sleeves, buttoned cuffs, knee-length box-pleated skirt. Fitted black wool-jersey sweater, scooped neckline, short inset sleeves, gilt-chain belt. Large white straw hat, black ribbon band. White handbag. Black leather sling-back sandals, strap-and-buckle fastening, peep toes, platform soles, thick high heels. **4** Grey and blue checked wool two-piece suit: single-breasted jacket, four-button fastening, narrow lapels, pointed collar, box-pleated patch pockets, buttoned flaps, self-fabric buckled belt; trousers flared from knee, no turn-ups. Pale-grey collar-attached shirt. Blue striped tie. Black leather step-in shoes. **5** Brown and beige checked wool two-piece suit: single-breasted fitted jacket, three-button fastening to under wide lapels, brown velvet collar, matching covered buttons, narrow inset sleeves, four flap pockets; trousers flare from knee-level. Beige wool sweater. Brown leather ankle-boots, round toes, high stacked heels.

Evening Wear

1 Two-piece dinner ensemble: hip-length black sequined top, semi-fitted bodice, inset sleeves gathered into cuffs, deep V-shaped neckline, long silver satin collar, matching cummerbund with large bow trim, vest inset and ankle-length flared skirt. Black satin shoes, square toes. **2** Dusty-pink silk-jersey evening dress, straight-cut bodice and ground-length skirt cut in one piece, gathered into high round neckline and on waist witn wide self-fabric sash, long narrow inset sleeves. Matching ground-length scarf. Close-fitting brimless cap, covering hair, embroidered and beaded in pink and silver. Silver kid shoes. **3** Pale-sage-green silk-satin two-piece evening pyjama suit: hip-length shirt-style jacket, single-breasted buttoned-strap fastening from hemline to under long pointed collar, narrow inset sleeves gathered into buttoned cuffs, self-fabric tie-belt, large hip-level patch pockets, top-stitched edges and detail; wide ground-length trousers, gathered from waist. Silver kid shoes. **4** Cream wool dinner dress, fitted bodice, slashed neckline, inset sleeves, flared hems decorated with inset bands of black wool to match hemline of ankle-length flared skirt and single band above waist seam. Black satin sling-back shoes, square toes, high thick heels. **5** Two-piece hostess ensemble: hip-length lilac wool-jersey top, high round neckline, deep armholes and hemline edged in purple, matching narrow suede belt; ankle-length black wool-jersey dress patterned with blue, lilac, purple and pink butterflies in various sizes, high polo-neck collar, inset sleeves gathered into buttoned cuffs, ankle-length flared skirt. Purple satin mules, peep toes, high platform soles and wedge heels.

Sports and Leisure Wear

1 Golf. Sage-green knitted-cotton shirt, front zip fastening to under long pointed collar, matching diagonal piped pockets above waist, short inset sleeves. Pink and green checked polyester mini-length flared skirt, no waistband, centre-front inverted box-pleat, two large hip-level patch pockets cut on bias. White leather step-in shoes, fringed tongues, blunt toes, flat heels. **2** Tennis. White rayon semi-fitted sleeveless dress, pintucked bib front, mock-strap opening to under wide round neckline, mini-length flared skirt. White cotton-towelling sweatband, matching wristband. White cotton ankle-socks. White canvas training shoes. **3** Country wear. Beige bouclé knitted-polyester jacket, front zip fastening from hem of deep ribbed waistband to ends of matching ribbed turned-down collar, wide batwing sleeves gathered into ribbed cuffs. Fitted grey flannel trousers, flared knee-level to hem, no turn-ups, central creases. Beige and grey knitted-polyester ribbed pull-on hat. Leather ankle-boots, square toes, top-stitched detail. **4** Holiday wear. White knitted-cotton two-piece patterned with uneven stripes of pink, turquoise, green and pale-blue: cropped top, low round neckline, short inset sleeves, top-stitched edges; hipster trousers, no hipband, wide legs, no turn-ups or creases. Large white straw hat. White leather sling-back sandals, strap fronts, high thick heels. **5** Holiday wear. Two-piece cotton-polyester beach suit: long bright-turquoise shirt, short inset sleeves, dark-blue buttoned-strap fastening from hem to under long pointed collar, worn open, matching shoulder yoke buttoned onto shaped patch pockets, patch pockets with mock-buttoned flaps and buttoned waistband of shorts.

Underwear and Negligee

1 White crochet-look nylon-doubleknit bra, moulded underwired cups, elasticated adjustable shoulder straps, back fastening. White nylon-doubleknit panty-girdle, shaped waist, top-stitched tummy control panel, long legs, elasticated nylon lace trim. **2** One-piece waist-to-toe grey wool undergarment, elasticated waistband, white cotton crotch panel, side opening, fitted legs incorporating knee-high ribbed dress socks. **3** Cream stretch-nylon body-shirt incorporating short panties, button opening from bust-level to under high round neckline, short inset sleeves, high-cut legs, fastening under crotch. **4** Pale-blue nylon sleeveless nightdress, low V-shaped neckline to high waistline marked by nylon-cord double-belt, large bow tied at front, bodice and ground-length skirt cut in one piece. **5** Black machine-embroidered cotton two-piece underwear set: unstructured bra, low V-shaped neckline, bow trim, adjustable satin-ribbon shoulder straps, back fastening; hipster briefs, elasticated waist and high-cut legs. **6** Ground-length nightdress, sleeveless high-waisted peach silk bodice, self-fabric-covered button trim under low V-shaped neckline, deep armholes, narrow cut-away shoulders, flared yellow silk skirt, centre-front inverted box-pleat, edges bound in silk to match bodice.

 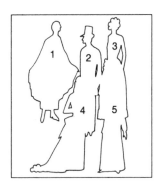 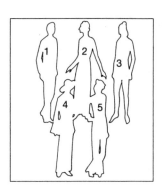 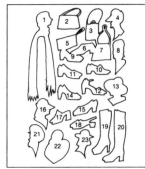

1973 Day Wear

1 White wool two-piece suit: knee-length wrapover coat, large white fur shawl collar, long inset sleeves, self-fabric tie-belt, hip-level pockets; straight-cut trousers, creases, no turn-ups. White felt hat, high crown, wide brim. White leather ankle-boots, platform soles, high thick heels.
2 Cream wool-crepe dress, brown cord-velvet shaped yoke, two self-fabric-covered buttons, wide-set collar, short inset sleeves, shaped cuffs, matching trim on hip-level offset patch pockets, semi-fitted bodice and flared skirt cut in one piece, top-stitched edges and detail. Brown velvet hairband, bow trim. Brown leather shoes, platform soles.
3 Grey and red flecked wool-tweed two-piece suit: long double-breasted jacket, wide lapels, large collar worn turned up, long inset sleeves, stitched cuffs, self-fabric buckled belt, welt pockets; wide flared trousers, top-stitched edges and detail. Red polyester blouse, long pointed collar. Hat in tweed to match suit, sectioned crown, narrow brim. Grey leather gloves; matching ankle-boots, blunt toes, platform soles, high thick heels.
4 White polyester dress spotted in red, semi-fitted bodice, high round neckline, self-fabric scarf tied on one side, flower trim, long inset sleeves, buttoned cuffs, self-fabric buckled belt, skirt fitted over hips, flared from hip to knee-level. Outsized bowler-style hat in fabric matching dress, high crown, wide band, narrow curled brim. Red leather bar-strap shoes, high thick heels.
5 Dark-brown leather jacket, front zip fastening, pointed collar, high yoke seam, mock-flap pockets, patch pockets with mock flaps and side opening, inset sleeves, ribbed-wool cuffs, matching waistband. Brown wool polo-neck sweater. Light-brown wool-flannel fitted trousers, wide flares from above knee, no turn-ups. Brown leather ankle-boots, platform soles.

Wedding Wear

1 Cream cotton-lawn wedding dress, large oval cape, mock bodice with boat-shaped neckline, pintucks and lace trim, sham-strap opening, self-fabric-covered buttons, bodice held by threaded lace-covered self-fabric belt at high-waist position, outside and inside edges of cape trimmed with bias-cut cream satin ribbon and lace, matching trim on ankle-length skirt. Close-fitting cream cotton-lawn bonnet, trimmed lace, fastening under chin. Cream leather ankle-strap shoes, cut-away detail above high thick heels and platform soles. **2** Formal wedding attire: fitted single-breasted grey wool tailcoat, single-button fastening, wide lapels, breast pocket, silk handkerchief. Single-breasted collarless pale-grey wool waistcoat. Black and grey striped wool trousers, straight-cut, no turn-ups. White shirt, imperial collar; black, grey and white striped silk cravat; pin. Grey top hat. Black shoes. **3** White nylon wedding dress, random white nylon-lace appliqué flower decoration on fitted bodice, tight sleeves and full gathered skirt, frilled hem, scalloped neckline and sleeve hems; strapless white nylon-taffeta under-dress. Wreath of fresh flowers worn as headdress. Matching bouquet.
4 Matt-ivory silk-satin pinafore-style wedding dress, low scooped neckline, fitted bodice and ground-length skirt cut in one piece, bias-cut waterfall frill set into side seams, continues around long train, large bow trim at back, pearl- and crystal-embroidered blouse, long tight sleeves, high round neckline. Long tulle veil attached to hair ornament. **5** Cream wool-crepe wedding dress, semi-fitted, flared from under bust to ground-length hem, no waist seam, low scooped neckline under bust, infilled to high round neckline, infill matching cuffs of sleeves and close-fitting brimless cap. Cream leather shoes.

Sports and Leisure Wear

1 Casual wear. Green collarless machine-knitted cardigan-jacket, single-breasted button fastening, ribbed edges in brown and cream matching cuffs of long inset sleeves and tops of patch pockets, wide self-colour rib inset on waistline. Green machine-knitted sleeveless sweater, V-shaped neckline. Green-grey flannel trousers, flared hems, no turn-ups. Brown brushed-cotton collar-attached shirt. Brown, green and cream checked cravat. Brown leather ankle-boots.
2 Holiday wear. Two-piece multicoloured spotted cotton beach suit: semi-fitted cropped top, cut-away armholes, high roll collar, long V-shaped slash from neckline to under bust; trousers cut without waistband, fitted over hips, wide flared legs; turban in matching fabric. Leather sandals, low wedge heels, peep toes.
3 Yoga. Grey knitted mini dress with built-in briefs, wide shoulder straps, fitted bodice, tiny flared skirt, white leather hip-belt, stud fastening, detachable purse.
4 Casual/Country wear. Two-piece green wool-flannel suit: short single-breasted jacket, button fastening, small revers, large collar, long inset sleeves, buttoned strap above wrist, patch pockets, buttoned flaps, self-fabric belt, round buckle, top-stitched edges and detail; trousers fitted over hips, flared from knee-level to hem, central creases. Dark-green wool polo-neck sweater. Rust-brown suede hat, sectioned crown. Brown leather shoulder bag; matching ankle-boots. **5** Casual wear. Blue denim dungarees, bib front, central patch pocket, adjustable shoulder straps, inset waistband, patch pockets either side fly-front fastening, fitted over hips, wide flares, multicoloured machine-embroidery. Gold panne-velvet top, high round neckline, long inset sleeves gathered into bow-tied rouleau bands. Gold kid boots, peep toes, high thick heels.

Accessories

1 Red and black crocheted-wool pull-on hat. Red, black, green and cream patterned crocheted-wool scarf, tasselled hem.
2 Burgundy leather bag, flap, clasp fastening, long handle.
3 Brown mock-patent-leather bag, flap, clasp fastening, small handle, long detachable rouleau handle. **4** Outsized pink suede peaked cap. **5** Small beige leather clutch bag, black patent panel in flap, zipped pockets, wrist handle. **6** Blue and red canvas lace-up shoes, platform soles, thick heels. **7** Shiny green leather shoulder bag, long handle, flap with applied matt-leather trim, clasp fastening.
8 Red silk-jersey turban. Plastic amber necklace and clip-on earrings. **9** Cream canvas shoes, green leather platform soles, low thick heels and strap trim.
10 Green patent-leather shoes, high tongues, strap-and-buckle trim, blunt toes, low thick heels.
11 Black patent-leather shoes, low-cut front and sides, metal trim on blunt toes and above low thick heels. **12** Shiny red leather shoes, ankle straps, buckle fastening, open sides, high straight heels. **13** Red waterproofed-cotton hat, top-stitched sectioned crown, matching wide brim. **14** Green snakeskin shoes, platform soles, high shaped heels, inset black suede trim on uppers. **15** Black and white patent-leather shoes, perforated detail, high thick heels. **16** Blue mock-suede sports visor, wide band edged in cream, matching outsized visor.
17 Yellow plastic mules, high pointed vamp, flared heels.
18 Cream leather sling-back shoes, peep toes, powder-blue platform soles and flared heels. **19** Knee-high brown suede boots, platform soles, high straight heels, side zip fastening.
20 Above-knee-high blue leather boots, platform soles, flared heels. **21** Tan leather beret.
22 Silver Lurex pull-on hat. Fox fur. **23** Blue felt hat, self-felt trim.

 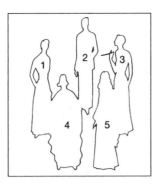  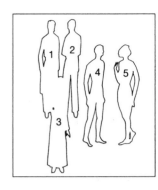

1974 Day Wear

1 Green wool two-piece suit: long single-breasted jacket, wide lapels, long inset sleeves, welt pockets, edges and detail finished with rows of machine top-stitching, green leather belt, matching covered buttons; knee-length flared skirt. Green satin blouse, tie at neck with rows of machine top-stitching. White and green wool-jersey turban-style hat. Green leather bag; matching shoes, ankle straps, cut-away sides, high heels. **2** Coffee rayon thirties-style dress patterned with multicoloured flowers, semi-fitted bodice, buttoned-strap opening, self-fabric belt, low sweetheart neckline, gathers from centre-front bust, short puffed sleeves, narrow skirt to below knee-level. Yellow lacquered-straw hat, white daisy trim. White gloves. Coffee leather shoes, double ankle straps, high thick heels. **3** Light-tan wool-flannel suit: single-breasted fitted jacket, three-button fastening, wide lapels, patch pockets, top-stitched mock flaps, matching edges and detail; flared trousers, deep turn-ups. Dark-tan cotton shirt, attached collar with long points. Cream, brown and tan patterned silk tie; matching breast pocket handkerchief. Leather ankle-boots. **4** Blue wool four-piece suit: long unfitted single-breasted collarless jacket, buttons in sets of three, edges bound with coffee, brown and cream zigzag-patterned wool to match welt pockets, hems of long inset sleeves, flared and pleated skirt and long scarf; collarless single-breasted waistcoat, self-fabric binding. Coffee lacquered-straw hat. Coffee leather bag and shoes. **5** Single-breasted mid-calf-length grey and yellow flecked showerproof wool-tweed coat, flared from shoulders, horn buttons, large shirt collar, long inset cuffed sleeves, diagonal welt pockets. Wide grey flannel trousers, no creases or turn-ups. Grey wool beret. Grey leather shoes, stacked heels.

Evening Wear

1 Midnight-blue silk-jersey evening dress, wide halter-straps form cross-over backless bodice, open V-shape on centre-front above wide draped cummerbund, floor-length gathered skirt, centre-front wide-spaced unpressed inverted box-pleat. Midnight-blue satin strap sandals. **2** Single-breasted fitted red velvet jacket, single-button fastening under wide lapels, fitted sleeves, large patch pockets. Collarless single-breasted black silk waistcoat, low V-shaped neckline, pointed hem. Flared black wool trousers, no turn-ups. White silk collar-attached shirt, buttoned-strap fastening. Large black silk bow-tie. Black suede ankle-boots. **3** White silk-crepe thirties-style evening dress, bias-cut bodice and floor-length flared skirt cut in one piece without waist seam, wide godets set into hem of side seams, upper bodice draped over bust on either side centre-front seam, fine self-fabric rouleau halter straps from centre of shaped neckline. Draped turban in matching fabric, bead brooch trim. White shoes. **4** Floor-length navy-blue and silver synthetic-chiffon evening dress overprinted in pink and white, full-length cape sleeves cut in one piece with bodice from high round neckline, narrow belt, bow trim, gathered skirt, navy-blue synthetic-silk underdress, fitted bodice, high round neckline, cut-away armholes, gathered skirt. Navy-blue silk shoes, peep toes, low platform soles. **5** White silk-chiffon evening dress printed with outsized red and pink poppies and golden corn, fitted bodice mounted over white silk, low scooped neckline, full-length unlined inset sleeves gathered into rouleau bands, wide waist sash, large black silk poppy trim on side waist above trailing ends, ground-length gathered skirt, underskirt of same shape. Red silk shoes.

Leisure Wear

1 Holiday wear. Two-piece white cotton beach suit patterned with red, yellow and orange berries and outsized green leaves: cropped top, cut-away armholes gathered into plain orange cotton binding around high round neckline; mid-calf-length flared skirt, plain orange cotton tie-belt. Lime-green headscarf tied into large bow on one side. Plastic jewelry in bright colours. Multicoloured plastic strap sandals, thick cork platform soles. **2** Holiday wear. Pale-green cotton-poplin beach dress patterned with bands of multicoloured flowers, four-tier mid-calf-length skirt gathered from high yoke, wide shoulder straps. Dark-green canvas beach shoes, low wedge heels, thin platform soles. **3** Holiday wear. Waist-length yellow knitted-wool single-breasted waistcoat, three-button fastening, front edges finished with dark-yellow rib to match armholes, tops of patch pockets and hem. Cream cotton flared trousers, side hip pockets, no turn-ups. Orange cotton shirt, pointed collar worn open, short inset cuffed sleeves. Tan and white leather step-in shoes. **4** Holiday wear. Red, white and black striped cotton shirt, pointed collar worn open, long fitted cuffed inset sleeves. White knitted-cotton sleeveless sweater, red and black stripes from above waist-level rib to under point of V-shaped neckline. White cotton-poplin flared trousers, pockets set under waistband, no turn-ups. **5** Cream cotton-muslin beach dress, buttons from hemline to under bust-level, low collarless neckline, short cape sleeves cut in one piece with upper bodice, gathered shaping under bust, fitted bodice from waist to under bust, ground-length flared skirt. Pale-coffee lacquered-straw hat, shallow crown, wide brim. Coffee canvas mules, peep toes, rope platform soles.

Underwear and Negligee

1 Deep-blue synthetic-silk dressing gown patterned with large yellow flowers, wrapover front, self-fabric tie-belt, long shawl collar, full-length inset sleeves, stitched cuffs, hip-level patch pockets. Dark-blue cotton-poplin pyjama trousers. Dark-blue leather slippers. **2** Sky-blue knitted-silk-jersey two-piece pyjama suit patterned with blue-grey herringbone design: long top, buttoned-strap fastening and high round neckline bound in plain navy-blue silk-jersey, matching tie-belt and full-length inset sleeve bindings, large hip-level patch pockets; wide trousers. Navy-blue leather slippers. **3** White knitted-cotton singlet, deep-cut armholes, self-bound and machine top-stitched, matching low scooped neckline. White cotton-poplin boxer shorts, red and yellow pattern, elasticated waistband, front fly opening, short wide legs. **4** Flesh-coloured stretch-nylon bra, wide scooped neckline, unstructured cups, adjustable stretch halter-straps, back fastening. Flesh-coloured briefs, elasticated sides. **5** Pale-mustard-yellow brushed-cotton nightdress, high waist position marked by cream satin belt tied into large bow on centre-front, long flared sleeves cut in one with unfitted bodice and edged in cream lace, matching two rows of lace forming centre-front decorative panel under high round neckline and hem of ankle-length skirt. Yellow satin slippers, embroidered trim.

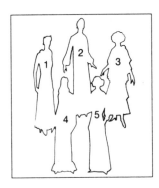
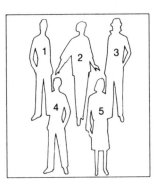
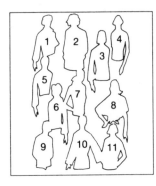

1975 Day Wear

1 Green showerproof cotton-poplin raincoat, single-breasted, wide lapels, epaulettes on dropped shoulderline, full sleeves set into large armholes, narrow cuffs, drawstring waist tied into bow at front, gathered skirts to below knee, shaped welt pockets. Beige blouse, cowl neck. Green silk scarf. Tan felt hat. Tan leather shoes, high straight heels. **2** Blue-grey wool-jersey two-piece suit: collarless jacket, edge-to-edge rouleau loop and self-covered-button fastening under low V-shaped neckline, matching fastening on cuffs of three-quarter-length inset sleeves, shoulder yoke, gathered shaping over bust, flared skirts, rounded edges; flared panelled skirt. Brimless navy-blue felt hat. Navy-blue feather boa. Navy-blue patent-leather bar-strap shoes, scalloped open sides and fronts, high heels. **3** Oatmeal and beige wool-tweed two-piece suit: long jacket, edge-to-edge fastening, three-quarter-length inset sleeves, deep turned-back cuffs, large patch pockets, twisted brown leather belt; straight skirt. Brown wool beret. Brown, oatmeal and beige flecked wool-tweed stole, thick brown wool fringe. Brown leather shoes, ankle straps, cut-away sides, high heels. **4** Tangerine wool two-piece trouser suit: single-breasted fitted jacket, wide lapels, large collar, narrow inset sleeves, patch pockets, top-stitched edges and detail; straight-cut trousers. Light brown wool sweater. Cream silk scarf patterned in tangerine. Brown wool beret. Leather shoes, flat heels. **5** Double-breasted navy-blue wool overcoat, wide lapels, large collar, shoulder epaulettes, button trim, self-fabric buckled belt, matching sleeve trim, hip-level welt pockets in knee-length skirts. Dark-grey flannel trousers, no turn-ups. Pale-grey wool collar-attached shirt. Navy-blue silk scarf. Black leather ankle-boots.

Evening Wear

1 Evening dress, hip-length fitted petticoat bodice, embroidered with shiny black beads and sequins from low neckline to hip seam, narrow black satin rouleau shoulder straps, ankle-length pleated black silk-crepe skirt. Black silk flower worn on right shoulder strap. Black satin shoes, peep toes, high straight heels. **2** Gold panne-velvet evening dress, wide square neckline above shaped yoke, full-length sleeves gathered into armholes and into fitted cuffs, ankle-length skirt gathered from yoke seam. Draped turban to match dress. Gold satin boots, thin platform soles. **3** Ankle-length ice-blue pleated silk evening dress, fitted bodice, high waist seam, low square neckline infilled with embroidered silk, elbow-length cape sleeves falling to hip-level at back, cream satin ribbon trim, matching hems of three-tier skirt. Cream and blue satin flower worn on left shoulder. Cream kid-leather ankle-strap shoes, open sides, high straight heels. **4** Dark-plum satin evening dress, low V-shaped neckline in bra top, high waist seam, low back, floor-length semi-fitted flared skirt edged with wide self-fabric gathered frill. Pale-pink triangular silk shawl, patterned with stylized gold flowers, wide gold-fringed edge. Gold leather strap sandals, thin platform soles. **5** Silver sequined evening dress, fitted bodice, apron front, narrow silver satin rouleau shoulder straps, low back, flared skirt fitted over hips. Silver kid shoes.

Sports and Leisure Wear

1 Ski wear. Two-piece red nylon ski suit: lined and padded jacket, front zip fastening from hemline to under yellow stand collar which matches colour of inset epaulettes, stripe on outer sleeve and buttoned sleeve cuffs, zipped pockets, top-stitched edges and detail; interlined trousers. Red knitted-wool pull-on hat. Red and yellow padded leather gloves. Red ski boots. **2** Country wear. Orange wool-tweed unfitted top, large wing collar, wide three-quarter-length sleeves, hems trimmed with rows of machine top-stitching to match tops of patch pockets. Yellow jersey sweater, draped polo-neck collar, long sleeves, narrow stitched cuffs. Straight-cut dark-yellow wool trousers. Dark-yellow beret. Tan and cream leather lace-up shoes. **3** Golf. Yellow knitted-wool sweater, low V-shaped neckline, full-length raglan sleeves, fawn, cream and light-brown pattern above rib to under chest. Beige wool shirt. Straight-cut cream wool trousers, yellow check, deep turn-ups. Oatmeal and yellow flecked wool-tweed hat, self-fabric band and loops. Leather step-in shoes. **4** Ski wear. Green weatherproof cotton-poplin two-piece ski suit: padded and lined semi-fitted jacket, front zip fastening, navy-blue buttoned waistband, matching stand collar, narrow inset sleeves, navy-blue buttoned cuffs, zipped pockets; straight-cut trousers, machine-top-stitched hems. Navy-blue knitted-wool pull-on hat. Navy-blue ski boots. **5** Golf. Weatherproof cotton-poplin two-piece suit: green semi-fitted top, zip fastening in bust-level strap to under neckline of grown-on hood, drawstring waist, bow on front, angled patch pockets, inset sleeves, buttoned cuffs; navy-blue flared skirt, green centre-front inverted box-pleat. Navy-blue wool tights. Navy-blue leather step-in shoes.

Knitwear

1 Blue and grey mix handknitted wool jacket, front zip fastening from hem to under large collar, wide kimono sleeves gathered into cuffs. Hat with plaited brim and long scarf in matching wool. **2** Green hand-knitted cardigan-jacket, openwork design, wrapover front, long ribbed shawl collar matching tie-belt, hem, cuffs of raglan sleeves and tops of patch pockets. **3** Lilac knitted-wool sleeveless slipover, low square neckline, deep-purple outlines matching armholes and trim above ribbed hem, cable-knit design on main body. **4** Pink hand-knitted cotton tank top, narrow halter straps, stripes of blue and green under neckline and above ribbed hem. **5** Tangerine knitted wool-tweed waistcoat, narrow roll collar, single-breasted fastening, deep rib from hem to under bust. **6** Sleeveless cream handknitted lace-stitch slipover, low scooped neckline and armholes edged with narrow rib, matching hem. **7** Strapless blue handknitted tank top, white stripe trim over bust imitating ruching, fine ribbed body, stitched hem. **8** Coral-pink hand-knitted cotton cape top, square neckline, fine shell edge, matching hem, narrow tie-belt. **9** White machine-knitted wool sweater, polo-neck, unfitted body decorated across chest-level with black and red geometric design matching upper part of inset sleeves, narrow red and black stripes above ribbed cuffs and hem. **10** Red, black, purple and orange patterned machine-knitted collarless cardigan-coat, wrapover front edged in black, matching tie-belt and welt pockets, long flared inset sleeves. Black knitted-wool polo-neck sweater. **11** Brown and tan chevron-striped machine-knitted wool-mixture slipover, wide round neckline and low-cut armholes edged in cream, matching deep welt. Brown machine-knitted polo-neck sweater.

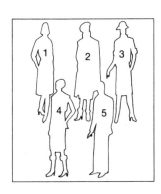

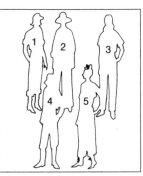
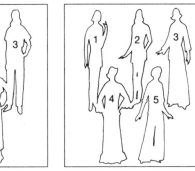

1976 Day Wear

1 Cream wool-jersey dress, bloused bodice, elbow-length cuffed sleeves, top-stitched seam from hem of flared skirt to under boat-shaped neckline, black patent-leather belt, round buckle. Black knitted-cotton polo-neck sweater. Black patent-leather shoes, cut-away sides, round toes, high heels. 2 Three-quarter-length lilac, blue, grey and white flecked wool-tweed sleeveless coat, shoulder-wide collar falling to hemline, large patch pockets on front. Straight skirt in matching fabric, hand-stitched edges and detail. Lightweight grey wool top, low V-shaped neckline, cuffed sleeves, hand-stitched edges and detail, blue suede belt. Blue knitted-cotton sweater, outsized polo-collar, long tight sleeves. Blue wool beret. Blue suede ankle-boots, leather straps, high heels. 3 White cotton dress, bloused bodice, low waist position marked by red leather belt, strap fastening buttoned in red from hem of straight skirt to under stand collar, edges bound in red cotton to match yoke seam and cuff edges on short inset sleeves. Red lacquered-straw hat. Leather shoes, white sling-backs, bar-straps and uppers, red toecaps and high heels. 4 Turquoise knitted-wool two-piece suit: edge-to-edge bolero jacket, loop-and-toggle fastening, blue, green, yellow and red pattern across bustline, edged in red and yellow; semi-fitted dress, polo collar, long tight sleeves, edged in red and yellow, pattern above hemline. Brimless turquoise felt hat. Turquoise suede boots, red fox-fur trim. 5 Single-breasted cream, yellow and grey striped wool jacket, two-button fastening, wide lapels, large patch pockets. Single-breasted collarless grey flannel waistcoat. Matching straight-cut trousers, pleats from waist. Collar-attached yellow cotton shirt. Yellow and grey striped wide silk tie. Yellow and white leather shoes.

Evening Wear

1 Blue, green and turquoise checked silk-taffeta evening dress, off-the-shoulder neckline edged with pleated crystal-blue silk-chiffon, matching deep hip peplum under wide blue satin belt with bow trim, and under wide satin band around hem of full skirt. Blue satin ribbon-bow hair decoration. 2 Fine apricot Terylene-jersey evening dress, fitted bodice and full-length skirt cut in one piece, no waist seam, cape overbodice and sleeves, short over bust, knee-level at sides and back, bare top connected by eight rhinestone straps. Matching strap sandals. 3 Two-piece black wool and mohair evening suit: fitted single-breasted jacket, wide satin lapels, diagonal flap pockets, narrow sleeves; straight-cut trousers, slight flare to hem, no turn-ups, satin trim on outside seam. White cotton collar-attached shirt, large collar, frilled front and cuffs, lace trim. Large black velvet bow-tie. Black suede elastic-sided shoes. 4 Four-piece evening ensemble: ivory silk-chiffon blouse threaded with gold, high round neckline bound and trimmed with gold tissue to match hems of full elbow-length sleeves; voluminous black silk-paper-taffeta skirt, frilled hem under gold and black velvet ribbon trim; short sleeveless quilted black velvet bolero; matching wide cummerbund. Gold tissue turban, twisted crown set onto wide headband. 5 Silver-grey silk-jersey evening dress, hip-length bloused bodice above top-stitched decoration, low neckline and small keyhole bound with silver and royal-blue striped ribbon braid to match side bodice trim, hems of inset flared sleeves, hem and hip-length side vent of straight skirt. Silver rouleau-loop hair decoration. Silver bar-strap shoes, round toes.

Sports and Leisure Wear

1 Casual wear. Pale-blue brushed-cotton-denim boilersuit, bloused top and trousers cut in one piece, buttoned-strap fastening under lapels faced in red to match cuffs of short sleeves, pointed collar, patch pockets, button trim, trousers rolled to mid-calf-length, self-fabric buckled belt, top-stitched edges and detail. Red and white checked cotton scarf. Denim peaked cap. Red knitted-cotton ankle socks. White leather strap sandals, low heels. 2 Holiday wear. Two-piece pink and white striped polyester and cotton beach suit: edge-to-edge flared collarless jacket, bound front edges, dropped shoulderline, deep cuffs buttoned onto wide sleeves with self-fabric tabs, matching trim on large patch pockets; wide trousers, pleated from buttoned waistband, fly front, pockets set into side seams. Deep-pink knitted-cotton blouse. Pink straw hat. Pink leather sandals. 3 Holiday wear. Blue and green striped cotton shirt, plain blue cotton buttoned-strap fastening and round collar, matching long buttoned epaulettes, top of patch pocket and cuffs of short sleeves, dropped shoulderline, top-stitched edges and detail. Blue cotton-poplin straight-cut trousers, pleated from waistband, self-fabric tie-belt. Blue leather mule sandals. 4 Casual wear. Green polyester and cotton jumpsuit, shirt top and trousers cut in one piece, two patch pockets with pointed flaps, matching pockets on upper part of cuffed sleeves, pointed collar, drawstring waist, fly front, straight-cut trousers. Yellow cowboy boots, scalloped upper edges. 5 Holiday wear. Green cotton-seersucker jumpsuit, shirred bodice under wide self-fabric frill edged in pink to match shoulder straps and bindings at ankle-level on full trousers. Green canvas bar-strap shoes, rope soles, low wedge heels.

Underwear and Negligee

1 Flesh-coloured Lycra moulded bra, narrow shoulder straps, back fastening. Cream rayon knickers, gathers from elasticated waist, wide legs trimmed with nylon lace. 2 Turquoise nylon camiknickers, fitted bra top, cream nylon lace trim, narrow adjustable shoulder straps, fitted body, hems of flared legs trimmed with cream nylon lace. 3 Two-piece silk lounging pyjamas: oyster silk-satin hip-length top patterned with large gold-yellow flowers and leaves, three-quarter-length kimono sleeves, scalloped lace-trimmed hems, matching slashed neckline and hem, plain gold silk-satin tie-belt; wide trousers in matching fabric. Gold satin slippers, peep toes. 4 Pale-peach silk collarless negligee, edge-to-edge, wide pale-cream trim to above frilled hem, self-fabric bow tie at bust-level, three-quarter-length flared sleeves split to elbow, lace trim. Cream satin house slippers, peep toes. 5 Two-piece sky-blue rayon pyjama suit: single-breasted collarless jacket, deep-blue rayon-satin strap fastening continuing around neck, piped in white to match cuffs of elbow-length inset sleeves, deep-blue rayon satin-covered buttons, curved seam with shaping under bust; flared trousers matching jacket, wide hems bound in white. Flat blue satin pumps, bow trim.

 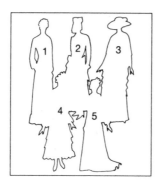 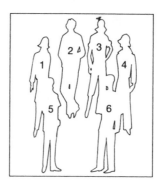 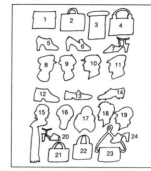

1977 Day Wear

1 Two-piece grey and white striped wool and mohair suit: single-breasted jacket, wide lapels, padded shoulders; straight-cut trousers, turn-ups, pleats from deep waistband, red leather belt. Pale-grey silk collar-attached shirt. White and red spotted silk bow-tie. Red leather step-in shoes, round toes, flat heels. White silk socks. **2** Beige suede hooded coat, sheepskin lining and cuffs, single-breasted wooden toggle fastening, flared inset sleeves, black, orange and yellow machine-embroidered decoration matching hem of flared skirts, self-fabric tie-belt, piped hip-level pockets. Black leather gloves and long boots, round toes, high heels. **3** Sage-green brushed-cotton three-piece ensemble with all-over pattern of multicoloured flowers: quilted sleeveless waistcoat, single-breasted fastening under round neckline, self-fabric covered buttons, piped edges, pleated hem, black braid trim; blouse, pleated neckline, black shoestring bow tie, full sleeves gathered into buttoned cuffs, pleated hems; full gathered skirt, deep gathered frill on hem. Long black leather boots, round toes. **4** Mid-calf-length dark-rust-brown overcoat, wrapover fastening with wide self-fabric tie-belt, wide lapels, large collar worn turned up, narrow yoke, inset sleeves, hip-level welt pockets, top-stitched edges and detail. Straight-cut grey flannel trousers, no turn-ups. Light-grey wool collar-attached shirt. Petrol-blue wool tie. Oxblood-red step-in shoes. **5** Fine rayon-jersey dress, dark-green yoke spotted in white and navy-blue, short T-shirt sleeves, padded shoulders, round neckline, hip yoke in matching colours, white bloused bodice spotted in dark-green and navy-blue, drawstring waist, knee-length skirt from hip-level in colours to match bodice. Navy-blue sling-back strap sandals, peep toes, high slender heels.

Wedding Wear

1 Ivory silk wedding dress, fitted lace bodice, high waist marked by scalloped edge, matching high stand collar, deep cuffs of long gathered sleeves and border above gathered frill on ground-length flared skirt. Headdress of tiny silk roses and lily of the valley. **2** Cream silk two-piece Victorian-style wedding suit: fitted single-breasted jacket, fastening with tiny buttons from waist-level to under large collar, self-fabric piping and frilled edge, matching front opening, edge of peplum and hems of long inset sleeves, large cream satin bow on centre-back waist, two small bows on waist either side centre-front; ankle-length flared skirt, deep scallops of pleated silk at mid-calf-level topped with satin bows, hem edged in silk pleating. Small cream silk hat, large bow trim, silk-tulle veil. Cream satin shoes, bow trim. **3** Pale-turquoise silk-chiffon wedding dress patterned with cream leaves, sleeveless fitted bodice, high stand collar, bias-cut cape set into side panel front and back covering arms to elbow and dipping to knee-level at front and mid-calf at back. Pale-turquoise transparent-nylon hat decorated with rows of machine top-stitching, wide brim, cream and turquoise silk flower trim. **4** Mid-calf-length white cotton wedding dress, low square neckline, edged pintucked band, self-fabric binding, lace trim and lace edging, matching bodice side panel seams, frilled cuffs of three-quarter-length full sleeves and edges of three-tier gathered skirt, wide cummerbund. Headdress of fresh flowers. White suede boots. **5** Ground-length white nylon wedding dress, fitted bodice, transparent yoke embroidered with pearl and crystal beads to match high stand collar and cuffs of gathered transparent sleeves, full skirt, long train, hem edged with pearl and crystal beads. Small spray of silk flowers on back of head, long silk-tulle veil.

Sports and Leisure Wear

1 Country wear. Two-piece lilac, blue and grey herringbone wool-tweed suit: knee-length semi-fitted dress, buttoned-strap fastening, shirt collar, cuffed shirt sleeves, flared skirt; narrow trousers. Lilac polo-neck sweater. Purple wool scarf, fringed hems. Purple leather ankle-boots. **2** Country wear. Rust and brown wool-tweed casual jacket, press-stud fastening, shirt collar, raglan sleeves, knitted cuffs, matching side hip-band, diagonal pockets, strap-and-stud trim. Brown needlecord trousers. Rust wool scarf. Brown leather elastic-sided ankle-boots. **3** Casual wear. Orange cotton jumpsuit, front zip fastening, shirt collar, semi-fitted top and trousers cut in one piece without waist seam, short cuffed sleeves, strap-and-button trim, matching epaulettes, two patch pockets, buttoned flaps, matching diagonally-set pockets. Orange and cream leather cowboy boots. **4** Golf. Two-piece beige wool trouser suit flecked in orange, brown and black: short jacket, front zip fastening, shirt collar, cuffed shirt sleeves, vertical welt pockets set into side panel seams, hipband with strap-and-button trim; flared trousers. Beige wool polo-neck sweater. Brown and cream wool-tweed hat. Cream and orange leather step-in shoes, fringed tongues. **5** Country wear. Black and red wool top; horizontally-striped scarf collar, buttoned-strap fastening and deep cuffs; sleeves and body in small check; piped pockets. Black stretch-wool trousers. Black leather elastic-sided ankle-boots. **6** Golf. Ochre knitted-wool cardigan-jacket, front zip fastening edged with panels of brown suede, matching side panel seams, welt pockets and shirt collar, inset sleeves, ribbed cuffs and hipband. Ochre knitted-wool polo-neck sweater. Light-brown, ochre and brown checked wool flared trousers. Brown wool peaked cap. Leather step-in shoes, fringed tongues.

Accessories

1 Maroon leather clutch bag, edged and trimmed in black suede. **2** Unstructured black leather handbag, double padded rouleau handles. **3** Tan leather bag, flap-and-clasp fastening, front pocket, short handle. **4** Green leather bag, double padded rouleau handles, front pocket with flap. **5** Navy-blue and white leather lace-up brogues, high straight heels. **6** Grey leather shoes, high fringed tongues, high straight heels. **7** Red leather sling-back shoes, ankle straps, high straight heels. **8** Brown cotton-corduroy peaked cap. **9** Blue denim peaked cap, top-stitched sectioned crown, button trim. **10** Orange, cream and brown checked wool peaked cap, button trim. **11** Olive-green waterproof-cotton peaked golfer's cap. **12** Beige suede lace-up ankle-boots, man-made soles and heels. **13** Black leather step-in shoes, high tongues, stitched fronts, stacked heels. **14** Red and cream leather lace-up golf shoes, laces tied through turned-down fringed tongues, spiked soles and heels. **15** Red wool-jersey hat, narrow turned-down top-stitched brim, small fitted crown, twisted padded self-fabric roll band. Long red wool scarf, fringed hems. **16** Sage-green wool beret, brooch trim. **17** Black sequined brimless evening cap. **18** Brimless red fox-fur hat. **19** Cream felt hat, narrow turned-down brim, rounded crown, double self-fabric bands. **20** Navy-blue leather sling-back shoes, peep toes, ankle straps, high straight heels. **21** Light-brown baby-snakeskin handbag, double handle, zip fastening. **22** Tan leather handbag, double handles through rings, top-stitched curved panel seam, zip fastening. **23** Light-brown canvas shoulder bag, long brown leather handle, matching trim. **24** Pale-blue denim mules, peep toes, cut-out flower motifs, wooden platform soles and high straight heels.

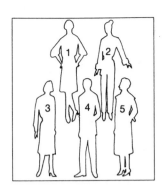
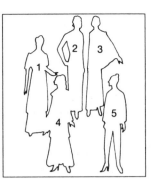
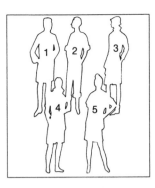
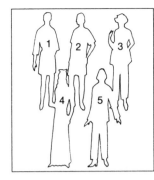

1978 Day Wear

1 Dusty-pink Tricel-jersey dress, high round neckline, centre-front split, shoulder yoke and narrow front panel cut in one piece, bloused bodice, sleeves gathered under shoulder pads and into buttoned cuffs on elbow, skirt gathered from shaped hip yoke, self-fabric tie-belt, top-stitched edges and detail. Cream leather T-strap shoes, pointed toes, high shaped heels. **2** Two-piece oatmeal wool trouser suit: wrapover jacket, long roll collar, fastened with self-fabric tie-belt, large hip-level patch pockets, gathered shaping from under narrow shoulder yoke, long wide inset sleeves, deep cuffs, shoulder pads, top-stitched edges and detail; narrow trousers. Cream silk blouse, stand collar, long sleeves. Cream suede ankle-boots, elongated square toes. **3** Grey flannel dress, semi-fitted bodice, buttoned-strap fastening to under bound round neckline, long raglan sleeves cut in one with pintucked cuffs, matching tucks on shoulderline above pads, self-fabric buckled belt, flared skirt, top-stitched edges and detail. Black leather shoes, white trim, peep toes, high shaped heels. **4** Two-piece cream silk-and-wool-mixture tweed suit: double-breasted shaped jacket, narrow lapels, large patch pockets; straight-cut trousers, no turn-ups. Cream silk collar-attached shirt. Cream silk tie. Light-beige suede lace-up shoes, top-stitched trim. **5** Grey-green wool wrapover coat, fastened with self-fabric buckled belt worn knotted at front, outsized collar, wide sleeves cut in one piece with floating yoke, belt trim above wrists, large hip-level patch pockets, flared skirts, top-stitched edges and detail. White wool sweater, outsized polo-neck collar. Matching pull-on hat. Knee-high dark-green leather unfitted boots, high heels, pointed toes.

Evening Wear

1 Salmon-pink silk-taffeta evening dress, fitted bodice, low square neckline, elbow-length circular-cut cap sleeves gathered into armholes over small shoulder pads, two-tier skirt, knee-length top tier gathered from high waist position, ankle-length underskirt. Gold kid strap sandals. **2** Midnight-blue silk-jersey evening dress, embroidered all over with crystal beads in various sizes, fitted bodice and ankle-length straight skirt cut in one piece without waist seam, navy-blue silk-jersey shoulder yoke, shallow stand collar and cuffs of long inset sleeves embroidered to match dress, padded shoulders. Silver kid strap sandals. **3** Blue-grey wool-crepe evening dress, wrist-length asymmetric shoulder cape gathered into brooch on one shoulder, lined in fuchsia-pink silk, ankle-length straight skirt lined to match, split from hem to hip-level. Fuchsia-pink satin T-strap sandals. **4** Two-piece royal-blue Tricel-jersey evening pants suit: long unfitted top, gathered from under off-the-shoulder frilled collar, long full sleeves gathered into armholes, elasticated on wrist; matching full harem pants elasticated on ankles. Silver kid strap sandals, high slender heels. **5** Three-piece evening ensemble: black velvet fitted strapless bodice; ankle-length black silk-jersey drainpipe trousers, black satin waistband, bow trim; wrist-length circular-cut black silk-chiffon shoulder cape, black satin stand collar, back opening, matching bound hem. Black satin strap sandals, high slender heels.

Sports and Leisure Wear

1 Sailing. Midnight-blue waterproof cotton-poplin bloused top, hood set into V-shaped neckline, self-fabric infill, long raglan sleeves elasticated at wrist, drawstring waist, top-stitched edges and detail. White cotton-sailcloth shorts, pleated from waist, fly front, pockets set into side seams. White canvas lace-up shoes, rubber soles and heels. **2** Sailing/Holiday wear. Red and white vertically-striped bloused top, shirt collar set into V-shaped neckline, self-fabric infill with horizontal stripes matching deep cuffs of wide elbow-length raglan sleeves. White cotton-poplin trousers, drawstring waist, large patch pockets at each side hip, straight-cut legs worn rolled to mid-calf-level. Red canvas T-strap shoes, openwork decoration on fronts, high wedge heels covered in rope. **3** Holiday wear. Collarless single-breasted orange wool waistcoat, deep armholes, small shaped flap pockets, button trim, top-stitched edges and detail; flared shorts in matching fabric, large patch pockets either side below hip-level, shaped flaps, button trim, pleated from deep waistband, green leather buckled belt. Yellow cotton blouse, shirt sleeves, button cuffs, collar worn open and turned up. Green cotton hat, sectioned crown, button trim, narrow brim turned down. Yellow cotton ankle socks. Green leather lace-up shoes, flat heels. **4** Beach wear. Blue and white checked cotton shirt worn open, shirt collar worn turned up, short inset sleeves, deep cuffs. Red and white knitted-cotton T-shirt, round neckline and hem bound in white. White cotton shorts, fly front, pockets set in side seams. Red leather T-strap sandals. **5** Beachwear. Outsized yellow knitted-cotton T-shirt-dress, wide round neckline, wide short sleeves cut in one piece with hip-length bloused bodice and mini-length skirt, split from hem to hip either side, top-stitched edges.

Negligee

1 Short bright-yellow cotton-towelling bathrobe, collarless wrapover front, wide self-fabric binding matching hems of three-quarter-length kimono sleeves, self-fabric tie-belt, large hip-length patch pockets. **2** Two-piece pale-blue cotton pyjama suit: single-breasted collarless jacket, press-stud fastening, wide self-fabric binding, short inset sleeves, single chest-level patch pocket; wide shorts, fly fastening, drawstring waist. Cream leather mule slippers, toolwork design on fronts. **3** Two-piece pink cotton pyjama suit: hip-length sleeveless top, stand collar embroidered with multicoloured flowers and leaves, matching wrapover bib front, self-fabric rouleau-bow fastening, gathers from under bust; mid-calf-length trousers. Pink velvet mule slippers, feather trim. **4** Fine white silk nightdress, wrapover front secured on hip with satin ribbons tied into large bow, low neckline, edges and hem trimmed with wide border of lace, double white satin rouleau straps, low back. White satin slippers, pointed toes, bow trim. **5** Two-piece pale-peach-pink satin pyjama suit patterned with peach-pink and white sprays of flowers: hip-length semi-fitted jacket, single-breasted buttoned-strap fastening from hem to under shaped stand collar, inset sleeves flare to wrists, hems bound in self-fabric to match hem of jacket, side split, hems of straight-cut ankle-length trousers and side splits on side seams. Cream silk mule slippers, peep toes, medium-high heels.

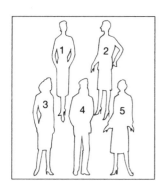

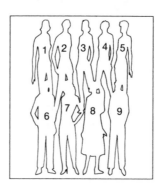
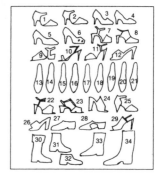

1979 Day Wear

1 Cream knitted-cotton dress patterned with pale-blue broken stripes, fitted bodice, slashed neckline, padded shoulders, three-quarter-length sleeves, plain pale-blue knitted-cotton cuffs, matching hip-level welt pockets in knee-length straight skirt, wide pale-blue leather belt. Cream leather shoes, pointed toes, dark-blue toecaps, heel trim and high spike heels. **2** Navy-blue linen double-breasted tailored jacket, narrow lapels, long inset sleeves, button trim, padded shoulders, wide stitched canvas and leather belt. Knee-length pale-grey linen wrapover skirt, spotted in pink. Navy-blue silk-jersey crownless turban. Navy-blue leather strap sandals, high spike heels. **3** Mint-green Tricel-jersey two-piece suit: collarless edge-to-edge jacket, loop-and-button fastening from waist to under low V-shaped neckline, bloused bodice, shaping gathers under narrow shoulder yoke, padded shoulders, narrow inset sleeves, draped cummerbund, hip-level skirts with rounded edges; narrow knee-length skirt. Dark-beige leather shoes, peep toes, high spike heels. **4** Burgundy wool-tweed single-breasted jacket, shirt-style collar worn turned up, patch pockets, buttoned shaped flaps, top-stitched edges and detail. Narrow dark-grey heavy-cotton trousers, pleated from waist, no turn-ups. Grey cotton-tweed collar-attached shirt. Grey and burgundy hand-knitted sweater, low V-shaped neckline. Grey cotton peaked cap. Dark-grey leather shoes, strap-and-buckle fastening, square toes. **5** Pale-blue silk-jersey dress, full bodice and skirt cut in one piece, gathered from narrow shoulder yoke, padded shoulders, full inset sleeves gathered into cuffs, dress buttons through from hem to under narrow peter-pan collar worn turned up. Pale-blue leather shoes, pointed toes, high spike heels.

Evening Wear

1 Blue-grey silk-taffeta strapless evening dress, fitted and boned bodice, edges and wrapover effect bound and frilled in cream silk-taffeta to match edges and hems of two-tier gathered skirts and hem of large bow on side hip, trimmed with large cream silk flowers. **2** White silk-chiffon full-length dinner dress, bloused bodice gathered from above wide belt, black bead embroidery matching narrow shoulder yoke and upper sleeve trim, gathered shaping over bust, ground-length full gathered skirt. **3** Two-piece black striped wool-and-silk-mixture evening suit: double-breasted jacket, narrow satin-faced roll collar, matching covered buttons, three patch pockets, square shoulders; narrow trousers, satin braid trim on outside seams, no turn-ups. White silk shirt, attached collar, round edges. Black satin bow-tie. Black patent-leather step-in shoes. **4** Primrose-yellow Tricel-jersey sleeveless evening dress, bloused bodice draped from padded shoulders to triangular inset panel on front under low V-shaped neckline, wide self-fabric belt, ground-length straight skirt, draped front panel. Gold kid shoes. **5** Two-piece black silk dinner ensemble, fabric decorated with wide-spaced rows of vertical pintucks: hip-length top, self-fabric belt tied into bow on side, hem edged and trimmed with lace and bands of fine pintucks to match yoke under slashed neckline, hems of long flared inset sleeves and hem of knee-length gathered skirt. Black silk flower worn on one shoulder. Black patent-leather shoes, pointed toes, high spike heels.

Sports and Leisure Wear

1 Swimwear. White Lycra swim-suit with outsized yellow and orange flower pattern, V-plunge neckline, halter fastening at back, covered button trim on centre-front seam, low back. **2** Swimwear. Mauve Lycra swimsuit, low V-shaped neckline to waist-level, ruched detail, halter fastening at back, low back. **3** Swimwear. Cerise, pink and blue striped and spotted Lycra swimsuit, tab front, threaded rouleau halter strap, back fastening, scooped back. **4** Swimwear. Green nylon and cotton swimsuit, keyhole under scooped neckline, narrow halter straps, back fastening, scooped back. **5** Swimwear. Backless Lycra swimsuit, deep V-shaped neckline incorporating wide halter straps from top of bikini briefs, back fastening, restraining rouleau strap under bust to back. **6** Exercise wear. Two-piece pink knitted-cotton tracksuit: bloused top, V-shaped neckline bound in red, drawstring waist matches hems of sleeves and trousers, bound pockets. Crownless pink plastic visor. Pink and red canvas trainers. **7** Holiday/Casual wear. Shiny silver-blue stretch-Lycra top, low scooped neckline, narrow shoulder straps. Blue Tricel-jersey trousers, gathered from waist to narrow hems, hip-level pockets. Blue suede belt, self-fabric buckle. Blue suede mules, peep toes, wooden soles and high heels. **8** Beachwear. Knee-length green cotton dress with black and white leaf pattern, gathered from bound scooped neckline, rouleau straps tied into bows on shoulders. White plastic mules, peep toes, cork soles and wedge heels. **9** Exercise wear. Two-piece red knitted-cotton tracksuit: unfitted top, front zip fastening from hem to under navy-blue stand collar which matches sleeve cuffs and trim on sleeve head; unfitted trousers, fly fastening, navy-blue cuffs on ankles. Red and navy canvas and leather trainers.

Footwear

1 Beige leather shoes, tan leather bar-straps, toecaps, heels and trim. **2** Grey leather shoes, green leather bar-straps, heels and trim. **3** White leather shoes, navy-blue toecaps and heels. **4** Black patent-leather shoes, grey leather trim. **5** Brown leather shoes, black leather heels and trim. **6** Red leather shoes, strap fronts. **7** Sling-back cream leather bar-strap sandals, peep toes. **8** Sling-back green leather T-strap sandals. **9** Cream leather sling-back shoes, low wedge heels, fronts banded in brown, peep toes. **10** Pearlized-blue leather sling-back sandals, tied ankle straps. **11** Beige leather sling-back shoes, ankle straps, black leather trim, peep toes. **12** Tan leather mules, peep toes, wooden soles and heels. **13** Brown leather step-in shoes, tasselled tie-trim. **14** White canvas lace-up shoes, brown leather soles and heels. **15** Brown suede lace-up ankle-boots, toecaps. **16** Red leather perforated shoes. **17** Tan suede shoes, cross-strap-and-buckle fastening. **18** Brown leather shoes, narrow cross-strap fastening. **19** Brown suede step-in perforated shoes. **20** Green leather step-in shoes. **21** Yellow leather lace-up shoes, hand-stitched trim. **22** Gold kid sling-back sandals, ankle straps, peep toes. **23** Sling-back blue leather T-strap sandals. **24** Tan leather perforated mules, crossed straps. **25** Blue suede shoes, scalloped edges, ankle straps, conical heels. **26** Mules, wooden soles, leather strap fronts. **27** Pink suede lace-up shoes, rubber soles and heels. **28** Orange leather T-strap sandals. **29** Gold kid rouleau-strap sandals, spike heels. **30** Green boots, top-stitched cuffs. **31** Brown leather lace-up ankle-boots, light-brown canvas sides. **32** Brown leather lace-up boots. **33** Tan leather boots, beige canvas uppers, vertical top-stitching. **34** Green leather lace-up boots.

The 1980s

Introduction · The 1980s

In the 1980s, youth culture no longer dominated fashion. In male dress, the peacock look of the seventies gave way to a more sophisticated, formal elegance. Men wanted clothes that were both business-like and comfortable, as well as being of a recognizably high quality in a decade that was greatly concerned with status. A typical outfit for men consisted of a double-breasted jacket worn with straight-cut trousers with pleats from the waist. For smart occasions, a designer-label jacket was often combined with blue denim jeans and an open-necked silk shirt.

Clothes by top designers were a leitmotif of the eighties. Department stores were rearranged to cater for a new way of merchandising, with in-house designer boutiques selling everything from coats and suits to accessories and perfumes – all under one designer label.

For women as well as men, minimal elegance was the aim. The 'executive look', which had first found expression as part of working women's dress in the 1970s, matured into what became known as 'power dressing'. This style was based on the male silhouette, and was achieved through a skirt suit which combined a wide, shoulder-padded jacket with a feminizing short skirt. The jacket hung from the shoulders, skimming the waist and disguising the hips. It was a strong, aggressive silhouette. Trouser suits, though still worn, were less in evidence than they had been in the seventies.

Glamour was reserved for the evening. In the early part of the decade, ball gowns in silk and satin with huge skirts and outsized bows and frills were much in vogue (wedding dresses were similarly styled). In the later eighties these rather fairytale garments gave way to overtly body-conscious styles such as mini-length, skimpy dresses in Lycra or leather, with strapless boned bodices reminiscent of corsets. Azzedine Alaïa, Gianni Versace and Thierry Mugler were among a number of designers who contributed provocative, body-hugging garments to the female wardrobe.

Many designers favoured natural materials, including silk, wool, cotton and linen. The Italians, in particular Giorgio Armani, were responsible for a vogue for softly tailored crumpled linens, and this fabric achieved widespread popularity. Trousers and jackets in linen or cotton became fashionable leisure wear for men.

Young Japanese designers produced avant-garde collections of oversized, often asymmetric clothes, predominantly in black, ink-blue and black-brown. These were often slashed and creased, with irregularly placed necklines, collars and sleeves.

Some fabrics were mixtures of new and old: polyester with cotton, for example, or Lycra with wool. Polyamides, rayon and nylon were also used together. The mixed fabrics took dyes well, giving rise to bright colours and jazzy printed patterns which were used for leisure wear and beach wear. Leisure and sports wear had by this time merged with casual wear. Tracksuits became familiar on the street, while white trainers and baseball caps found particular favour with the young.

Accessories for both men and women were refined and of high quality. Men chose classic shoes for business wear, and for leisure use coloured deck shoes in canvas, suede or leather were popular.

Women's shoes ranged from slingbacks with medium-high, slender heels to mannish designs with laces or buckles and straps. Also popular were knee-high boots with either high spiked heels or low, stacked cuban heels. Black or dark stockings or tights were especially favoured as skirts grew shorter later in the decade. The most popular bags were shoulder bags with long, adjustable straps and quilted leather bags with chain handles.

Hats were reserved for occasions such as races and weddings. Women's special-occasion hats tended to be shallow-crowned with wide brims. Men rarely wore hats at all, apart from top hats at weddings, though caps were still common at country sporting occasions.

As is usually the case, men's fashions in this decade developed more slowly than women's, so they have been shown on average with one example per page.

In the main, the fashions I have used are such as would have been worn by men and women of the middle or upper-middle classes and by people who, while not necessarily being 'dedicated followers of fashion', would have had a keen interest in the latest styles.

The sources from which I have drawn – chiefly from Great Britain, North America, France and Italy – include contemporary magazines, catalogues and journals, museum collections, original dated photographs, and my own costume collection.

This section of the Sourcebook is divided into ten parts, each of which includes four subdivisions covering Day Wear, Evening Wear (alternately, on two occasions, Wedding Wear), Sports and Leisure Wear, and a section on either Underwear or Accessories. Following the main illustrations are ten pages of schematic drawings accompanied by detailed notes about each example, giving particulars of colour, fabric, cut and trimming, as well as accessories and other useful information.

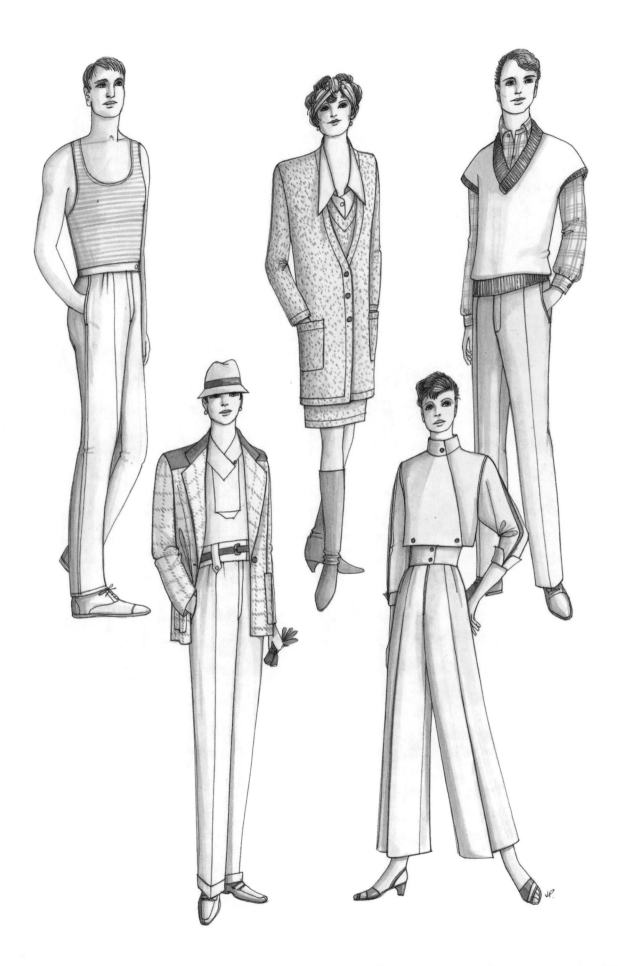

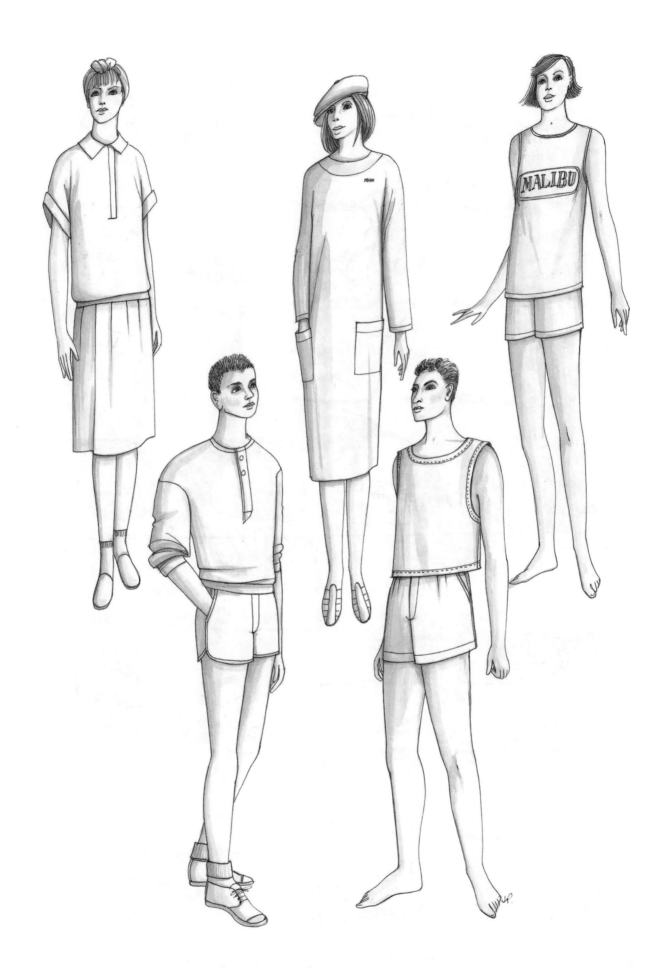

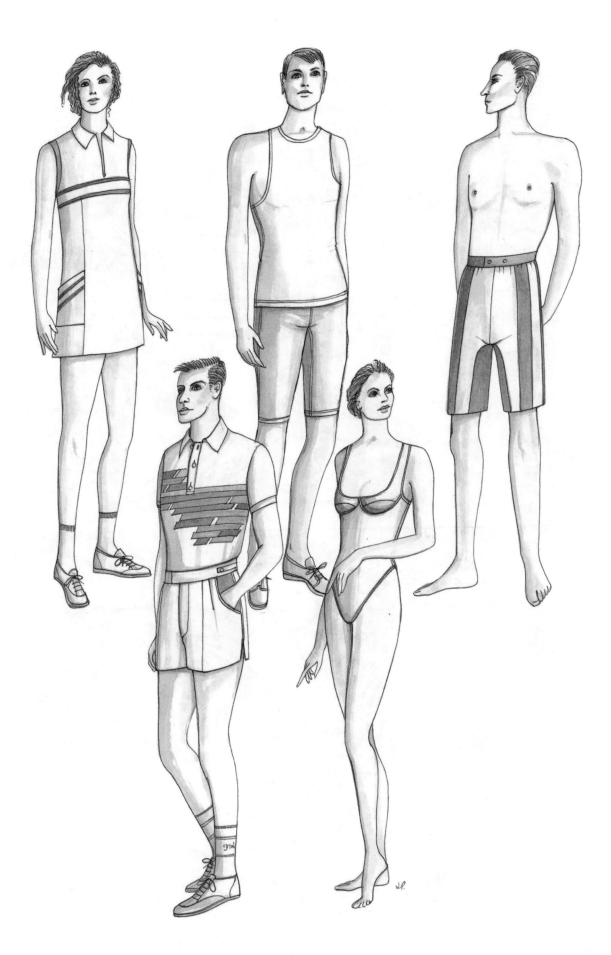

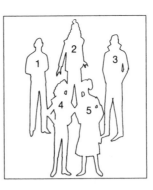
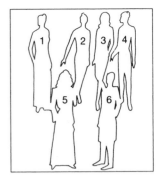

1980 Day Wear

1 Navy-blue crepe-de-chine dress, bloused bodice and below-knee-length skirt cut without waist seam, gathered in on waist by navy-blue leather buckled belt, padded shoulders, full-length inset sleeves, white crepe-de-chine frilled cuffs gathered under cherry-red ribbon bands, matching collar and bow-tie. Navy-blue leather shoes, almond-shaped toes, high stacked heels. **2** Light-brown rayon dress, random pattern of black spots, unfitted bodice and knee-length skirt cut without waist seam, knife-pleats from under shaped yoke, padded shoulders, full-length inset sleeves, button trim above hem, white top-stitched collar, brown petersham ribbon bow-tie. Brown patent-leather sling-back shoes, round toes, bow trim, thick medium-high heels. **3** Pink, yellow and green knitted-wool sweater dress, all-over geometric patterns, mini-length skirt, ribbed hemline, deep yoke, high round neckline, padded shoulders, long cuffed inset sleeves, dropped shoulderline. Pink and green striped knitted-wool tights. Green leather step-in shoes, round toes, flat heels. **4** Dark-brown wool-tweed jacket, single-breasted fastening, flap pockets. Light-brown wool tapered trousers, pleats from waist, no turn-ups. Burgundy and beige Argyle check lambswool sweater, V-shaped neckline. Pale-blue wool collar-attached shirt worn over light-brown knitted-wool polo-neck sweater. Pale-blue scarf, fringed hems. Brown leather step-in shoes. **5** Dark mustard-yellow leather two-piece suit: wrapover hip-length jacket, self-fabric tie belt, wide lapels, brown fur collar, matching cuffs on full-length inset sleeves, padded shoulders, hip-level pockets set into vertical panel seams; knee-length straight skirt, seamed on low hip-level, top-stitched edges and detail. Cream silk T-shirt. Brown leather shoes.

Evening Wear

1 Navy-blue wool two-piece evening suit: edge-to-edge jacket, fastening with linked buttons, long shawl collar faced with blue silk, piped pockets; tapered trousers, no turn-ups. White cotton collar-attached shirt, concealed fastening, top-stitched edges, navy-blue silk bow-tie. Black leather lace-up shoes. **2** Black sequined evening dress, semi-fitted bodice, narrow ankle-length skirt, back vent to knee-level, deep V-shaped neckline, padded shoulders, full-length inset sleeves. Black satin shoes, pointed toes. **3** Pleated polyester-crepe evening dress, asymmetric upper bodice draped from one shoulder in lilac, draped asymmetric midriff and bow-knot detail in yellow, ankle-length skirt in bright-pink. Pink suede strap sandals. **4** Royal-blue polyester-crepe three-piece evening suit: short edge-to-edge jacket, small collar worn turned up, padded shoulders, full-length inset sleeves, top-stitched edges; chemise top gathered from straight neckline, narrow shoestring straps; ankle-length drainpipe trousers split on outside seams above hems, gathers from waist, side-hip pockets, pink polyester satin belt. Royal-blue satin strap sandals, high spike heels. **5** Sleeveless cream satin ballgown, woven pattern of silver and gold butterflies, bloused bodice, full-length gathered skirt worn over stiffened petticoats, off-the-shoulder neckline edged with deep frill of cream silk organdie, woven pattern of silver and gold butterflies and scattered with silver and gold sequins, matching gathered scalloped frill above hemline, large organdie bow trim on one side of neckline.

Sports and Leisure Wear

1 Cricket. Handknitted cream cotton sweater, low V-shaped neckline edged in blue and green, matching bands above ribbed cuffs of full-length inset sleeves. Cream wool-flannel tapered trousers, hip-level pockets, no turn-ups. Cream brushed-cotton collar-attached shirt. Green wool peaked cap, blue trim. Cream leather lace-up spiked cricket boots. **2** Ski wear. Sleeveless red wool jacket, zip fastening to under high stand collar; red, blue, purple and yellow geometric-patterned yoke, matching lining, hip-level welt pockets, button trim. Red wool sweater, high round neckline, full-length cuffed sleeves. Wool and nylon ski pants. Brimless red knitted-wool hat, matching jacket pattern. **3** Casual wear. Dark-yellow leather jacket, zip fastening to under large collar, stitched and tucked yoke, full-length sleeves, chest-level zipped pockets, matching vertical pockets above hemline. Dark-brown cotton tapered trousers, knee-level seam, inset zipped pocket, side-hip pockets, no creases or turn-ups. Burnt-orange knitted-wool sweater, V-shaped neckline, full-length sleeves. Cream cotton collar-attached shirt. White canvas trainers, yellow trim. **4** Casual wear. Turquoise brushed-cotton all-in-one jumpsuit, zip fastening from hip-level to under stand collar, full-length shirt-style sleeves, inset elasticated half-belt, button trim, matching low hip-level pockets, tapered legs. Sleeveless turquoise cotton jacket, multicoloured printed pattern, zip fastening under large collar, zipped side-hip pockets, elasticated hipband. Long tan leather boots, flat heels. **5** Holiday wear. Yellow cotton dress, white seagull print, yoke bodice, gathered halter straps, three-tier skirt, central panel white with red seagulls, matching yellow and white print stole. Striped cotton shoes, rope soles.

Underwear and Negligee

1 White rayon-satin nightdress, ankle-length skirt gathered from under shaped cups, wide V-shaped neckline formed by two wide-set embroidered-velvet ribbon shoulder straps infilled with fine rayon-lace. **2** Pale-peach Lycra-satin soft cup bra, lace trim, front fastening, adjustable shoulder straps, hip-level bikini briefs in matching fabric, rayon-lace side panels, high-cut legs. **3** Black silk one-piece camisole and French knickers, low shaped neckline edged with black scalloped lace to match side edges of high-cut legs, narrow self-fabric shoulder straps, crotch fastening. **4** Primrose-yellow Lycra-satin bra, low scooped neckline forming half-cups, scalloped lace infill, back fastening, low-cut bikini briefs in matching fabric, top edge trimmed with scalloped lace, high-cut legs. **5** Wine-red panne-velvet dressing gown, wrapover bloused bodice, roll collar, scalloped edge embroidered with self-colour flowers and leaves, padded shoulders, bishop-style inset sleeves gathered into rouleau cuffs, matching tie-belt, ankle-length gathered skirts. **6** Dark-blue wool dressing gown, front edges and roll collar piped in red to match ends of self-fabric tie-belt, mock cuffs of full-length inset sleeves and top edges of patch pockets, breast pocket with embroidered monogram. Red cotton pyjamas. Red leather step-in slippers.

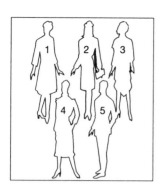

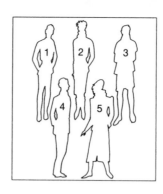
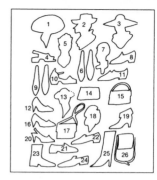

1981 Day Wear

1 Sage-green wool dress, knee-length skirt flared from high waist position, unpressed pleats from side-front panel seams in upper bodice, high round neckline, deep slash on centre front, padded shoulders, three-quarter-length flared inset sleeves, hems trimmed with black braid, matching skirt hem, top-stitched edges and detail. Black suede shoes, black patent-leather toecaps and high spike heels.
2 Bright-red acetate and nylon two-piece suit, spotted in dark-red, black and white: single-breasted unfitted hip-length jacket, white peter-pan collar, gathered shaping from under yoke seam, padded shoulders, full-length inset sleeves gathered into narrow cuffs, self-fabric belt and covered buckle; knee-length gathered skirt. Small black felt hat, low crown, red plastic band, narrow brim. Black leather shoulder bag; matching shoes, peep toes.
3 Black knitted-wool sweater dress, outsized polo-neck collar, full-length sleeves, ribbed cuffs, straight knee-length skirt. Charcoal-grey wool-flannel wrap, bias-cut, single armhole, worn draped over one shoulder. Black leather shoes, almond-shaped toes, high heels.
4 Coffee-coloured silk dress spotted in brown, bloused bodice buttoned from waist to under frilled neckline, matching edge of square yoke and hemline of knee-length skirt, padded shoulders, full-length inset sleeves gathered into cuffs, self-fabric tie-belt, hip-level pockets set into side seams. Dark-brown leather sling-back shoes, peep toes, high spike heels. **5** Dark-cream linen jacket flecked with black and brown, single-breasted two-button fastening, narrow lapels, patch pockets, side vents. Black linen tapered trousers, no turn-ups. Cream linen collar-attached shirt. Pink silk tie, black and brown pattern. Black lace-up shoes, perforated detail.

Evening Wear

1 Turquoise satin two-piece evening ensemble: edge-to-edge bolero jacket, outsized collar faced with pintucked grey silk, matching cuffs of full-length bishop sleeves, appliqué of pink and green waterlilies on hem of sleeves, matching hemline of ground-length gathered skirt of dress, fitted strapless bodice, pintucked decoration from central seam. **2** Primrose-yellow silk-taffeta ballgown, fitted and boned bodice, waistline with centre-front point, off-the-shoulder neckline edged with wide frill, central bow trim, matching detail above two-tier frill on hem of elbow-length outsized puffed sleeves, ground-length gathered skirt worn over stiffened petticoats. **3** Gold lamé evening dress, bloused bodice, horizontal tucks forming yoke above bustline, matching detail above hemline of ankle-length gathered skirt, high neckline, padded shoulders, elbow-length sleeves gathered on shoulders and into narrow cuffs on hem, self-fabric tie-belt. Gold kid strap sandals. **4** Black silk-taffeta evening gown, fitted and boned bodice, off-the-shoulder neckline caught up to centre-front neck by self-fabric rouleau band, edge of neckline trimmed with narrow frill to match hemline of ground-length gathered skirt and trim on edge of draped black satin belt, full-length sleeves. **5** White silk-jersey evening dress, low neckline, self-fabric rouleau straps, semi-fitted bodice and ankle-length skirt cut without waist seam; white, silver and crystal bead embroidery from under neckline to knee-level, bunches of white ostrich feathers trim from knee-level to hemline. White satin shoes, pointed toes.

Sports and Leisure Wear

1 Tennis. White knitted-cotton shirt striped in yellow and blue, V-shaped neckline, plain-blue collar matching cuffs of short inset sleeves. White cotton shorts, side-hip pockets. White canvas trainers, white cotton ankle socks. **2** Casual wear. Light-brown leather collarless jacket, fitted upper bodice, horizontal tucks above self-fabric belt to bust-level, asymmetric fastening, padded shoulders, stitched epaulettes, full-length sleeves, stitched cuffs, pockets set into diagonal seams of skirt, top-stitched edges and detail. Brown velvet breeches, knee-level cuffs. Brown wool sweater, outsized polo-neck collar, long sleeves, matching tights. Long brown leather boots, decorative ruching above ankles, almond-shaped toes. **3** Holiday wear. Pale-green two-piece safari suit: unfitted hip-length jacket, single-breasted fastening with press-studs, shirt collar, shaped yoke, epaulettes, button trim; bermuda-length shorts, turn-ups, dark-green leather belt. White cotton T-shirt. Dark-green leather T-strap sandals, openwork detail, crepe soles. **4** Ski wear. Pink rayon and wool mixture two-piece ski suit: jacket zip fastening from hem to under dark-blue collar, matching yoke and upper part of full-length inset sleeves, elasticated inset waistband, hip-level zipped pockets, top-stitched edges and detail; mid-calf-length trousers, elasticated hems. Ski boots. Blue and pink knitted-wool hat worn over pink wool cowl. White ski boots, dark-blue trim. **5** Country wear. Dark-cream cotton-velvet cord jacket, single-breasted fastening, brown suede yoke, padded shoulders, full-length sleeves, gathered on shoulders, flap pockets. Cream, brown and red checked wool mid-calf-length culottes, off-centre knife-pleats, hip-level pockets. Brick-red wool polo-neck sweater flecked with brown. Brown leather pumps.

Accessories

1 White straw hat, wide brim, outsized sunglasses. **2** Dark-brown felt hat, crown with flat top, turned-up brim. **3** Navy-blue straw hat, shallow crown, wide brim. **4** Brown leather sling-back strap sandals, low heels, open toes. **5** Cherry-red felt hat, moulded crown, turned-up brim. **6** Navy-blue and white leather shoes, half-and-half design, almond-shaped toes. **7** White knitted-wool beret, red and black pattern, matching scarf. **8** Green leather step-in shoes, knotted thong detail, low heels. **9** Half-and-half red and navy-blue peep-toe shoes. **10** Beige suede shoes, open sides, narrow strap fastening, peep toes, low semi-wedge heels. **11** Orange-red leather lace-up shoes, flat heels. **12** Brown leather shoes, cream mesh fronts, peep toes, high tapered heels. **13** Brown felt hat, fur trim. **14** Grey leather clutch bag, shaped flap threaded through self-leather strap, top-stitched trim. **15** Dark-red leather handbag, flap, short handle, top-stitched detail. **16** Black leather shoes, high tapered heels, almond-shaped toes. **17** Wine-red shoulder bag, scalloped flap embroidered in gold thread. **18** Lime-green wool beret. **19** Cream leather ankle boots, wide turned-down cuffs. **20** Black leather sling-back shoes, bow trim, high tapered heels. **21** Blue velvet slippers, red quilted silk linings, gold monogram. **22** Brown leather step-in shoes, rounded tongues, self-leather strap trim, top-stitched detail. **23** Black leather boots, self-leather stirrup trim, side-zip fastening. **24** Brown leather step-in shoes, square tongues, inset bands of green and grey over instep. **25** White leather knee-high boots, top-stitched in gold thread on cuffs and above ankle seam, almond-shaped toes, high tapered heels. **26** White leather bag, flap, gold thread embroidery, long adjustable handle.

 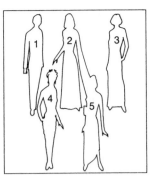 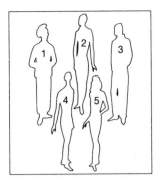 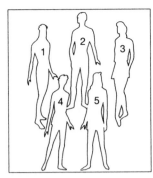

1982 Day Wear

1 Single-breasted beige suede jacket, self-suede button fastening from hemline to under stand collar, deep yoke, padded shoulders, drop head three-quarter-length inset sleeves gathered into narrow cuffs, top-stitched edges and detail, dark-blue leather belt, stepped buckle fastening. Knee-length bright-pink wool gathered skirt. Dark-blue leather strap sandals, high spike heels. **2** Charcoal-grey linen dress, bloused bodice, concealed strap fastening, plain white collar, matching cuffs of full-length inset sleeves, box-pleat detail from padded shoulders to wrists, above-knee-level straight skirt, buckled black leather belt. Black leather strap sandals. **3** Black and white striped knitted-wool three-piece suit: above knee-length edge-to-edge collarless coat, three-quarter-length kimono-style sleeves with seams, edges and hems bound in black; long sweater top, low V-shaped neckline; plain-black above-knee-length straight skirt. Black lacquered-straw hat, high crown, wide straight brim. Black leather shoes, almond-shaped toes, high straight heels. **4** Pale-blue, grey and white striped cotton jacket, single-breasted two-button fastening, narrow lapels, full-length sleeves worn pushed up to elbow-level, piped pockets. Tapered pale-blue cotton trousers, no turn-ups, dark-blue leather belt. Pale-grey cotton collar-attached shirt, concealed strap fastening, single breast patch pocket; red, grey and blue spotted silk bow-tie. Dark-blue leather step-in shoes. **5** Dark-red wool two-piece suit: double-breasted hip-length jacket, notched shawl collar, padded shoulders, full-length inset sleeves, piped pockets; straight-cut trousers, no creases or turn-ups. White silk collarless T-shirt. Black leather strap sandals, high straight heels.

Evening Wear

1 Dark-blue wool and mohair two-piece evening suit: long double-breasted jacket, wide lapels faced in blue silk, matching covered buttons and piped pockets; tapered trousers, no turn-ups. White silk collar-attached shirt, dark-blue velvet bow-tie. Dark-blue leather step-in shoes. **2** Ground-length white silk-chiffon evening dress, layered skirt gathered from base of hip-length white guipure-lace fitted and boned strapless bodice, ground-length white silk-chiffon stole worn across throat to trail at back. White satin shoes. **3** Fine silk-satin evening dress patterned in various purples, oranges and reds, fitted strapless boned bodice horizontally ruched to hip-level at one side. Purple satin strap sandals, ruched fronts, peep toes, ankle straps, high heels. **4** Strapless red silk-jersey cocktail dress, hip-length fitted strapless bodice, gold bead embroidery following lines of low neckline, above-knee-length wrapover draped skirt. Gold kid strap sandals, ankle straps, high heels. **5** Silk-taffeta evening dress, lower part of fitted and boned strapless bodice in dark blue, upper bodice with centre-front split in pale lilac-grey, matching ankle-length skirt, wide sweeping curved slash to knee-level at one side, narrow fuchsia-pink belt trimmed on centre front with outsized bow. Lilac-grey satin shoes, peep toes.

Sports and Leisure Wear

1 Jogging. Pink cotton-jersey two-piece suit: hip-length bloused jacket, large half-circle patch pockets, front-zip fastening from hem to under ribbed charcoal-grey stand collar, matching elasticated ribbing on hem, cuffs of full-length raglan sleeves and cuffs of ankle-length unfitted trousers. White canvas lace-up trainers. **2** Swimwear. Dark-plum-red Lycra swimsuit, low V-shaped neckline formed between wide halter straps, ruched detail at base of side seams above high-cut legs. **3** Casual wear. Pale-yellow knitted-cotton sweater, high round neckline, blue and white striped trim, matching heads of full-length inset sleeves, ribbed cuffs matching hemline. Tapered cream cotton trousers, pleated from waistband, side-hip pockets, wide turn-ups. Cream cotton collar-attached shirt, collar worn open. Dark-cream leather lace-up shoes. **4** Surfing. Black Lycra all-in-one suit, low-cut armholes, wide shoulder straps, Velcro fastenings, V-shaped insert of purple and yellow stripes under low scooped neckline, matching stripes on lower front leg patches, all edges and detail outlined in lilac. **5** Beach wear. White Lycra poolside swimsuit, draped halter straps, deep V-shaped neckline, wrapover above waistline, low back, high-cut legs, self-fabric belt, gold clasp fastening.

Underwear

1 White elasticated-cotton strapless bra, underwired and padded cups, white cotton-lace trim, back fastening. White Lycra pantie-girdle, deep waistband, top-stitched front-firming panel, long legs, fine tuck trim. **2** White knitted-cotton briefs, elasticated waistband, double fabric front panel, Y-shaped stitched seams, high-cut legs. **3** Primrose-yellow silk chemise top, self-fabric rouleau shoulder straps, low scalloped neckline edged with wide panel of embroidered and lace-trimmed white silk-satin, matching hems of wide flared knickers, cut high on side seams, gathers from elasticated waistline. **4** Peach-pink Lycra bra, underwired cups cut in one with adjustable shoulder straps, side padding, wide lace trim, back fastening. Peach-pink silk knickers, flared legs, high cut on side seams, scalloped lace trim, gathers from elasticated waistline. **5** Black silk-satin mini-length slip, panel seams from under fitted cups, inset black embroidered lace under bust, matching trim above low neckline and on flared hemline, adjustable shoulder straps.

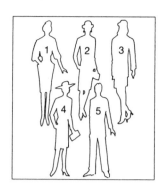 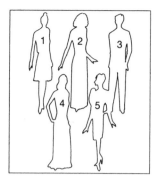 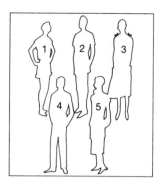 

1983 Day Wear

1 Green silk blouse patterned with self-colour satin leaves, blouse bodice draped from button fastening on padded shoulders, three-quarter-length inset sleeves gathered on shoulders and into cuffs. Above-knee-length dark-green wool skirt, pockets set into hip-level pleats, black suede belt. Black leather shoes, almond-shaped toes. **2** Brown, grey and black striped wool coat-dress, double-breasted fastening, pointed lapels and collar, side panel seams, breast pockets, hip-level pockets set into side seams, padded shoulders, full-length inset sleeves. Grey felt hat, high crown, self-colour petersham band, curled brim. **3** Three-quarter-length camel-coloured wool coat, double-breasted fastening, wide lapels, long collar, hip-level welt pockets, full-length two-piece sleeves, padded shoulders, top-stitched edges and detail. Emerald-green wool polo-neck sweater-dress, straight above-knee-length skirt. Navy-blue leather gloves and knee-high fitted boots, pointed toes, high heels, side-zip fastening.
4 Cherry-red wool two-piece suit: short fitted jacket, double-breasted fastening, wide lapels, padded shoulders, full-length inset sleeves, button trim above hem; straight above-knee-length skirt, pleats from waist. Black silk blouse, high round neckline. Black straw hat, shallow crown, self-colour petersham band, wide brim. Large black leather clutch bag. Cherry-red leather sling-back shoes, almond-shaped toes, high heels. **5** Cream linen-tweed two-piece suit: long double-breasted jacket, inset half-belt from side seam to side seam, large patch pockets, wide shoulder, top-stitched edges and detail; tapered trousers, turn-ups. Pale-cream linen collar-attached shirt. Pink silk tie and pocket handkerchief. Light-brown leather lace-up brogues.

Evening Wear

1 Royal-blue acetate-jersey cocktail dress, bloused bodice, fine self-fabric rouleau shoulder straps, low scalloped neckline edged in tiny gold beads to match centre-front seam, above-knee-length accordion-pleated skirt, mock ties from side waist. Gold kid strap sandals.
2 Fuchsia-pink silk-chiffon evening dress, pleated halter cross-over straps form upper part of fitted and draped bodice, matching shaped hip sash and front fall, multilayered ground-length full skirt. **3** Cream silk evening jacket, single-breasted one-button fastening, double-breasted lapels faced with cream satin, piped pockets. Tapered black wool trousers, no turn-ups. White silk shirt, attached wing collar. Black silk-satin bow-tie. Black kid lace-up shoes. **4** Gold lamé evening dress, fitted bias-cut bodice, drapery from central knot over wired cups, draped shoulder straps and hip sash with waterfall ends, ground-length bias-cut skirt. **5** Cocktail dress, royal-blue silk-velvet bodice and above-knee-length straight skirt cut without waist seam, upper bodice draped in black silk-taffeta, wide off-the-shoulder low V-shaped neckline, point trimmed with large black taffeta bow, outsized puff sleeves gathered into deep cuffs. Black silk shoes, pointed toes, high straight heels.

Sports and Leisure Wear

1 Tennis. Waist-length white cotton blouse, low square neckline, cap sleeves, top-stitched edges. White cotton-poplin tailored shorts, flared legs, turn-ups. White knitted-cotton socks, white canvas lace-up sports shoes. **2** Tennis. White knitted-cotton shirt; collar, strap fastening and short inset sleeves in dark-blue knitted cotton. White cotton-poplin tailored shorts, buttoned waistband, side-hip pockets, red and blue logo on outside leg above hemline at one side. White knitted-cotton socks, white trainers. **3** Holiday wear. Yellow and white striped cotton sundress, straight hip-length bodice with horizontal stripes, straight neckline bound with vertically striped band, matching below-knee-length gathered skirt, large horizontally-striped patch pockets, narrow self-fabric shoulder straps, bow-ties on shoulders. Yellow canvas pumps, decorative laces. **4** Golf. Beige and cream knitted-wool collarless cardigan, single-breasted fastening, ribbed edges matching cuffs of full-length inset sleeves and edges of three patch pockets. Light-brown wool tapered trousers, side-hip pockets, turn-ups. Cream, brown and green checked brushed-cotton shirt. Brown leather step-in shoes. **5** Country wear. Olive-green knitted-wool two-piece jumper suit: long top, deep ribbed hem, cable-stitched front panel, matching detail above ribbed hems of full-length inset sleeves, cable repeated on dropped shoulderline, padded shoulders; straight mid-calf-length skirt. Nut-brown wool scarf, fringed ends, matching pull-on knitted-wool hat with ribbed edge. Matching wool tights. Dark-brown-green leather lace-up shoes, almond-shaped toes, flat heels.

Accessories

1 White leather shoes, blue striped trim on toes and low wedge heels. **2** Red felt hat, wide brim. **3** Cream leather shoes, brown trim, almond-shaped toes, tapered heels. **4** Brown mock-snakeskin boots, ruched above ankles, low tapered heels. **5** Grey leather shoes, low wedge heels. **6** Asymmetric sling-back red leather sandals, wide front strap, black braid trim, peep toes, high spike heels. **7** Black leather shoes, high straight heels. **8** Beige leather sandals, single front strap, ankle strap, buckle fastening, tapered heels. **9** Yellow leather shoes, asymmetric open sides, ruched fronts, open toes, low wedge heels. **10** Black knitted-wool pull-on hat, stalk trim. **11** Tan leather boots, ruched on ankles above decorative seaming, mock-snakeskin inset collar, low heels. **12** Green strap sandals, low wedge heels. **13** Navy-blue leather shoes, fronts trimmed white, matching sling-back straps. **14** Gold-brown bag, flap, stud fastening, long strap. **15** Black leather strap sandals, high tapered heels. **16** Maroon-red canvas bag, double flap, stud fastening, long handle. **17** Yellow straw hat, low crown, flat top, blue ribbon band, wide flat brim. **18** Knee-high black leather boots, ruched on ankles, low tapered heels. **19** Off-white plastic leather-look clutch bag, suede-look trim. **20** Unstructured white felt hat, high crown, black band, wide brim. **21** Brown leather step-in shoes, grey and tan inset trim. **22** Black leather step-in shoes, mock tie, fringed ends. **23** Dark-grey leather step-in shoes, self-leather crossed strap detail. **24** Black leather step-in shoes, high tongues, bar straps, cut-out detail. **25** Black leather shoes, laced through metal rings, decorative seaming. **26** Green leather moccasins, self-leather laces. **27** Ankle-high white trainers, Velcro fastenings.

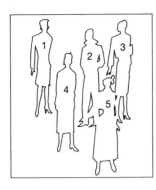
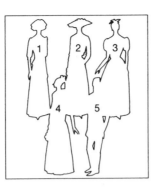
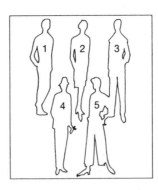
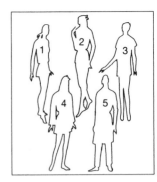

1984 Day Wear

1 Grey, brown and black checked wool- and silk-tweed jacket, double-breasted fastening, wide lapels, padded shoulders, full-length inset sleeves, hip-level piped pockets. Above-knee-length straight skirt, centre-front unpressed knife-pleat. Black leather shoes, pointed toes, high heels. **2** Short black leather jacket, zip fastening to under collar with decorative ring-and-strap fastening, matching epaulettes, sleeves gathered into cuffs, V-shaped tucked seam from centre-shoulder to centre-front of hip band, diagonal piped pockets. Fitted blue denim jeans, top-stitched edges and detail. White cotton T-shirt. Black leather cowboy boots, pointed toes, stacked heels. **3** Collarless yellow crepe dress, blue and grey random pattern, box-pleated bloused bodice, centre-front button fastening to under high round neckline, padded shoulders, inset sleeves gathered into deep cuffs, knee-length skirt, unpressed pleats over hips, centre-front box-pleat, self-fabric belt gathered through ring. Grey leather bag, matching shoes, pointed toes, high stiletto heels. **4** Beige wool three-piece suit: long unfitted edge-to-edge jacket, wide lapels, full-length kimono-style sleeves, wide turned-back cuffs, padded shoulders, top-stitched edges and detail; collarless waistcoat, pointed edges knotted to form fastening; mid-calf-length skirt, hip-level pockets in side seams. Cream knitted-silk-tweed collarless sweater. Cream wool beret. Brown and beige leather lace-up shoes. **5** Cream wool dress flecked with navy-blue, bloused bodice and full-length cuffed sleeves cut in one piece, draped cowl neckline, padded shoulders, gathered skirt, side-hip pockets, navy-blue woven plastic belt, large round buckle. Blue and white patterned turban. Navy-blue plastic strap sandals.

Wedding Wear

1 Pink silk-moiré taffeta three-piece wedding suit: collarless fitted jacket, single-breasted fastening from waist seam to under bustline, wide neckline split to show low neckline of blouse, padded shoulders, three-quarter-length inset sleeves gathered into narrow cuffs, short peplum; ground-length flared skirt, centre-front mock-button fastening. Pillbox hat matching suit fabric, short silk-tulle veil. **2** Ivory-white silk-jersey wedding dress, four tiers of wrapover curved panels, top-stitched edges, fitted bodice, slashed neckline, padded shoulders, full-length inset sleeves fitted from wrist to elbow, ground-length flared skirt. Layered ivory-white silk-organdie crownless hat trimmed with silk flowers. **3** White silk-satin wedding dress, fitted bodice draped from centre-front padded motif to follow lines of wide V-shaped off-the-shoulder neckline, padded motif and drapery repeated on the puffed sleeves, bead edging matching neckline and pointed waist seam, lace undersleeves, ground-length gathered skirt worn over stiffened petticoats. Beaded white satin headdress, long silk-tulle veil. Long white stretch-satin gloves. **4** Pale-cream fine wool wedding dress, unfitted hip-length bodice, diagonal tucked decoration, high round neckline, padded shoulders, full-length inset sleeves, gathered on head, buttons from wrist to below elbow-level, ground-length skirt gathered from hip seam. Silk flower headdress, long silk-tulle veil. **5** Three-piece morning suit: single-breasted dark-grey wool tailcoat, single-button fastening, double-breasted lapels; light-grey wool collarless waistcoat; charcoal-grey and black striped wool tapered trousers, no turn-ups. White cotton shirt worn with wing collar and silver-grey and black patterned silk cravat. Black leather lace-up shoes.

Sports and Leisure Wear

1 Exercise wear. Sleeveless blue and white striped cotton vest, low scooped neckline. Navy-blue cotton-jersey trousers, tapered legs, pockets set into top-stitched side seams, pleats from buttoned waistband, pintucked central creases. White trainers. **2** Country wear. Burnt-orange wool three-piece suit: long collarless coat-jacket, single-breasted fastening with suede-covered buttons, padded shoulders, full-length inset sleeves, large hip-level patch pockets; sweater with low V-shaped neckline; straight above-knee-length skirt, top-stitched edges and detail. Orange stretch-wool turban. Long tan leather boots, ruched at ankle, almond-shaped toes, low tapered heels. **3** Casual wear. Grey knitted-wool sweater, low V-shaped neckline, deep ribbed edge, matching hemline and short cap sleeves. Blue-grey wool tapered trousers, side-hip pockets, no turn-ups. Green, turquoise and grey checked wool collar-attached shirt. Black leather step-in shoes. **4** Golf. Brown and brick-red checked wool single-breasted jacket, wide lapels, brown suede collar, matching yoke and covered button, large patch pockets, padded shoulders, full-length inset sleeves. Cream wool shirt, flat wrapover collar above mock boiled-front. Dark-cream wool trousers, wide waistband, brown suede belt, buttoned loops, tapered legs, wide turn-ups. Brown suede gloves, matching step-in shoes, fringe trim. **5** Holiday wear. Waist-length yellow cotton jacket, asymmetric fastening, double-breasted on hemline, single-breasted on stand collar, padded shoulders, three-quarter-length inset cuffed sleeves, box-pleat decoration. Ankle-length black cotton trousers, deep waistband, button fastening, wide legs, off-centre knife-pleats. Black leather strap sandals, low heels.

Underwear and Negligee

1 Lilac polyester-satin strapless camiknickers, elasticated neckline edged with wide scalloped lace to match front panel and hems of straight-cut legs, elasticated drawstring waist, crotch fastening. **2** Royal-blue polyester-satin camiknickers, low V-shaped neckline formed by cross-over bloused bodice, elasticated waist seam, asymmetric overskirt with curved edge, high-cut legs, self-fabric rouleau shoulder straps, all main edges trimmed with self-colour polyester lace. **3** Hip-length pale-pink silk nightshirt, short sleeves cut in one with body, narrow pale-blue stitched cuffs, matching collar and short pointed wrapover front panel, hemline curves up to side seams, top-stitched edges and detail. **4** Pale-blue shiny acetate and nylon kimono-inspired dressing gown, patterned with random dull self-colour stripes and bright-blue flowers, wrapover front, wide self-fabric bindings, matching tie-belt, padded shoulders, full-length kimono-style sleeves gathered into narrow cuffs, mini-length skirts. **5** Red polyester-satin dressing gown, wrapover front, wide shawl collar, full-length inset sleeves worn pushed up to elbow-level, self-fabric tie-belt, large hip-level patch pockets, top-stitched edges and detail. Black polyester-satin pyjama trousers.

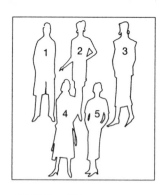
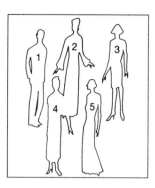
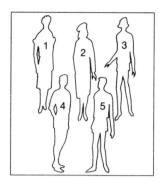
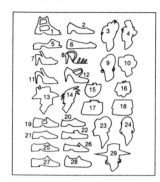

1985 Day Wear

1 Black showerproofed cotton topcoat, single-breasted fastening, inset sleeves, strap-and-button trim, matching epaulettes, saddle-stitched trim. Double-breasted dark-salmon-pink cotton jacket, narrow lapels, piped pockets. Grey and blue checked cotton tapered trousers, no turn-ups. Grey cotton collar-attached shirt, gold and blue striped polyester tie. Navy-blue step-in shoes. **2** Grey knitted-wool two-piece jumper suit: long unfitted top, wide neckline, padded shoulders, deep inset sleeves, button trim on top-stitched side seams above hemline, matching detail on shoulders, above-knee-length straight skirt. Black leather shoes. **3** Edge-to-edge mustard-yellow and black flecked wool-tweed jacket, padded shoulders, wide cap sleeves, high stand collar, triangular-shaped patch pockets, top-stitched edges and detail. Hip-length collarless black wool shirt, full-length cuffed sleeves. Mid-calf-length mustard-yellow wool straight skirt, inset front panel. Black ribbed-wool tights, black leather pumps, flat heels. **4** Camel-coloured wool coat, wrapover front, self-fabric tie-belt, wide lapels, large collar, padded shoulders, full-length raglan sleeves, split cuffs, large patch pockets, top-stitched edges and detail. Black and terracotta checked wool single-breasted jacket, wide lapels, flap pockets. Black wool polo-neck sweater. Black wool straight mini-skirt. Black leather shoes, almond-shaped toes, medium-high tapered heels. **5** Grey and white striped polyester and cotton dress, bloused bodice, yoke, decorative front panel, padded shoulders, short inset sleeves, stitched cuffs, low V-shaped neckline, plain white collar, black satin bow trim, mid-calf-length panelled skirt, box-pleat hem, side-hip pockets. Grey leather lace-up shoes.

Evening Wear

1 Black wool and silk three-piece evening suit: single-breasted jacket, single-button fastening, double-breasted lapels faced with black silk, piped pockets; collarless single-breasted waistcoat, straight hemline; tapered trousers, black silk braid trim on outside seam, no turn-ups. White silk shirt, attached wing collar; black silk bow-tie. Black patent-leather lace-up shoes. **2** Royal-blue silk-jersey evening dress, draped bodice and ground-length skirt cut without waist seam, wide and low sweetheart neckline, padded shoulders, full-length bishop-style sleeves gathered into deep cuffs. **3** Bright-green silk-chiffon cocktail dress, draped and ruched from low neckline of boned strapless bodice to hemline of mini-length skirt. Long black stretch-satin gloves. Black satin sling-back strap sandals, high stiletto heels. **4** Ink-blue silk-jersey evening dress, bias-cut wrapover bodice and skirt draped from self-fabric knot at base of low asymmetric neckline, hemline below-knee-length at front and ankle-length at back, short inset sleeves, padded shoulders. Gold kid strap sandals, asymmetric sling-back straps, high spike heels. **5** Fuchsia-pink silk evening dress, low neckline, fitted strapless boned bodice, draped and ruched from central seam to low hip-level, ground-length skirt flared from hip-level, godet of unpressed pleats centre-front hip-level.

Sports and Leisure Wear

1 Tennis. Hip-length white knitted-cotton unfitted T-shaped top, short wide sleeves, narrow turned-back cuffs, flat peter-pan collar, offset strap with concealed fastening, hip-level band. Knee-length white cotton skirt, unpressed knife-pleats from waist. White stretch-cotton towelling headband. White canvas step-in shoes, elasticated sides, rubber soles, round toes, short white cotton socks. **2** Holiday wear. Pale-grey knitted-cotton T-shaped sweater-dress, wide round neckline, top-stitched facings above manufacturer's logo, padded shoulders, full-length sleeves cut in one with unfitted bodice, top-stitched hems, large hip-level patch pockets, top-stitched cuffs, straight knee-length skirt, no waist seam. White cotton peaked cap. White leather step-in strap sandals, round toes, flat heels. **3** Beach wear. Hip-length pink knitted-cotton sleeveless vest, top-stitched low neckline, matching deep armholes, printed logo across chest, top-stitched hem. Pink knitted-cotton shorts, wide legs, top-stitched hems. **4** Tennis. Collarless white knitted-cotton shirt, high round neckline, top-stitched edge, short cloth-bound fly fastening, two-button fastening, full-length inset sleeves worn pushed up to elbow-level, dropped shoulder seam. White cotton shorts, short legs, curved wrapover side seams, inset pockets, fly front, top-stitched edges and detail. White knitted-cotton ankle socks, white canvas tennis shoes, rubber soles. **5** Beach wear. Waist-length yellow knitted-cotton vest, wide neckline, top-stitched edges, matching deep armholes and hemline. Blue cotton-poplin shorts, pleats from waist, side-hip pockets, short legs, top-stitched.

Accessories

1 Yellow leather strap sandals, double strap-and-buckle fastening, open sides, flat heels. **2** Brown suede shoes, low heels. **3** Red cotton-towelling turban. **4** White Lycra turban, large bow trim. **5** Tan leather mules, open toes, low stacked heels. **6** Red leather shoes, low wedge heels. **7** Navy-blue sling-back shoes, tapered heels. **8** Green leather strap sandals, asymmetric sling-back straps, stiletto heels. **9** Red wool beret. **10** Cream felt hat, high crown, turned-back brim. **11** Grey leather sling-back shoes, black patent-leather toecaps and heels. **12** Beige suede shoes, asymmetric cross straps, tapered heels. **13** White felt hat, high crown, draped black taffeta band and bow, wide brim. **14** Brimless grey felt hat, black feather trim. **15** Black silk evening bag, gold clasp fastening and trim. **16** Cream satin shell-shaped evening bag, embroidered pearl beads, clasp fastening. **17** Black suede clutch bag, flap with central ruched detail. **18** Brown leather clutch bag, green and black inset trim. **19** Brown leather sandals, open sides, strap-and-buckle fastening, perforated fronts. **20** Navy-blue canvas step-in beach shoes, rope soles. **21** Grey leather step-in shoes, top-stitched detail, button trim. **22** Black leather step-in shoes, top-stitched detail, button trim. **23** Pale-grey felt hat, large crown, wide black band, narrow turned-up brim. **24** Red wool fitted hat, turned-back brim. **25** Brown leather lace-up shoes, top-stitched edges. **26** White leather sandals, strap fronts, strap-and-buckle fastening. **27** White trainers, blue side flashes. **28** White trainers, red striped flashes. **29** Black felt hat, high flat crown, wide brim.

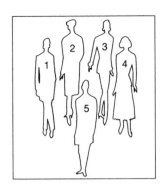

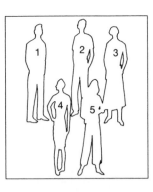
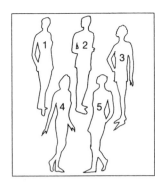

1986 Day Wear

1 Oatmeal and beige silk-tweed collarless jacket, asymmetric two-button fastening on hip-level below wide self-binding of front edges and neckline, padded shoulders, full-length inset sleeves, button trim on wrists, hip-level welt pockets. Narrow dark-beige wool-and-silk mixture trousers. Cream silk collarless blouse, wrapover neckline, self-fabric binding, button trim. Beige leather strap sandals. **2** Below-knee-length camel-coloured wool coat, double-breasted fastening from hip-level to under wide-set collar, padded shoulders, full-length raglan sleeves, rounded split seams at wrist-level, hip-level bound pockets, top-stitched edges and detail. Black leather beret, matching shoes, almond-shaped toes, tapered heels. Beige leather gloves. **3** Charcoal-grey wool two-piece suit: hip-length fitted single-breasted jacket, two-button fastening, rounded wide lapels, matching collar and cuffs of full-length inset sleeves, padded shoulders, below-waist-level welt pockets; above-knee-level straight skirt, hem rounded up to centre-front. Black leather sling-back shoes, almond-shaped toes, medium-high tapered heels. **4** Short fitted collarless wool jacket, all-over pattern of blues, greys and pinks, asymmetric fastening from waist-level to above bustline, padded shoulders, full-length sleeves gathered into armholes, top-stitched edges and detail. Accordion-pleated blue and grey wool mid-calf-length skirt. Wine-red leather boots, almond-shaped toes. **5** Knee-length camel-coloured wool overcoat, single-breasted one-button fastening, wide lapels, padded shoulders, hip-level welt pockets. Black wool tapered trousers, no turn-ups. Dark-beige wool collar-attached shirt. Grey and blue striped silk tie. Black leather gloves; matching shoes, strap-and-buckle trim.

Evening Wear

1 Silver-grey silk-chiffon strapless blouse, blue and pink flocked-velvet flower pattern, boned bodice wrapover drapery to large self-fabric bow on side-hip. Navy-blue ankle-length straight skirt. Side split from hemline to knee-level at one side. Navy-blue silk shoes, almond-shaped toes, low tapered heels. **2** Black silk two-piece suit: double-breasted jacket, wide lapels faced in satin, matching covered buttons, piped pockets, tapered trousers, no turn-ups. Red silk collar-attached shirt worn without tie, matching red silk handkerchief in breast pocket. Black suede lace-up shoes. **3** Yellow polyester-chiffon cocktail dress, spotted in red, fitted and draped high-length strapless bodice, red velvet ribbon belt, bow-tie on one side, gathered three-tier skirt to above knee-length, worn over stiffened petticoats. Red satin shoes, pointed toes, stiletto heels.
4 Bright-pink, crinkle-pleated silk-satin evening dress, fitted bodice, padded shoulders, short cap sleeves, black satin polo collar, matching wide belt, flared ankle-length skirt. Above-elbow-length black stretch-satin gloves. Black satin shoes, pointed toes, high stiletto heels. **5** Smoke-blue and charcoal-grey striped silk blouse, fitted bodice, off-the-shoulder neckline, cuffed edge. Above-knee-length cerise-pink silk-taffeta gathered skirt, worn over navy-blue silk petticoats with scalloped hems, wide buckled belt in matching fabric. Navy-blue satin shoes, pointed toes, high stiletto heels.

Sports and Leisure Wear

1 Casual wear. Pale-turquoise unstructured cotton jacket, two-button single-breasted fastening, wide lapels, patch pockets. Cream cotton tapered trousers, side-hip pockets, no creases or turn-ups. Turquoise knitted-cotton collar-attached shirt. Light-brown leather shoes, strap-and-buckle fastening. **2** Exercise wear. Pale-grey knitted-cotton T-shirt. Grey knitted-cotton jogging pants, gathered from elasticated waistband, mock fly opening, side-hip pockets, tapered legs gathered into elasticated band at ankle-level. White trainers, Velcro strap fastenings. **3** Country wear. Brown wool-tweed single-breasted jacket, wide lapels, brown velvet collar, patch pockets. Mid-calf-length light-brown wool skirt, unpressed pleats from waist, centre-front inverted box-pleat, brown leather belt. Collarless knitted-wool waistcoat, brown, black and mustard pattern, single-breasted fastening, plain brown ribbed edging. Cream and brown checked brushed-cotton shirt, attached collar worn open; brown and black patterned silk scarf. Dark-brown leather boots, front lacing, almond-shaped toes, flat heels. **4** Beach wear. Blue and white printed cotton two-piece beach suit: strapless bra top, fabric draped over wired cups and through centre-front knot of fabric; knee-length wrapover skirt, loop-and-button fastening at one side of curved waistband, asymmetric drapery from waistband to side hip. **5** Exercise wear. Royal-blue cotton-velour two-piece leisure suit: hip-length unfitted jacket, zip fastening from hipband to under pointed collar, padded shoulders, inset sleeves gathered into stretch cuffs, patch pockets set into top-stitched panel seams; unfitted pants gathered from waist and into stretch cuffs on ankles. White canvas pumps, elasticated front panels, rubber soles.

Underwear

1 White Lycra bra, underwired, formed and seamed cups, light underpadding, lace trim, adjustable shoulder straps, back fastening. White cotton and Lycra briefs, high-cut legs, cross-over side panels, double fabric front V-shaped panel, lace trim.
2 White cotton-polyester boxer shorts, patterned with outsized red, blue and yellow spots, elasticated waistband, open fly fronts, wide legs, side seams split above hemline. **3** Fine cream cotton and Lycra-lace mini-slip, low scalloped neckline, matching hemline, cream satin rouleau shoulder straps and underarm bindings, flesh-coloured briefs, high-cut legs on sides to elasticated waistband. **4** Black Lycra and Lycra-lace body suit, bra top draped with plain black Lycra from centre-front under bust to above waist-level on sides to low back, low neckline, narrow Lycra shoulder straps, bow trim, main body in stretch-Lycra-lace, high-cut legs trimmed with fine lace edging, matching under arm to back, fastening under crotch. **5** White stretch-Lycra-lace bodysuit, deep plunge neckline to waist-level, scalloped edges, infilled with plain white Lycra, matching adjustable shoulder straps and underarm binding, high-cut legs, fastening under crotch.

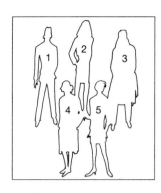

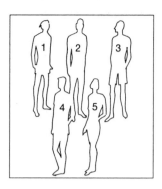

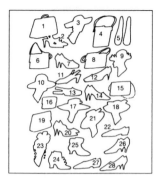

1987 Day Wear

1 Charcoal-grey and blue striped wool two-piece suit: single-breasted fitted jacket, single-button fastening, wide lapels, padded shoulders, full-length inset sleeves, flap pockets; tapered trousers, pleats from waistband, blue leather belt. Knitted charcoal-grey wool polo-neck sweater. Brimless charcoal-grey wool hat. Black leather boots. **2** Dark-grey two-piece suit: waist-length single-breasted jacket, two-button fastening, wide stitched band around hem, brooch trim on centre-front, narrow lapels, padded shoulders, full-length inset sleeves gathered into cuffs; high waistband and mini-length skirt cut in one piece, vertical panel seams. Black leather shoes, medium-high tapered heels. **3** Below-knee-length sage-green wool overcoat, wrapover front, self-fabric tie-belt, wide lapels with buttonholes, large collar, raglan sleeves, buttoned flaps at wrist-level, flap pockets, top-stitched edges and detail. Green and brown flecked wool-tweed single-breasted jacket, patch pockets. Dark-green-brown wool tapered trousers, pleats from waist, side-hip pockets, no turn-ups. Cream cotton collar-attached shirt, buttoned-down pointed collar. Brown wool tie. Brown leather lace-up shoes. **4** Red knitted-wool three-piece suit: below-knee-length edge-to-edge coat, roll collar, padded shoulders, sleeves gathered at wrists, large hip-level patch pockets; hip-length polo-neck sweater, self-fabric buckled belt; straight mini-length skirt. Dark-grey wool tights. Deep-red suede lace-up shoes, ridged thick soles, flat heels. **5** Scarlet wool-jersey mini-dress, high round neckline, facings top-stitched to match cuffs of three-quarter-length sleeves and inset seam, padded shoulders, black patent-leather hip-level belt. Black patent-leather sling-back shoes.

Wedding Wear

1 White silk-jersey wedding dress, fitted bodice and ground-length flared skirt cut without waist seam, upper bodice draped with self-fabric cross-over panel, white silk-organdie off-the-shoulder collar. Hair decorated with fresh flowers. Full-length stretch-silk gloves. **2** Pale-cream silk-jersey wedding dress, strapless bloused bodice, ground-length flared skirt, transparent cream silk bloused overbodice patterned with cream flocked-velvet flower pattern, slashed neckline, cap sleeves, self-fabric sash draped over hips, gathered front panel to hemline of dress. Cream silk bow hair decoration. Three-quarter-length stretch-fabric gloves. **3** White silk three-piece wedding suit: short edge-to-edge jacket, curved front edges, grown-on collar, padded shoulder, full-length leg-of-mutton-style sleeves; chemise blouse, straight neckline; ankle-length flared skirt, wide waistband, large bow trim on centre-front. **4** White silk wedding dress, fitted bodice, low scooped neckline, full-length leg-of-mutton sleeves, lace trim above and below bow-trimmed waist-belt, matching edging on long detachable train, ground-length straight skirt. Long silk-tulle veil scattered with silk flowers. **5** Ivory-white silk wedding dress, hip-length fitted bodice, self-fabric covered buttons on centre-front from under bow trim on bustline to pointed hip seam, off-the-shoulder neckline and cap sleeves with scalloped edges which match hemline of full-length gathered skirt. Full-length stretch-fabric gloves.

Sports and Leisure Wear

1 Tennis. Mini-length white polyester-cotton dress, semi-fitted bodice and flared skirt cut without waist seam, high round neckline, collar split at front to red braid trim above bustline, matching braid trim on hip-level asymmetric patch pockets and armhole bindings. White cotton socks, white canvas tennis shoes. **2** Jogging. Light-blue knitted-cotton vest, high round neckline, cut-away armholes and hemline with top-stitched edges and seams. Black canvas running shoes. **3** Beach wear. Yellow polyester and cotton shorts, orange stripes set into side panels, matching inside legs and buttoned waistband. **4** Tennis. White knitted-cotton shirt, pointed collar, strap fastening, short inset sleeves, stitched cuffs, multicolour printed geometric pattern across chest. White cotton tailored shorts, waistband with adjustable buttoned side straps, short legs split on side seams above hemline, side-hip pockets lined in blue. White cotton socks patterned with fine blue stripes and manufacturer's logo, white canvas tennis shoes. **5** Beach wear. Gold Lycra one-piece swimsuit, bra top moulded and seamed, underwired cups cut in one with wide shoulder straps, high-cut legs, top-stitched edges and seams.

Accessories

1 Yellow ostrich leather bag, front flap, strap-and-clasp fastening, short handle. **2** Beige leather sling-back shoes, high vamps, cut-away front, high tapered heels. **3** Natural straw hat, blue band. **4** Red leather bucket-shaped bag, strap-and-stud fastening, long handle, top-stitched trim. **5** Tan leather step-in shoes, tassel trim, round toes, flat heels. **6** Cream leather shoulder bag, green and brown trim, long handle. **7** Brown leather shoes, high tapered heels. **8** Grey leather shoulder bag, blue and red trim, long handle. **9** Wine-red felt hat, self-felt leaves in brim. **10** Black felt hat, high crown, draped white silk band, wide brim. **11** Black leather sling-back shoes, medium-high tapered heels. **12** Black leather shoes, red suede shaped inset, stiletto heels. **13** Beige suede sling-back shoes, high vamps, flat heels. **14** Red leather shoes, silver inset stripe above heels, matching toecaps and tapered heels. **15** Black quilted-leather shoulder bag, chain handle. **16** Brown crocodile clutch bag. **17** White straw hat, shallow crown, black band, wide brim. **18** Cream straw hat, shallow crown, red band, matching edges of wide brim and bow trim. **19** Dark-grey leather clutch bag, flap, two strap-and-stud fastenings. **20** Black suede shoes, scalloped edges, tapered heels. **21** White straw hat, high crown, flat top, petersham band and bow, wide brim. **22** Brown leather step-in shoes, strap-and-button trim, elasticated sides, flat heels. **23** Red velvet hair decoration, petersham bow trim. **24** Red suede ankle boots, trimmed self-suede bows, louis heels. **25** Black leather lace-up ankle boots, fake-fur trim, louis heels. **26** Black leather elastic-sided ankle boots, medium-high tapered heels. **27** Tan leather pumps, flat heels. **28** Black leather shoes, petersham bow trim.

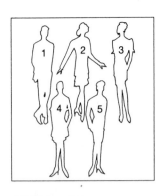
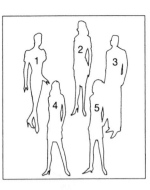
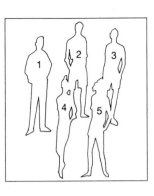
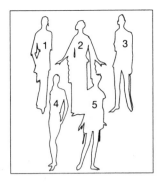

1988 Day Wear

1 Black and blue-grey checked wool-tweed jacket, single-breasted fastening, narrow lapels, flap pockets. Yellow knitted-wool collarless cardigan, single-breasted button fastening, welt pockets. Blue denim tapered jeans, side-hip pockets, top-stitched edges and seams. Pale-blue cotton collar-attached shirt. Red and blue patterned silk tie. Black leather lace-up ankle boots. **2** Brown and beige checked-pattern linen jacket, single-breasted concealed fastening, hip-level button trim, high round neckline, padded shoulders, full-length inset sleeves, button trim on wrists, hip-level piped pockets. Two-tier mini-length pleated linen skirt, brown and beige leaf pattern. Brown leather shoes, almond-shaped toes, tapered heels. **3** White cotton dress, navy-blue spot pattern, bloused bodice, padded shoulders, short puffed sleeves, knot trim, high round neckline bound in plain red, matching pleated belt and mock underskirt, above-knee-length straight skirt. Navy-blue leather shoes, pointed patent-leather toecaps. **4** Black and white checked linen collarless jacket, fitted bodice, edge-to-edge, double loop-and-button fastening, outsized lapels, padded shoulders, inset sleeves, button trim, bias-cut skirts, waterfall at back to above hemline of straight black linen skirt, matching black linen blouse. White leather sling-back shoes, black patent-leather toecaps. **5** Cream linen fitted single-breasted jacket, light-brown pattern, single-button fastening, narrow rounded lapels and collar, matching edges of short skirts and welt pockets, padded shoulders, inset sleeves, button trim. Straight plain cream linen above-knee-length skirt, matching blouse with low sweetheart neckline. Brown leather shoes.

Evening Wear

1 Bright-pink Lycra mini-length dress, fitted and panelled bodice and skirt cut in one piece without waist seam, low off-the-shoulder neckline, draped taffeta stole collar. Black satin shoes, pointed toes, high stiletto heels. **2** Black silk-jersey mini-length dress, wrapover and draped fitted bodice, matching off-the-shoulder neckline, three-quarter-length sleeves and above-knee-length wrapover skirt. Black satin shoes, pointed toes, high stiletto heels. **3** Dark-blue wool and silk two-piece evening suit: double-breasted jacket, long shawl collar faced with dark-blue silk to match covered buttons and piped pockets; tapered trousers, braided outside seams, no turn-ups. White cotton shirt, attached wing collar, concealed fastening. Dark-blue silk bow-tie. Black patent-leather lace-up shoes. **4** Gold lace mini-length dress, fitted bodice, low rounded square neckline bound with gold-coloured satin, matching fitted underdress, full-length unlined inset sleeves, scalloped hems, matching hemline of fitted skirt. Gold kid shoes, pointed toes, high stiletto heels. **5** Royal-blue Lycra strapless mini-length dress, tight skirt and fitted bodice ruched from hemline to under bust, pink lace blouse, collarless neckline bound with pink satin to match hems of full-length inset sleeves, padded shoulders. Royal-blue suede sling-back shoes, high vamps, pointed toes, low heels.

Sports and Leisure Wear

1 Casual wear. Hip-length blue denim jacket, single-breasted button fastening from hipband to under shirt collar, full-length cuffed sleeves, dropped shoulderline, patch pockets under yoke seam, top-stitched edges and detail. Tapered blue denim jeans, side-hip pockets, top-stitched edges and detail. Black knitted-wool cardigan, front-zip fastening. Pale-blue knitted-cotton shirt, small collar, short strap fastening. White trainers. **2** Holiday wear. Fine beige cotton-denim shirt, buttoned collar points, buttoned-strap fastening, full-length sleeves rolled to elbow-level, two breast patch pockets, buttoned flaps, box-pleat detail, narrow shoulder yoke, top-stitched edges and detail. Dark-beige denim tailored knee-length shorts, red leather belt threaded through wide waistband. Dark-blue knitted-cotton sweater, long sleeves tied around hips. Blue canvas lace-up shoes, rubber soles and heels. **3** Beach wear. Multicolour floral patterned cotton knee-length shorts, elasticated waistband. **4** Cycling. Cropped black Lycra top, low scooped neckline, cut-away armholes. Knee-length black Lycra fitted shorts, top-stitched edges. Black leather pumps, round toes, flat heels. **5** Beach wear. Two-piece cotton and Lycra bikini set: mini bra top, small triangular cups, bicolour bright-yellow and royal-blue, narrow rouleau securing band under bust, matching halter straps; briefs with high-cut legs, bright-yellow front panel, royal-blue side panels.

Underwear and Negligee

1 White cotton broderie-anglaise three-piece sleep suit: long edge-to-edge jacket, pointed scalloped front edges which match edges of three-quarter-length flared inset sleeves, hems of self-fabric tie-belt and low neckline of hip-length camisole top, concealed front fastening; full-length trousers flared from knee-level. Green kid slippers, green silk pompon trim. **2** Oyster silk-satin negligee, wrapover front, fastening on side-hip with self-fabric ties, collarless neckline and front edges trimmed with self-colour scalloped-edge lace, matching three-quarter-length trailing sleeves, set into dropped shoulderline, ankle-length flared skirts. **3** Pale-blue satin two-piece underwear set: cropped camisole top, front fastening with self-fabric-covered buttons to under low V-shaped neckline, lace trim, shaping in under bust seams, cut-away armholes; short hipster knickers, flared legs split on curved side seams above hemline. **4** Cream knitted-thermal-cotton two-piece underwear suit, waist-length wrapover top, permanent side fastening above ribbed waist, low neckline piped with cream satin, full-length inset sleeves, ribbed hems, matching ankle-length footless tights. **5** White cotton three-piece lingerie suit, blue and pink butterfly pattern: mini-length wrapover collarless robe, narrow self-fabric tie-belt, short cap sleeves, padded shoulders; strapless bra top, underwired cups, boned front panels, front fastening; short knickers, loop-and-button front fastening.

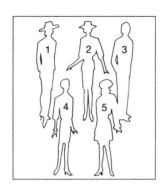
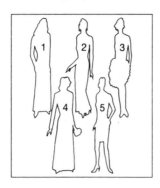
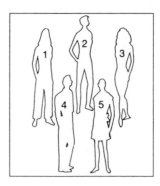

1989 Day Wear

1 Pink-beige wool two-piece suit: single-breasted jacket, two-button fastening, narrow lapels, edges bound with brown velvet to match hems of full-length inset sleeves, covered buttons and trim on large patch pockets, straight above-knee-length skirt. Brown felt hat, high crown, flat top, brown velvet trim, narrow brim, turned-up edge. Brown leather shoes, pointed toes, stiletto heels. **2** Bright-yellow wool two-piece suit: hip-length wrapover jacket, outsized lapels, padded shoulders, fine yellow-and-black striped yoke, matching cuffs of elbow-length inset sleeves and frilled trim on black patent-leather belt; straight above-knee-length skirt. Yellow felt hat, black half-band at front. Black patent-leather shoes, pointed toecaps. **3** Navy-blue wool double-breasted blazer, dull metal buttons, narrow lapels, flap pockets. Navy-blue and grey checked wool tapered trousers. White cotton collar-attached shirt. Blue and yellow patterned silk tie. Navy-blue leather step-in shoes. **4** Red and white rayon-crepe dress, patterned with flowers, bloused bodice, off-centre fastening, single button under high round neckline, three-quarter-length inset sleeves, gathered on hems and padded shoulders, swathed hip yoke, white and red spotted epaulettes, matching straight above-knee-length skirt. Red leather sling-back shoes, thick straps, pointed toes, low heels. **5** Egg-yellow wool edge-to-edge coat, narrow lapels, collar worn turned up, padded shoulders, full-length cuffed sleeves, seamed at short sleeve-level, large patch pockets, wide black suede buckled belt. Black knitted-wool polo-neck sweater-dress, straight above-knee-length skirt. Black felt hat, wide turned-back brim. Black suede gloves. Black knitted-wool tights. Black suede shoes.

Evening Wear

1 Black silk and wool two-piece evening suit: edge-to-edge hip-length semi-fitted jacket, fastening from curved hem to under high round neckline with loops and buttons, gold braid edging, matching hems of full-length inset sleeves, padded shoulders, either side centre-front and hems of jacket and sleeves embroidered with fine gold russian braid, beads and sequins in a paisley-style pattern; straight ankle-length skirt, back split. Black satin shoes, pointed toes. **2** Black silk-jersey evening dress, fitted bodice and ankle-length skirt cut in one piece without waist seam, fitted bra top, cups embroidered with tiny silver beads and sequins, fine self-jersey rouleau shoulder straps. Black satin shoes, pointed toes, tapered heels. **3** Pink, red and gold patterned silk cocktail dress, hip-length fitted boned strapless bodice, straight across neckline, straight above-knee-length skirt, trimmed with swirls of accordion-pleated self-fabric. Red satin shoes, pointed toes. **4** Gold lamé evening dress, fitted bodice ruched from hip-level to under bustline, upper bodice draped over bust from padded shoulders, forming low square neckline, full-length inset sleeves, ground-length pleated skirt. Gold sequined clutch bag; gold kid shoes, pointed toes. **5** Red leather top and skirt, fitted and boned corset-style bodice, low hip-level centre point, seamed bra top, narrow shoulder straps, straight mini-length skirt. Black velvet shoes, two laced bar straps, pointed toes, high stiletto heels.

Sports and Leisure Wear

1 Holiday wear. Pink Lycra top, front midriff open from side to high-centre-front point under bust, drapery from point of low V-shaped neckline, low-cut and cut-away armholes, top-stitched edges. Pink and yellow patterned harem trousers, full legs gathered from low hip yoke seam, elasticated hems, narrow waistband. Pink leather mules, open toes, flat heels. **2** Exercise wear. Stretch-Lycra all-in-one bodysuit, low scooped neckline edged in yellow, matching hip-length side-hip panels, orange bust-level yoke and short sleeves, lime-green body and legs, edges and seams outlined in black, top-stitched hems. **3** Beach wear. Ice-blue shiny stretch-Lycra swimsuit, waist-length wrapover V-shaped neckline formed between pleated halter straps, low back, high-cut legs. **4** Casual wear. Red and white striped cotton shirt, pointed collar, worn open, buttoned-strap fastening, two large breast patch pockets, buttoned flaps, narrow shoulder yoke, full-length sleeves worn rolled to elbow-level. White polyester-cotton tapered trousers, side-hip pockets, pleats from waistband, blue leather belt. Red leather step-in shoes, mock lace-up fastenings, white man-made soles and heels. **5** Cycling. Green cotton top, wrapover front, side-waist tie, notched roll collar, padded shoulders, cap sleeves. Mini-length red cotton divided skirt, gathers from under narrow hip yoke, flared legs, top-stitched edges. Blue leather step-in shoes, high tongues, round toes, flat heels.

Accessories

1 Natural straw hat, high crown, curled brim. **2** White canvas shoes, open fronts and toes, white and red spotted straps and bow trim. **3** White silk hat, draped crown, self-fabric bow trim, wide brim. **4** Black leather shoulder bag, gilt trim, long handle. **5** Brown felt hat, large crown, wide brim. Fake-fur collar. **6** Black felt hat, tall crown, russian braid trim, straight brim. Black and red patterned polyester scarf. **7** Navy-blue leather sling-back shoes, flat heels. **8** White leather shoes, brown toecaps, trim and high louis heels. **9** Tan leather bag, flap, concealed fastening, saddle-stitched trim, short handle. **10** Green felt hat, tall crown, flat top, wide brim. Green silk scarf. **11** White straw hat, large crown, turned-up outsized brim trimmed in brown. **12** Dark-blue drawstring bag, gilt trim, long handle. **13** Natural straw hat, pointed crown, turned-up brim, blue and brown striped trim. **14** Cream shoes, sage-green snakeskin cross-over straps. **15** Brimless mock-leopard-skin hat, ruched crown; matching fur earrings. **16** Black fur hat, large crown covered in ostrich feather spikes, wide brim. **17** Mock-leopard-skin pumps, flat heels. **18** Mock-snakeskin elastic-sided boots, pointed toes, flared heels. **19** Mock-tiger-skin shoes, pointed toes, strap-and-buckle fastening. **20** Brown felt hat, large crown, fake-fur trim. **21** Brown and cream two-tone shoes, laced through metal rings. **22** Tan leather shoes, almond-shaped toes, strap-and-buckle fastenings. **23** Olive-green lace-up shoes, decorative self-leather thonging, top-stitched detail.

Chart of the Development of 1920s Fashion

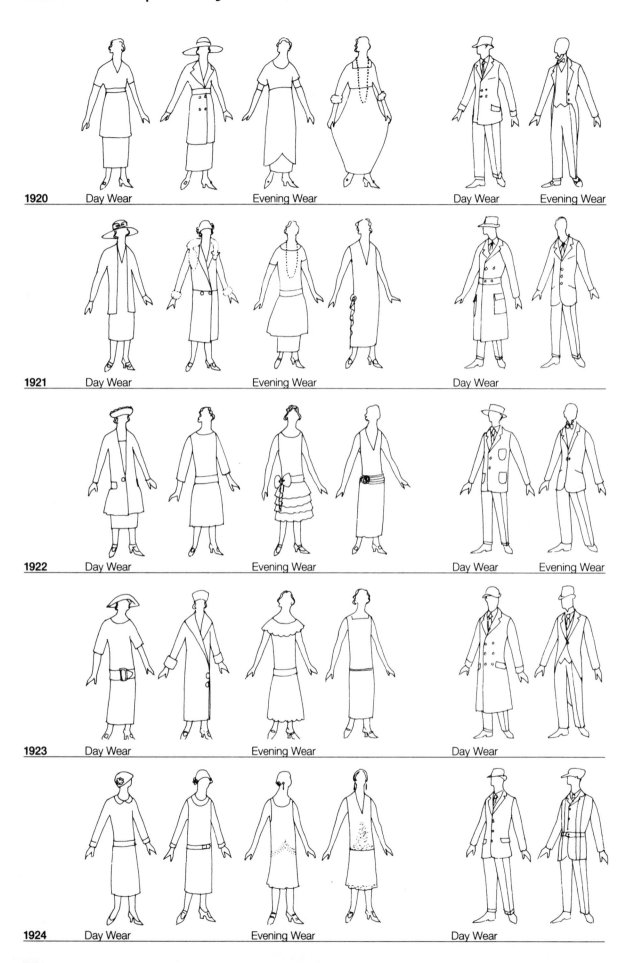

1920 Day Wear   Evening Wear   Day Wear   Evening Wear

1921 Day Wear   Evening Wear   Day Wear

1922 Day Wear   Evening Wear   Day Wear   Evening Wear

1923 Day Wear   Evening Wear   Day Wear

1924 Day Wear   Evening Wear   Day Wear

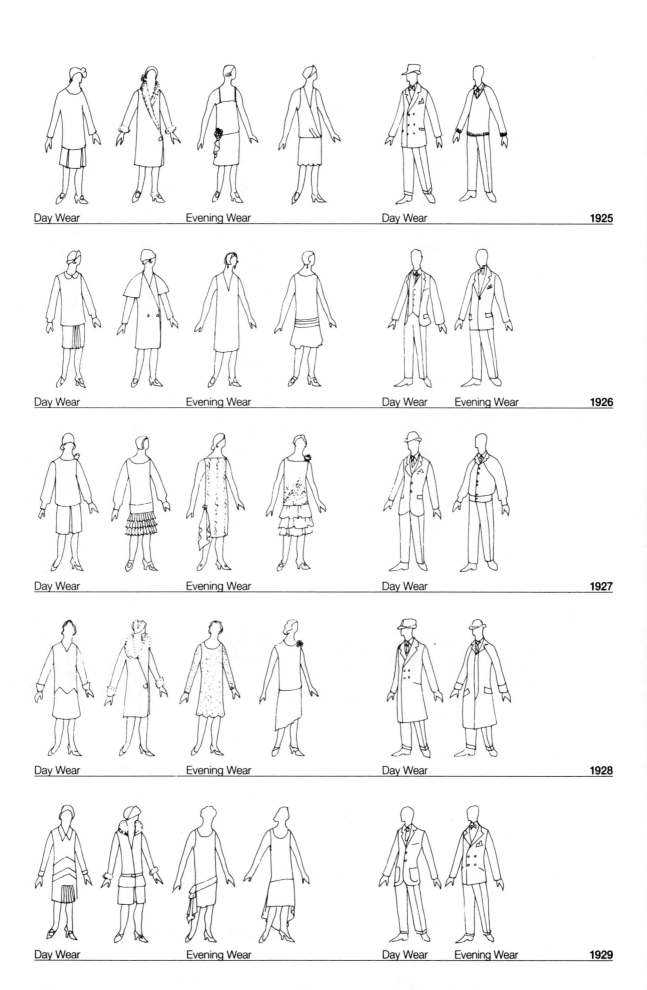

Day Wear   Evening Wear   Day Wear   **1925**

Day Wear   Evening Wear   Day Wear   Evening Wear   **1926**

Day Wear   Evening Wear   Day Wear   **1927**

Day Wear   Evening Wear   Day Wear   **1928**

Day Wear   Evening Wear   Day Wear   Evening Wear   **1929**

Chart of the Development of 1930s Fashion

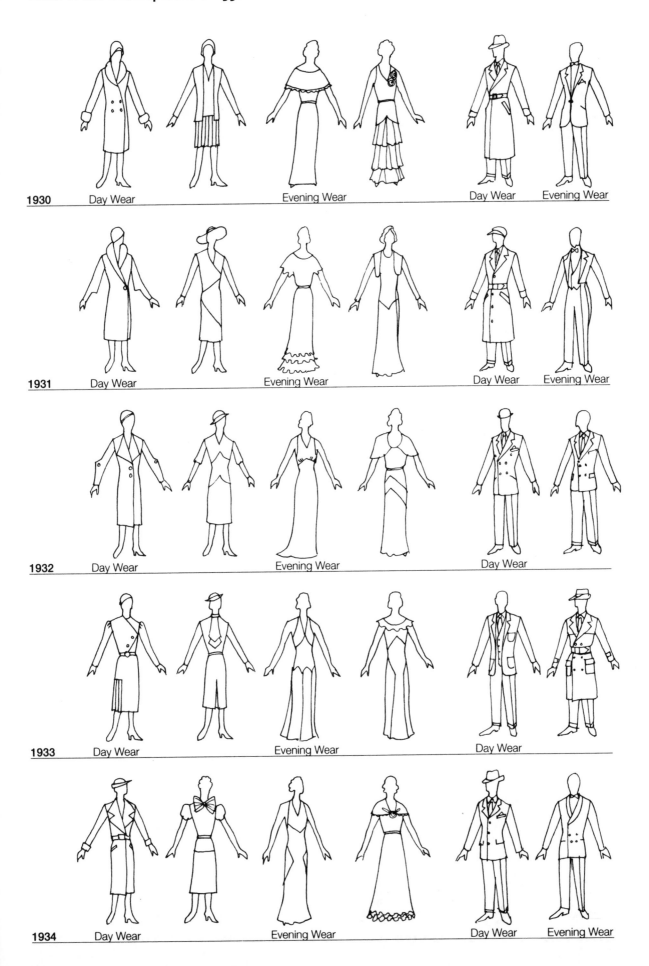

1930   Day Wear   Evening Wear   Day Wear   Evening Wear

1931   Day Wear   Evening Wear   Day Wear   Evening Wear

1932   Day Wear   Evening Wear   Day Wear

1933   Day Wear   Evening Wear   Day Wear

1934   Day Wear   Evening Wear   Day Wear   Evening Wear

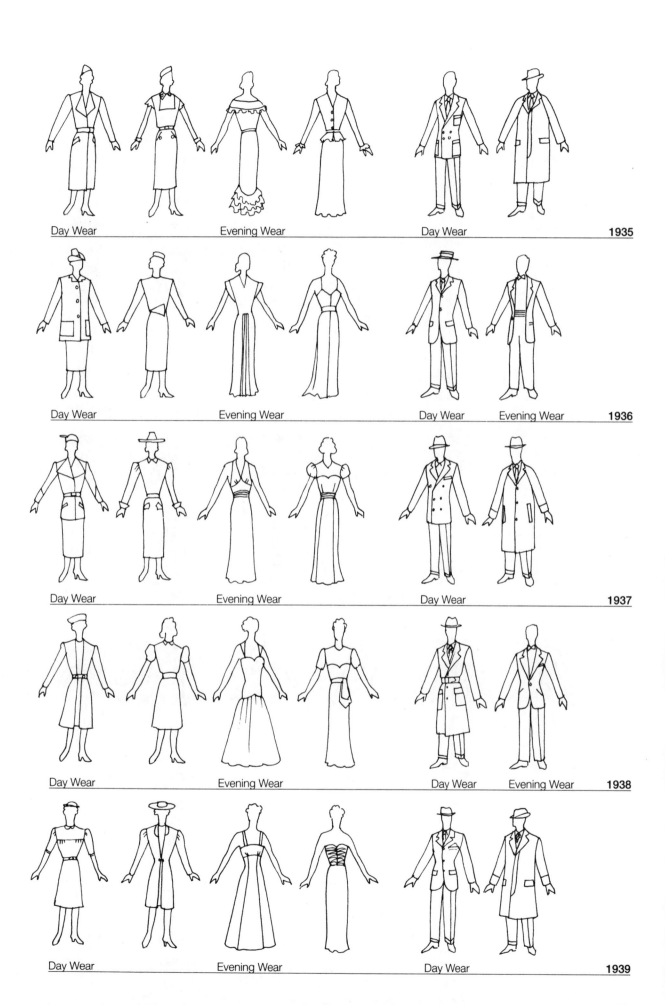

Day Wear   Evening Wear   Day Wear   **1935**

Day Wear   Evening Wear   Day Wear   Evening Wear   **1936**

Day Wear   Evening Wear   Day Wear   **1937**

Day Wear   Evening Wear   Day Wear   Evening Wear   **1938**

Day Wear   Evening Wear   Day Wear   **1939**

Chart of the Development of 1940s Fashion

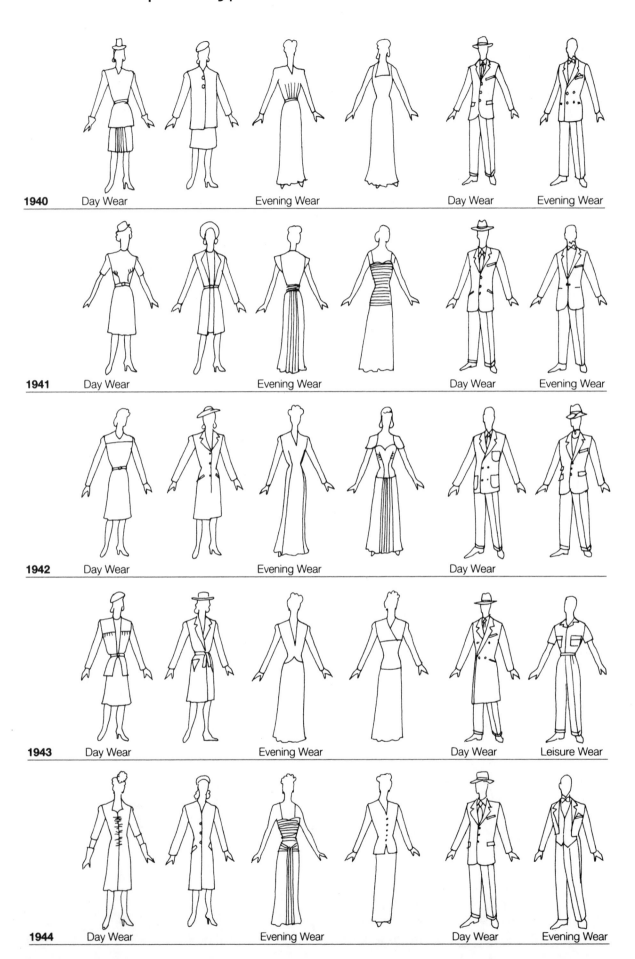

1940   Day Wear   Evening Wear   Day Wear   Evening Wear

1941   Day Wear   Evening Wear   Day Wear   Evening Wear

1942   Day Wear   Evening Wear   Day Wear

1943   Day Wear   Evening Wear   Day Wear   Leisure Wear

1944   Day Wear   Evening Wear   Day Wear   Evening Wear

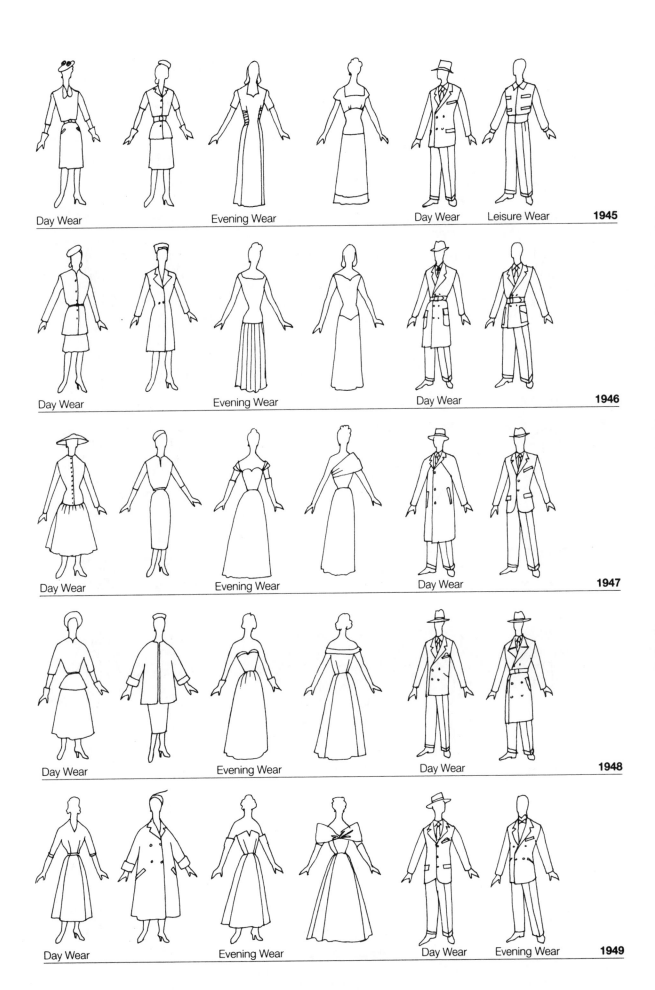

Day Wear   Evening Wear   Day Wear   Leisure Wear   **1945**

Day Wear   Evening Wear   Day Wear   **1946**

Day Wear   Evening Wear   Day Wear   **1947**

Day Wear   Evening Wear   Day Wear   **1948**

Day Wear   Evening Wear   Day Wear   Evening Wear   **1949**

Chart of the Development of 1950s Fashion

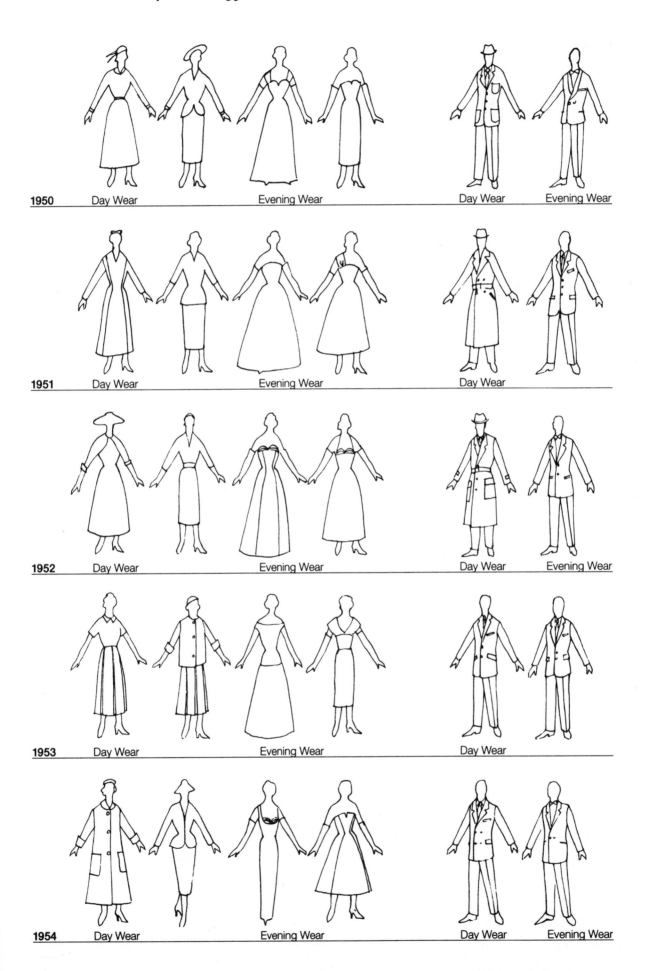

1950 Day Wear   Evening Wear   Day Wear   Evening Wear

1951 Day Wear   Evening Wear   Day Wear

1952 Day Wear   Evening Wear   Day Wear   Evening Wear

1953 Day Wear   Evening Wear   Day Wear

1954 Day Wear   Evening Wear   Day Wear   Evening Wear

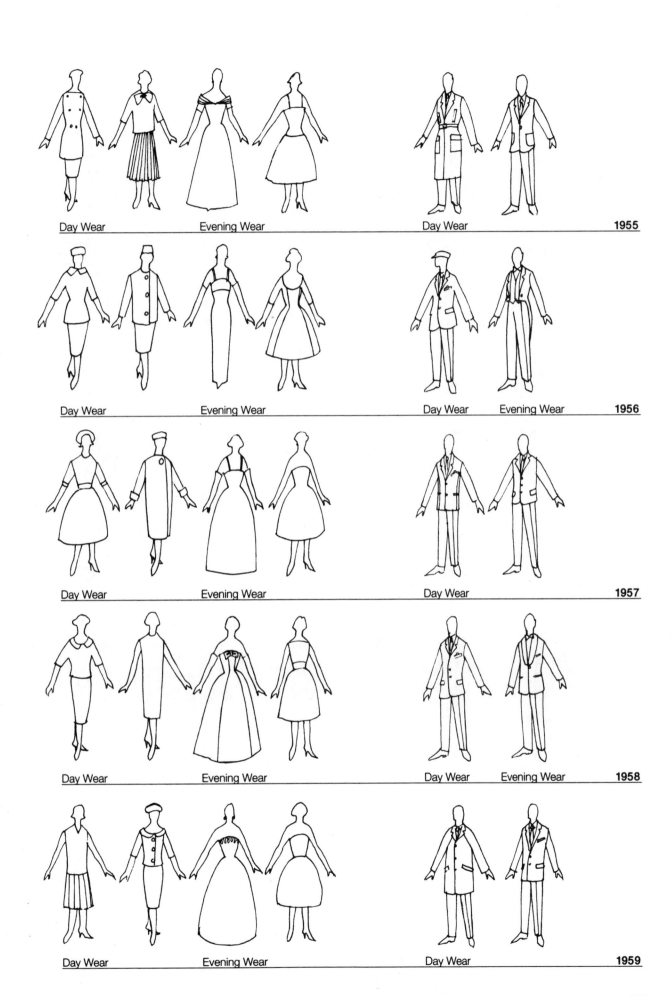

Day Wear   Evening Wear   Day Wear   **1955**

Day Wear   Evening Wear   Day Wear   Evening Wear   **1956**

Day Wear   Evening Wear   Day Wear   **1957**

Day Wear   Evening Wear   Day Wear   Evening Wear   **1958**

Day Wear   Evening Wear   Day Wear   **1959**

Chart of the Development of 1960s Fashion

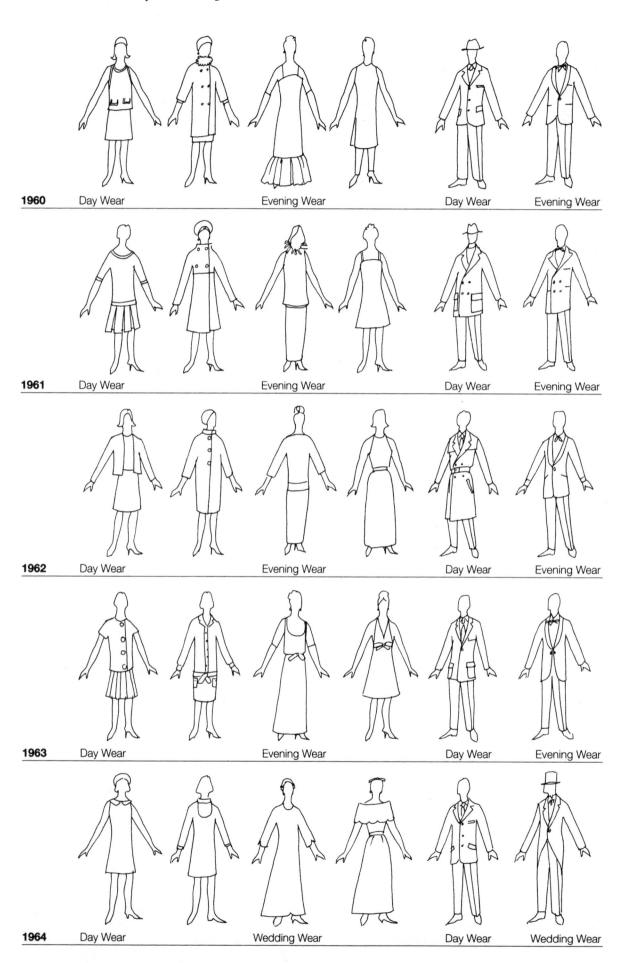

| **1960** | Day Wear | Evening Wear | Day Wear | Evening Wear |

| **1961** | Day Wear | Evening Wear | Day Wear | Evening Wear |

| **1962** | Day Wear | Evening Wear | Day Wear | Evening Wear |

| **1963** | Day Wear | Evening Wear | Day Wear | Evening Wear |

| **1964** | Day Wear | Wedding Wear | Day Wear | Wedding Wear |

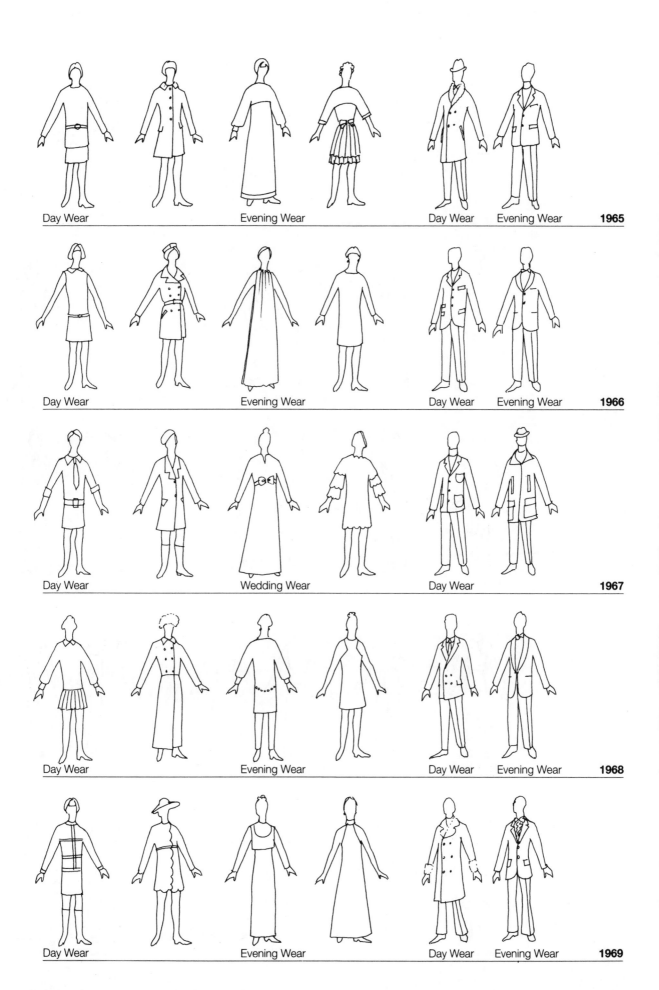

Day Wear   Evening Wear   Day Wear   Evening Wear   **1965**

Day Wear   Evening Wear   Day Wear   Evening Wear   **1966**

Day Wear   Wedding Wear   Day Wear   **1967**

Day Wear   Evening Wear   Day Wear   Evening Wear   **1968**

Day Wear   Evening Wear   Day Wear   Evening Wear   **1969**

Chart of the Development of 1970s Fashion

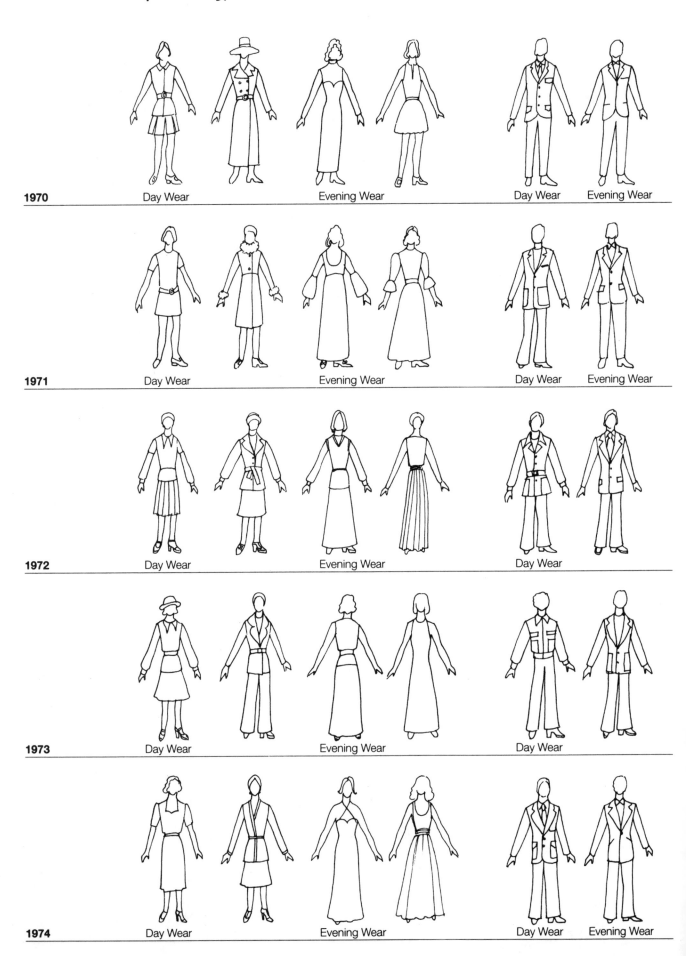

1970 Day Wear   Evening Wear   Day Wear   Evening Wear

1971 Day Wear   Evening Wear   Day Wear   Evening Wear

1972 Day Wear   Evening Wear   Day Wear

1973 Day Wear   Evening Wear   Day Wear

1974 Day Wear   Evening Wear   Day Wear   Evening Wear

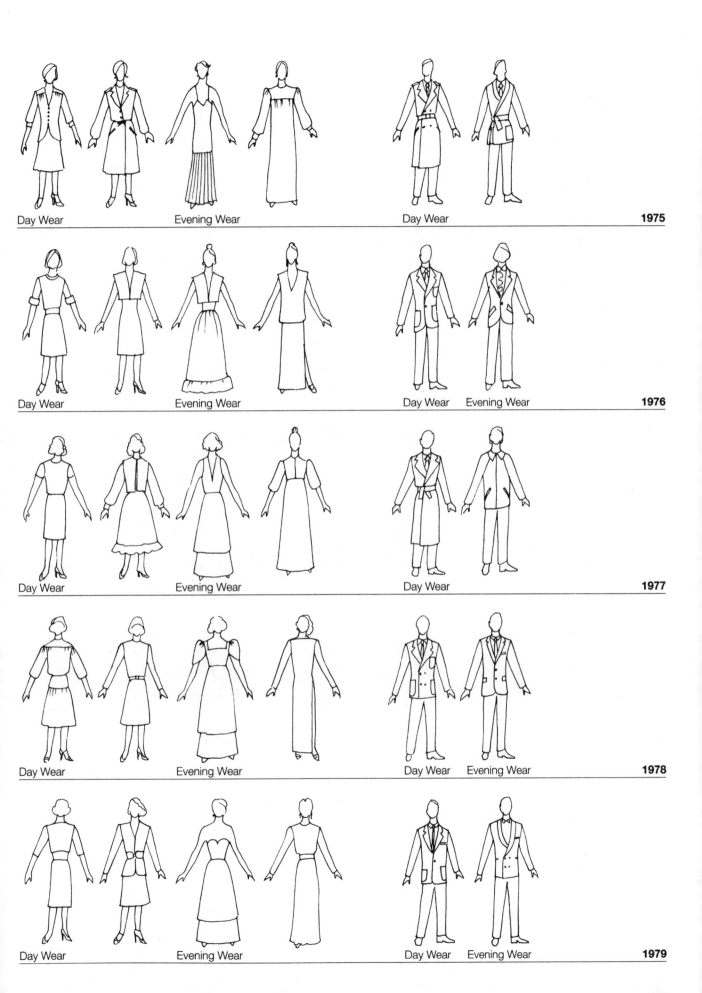

Day Wear   Evening Wear   Day Wear   **1975**

Day Wear   Evening Wear   Day Wear   Evening Wear   **1976**

Day Wear   Evening Wear   Day Wear   **1977**

Day Wear   Evening Wear   Day Wear   Evening Wear   **1978**

Day Wear   Evening Wear   Day Wear   Evening Wear   **1979**

Chart of the Development of 1980s Fashion

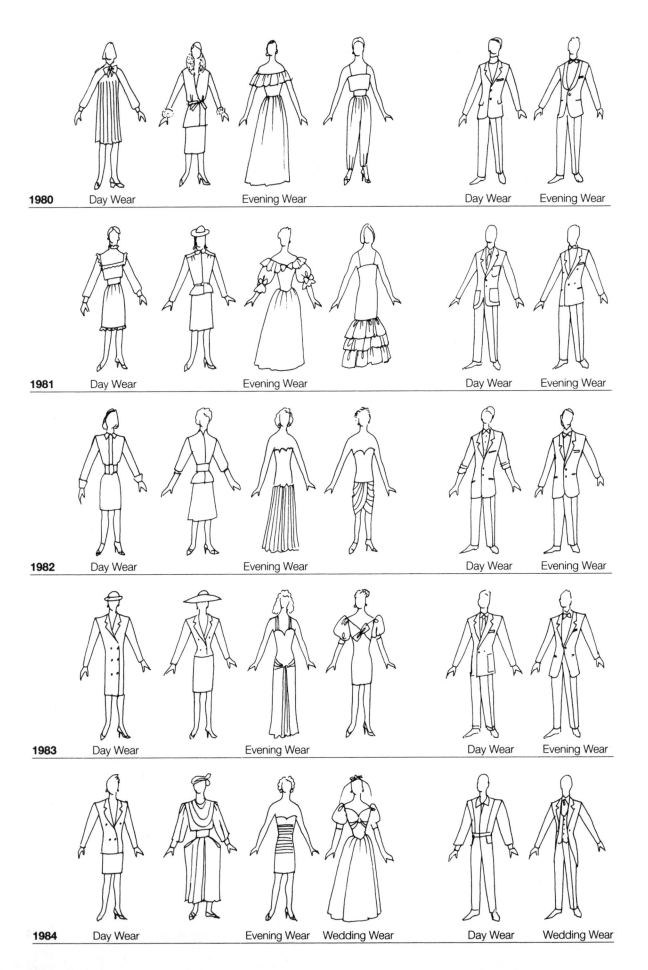

| 1980 | Day Wear | Evening Wear | | Day Wear | Evening Wear |

| 1981 | Day Wear | Evening Wear | | Day Wear | Evening Wear |

| 1982 | Day Wear | Evening Wear | | Day Wear | Evening Wear |

| 1983 | Day Wear | Evening Wear | | Day Wear | Evening Wear |

| 1984 | Day Wear | Evening Wear | Wedding Wear | Day Wear | Wedding Wear |

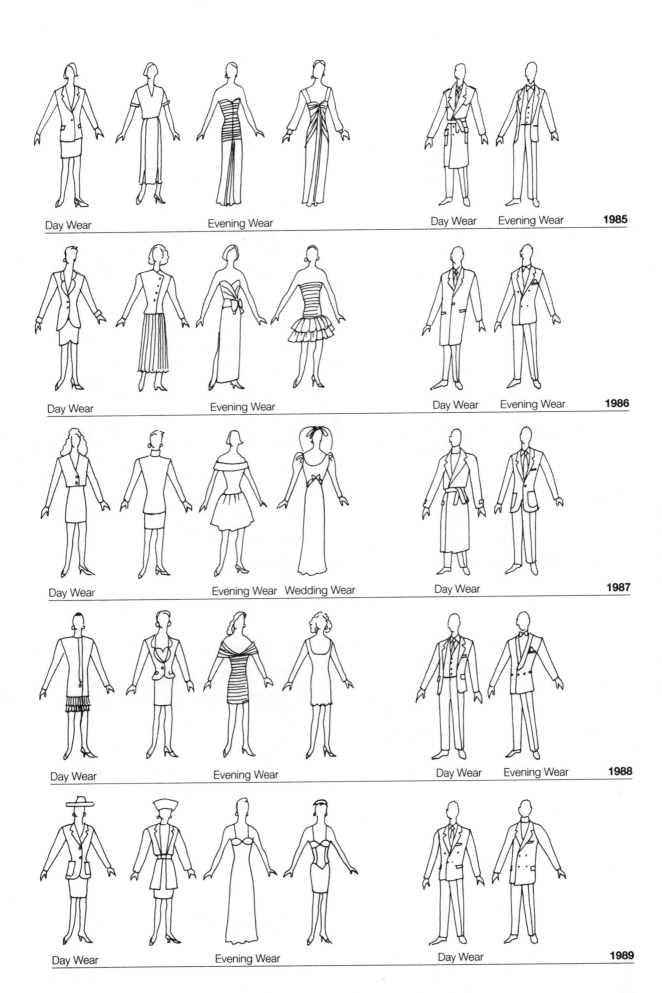

Day Wear   Evening Wear   Day Wear   Evening Wear   **1985**

Day Wear   Evening Wear   Day Wear   Evening Wear   **1986**

Day Wear   Evening Wear   Wedding Wear   Day Wear   **1987**

Day Wear   Evening Wear   Day Wear   Evening Wear   **1988**

Day Wear   Evening Wear   Day Wear   **1989**

Biographies of 1920s Designers

Beer Dates unknown. Designer. Born Germany. Opened his own couture house in Paris in 1905. During the 1920s Beer was best known for elegant, conservative outfits and luxurious underwear.

Brooks Brothers Established as Brooks Clothing Company in New York in 1818, Brooks Brothers pioneered ready-to-wear clothes for men. Best known for button-down shirts, foulard ties, Shetland sweaters, polo coats and for their use of madras fabric and Harris tweed.

Burberry, Thomas 1835–1926. Store owner. Born Dorking, England. After an apprenticeship with a draper, Burberry opened his own business, T. Burberry & Sons, in Basingstoke, Hampshire, in 1856. In 1891 he established a wholesale business in London, specializing in waterproofed gaberdine clothes for sports and leisure wear. Best known for the 'Burberry' trenchcoat which he designed for the British Royal Flying Corps during World War I and which became widely popular on the general market after the war.

Callot Sœurs Couture house. Founded in Paris in 1895 by Marie Callot Gerber, Marthe Callot Bertrand and Regina Callot Chantrelle. Callot Sœurs began by selling ribbons and lingerie, but became known for their elaborately decorated day dresses and heavy evening gowns. Though the house became less prominent in the late 1920s, it continued to produce high-quality clothes for discerning clients wishing to avoid the harsh simplicity many other designers adopted during this period. The house closed in 1937.

Carnegie, Hattie (Henrietta Kanengeiser) 1889–1956. Designer, manufacturer. Born Vienna, Austria. Carnegie began her career at the age of 15 at Macy's department store in New York, dressing hats. She moved into clothing design in 1913 and launched her first collection in 1918. Her first ready-to-wear collection followed in 1928. Carnegie was best known for grey tailored suits and black dresses which sold in her own retail stores across America. Her success was largely due to an ability to adapt Paris haute-couture fashions to the US market, where her smart but conventional clothes became highly sought after.

Chanel, Gabrielle (Coco) 1883–1971. Designer. Born Saumur, France. Chanel began her career as a milliner in Paris in 1910, under the label 'Chanel Mode'. In 1913 she opened her first hat shop in Deauville and two years later started a dress shop in Biarritz. In 1916 she introduced jersey, and her first published design, for a chemise dress, appeared in *Harper's Bazaar*. The 1920s saw her career flourish wth the founding of her Paris house at 31, rue Cambon, and the launch of her most famous perfume, 'No. 5'. In the same decade she was responsible for introducing the 'little black dress', wide-legged yachting pants, lightweight evening chemises, geometrically patterned beaded dresses and the first of her famous tweed suits. She also began her unconventional mixing of fabrics – plain with patterned jersey, or tweed with floral silk.

Chéruit, Madeleine Dates unknown. Designer, Born France. After training with Raudnitz in Paris in the 1880s, Chéruit opened her own couture house in 1906. During the 1920s she was well known for refined, elegant day wear and ornate evening wear. Chéruit's dresses painted with Cubist designs were also a great success in 1925. Her popularity waned towards the end of the decade and in 1935 the house was taken over by Schiaparelli.

Daché, Lilly 1904–89. Milliner. Born Bègles, France. After an apprenticeship with a milliner in Bordeaux, Daché worked briefly for Suzanne Talbot and then for Caroline Reboux in Paris. In 1924 she joined a small New York milliners, which she bought out almost immediately. She quickly became famous for her turbans, cloche hats, snoods and caps.

Delaunay, Sonia 1884–1979. Artist. Born Odessa, Russia. Delaunay studied painting in St Petersburg before moving to Paris in 1905. In 1925 she collaborated with the textile company Bianchini-Férier to produce fabric with characteristic abstract patterns in bright colours. She also worked with Jacques Heim, who made her patchwork designs into coats. Delaunay influenced many designers of the 1920s, including Patou.

Drécoll Couture house. It is unknown when the house was founded but it became well known for luxurious tea gowns and evening dresses. It closed in 1929.

Fortuny, Mariano 1871–1949. Textile and dress designer. Born Granada, Spain. Fortuny first studied painting and drawing in Spain and then chemistry and dyeing processes in France and Germany. He invented his own textile printing and pleating processes and designed experimental, loose-fitting, exotic garments. His clients included the dancer Isadora Duncan. During the 1920s, Fortuny developed his celebrated Delphos and Peplos designs, creating sleeveless versions of his columnar dresses made from finely pleated thin silk satin. Influenced by Eastern and African garments such as the kimono, burnous and sari, Fortuny was also famous for patterned prints, gowns and veils weighted with beads, and for his use of rich silks and velvets.

Hartnell, Norman 1901–79. Designer. Born London, England. Hartnell worked at Madame Désirée, Esther's and with Lucile before opening his own premises in London in 1923. His career took off during the late 1920s when he became famous for his extravagant wedding dresses, though he also designed for the theatre and for films.

Jenny Couture house. Founded in 1909 by Jenny Sacerdote, who trained at Paquin. Jenny's simple clothes were popular with American clients, though the house was also well known for elaborately beaded evening dresses. Jenny closed in 1938.

Lanvin, Jeanne 1867–1946. Designer. Born Brittany, France. After an apprenticeship with Suzanne Talbot, Lanvin opened her own millinery shop in Paris in 1890. She began making clothes commercially after customers commented on the garments she made for her younger sister and daughter. Lanvin became famous for her mother/daughter outfits which were significant in the development of fashion for blurring the distinction between clothing for different age groups. Lanvin was to exert an enormous influence over the fashions of the 1920s, creating the decade's basic shape at the beginning of World War I with the chemise dress. Other designs which became characteristic of the period include her breton suits and beaded evening dresses. She was also the first couturier to design clothes for entire families, presenting her first line of menswear in 1926. The following year the first of Lanvin's famous perfumes, 'Arpège', was produced. Lanvin refused to be constricted by contemporary trends, offering an alternative to the straight silhouette of the 1920s with variations on the full-skirted 'robes de style' she first created during the 1910s. Preferring embroidery and appliquéd motifs to patterned material, she transformed motifs from orientalism, botanical etchings and Renaissance, Aztec and modern art into her own individual designs. She was also famous for her use of a particular shade of blue, which became known as 'Lanvin blue'.

Lelong, Lucien 1889–1958. Designer. Born Paris, France. Lelong trained at the Hautes Etudes des Commerciales in Paris and established his own business after World War I. During the 1920s he became known for his skilful use of beautiful fabrics in creating elegant, understated dresses and evening wear. He was one of the first designers to produce stockings and lingerie.

Madeleine et Madeleine Couture house. Founded in 1919, the house was highly influential in the early 1920s, producing varied and original garments made from luxurious materials. In 1926 it merged with Anna, who, earlier that year, had created 'le smoking', a highly popular man-tailored suit.

Martial et Armand Dates unknown. Couture house. This minor, though longstanding, Parisian house was known more for its skill and workmanship than for innovative fashion design.

Molyneux, Captain Edward 1891–1974. Designer. Born London, England. Molyneux began his career producing illustrations for magazines and advertisements, and in 1911 was employed as a sketcher by Lucile. After serving as a captain in World War I, he opened his own couture house in Paris in 1919, becoming famous for simple tailored suits and skirts in muted tones which were seen as archetypally English in their restrained elegance. Between 1925 and 1932 he opened further branches in Monte Carlo, Cannes, Biarritz and London.

Paquin, Mme ?–1936. Designer. Trained at Maison Rouff until she established her own house in Paris in 1891. She was one of the first designers to open shops abroad, founding branches in London, Buenos Aires and Madrid in 1902. Though she was famous for glamorous, romantic, fairytale garments, Paquin also designed for the more active woman of her era, creating tailored suits specifically cut to ease walking. She collaborated with the celebrated fashion artists of the day, producing dresses from designs by George Barbier, Paul Iribe, Léon Bakst and Etienne Drian. The success of her exuberant, exotic styles was acknowledged in 1913 when she became the first female designer to be awarded the Légion d'Honneur. The House of Paquin remained open after her retirement in 1920, finally closing in 1956.

Patou, Jean 1880–1936. Designer. Born Normandy, France. Patou opened the small firm Maison Parry in 1912, achieving a brief success before the advent of World War I forced the firm's closure. In 1919 he reopened under his own name, producing bell-skirted, high-waisted dresses. His Cubistic sweaters were also very popular. Patou had enormous influence over 1920s fashions, in particular with his sports and bathing wear, which included the calf-length pleated skirts and sleeveless cardigans worn by the tennis player Suzanne Lenglen. In 1924 he became one of the first designers to put his own initials on his clothing and in 1927 was one of the first to revert to the natural waistline.

Poiret, Paul 1879–1944. Designer. Born Paris, France. Poiret worked for Doucet from 1896, moving to Worth in 1900. In 1904 he established his own house with the help of Doucet and the patronage of the actress Réjane. Poiret is widely credited with releasing women from the corseted, hourglass-shaped designs of the period, creating elegant, gently fitted dresses with fewer underclothes. He was heavily influenced by the Ballets Russes, incorporating turbans and harem pants into his collections. In 1908 and 1909 he commissioned Paul Iribe and Georges Lepape to illustrate his clothes in brochures. Poiret's 1911 design for a hobble skirt, drawn in at the ankles, caused a huge furore and brought him a certain notoriety. His house closed during World War I and, though it reopened after the war and made some attempts to attract a younger clientele, Poiret found himself in the late 1920s facing financial ruin. The company finally shut its doors in 1929.

Premet Couture house. Founded in Paris in 1911 by Mme Premet. Major successes of the 1920s were the 'Garconne' two-piece and the 'Gamine' outfits of 1923, which were very popular with American buyers. The house closed in the late 1920s.

Reboux, Caroline 1837–1927. Milliner. Born Paris, France. Reboux opened her own shop in 1870 and by the 1920s had become the leading Paris milliner, with a successful establishment in the rue de la Paix. During this period she created hats for most major designers and is credited with having popularized the cloche.

Redfern, John Dates unknown. Born England. During the 1850s Redfern worked as a tailor on the Isle of Wight and in the late 19th century began designing sports clothes and tailored suits for women. He reached the pinnacle of his success when he was appointed dressmaker to Queen Victoria in 1888. Though at its peak the company attracted a stylish, international clientele, by the 1920s Redfern was concentrating on simple, luxurious clothes for older women.

Vionnet, Madeleine 1876–1975. Designer. Born Aubervilliers, France. At the age of 11 Vionnet was apprenticed to a dressmaker. Six years later she joined the House of Vincent in rue Cadot, Paris, rising to head seamstress after two years. In 1898 she travelled to London, where she worked for the dressmaker Kate O'Reilly. Returning to Paris in 1900, she spent two years as head seamstress at Callot Sœurs before moving to Doucet in 1907. In 1912 she opened her own house at 222, rue de Rivoli. This closed two years later but reopened in 1918. The late 1920s and 1930s saw Vionnet at the height of her success. Always an innovative designer, she drew inspiration from many sources, in particular Ancient Greek civilization – she was much influenced by the design of the peplos. Simplicity and austerity are at the core of her work. Vionnet was a supreme technician, draping her toiles on a wooden doll to achieve perfect proportions between body and dress. She is best remembered for her mastery of the bias cut.

Worth Couture house. Founded in 1858 by the English couturier Charles Frederick Worth, the House of Worth remained in family hands after his death in 1895 and in the 1920s, under his son Jean-Charles Worth, it was renowned for refined, sumptuous clothes which were always at the height of fashion.

Biographies of 1930s Designers

Adrian (Adrian Adolph Greenburg)
1903–59. Costume designer. Born Naugatuck, Connecticut, USA. In the 1930s Adrian was Hollywood's most influential designer. His many widely copied designs include a slouch hat worn by Greta Garbo in the 1929 film *A Woman of Affairs* and a white organdie dress with ruffled sleeves created for Joan Crawford in *Letty Lynton* in 1932. As well as his work for films, he also made chic, wearable suits, sometimes decorated with appliqué.

Augustabernard (Augusta Bernard)
1886–1946. Designer. Born Biarritz, France. Augustabernard opened her own business in Biarritz in 1920, moving to Paris in 1923. She became famous for dramatic, well-cut evening dresses in pale, sombre colours and for uncomplicated day clothes, often in tweed. She was known for decorating her elegant, slender evening gowns with flounces, scalloped tiers and scarves attached at the hip or shoulder. She retired in 1934.

Bruyère, Marie-Louise Dates unknown. Designer. Bruyère trained at Callot Sœurs, joined Lanvin in 1920 and opened her own house in 1928. She had a reputation for exclusivity. In the 1930s, her three-quarter-length coats worn over afternoon dresses were particularly successful.

Carnegie, Hattie (Henrietta Kanengeiser) 1889–1956. Designer, manufacturer. Born Vienna, Austria. Carnegie began her career at the age of 15 at Macy's department store, New York, dressing hats. She moved into clothing design in 1913 and launched her first collection in 1918. Her first ready-to-wear collection followed in 1928. Carnegie was best known for grey tailored suits and black dresses which she sold in her own retail stores across America. Her success was largely due to an ability to adapt Paris haute-couture fashion to the US market, where her chic, conservative clothes became highly sought after.

Chanel, Gabrielle (Coco) 1883–1971. Designer. Born Saumur, France. Chanel began her career as a milliner in Paris in 1910, under the label 'Chanel Mode'. In 1913 she opened her first hat shop in Deauville and two years later started a dress shop in Biarritz. In 1916 she introduced jersey, and her first published design, for a chemise dress, appeared in *Harper's Bazaar*. The 1920s saw her career flourish with the founding of her Paris house and the launch of her most famous perfume, 'No. 5'. In the same decade she was responsible for introducing the 'little black dress', wide-legged yachting pants, lightweight evening chemises, geometrically patterned beaded dresses and the first of her famous tweed suits. She also began her

unconventional mixing of fabrics – plain with patterned jersey, or tweed with floral silk. In the 1930s Chanel continued to develop her range of costume jewelry: her long gilt chains, rows of pearls and mixtures of semi-precious stones achieved particular popularity. During this period her evening wear became more feminine and ornate, though she also began using fabrics such as linen and cotton organdie which had previously been used only for day clothes. Chanel closed her house in 1939 but reopened in 1954.

Daché, Lilly 1904–89. Milliner. Born Bègles, France. After an apprenticeship with a milliner in Bordeaux, Daché worked briefly for Suzanne Talbot and then for Caroline Reboux in Paris. In 1924 she joined a small New York milliners, which she bought out almost immediately. She quickly became famous for her turbans, cloche hats, snoods and caps.

Grès Couture house. Founded in 1941 by Paris-born Germaine Krebs (1903–93). Krebs had trained with Premet and in 1934 she opened a couture house, 'Alix', in association with Julie Barton. 'Alix' closed in 1939. 'Madame Grès', as Krebs became known at her own house, was famous for draped and pleated dresses – in silk and wool – which resemble classical Greek robes, often cut on the bias and with dolman sleeves. She adopted a sculptural approach to dressmaking, each garment being modelled on the mannequin by hand with minimal use of patterns or cutting.

Hartnell, Norman 1901–79. Designer. Born London, England. Hartnell worked at Madame Désirée, Esther's and with Lucile before opening his own premises in London in 1923. His career took off during the late 1920s when he became famous for his extravagant wedding dresses, though he also designed for the theatre and for films. He was appointed dressmaker to the British royal family in 1938 and created Elizabeth II's wedding dress and coronation gown as well as designing many outfits for her overseas tours. His designs were central in forming the image of the royal family.

James, Charles 1906–78. Designer. Born Sandhurst, England. James began his fashion career when he opened a hat shop in Chicago in 1924 under the name of a schoolfriend 'Charles Boucheron'. He created his first dress collection in New York in 1928, his first London collection in 1929, and his first Paris collection in 1934. By 1940 he had returned to New York and established a house under his own name. An architect of dress, James created superbly cut, sculpted ball gowns using large quantities of lavish fabrics often arranged

asymmetrically in bunches and folds. He was also well known for his highly structured coats, his dresses with spiral zips and his quilted ivory-satin jackets.

Lanvin, Jeanne 1867–1946. Designer. Born Brittany, France. After an apprenticeship with Suzanne Talbot, Lanvin opened her own millinery shop in Paris in 1890. She began making clothes commercially after customers commented on the garments she made for her younger sister and daughter. Lanvin became famous for her mother/daughter outfits which were significant in the development of fashion for blurring the distinction between clothing for different age groups. She created the basic shape for the 1920s at the beginning of World War I with the chemise dress. Other designs which became characteristic of the period include her breton suits and beaded evening dresses. She was also the first couturier to design clothes for entire families, presenting a line of menswear in 1926. The following year the first of Lanvin's famous perfumes, 'Arpège', was produced. During the 1930s she often used parallel stitching and embroidered sequins, and continued to show her famous 'robes de style' which were inspired by eighteenth-century dresses. Preferring embroidery and appliquéd motifs to patterned material, she transformed motifs from orientalism, botanical etchings and Renaissance, Aztec and modern art into her own individual designs. She was also famous for her use of a particular shade of blue, which became known as 'Lanvin blue'.

Lelong, Lucien 1889–1958. Designer. Born Paris, France. Lelong trained at the Hautes Etudes des Commerciales in Paris and established his own business after World War I. He became known for his skilful use of beautiful fabrics in creating elegant, understated dresses and evening wear. He was one of the first designers to produce stockings and lingerie. In the late 1930s Lelong designed tight-waisted, full skirts which were precursors to Dior's 'New Look' of 1947.

Louiseboulanger (Louise Boulanger)
1900–? Designer. Born France. At the age of 13 Louiseboulanger was apprenticed to a dressmaking business. She was then employed by Chéruit until she founded her own business in 1923. She created refined, graceful garments, often using heavy fabrics such as taffeta and moiré in warm colours. Her innovations include the 'pouf' silhouette and knee-length evening skirts which fell to the ankles at the back. The house closed in 1939.

Mainbocher (Main Rousseau Bocher)
1891–1976. Designer. Born Chicago, Illinois, USA. In 1922 Mainbocher was

employed by *Harper's Bazaar* as a fashion artist and by 1923 was editor-in-chief of French *Vogue*, a post he held until 1929. He was the first American couturier to achieve success in Paris, opening his own house there in 1930. During the 1930s he became famous for embroidered, apron-style evening dresses, for his use of the bias cut, and for creating a fashion for 'Wallis blue' with the wedding dress he designed for the Duchess of Windsor. He opened a salon in New York in 1940.

Maxwell, Vera (Vera Huppé) 1901–95. Designer. Born New York, USA. Maxwell started her career by making clothes for herself. By 1936 she was attracting the attention of the fashion press and from the late 1930s her designs were being bought by Seventh Avenue firms such as Adler and Adler. Maxwell established her own business in 1947, creating classic, wearable separates and suits, wraparound jersey dresses and riding jackets. She was influenced by men's country clothes and used natural dyes to produce autumnal tones.

McCardell, Claire 1905–58. Designer. Born Frederick, Maryland, USA. McCardell studied at Parsons School of Design in New York, and also in Paris. During the late 1920s and 1930s she worked with Richard Turk at Townley Frocks, and then for Hattie Carnegie. One of her first highly successful designs was the waistless, bias-cut 'monastic dress' of 1938. Returning to Townley Frocks in 1940 to design under her own name, McCardell produced easy-fitting clothes made from cotton, denim, gingham and jersey which were hugely influential.

Molyneux, Captain Edward 1891–1974. Designer. Born London, England. Molyneux began his career producing illustrations for magazines and advertisements, and in 1911 was employed as a sketcher by Lucile. He opened his own couture house in Paris in 1919, becoming famous for simple tailored suits and skirts in muted tones which were seen as archetypally English in their restrained elegance. In the 1930s, a decade dominated by Schiaparelli's eccentric, humorous style, Molyneux's streamlined designs were particularly sought after. Between 1925 and 1932 he opened further branches in Monte Carlo, Cannes, Biarritz and London.

Morton, Digby 1906–83. Designer. Born Dublin, Ireland. In the late 1920s, after studying art and architecture in Ireland, Morton worked for Lachasse in London. He established his own business in 1933, becoming well known for his use of Aran knits and Donegal tweeds, often combined with silk blouses. Morton is also widely credited with having adapted the traditional tailor-made suit to make it more graceful and up-to-date.

Patou, Jean 1880–1936. Designer. Born Normandy, France. Patou opened the small firm Maison Parry in 1912, achieving a brief success before the advent of World War I forced the firm's closure. In 1919 he reopened under his own name, producing bell-skirted, high-waisted dresses. His Cubistic sweaters were also very popular. Patou was enormously influential with his sports and bathing wear, which included the calf-length pleated skirts and sleeveless cardigans worn by the tennis player Suzanne Lenglen. In 1924 he initiated a trend by putting his own initials on his clothing and in 1927 was one of the first designers to revert to the natural waistline, heralding the shape that came to predominate during the 1930s. The House of Patou continued to be hugely successful after his death.

Philippe et Gaston (Philippe Hecht and Gaston Kaufmann) Couture house. After training at Jenny, Kaufmann joined Hecht to form a couture house which opened in 1922. Philippe et Gaston had particular success with their pearl-embroidered evening dresses and ensembles for day wear, continuing to attract the attention of the fashion press until the house closed in 1937.

Piguet, Robert 1901–53. Designer. Born Yverdon, Switzerland. After training as a banker, Piguet moved to Paris in 1918 and worked for Redfern and Poiret. Opening in 1933, the House of Piguet was known for romantic evening gowns and elegant suits and dresses, often in grey, beige or blue. Piguet also made costumes for the stage and frequently employed other designers, including Balmain, Dior, Galanos and Givenchy.

Ricci, Nina (Maria Nielli) 1883–1970. Designer. Born Turin, Italy. After training with a couturier, Ricci opened her own house in 1932. She worked by draping fabric round the mannequin to create distinctive, luxurious garments. Ricci designed clothes that were classical rather than innovative in style and which were popular with older clients.

Rochas, Marcel 1902–55. Designer. Born Paris, France. Rochas established his house in 1924, becoming one of the most important and influential designers of the 1930s. Inspired by Javanese and Balinese traditional costumes, he introduced broad-shouldered garments to his collections in 1933, creating a look usually attributed to Schiaparelli. Other innovative designs included sculpted wool coats with widely stitched seams, trouser suits in grey flannel and the 'guêpière' bustier of 1943. Rochas was also famous for imaginative embroidery and appliqués and bizarre decorative features such as stuffed birds and buttons shaped like butterflies, lipstick and pipes. He often worked with flower-patterned fabric and was one of the first designers to add pockets to skirts.

Rouff, Maggy (Maggie Besançon de Wagner) 1896–1971. Designer. Born Paris, France. After working in her parents' company, Drécoll, Rouff founded her own house in 1929. She became famous for comfortable couture garments which often featured feminine details such as fichu collars, puffed sleeves, 'bustle'-draped skirts and bow motifs. During the 1930s Rouff created closely fitted dresses with shirring, sometimes decorated with diagonal tiers of ruffles. She also introduced many innovations into sportswear, including her jersey 'plus-fours'. Rouff was known for her imaginative use of colour.

Schiaparelli, Elsa 1890–1973. Designer. Born Rome, Italy. Schiaparelli moved to Paris in 1922 and opened a boutique, 'Pour le Sport', in 1927. The following year she showed her first collection. Her clothes were chic and eccentric, strongly influenced by modern art movements. She commissioned artists such as Salvador Dalí and Jean Cocteau to design fabrics and accessories and produced a range of surreal garments, often with *trompe-l'œil* effects. Her many innovations included unusually shaped buttons, padlock fastenings, lip-shaped pockets, and hats in the form of ice-cream cones, shoes or lamb cutlets. In 1933 her broad-shouldered pagoda sleeve set the basic shape for fashion until the New Look. Known for her gifted use of colour, Schiaparelli promoted 'Shocking Pink' and was the first designer to use plastic zippers decoratively.

Stiebel, Victor 1907–76. Designer. Born Durban, South Africa. Stiebel began an apprenticeship with Reville and Rossiter in 1929 and in 1932 opened his own house. He created romantic evening wear in the neo-classical style and was well known for his restrained day clothes, usually in soft fabrics such as jersey.

Valentina (Valentina Nicholaevna Sanina) 1899–1989. Designer. Born Kiev, Russia. Valentina established her house in 1928. While her day wear was often simple and practical, sometimes displaying peasant influences, she was best known for her dramatic evening wear and swirling capes. She was also a skilled designer of millinery, especially snoods, turbans and veils.

Vionnet, Madeleine 1876–1975. Designer. Born Aubervilliers, France. At the age of 11 Vionnet was apprenticed to a dressmaker. Six years later she joined the House of Vincent in Paris, rising to head seamstress after two years. In 1898 she travelled to London, where she worked for the dressmaker Kate O'Reilly. Returning to Paris in 1900, she spent two years as head seamstress at Callot Sœurs before moving to Doucet in 1907. In 1912 she opened her own house. The late 1920s and 1930s saw Vionnet at the height of her success. Always an innovative designer, she drew inspiration from many sources, in particular Ancient Greek civilization – she was much influenced by the design of the peplos. Simplicity and austerity are at the core of her work. Vionnet was a supreme technician, draping her toiles on a wooden doll to achieve perfect proportions between body and dress. She is best remembered for her mastery of the bias cut. She retired in 1939.

Worth Couture house. Founded in 1858 by the English couturier Charles Frederick Worth, the House of Worth remained in family hands after his death in 1895. In the 1920s and 1930s the house was run first by Jean-Charles Worth, grandson of the founder, and then from 1936 by Roger and Maurice Worth, who maintained its reputation for refined, sumptuous, highly fashionable clothes. The company was eventually taken over by Paquin in 1954.

Biographies of 1940s Designers

Adrian (Adrian Adolph Greenburg) 1903–59. Costume designer. Born Naugatuck, Connecticut, USA. In the 1930s Adrian was Hollywood's most influential designer. His many widely copied designs include a slouch hat worn by Greta Garbo in *A Woman of Affairs* (1929) and a white organdie dress with ruffled sleeves for Joan Crawford in *Letty Lynton* (1932). Several 1930s designs, such as his pillbox hat for Garbo in *As You Desire Me* (1932) and Hedy Lamarr's snood in *I Take This Woman*, were precursors to 1940s trends. As well as his work for the cinema, he also created chic, wearable suits, sometimes decorated with appliqué. Following his retirement in 1942, Adrian opened a boutique in Beverly Hills, California.

Amies, Hardy 1909–2003. Designer. Born London, England. Amies started his career in fashion at Lachasse in 1934. In 1945 he opened his own couture house and became known for refined, well-cut women's suits in tweed and wool and for sumptuous puff-sleeved ball gowns.

Balenciaga, Cristobal 1895–1972. Designer. Born Guetaria, Spain. At the age of 20 Balenciaga opened his first house in San Sebastian. When he moved to Paris in 1937 he was already Spain's leading couturier, producing austere, elegant, well-cut clothes in sombre colours recognizable for their stark Spanish style. In 1939 his tight-waisted dresses with dropped shoulderlines were clear forerunners of Dior's New Look of 1947. During the 1940s Balenciaga's reputation for highly influential, dramatic designs grew. 1946 saw the launch of his 'barrel line' as well as embroidered boleros based on toreadors' costumes. His many innovations include the pillbox hat, first shown in 1946, and the stand-away collar.

Balmain, Pierre 1914–82. Designer. Born St Jean de Maurienne, France. Balmain started his career with Molyneux. In 1941 he began working at Lelong where he met Dior. Balmain set up his own couture house in 1945 and found instant success with his bell-shaped skirts with nipped-in waists similar to those later produced by Dior for the New Look. Though he tended to favour a narrow silhouette for his suits and dresses, Balmain was also known for his full half-belted coats and romantic full-skirted ball gowns.

Carnegie, Hattie (Henrietta Kanengeiser) 1889–1956. Designer, manufacturer. Born Vienna, Austria. Carnegie began her career at the age of 15 at Macy's department store, New York, dressing hats. She moved into clothing design in 1913 and launched her first collection in 1918. Her first ready-to-wear collection followed in 1928. Carnegie was best known for grey tailored suits and black dresses which she sold in her own retail stores

across America. Her success was largely due to an ability to adapt Paris haute-couture fashions to the US market, where her chic, conservative clothes became highly sought after.

Creed, Charles 1909–66. Designer. Born Paris, France. Creed studied tailoring and art in Vienna, then worked for Linton Tweeds in Carlisle and the department store Bergdorf Goodman in New York. He joined his family's tailoring firm in Paris in the 1930s. The house closed during World War II, though Creed continued to design while on leave from the army and contributed to the Utility Scheme. He opened his own house after the war, establishing a reputation for refined, precisely cut suits in wool and tweed. During the late 1940s he also collaborated with a number of US sportswear manufacturers.

Dessès, Jean (Jean Dimitre Verginie) 1904–70. Designer. Born Alexandria, Egypt, of Greek parents. Dessès began his career at the age of 21 with Maison Jane. He opened his own house in 1937 and launched his first ready-to-wear line, 'Jean Dessès Diffusion', in 1949. During the 1940s he was known for his draped evening dresses inspired by Ancient Greek and Egyptian garments, and for his embroidered ball gowns and sheath dresses worn with close-fitting jackets.

Dior, Christian 1905–57. Designer. Born Granville, France. Dior began his fashion career in Paris at the age of 30, selling fashion sketches to newspapers. He joined Robert Piguet in 1938 and worked briefly for Lelong in 1942 before opening his own house in 1946. In 1947 his first collection, the 'Corolle line', soon nicknamed the 'New Look', was sensationally successful. His curved bodices and huge skirts with nipped-in waists brought a new femininity and glamour to fashion after the severe broad-shouldered, narrow-skirted lines produced under wartime rationing. While some were shocked by the enormous quantities of cloth required for such an exaggerated silhouette, most women followed the style and the 'Corolle line' remains the most famous single collection ever presented. In his 1948 and 1949 collections Dior developed the New Look shape, adding flounced sleeves or bulk at chest-level above a tightly belted waist. He also included jackets featuring *trompe-l'œil* details and full skirts with uneven hemlines.

Fath, Jacques 1912–54. Designer. Born Maison-Lafitte, France. During the 1930s Fath worked as a stockbroker at the Paris Bourse while at the same time studying costume and fashion design. He opened his own house in 1937, achieving worldwide fame by the late 1940s. Fath attracted a young, sophisticated clientele with his extravagant, flirtatious evening

dresses and jaunty day clothes, often with decorative pleats, darts and angled collars.

Grès Couture house. Founded in 1941 by Paris-born Germaine Krebs (1903–93). Krebs had trained with Premet and in 1934 she opened a couture house, 'Alix', in association with Julie Barton. 'Alix' closed in 1939. 'Madame Grès', as Krebs became known at her own house, was famous for draped and pleated dresses – in silk and wool – which resemble classical Greek robes, often cut on the bias and with dolman sleeves. She adopted a sculptural approach to dressmaking, each garment being modelled on the mannequin by hand with minimal use of patterns or cutting.

Hartnell, Norman 1901–79. Designer. Born London, England. Hartnell worked at Madame Désirée, Esther's and with Lucile before opening his own premises in London in 1923. His career took off during the late 1920s when he became famous for his extravagant wedding dresses, though he also designed for the theatre and for films. He was appointed dressmaker to the British royal family in 1938 and created Elizabeth II's wedding dress and coronation gown, as well as designing many outfits for her overseas tours. His designs were central in forming the image of the royal family. He also became known for fine tailoring and for his use of woollen tweed in suits and coats. In the 1940s Hartnell went on to produce his own ready-to-wear lines.

Heim, Jacques 1899–1967. Designer. Born Paris, France. Heim designed womenswear for his parents' fur business until the 1930s, when he founded his own couture house. His company closed during World War II. In 1946 he opened a chain of sportswear boutiques.

James, Charles 1906–78. Designer. Born Sandhurst, England. James began his fashion career when he opened a hat shop in Chicago in 1924 under the name 'Charles Bouchéron'. He created his first dress collection in New York in 1928, his first London collection in 1929, and his first Paris collection in 1934. By 1940 he had returned to New York and established a house under his own name where he based his operation for most of the 1940s and 1950s. An architect of dress, James created superbly cut, sculpted ball gowns using large quantities of lavish fabrics often arranged asymmetrically in bunches and folds. He was also well known for his highly structured coats, his dresses with spiral zips and his quilted ivory-satin jackets.

Lelong, Lucien 1889–1958. Designer. Born Paris, France. Lelong trained at the Hautes Etudes des Commerciales

in Paris and established his own business after World War I. He became known for his skilful use of beautiful fabrics in creating elegant, understated dresses and evening wear. He was one of the first designers to produce stockings and lingerie, and in the late 1930s he designed tight-waisted, full skirts which were precursors to Dior's 'New Look' of 1947. During World War II Lelong was president of the Chambre Syndicale de la Haute Couture and was instrumental in persuading the occupying German forces not to move Parisian couture houses to Berlin. His last collection in 1947 included narrow dresses, pleated harem hemlines and broad-shouldered suits with cutaway fronts and nipped-in waists.

Mainbocher (Main Rousseau Bocher) 1891–1976. Designer. Born Chicago, Illinois, USA. Mainbocher was the first American couturier to achieve success in Paris, opening his own house there in 1930. He became famous for embroidered, apron-style evening dresses, for his use of the bias cut and for creating a trend for 'Wallis blue' with the wedding dress he designed for the Duchess of Windsor. He opened a salon in New York in 1940. During World War II Mainbocher responded to the problem of fabric rationing by producing short evening dresses and maintaining a restrained, narrow silhouette. He also designed uniforms for WAVES and the American Red Cross, among others.

Maxwell, Vera (Vera Huppé) 1901–95. Designer. Born New York, USA. Maxwell started her career by making clothes for herself. By 1936 she was attracting the attention of the fashion press and from the late 1930s her designs were being bought by Seventh Avenue firms such as Adler and Adler. Maxwell established her own business in 1947, creating classic, wearable separates and suits, wraparound jersey dresses and riding jackets. She was influenced by men's country clothes and used natural dyes to produce autumnal tones.

McCardell, Claire 1905–58. Designer. Born Frederick, Maryland, USA. During the late 1920s and 1930s McCardell worked with Richard Turk at Townley Frocks, and then for Hattie Carnegie. One of her first highly successful designs was the waistless, bias-cut 'monastic dress' of 1938. McCardell returned to Townley Frocks in 1940 to design under her own name, producing easy-fitting clothes which were hugely influential. During World War II she responded to the strict rationing of silk and wool with a creative and innovative use of fabrics such as cotton, denim and jersey. Her wraparound 'popover' dress of 1942 became one of her most popular and durable designs.

Molyneux, Captain Edward 1891–1974. Designer. Born London, England. Molyneux began his career producing illustrations for magazines and advertisements, and in 1911 was employed as a sketcher by Lucile. He opened his own couture house in Paris in 1919, becoming famous for simple tailored suits and skirts in muted tones which were seen as archetypally English in their restrained elegance. Between 1925 and 1932 he opened further branches in Monte Carlo, Cannes, Biarritz and also London, where he continued to work during World War II, producing graceful, streamlined garments. Molyneux retired in 1950. An attempted comeback in 1965 was unsuccessful – unlike Chanel, he could not adapt his understated classicism to the new times.

Morton, Digby 1906–83. Designer. Born Dublin, Ireland. Morton worked for Lachasse in London in the late 1920s and established his own business in 1933. He became well known for his use of Aran knits and Donegal tweeds often combined with silk blouses. Morton is also widely credited with having adapted the traditional tailor-made suit to make it more graceful and up-to-date. He created the uniforms for the Women's Voluntary Service in 1939 and in the late 1940s and 1950s produced designs for various US manufacturers.

Norell, Norman (Norman Levinson) 1900–72. Designer. Born Noblesville, Indiana, USA. From 1922 Norell worked as a costume designer and for the Seventh Avenue firm Charles Armour. In 1928 he joined Hattie Carnegie, where he remained until he founded Traina-Norell with Anthony Traina in 1941. During the 1940s and 1950s Norell made his reputation as one of America's finest designers, known not only for sophisticated, elaborately trimmed evening wear but also for his fur trenchcoats, sequined sheath dresses and empire-line dresses.

Piguet, Robert 1901–53. Designer. Born Yverdon, Switzerland. Piguet moved to Paris in 1918 and worked for Redfern and Poiret. Opening in 1933, the House of Piguet was known for romantic evening gowns and elegant suits and dresses, often in grey, beige or blue. Piguet also made costumes for the stage and frequently employed other designers, including Balmain, Dior, Galanos and Givenchy.

Rochas, Marcel 1902–55. Designer. Born Paris, France. Rochas established his house in 1924, becoming an influential designer whose work at times heralded styles which became current years later. Inspired by Javanese and Balinese traditional costumes, he introduced broad-shouldered garments to his collections in 1933, creating a look usually attributed to Schiaparelli. Other innovative designs included sculpted wool coats with widely stitched seams, trouser suits in grey flannel and the tight-waisted 'guêpière' corset of 1942 which presaged the more feminine shapes of the 1950s. Rochas was also famous for imaginative embroidery and appliqués and bizarre decorative features such as stuffed birds and buttons shaped like butterflies, lipstick and pipes. He often worked with flower-patterned fabric and was one of the first designers to add pockets to skirts.

Schiaparelli, Elsa 1890–1973. Designer. Born Rome, Italy. Schiaparelli moved to Paris in 1922 and opened a boutique, 'Pour le Sport', in 1927. The following year she showed her first collection. Her clothes were chic and eccentric, strongly influenced by modern art movements. She commissioned artists such as Salvador Dalí and Jean Cocteau to design fabrics and accessories and produced a range of surreal garments, often with *trompe-l'œil* effects. Her many innovations included unusually shaped buttons, padlock fastenings, lip-shaped pockets, and hats in the form of ice-cream cones, shoes or lamb cutlets. In 1933 her broad-shouldered pagoda sleeve set the basic shape for fashion until the New Look. The house of Schiaparelli closed during the war and re-opened in 1945. Known for her gifted use of colour, Schiaparelli promoted 'Shocking Pink' and was the first designer to use plastic zippers decoratively.

Trigère, Pauline 1912–2002. Designer. Born Paris, France. As a child Trigère helped her mother in her dressmaking business and later worked as a cutter for Martial et Armand. After moving to New York and working for Travis Banton at Hattie Carnegie, she opened her own house in 1942. Trigère achieved instant success with her finely tailored, original designs, often created by draping fabric directly on the model. Among her many innovations were removable scarves and collars, dresses with jewelry attached and reversible coats and capes. She was also known for her use of the bias cut. In the late 1940s Trigère launched a ready-to-wear line.

Valentina (Valentina Nicholaevna Sanina) 1899–1989. Designer. Born Kiev, Russia. Valentina established her house in 1928. She designed costumes for many theatrical productions as well as offstage clothes for actresses, including Katharine Hepburn, Greta Garbo and Gloria Swanson. While her day wear was often simple and practical, sometimes displaying peasant influences, she was best known for her dramatic evening wear and swirling capes. She was also a skilled designer of millinery, especially snoods, turbans and veils. During the late 1940s Valentina achieved considerable success with her full ballerina-style skirts worn with ballet slippers.

Biographies of 1950s Designers

Amies, Hardy 1909–2003. Designer. Born London, England. Amies started his career in fashion at Lachasse in 1934. In 1945 he opened his own couture house and became known for refined, well-cut women's suits in tweed and wool and for sumptuous puff-sleeved ball gowns. He was hugely successful during the 1950s, receiving the Royal Warrant to design clothes for the Queen in 1955. In 1961 he began designing menswear. In 1989 he was awarded a knighthood.

Balenciaga, Cristobal 1895–1972. Designer. Born Guetaria, Spain. At the age of 20 Balenciaga opened his first house in San Sebastian. When he moved to Paris in 1937 he was already Spain's leading couturier, producing austere, elegant, well-cut clothes in sombre colours recognizable for their stark Spanish style. In 1939 his tight-waisted dresses with dropped shoulderlines were clear forerunners of Dior's New Look. His many innovations include the pillbox hat, the stand-away collar, and the sack dress of 1956. During the 1950s he also began to use lambswool dyed in acid pinks and yellows and made short dresses and coats with dropped hemlines at the back.

Balmain, Pierre 1914–82. Designer. Born St Jean de Maurienne, France. Balmain started his career with Molyneux. In 1941 he began working at Lelong where he met Dior. When Balmain set up his own couture house in 1945 he created bell-shaped skirts with nipped-in waists similar to those later produced by Dior for the New Look. Though he tended to favour a narrow silhouette for his suits and dresses, Balmain was also known for his full half-belted coats and romantic full-skirted ball gowns. During the 1950s he created his famous sheath dresses, worn under jackets, as well as stoles for day wear and cossack-style wraps.

Cardin, Pierre 1922–. Designer. Born San Biagio di Callalta, near Venice, Italy, to French parents. Cardin worked for a tailor in Vichy from the age of 17. He moved to Paris in 1944 and found work with Paquin, Schiaparelli and Dior. In 1947 he designed the costumes for Jean Cocteau's film *La Belle et la bête* and over the following years established a reputation as a theatrical costumier. Cardin opened his own house in 1950 and presented his first collection three years later. During the early 1950s he produced simple, elegant couture such as his popular bubble skirts and coats with hemlines dropped at the back. By the 1960s, he had developed into a highly innovative and influential designer for both men and women.

Cashin, Bonnie 1915–2000. Designer. Born Oakland, California, USA. Cashin began her career as a costume designer before opening her own business in New York in 1953. She became famous for casual, practical, loose-fitting clothes inspired by her native Californian landscape. Over the next decade she introduced the idea of layered dressing and was acclaimed for mixing natural fabrics such as leather, cashmere, linen and suede. She was also known for her Chinese-style jackets, fringed suede dresses and stylish ponchos.

Cassini, Oleg (Oleg Cassini Loiewski) 1913–. Designer. Born Paris, France, of Russian parents. Cassini worked in Paris, New York and Hollywood before opening his own firm in 1950. He became famous for glamorous ready-to-wear suits and sheath and cocktail dresses.

Chanel, Gabrielle (Coco) 1883–1971. Designer. Born Saumur, France. Chanel began her career as a milliner in Paris in 1910, under the label 'Chanel Mode'. In 1913 she opened her first hat shop in Deauville and two years later started a dress shop in Biarritz. The 1920s saw her career flourish wth the founding of her Paris house and the launch of her most famous perfume, 'No. 5'. Chanel was hugely influential with her 'little black dress', wide-legged yachting pants, geometrically patterned beaded dresses and unconventional mixing of fabrics – plain with patterned jersey, or floral silk with tweed. She also became famous for costume jewelry: her long gilt chains, rows of pearls and mixtures of semi-precious stones were especially popular. Though Chanel closed her house in 1939, when she reopened in 1954 with the launch of her jersey suit, her vision of clothes which combined practicality with elegance was perfectly in tune with the times. During the 1950s she introduced low-heeled two-tone sling-back pumps and shoulderbags with gilt-chain handles. Her famously wearable tweed suit, which she had created before World War II, became a fashion classic and remains so today.

Dessès, Jean (Jean Dimitre Verginie) 1904–70. Designer. Born Alexandria, Egypt. Dessès began his career at the age of 21 with Maison Jane. He opened his own house in 1937. During the 1940s and 1950s he was known for his draped evening dresses, inspired by Ancient Greek and Egyptian garments, and for his embroidered ball gowns and sheath dresses.

Dior, Christian 1905–57. Designer. Born Granville, France. Dior began his fashion career in Paris at the age of 30, selling fashion sketches to newspapers. He joined Robert Piguet in 1938 and worked briefly for Lelong in 1942 before opening his own house in 1946. In 1947 his first collection, the 'Corolle line', soon nicknamed the 'New Look', was sensationally successful. His curved bodices and huge skirts with nipped-in waists brought a new femininity and glamour to fashion after the severe broad-shouldered, narrow-skirted lines produced under wartime rationing. In the 1950s Dior continued to create highly influential and increasingly sophisticated designs such as three-piece outfits of cardigan, top and skirt, box-shaped jackets with short skirts and his own versions of the caftan and cheongsam. Other widely copied innovations included the princess line, coolie hats, three-quarter-length sleeves and horseshoe collars.

Fath, Jacques 1912–54. Designer. Born Maison-Lafitte, France. During the 1930s Fath worked as a stockbroker at the Paris Bourse while at the same time studying costume and fashion design. He opened his own house in 1937, achieving worldwide fame by the late 1940s. Fath attracted a young, sophisticated clientele with his extravagant, flirtatious evening dresses and jaunty day clothes, often with decorative pleats, darts and angled collars.

Galanos, James 1924–. Designer. Born Philadelphia, Pennsylvania, USA. Following a year-long apprenticeship with Piguet in Paris in 1947, Galanos founded his own house, based in Los Angeles, in 1951. His first show in 1953 brought immediate success. He is known for his high standards of tailoring and cutting and for his use of luxurious fabrics. During the 1950s he was innovative in showing suits with horseshoe necklines and evening wear with large prints.

Givenchy, Hubert de 1927–. Designer. Born Beauvais, France. After briefly studying law in Paris, Givenchy worked for Fath, Piguet, Lelong and Schiaparelli before opening his own business in 1952. In the 1950s he created many popular designs, including his famous Bettina blouse, his sack dress of 1955 and his sheath dress of 1957. In the course of the decade his young, playful style became more sombre under the influence of Balenciaga.

Grès, Madame Alix 1903–93. Designer. Born Paris, France. Following her training at Premet, Grès opened her own couture house in 1934 under the name 'Alix', reopening after World War II under the name 'Grès'. She became famous for her draped and pleated dresses – in silk and wool – which resemble classical Greek robes, often cut on the bias and with dolman sleeves. Grès adopted a sculptural approach to dressmaking, each garment being modelled on the mannequin by hand with minimal use of patterns or cutting.

Hartnell, Norman 1901–79. Designer. Born London, England. Hartnell worked at Madame Désirée, Esther's and with Lucile before opening his own premises in London in 1923. He is best known as dressmaker to the British royal family and created Elizabeth II's wedding dress and coronation gown as well as many outfits for her overseas tours. In 1977 he was awarded a knighthood. Hartnell also produced elegantly tailored coats and suits and lavishly embroidered evening gowns.

Heim, Jacques 1899–1967. Designer. Born Paris, France. Heim designed womenswear for his parents' fur business until the 1930s, when he founded his own couture house. He became famous for his 'Atome' two-piece bathing suit of 1950 – the first bikini. He was the first couturier to use cotton for beachwear. During the 1950s he was also known for his halterneck tops worn with knee-length madras shorts.

James, Charles 1906–78. Designer. Born Sandhurst, England. James began his fashion career when he opened a hat shop in Chicago in 1924 under the name 'Charles Bouchéron'. He created his first dress collection in New York in 1928, his first London collection in 1929, and his first Paris collection in 1934. By 1940 he had returned to New York and established a house under his own name where he based his operation for most of the 1940s and 1950s. An architect of dress, James created superbly cut, sculpted ball gowns using large quantities of lavish fabrics often arranged asymmetrically in bunches and folds. He was also well known for his highly structured coats, his dresses with spiral zips and his quilted ivory-satin jackets.

Laroche, Guy 1923–89. Designer. Born La Rochelle, France. Laroche worked in millinery and then for Jean Dessès before opening his own house in 1957. His practical but feminine designs of the late 1950s were highly successful and in 1960 he launched his own ready-to-wear line. He is best known for his fine tailoring and cutting.

Mainbocher (Main Rousseau Bocher) 1891–1976. Designer. Born Chicago, Illinois, USA. Mainbocher was the first American couturier to achieve success in Paris, opening his own salon in 1930. He became famous for embroidered, apron-style evening dresses, for his use of the bias cut and for creating a trend for 'Wallis blue' with the wedding dress he designed for the Duchess of Windsor. Mainbocher opened a salon in New York in 1940. During the 1950s he was best known for his elegant knee-length skirts and for his short jackets with prim bows and peter-pan collars.

Maxwell, Vera (Vera Huppé) 1901–95. Designer. Born New York, USA. Maxwell established her business in 1947, creating classic, wearable clothes such as separates and suits, wraparound jersey dresses and riding jackets. She was influenced by men's country clothes and used natural dyes to produce muted, autumnal tones.

McCardell, Claire 1905–58. Designer. Born Frederick, Maryland, USA. During the late 1920s and 1930s McCardell worked with Richard Turk at Townley Frocks, and then for Hattie Carnegie. Returning to Townley Frocks in 1940 to design under her own name, McCardell produced easy-fitting clothes made from cotton, denim, gingham and jersey which had a huge impact in the 1950s. Her many popular designs included the 'popover' dress, with side slits and ties; playsuits; dirndl skirts; strapless, elasticated tube tops and the diaper bathing suit. She often used metal fastenings and large patch pockets as decorative details and was the first designer to introduce ballet-type pumps for everyday wear.

Norell, Norman (Norman Levinson) 1900–72. Designer. Born Noblesville, Indiana, USA. From 1922 Norell worked as a costume designer and for the Seventh Avenue firm Charles Armour. In 1928 he joined Hattie Carnegie, where he remained until he founded Traina-Norell with Anthony Traina in 1941. During the 1940s and 1950s Norell made his reputation as one of America's finest designers, known not only for sophisticated, elaborately trimmed evening wear but also for his fur trenchcoats, sequined sheath dresses and empire-line dresses.

Pucci, Emilio (Marchese di Barsento) 1914–85. Designer. Born Naples, Italy. In the mid-1940s, as a member of the Italian Olympic ski team, Pucci was photographed by Toni Frissell for *Harper's Bazaar* wearing ski pants he had designed himself. The magazine then published some of his designs for women's winter clothes which were quickly bought by several New York stores. He founded his own couture house, Emilio, in 1950, producing capri pants, casual suits and other sportswear. Using bold acid colours, Pucci created prints inspired by medieval heraldic banners – psychedelic designs which are now synonymous with the fashions of the late 1950s and 1960s.

Saint Laurent, Yves 1936–. Designer. Born Oran, Algeria. Saint Laurent's career in fashion took off in 1954 when he won first prize for a design for a cocktail dress in a competition held by the International Wool Secretariat. In 1955 he began working for Dior, taking over the house at the age of 21 when Dior died. Saint Laurent attracted controversy with designs such as his precisely tailored 'Trapeze' dress of 1958 and his leather jackets and turtle-neck sweaters of 1960. Though hugely popular, his youthful style was not appreciated by Dior's more conventional clientele – when he returned from military service in Algeria in 1961 he found he had been replaced by Marc Bohan.

Schiaparelli, Elsa 1890–1973. Designer. Born Rome, Italy. Schiaparelli moved to Paris in 1922 and opened a boutique, 'Pour le Sport', in 1927. The following year she founded her own couture house, creating chic, eccentric clothes strongly influenced by modern art movements. She commissioned artists such as Salvador Dalí and Jean Cocteau to design fabrics and accessories and produced a range of surreal garments, often with *trompe-l'œil* effects. Her many innovations included unusually shaped buttons, padlock fastenings, lip-shaped pockets, and hats in the form of ice-cream cones, shoes or lamb cutlets. In 1933 her broad-shouldered pagoda sleeve set the basic shape for fashion until the New Look. Known for her gifted use of colour, Schiaparelli promoted 'Shocking Pink' and was the first designer to use plastic zippers decoratively. Her last show took place in 1954.

Trigère, Pauline 1912–2002. Designer. Born Paris, France. Trigère worked for Hattie Carnegie before opening her own house in New York in 1942. Trigère achieved instant success with her finely tailored, original designs. Among her many innovations were removable scarves and collars, dresses with jewelry attached and reversible coats and capes.

Valentina (Valentina Nicholaevna Sanina) 1899–1989. Designer. Born Kiev, Russia. Valentina established her house in 1928. While her day wear was often simple and practical, sometimes displaying peasant influences, she was best known for her dramatic evening wear and swirling capes. She was also a skilled designer of millinery, especially snoods, turbans and veils. During the late 1940s and 1950s Valentina had particular success with her full ballerina-length skirts and slippers.

Biographies of 1960s Designers

Balenciaga, Cristobal 1895–1972. Designer. Born Guetaria, Spain. At the age of 20 Balenciaga opened his first house in San Sebastian. When he moved to Paris in 1937 he was already Spain's leading couturier, producing austere, elegant, well-cut clothes in sombre colours recognizable for their stark Spanish style. In 1939 his tight-waisted dresses with dropped shoulderlines were clear forerunners of Dior's New Look. His many innovations include the pillbox hat, the stand-away collar, and the sack dress of 1956. In the 1960s he was one of the first couturiers to design bodystockings, and produced highly successful loose jackets with dolman sleeves. His couture house closed in 1968.

Bates, John 1938–. Designer. Born Ponteland, England. Bates started the company Jean Varon in the early 1960s and soon became known as one of the decade's most audacious designers, producing the briefest of mini-skirts, trouser suits, catsuits and broderie anglaise evening wear. He also made garments from Op Art-inspired fabrics. Among his widely copied designs were a black leather outfit and a white vinyl coat he created for the actress Diana Rigg in the British TV series *The Avengers*.

Beene, Geoffrey 1927–2004. Designer. Born Haynesville, Louisiana, USA. Beene studied at the Traphagen School of Fashion in New York. In the late 1940s he moved to Paris where he trained at the Académie Julian and at Molyneux. On his return to New York in 1948, he worked for a number of ready-to-wear companies before he founded his own firm in 1963. Beene designed graphically striking garments which combine couture quality with the ease of modern sportswear. He showed originality in mixing fabrics and in the use of synthetic materials.

Blass, Bill 1922–2002. Designer. Born Fort Wayne, Indiana, USA. After World War II Blass joined Anne Miller & Co. who merged with Maurice Rentner Ltd in 1959. He became vice president in 1962 and from 1970 the company went under his own name. During the 1960s Blass was known for his dresses extravagantly trimmed with ruffles and lace. Though he often borrowed from the male wardrobe for his sportswear, Blass tailored his suits with a curved silhouette which flattered the female shape.

Bohan, Marc 1926–. Designer. Born Paris, France. Bohan worked freelance for Piguet, Molyneux and Patou, among others, before he was appointed director of Dior's English operations in London in 1958. In 1961 he succeeded Saint Laurent as head designer in Paris. He quickly established a reputation for maintaining the refined, romantic image of Dior while adapting popular, youthful styles to haute couture. Among his most influential designs of the 1960s were the cossack-style fur-trimmed coats and full skirts he created in 1966. He is also known for his elegant evening gowns in rich fabrics.

Cardin, Pierre 1922–. Designer. Born San Biagio di Callalta, near Venice, Italy. Cardin worked for a tailor in Vichy from the age of 17. He moved to Paris in 1944 and found work with Paquin, Schiaparelli and Dior. He opened his own house in 1950. By the 1960s he had developed into a highly innovative and influential designer for men and women. His designs were bold and uncompromising: cut-out dresses, mini-skirts, brightly coloured wigs and dresses with necklines cut to the navel. In 1964 he showed his 'Space Age' collection which included catsuits, batwing jumpsuits and helmets.

Cashin, Bonnie 1915–2000. Designer. Born Oakland, California, USA. Cashin began her career as a costume designer before opening her own business in New York in 1953. She created casual, practical clothes. During the 1960s she introduced the idea of layered dressing and was acclaimed for mixing natural fabrics such as leather, linen and cashmere. She was also known for her Chinese-style jackets, fringed suede dresses and stylish ponchos.

Cassini, Oleg (Oleg Cassini Loiewski) 1913–. Designer. Born Paris, France. Cassini worked in Paris, New York and Hollywood before opening his own firm in 1950. He became famous for glamorous ready-to-wear suits and sheath and cocktail dresses. He was appointed official designer to Jacqueline Kennedy (Onassis) in 1961. The two-piece suit with three-quarter-length sleeves he made for her was widely copied.

Castillo, Antonio 1908–84. Designer. Born Madrid, Spain. Castillo designed dresses, hats and jewelry for Paquin and Piguet from 1936 until 1945 when he joined Elizabeth Arden's salon in New York. Returning to Paris in 1950, he was made designer for the house of Lanvin. Castillo founded his own company in 1964. He was known for luxurious, elegant garments with intricate detail.

Clark, Ossie 1942–96. Designer. Born Liverpool, England. From 1957 to 1961 Clark attended Manchester College of Art and the Royal College of Art in London. He began designing for the boutique Quorum while still a student and became a full-time designer in 1966. Clark was responsible for some of the most innovative styles of the 1960s, including hot-pants, maxi-coats and gypsy-style dresses.

Courrèges, André 1923–. Designer. Born Pau, France. After studying engineering, Courrèges joined Balenciaga in 1945. In 1961 he set up his own house. Courrèges fused the precise technique he had learnt at Balenciaga with the functionalism of his training as an engineer to produce some of the most avant-garde designs of the 1960s. His early collections included mini-dresses and trouser suits in white and silver, futuristic accessories such as goggles, and his famous white mid-calf boots. In the late 1960s he produced catsuits and cut-out dresses.

De la Renta, Oscar 1932–. Designer. Born Santo Domingo, Dominican Republic. De la Renta studied at the Academia de San Fernando in Madrid. His first design, a debutante gown for the daughter of the US ambassador to Spain, was featured on the cover of *Life* and led to a job with Balenciaga. In 1961 he was made assistant to Castillo at Lanvin in Paris and moved with Castillo to Elizabeth Arden in New York in 1963. In 1965, he began working for Jane Derby but on her retirement in the same year he founded his own house. De la Renta is best known for his dramatic evening wear, often lavishly trimmed. His 1967 Gypsy collection was a precursor to the 1970s vogue for peasant styles.

Fratini, Gina 1934–. Designer. Born Kobe, Japan, of English parents. Fratini studied fashion at the Royal College of Art in London. From her first collection in 1966, she became known for an essentially romantic style, expressed in frilly, floating dresses and flowing evening gowns.

Galanos, James 1924–. Designer. Born Philadelphia, Pennsylvania, USA. Galanos was apprenticed to Piguet in Paris in 1947, and in 1951 founded his own house in Los Angeles. His first show in 1953 brought immediate success. He is known for his high standards of tailoring and for his use of luxurious fabrics. During the 1960s he designed many close-fitting, classically draped evening dresses.

Galitzine, Princess Irene 1916–. Designer. Born Tiflis, Russia. Galitzine studied art and design in Rome. From the mid-1940s she worked for Fontana until she set up her own business in 1949. In 1960 she introduced her most famous design, the wide-legged 'Palazzo Pyjamas'. Galitzine produced garments that epitomized 1960s Italian high style: open-sided dresses, toga tops worn over trousers and, in 1966, a futuristic quilted vinyl jumpsuit. In 1968 she turned to freelance designing but reopened her house under the name 'Princess Galitzine' in 1970.

Gernreich, Rudi 1922–85. Designer. Born Vienna, Austria. Gernreich began designing for the Los Angeles boutique 'Jax' in 1948 and started his own firm in 1964. He is considered the most radical of the 1960s American designers. Among his most experimental designs were jackets with one notched and one rounded lapel and elasticated swimsuits with no inner structuring. In 1964 he launched the 'no-bra bra' which allowed a natural body shape, the highly controversial topless bathing suit and a flesh-coloured bodystocking in stretch nylon. He also promoted unisex clothing with designs for kaftans, bell-bottom trousers and cropped tops.

Givenchy, Hubert de 1927–. Designer. Born Beauvais, France. Givenchy worked for Fath, Piguet, Lelong and Schiaparelli before opening his own business in 1952. During the 1950s his young, playful style became more sombre under the influence of Balenciaga. Givenchy was hugely influential, particularly through his designs for Audrey Hepburn in the 1961 film *Breakfast at Tiffany's*. During the 1960s his chic, simple and highly wearable designs became increasingly sophisticated.

Halston, Roy 1932–90. Designer. Born Des Moines, Iowa, USA. Halston opened a millinery salon in 1953 in Chicago before moving to New York in 1958 to work for the milliner Lilly Daché and then for Bergdorf Goodman. He founded a ready-to-wear firm in 1966, gaining a reputation for sexy, glamorous clothes with a slim silhouette. He was influential in the late 1960s with sophisticated designs for halterneck jumpsuits and dresses, wide-legged trousers and cashmere sweaters.

Hulanicki, Barbara 1936–. Designer. Born Palestine, of Polish parents. After studying at Brighton Art College, Hulanicki won a London *Evening Standard* competition for beachwear in 1955. She then worked as an illustrator for various magazines, including *Vogue* and *Tatler*. Hulanicki sold her first designs by mail order. In 1964 she opened the Biba shop in Kensington which became famous for its stylishly decadent atmosphere with lavish decor inspired by 1930s interiors and art nouveau. Here, affordable mini-skirts and unisex T-shirts dyed in rich, muted colours were eagerly snapped up by a young clientele. Other signature items included floppy felt hats, feather boas and velvet trouser suits.

Johnson, Betsey 1942–. Designer. Born Hartford, Connecticut, USA. Johnson studied fine art at Syracuse University in New York and was appointed guest editor of *Mademoiselle* in 1964. She then worked as a freelance designer and in 1965 began supplying the New York shop 'Paraphernalia'. During the 1960s she produced inexpensive, inventive garments such as a transparent vinyl dress with adhesive star motifs, a silver motorcycle suit and a 'noise' dress fringed with grommets. Her cowhide mini-skirts and slinky T-shirt dresses were also popular. In 1969 she opened a boutique called 'Betsey, Bunkey, and Nini'.

Khanh, Emanuelle 1937–. Designer. Born Paris, France. Khanh began her career in fashion in the 1950s as a model for Balenciaga and Givenchy. Her success as a designer was assured with an article featuring her 'Yé Yé' styles in a 1961 edition of *Elle*. During the 1960s she created collections for various houses, including Dorothée Bis, Cacharel, Missoni and Krizia. Khanh was at the forefront of young Parisian fashion, producing feminine designs with a nostalgic 1930s feel. She was known for close-fitting jackets and dresses, sometimes featuring long collars.

Missoni, Ottavio and Rosita Knitwear designers. Ottavio born 1921 in Dalmatia; Rosita born 1931 in Lombardy, Italy. After founding the Missoni company in 1953, the couple produced their first knitwear collection for Rinascente stores in 1954. In 1958 they launched their own label. They rose to prominence in the 1960s and 1970s, creating fluid, boldly patterned dresses, coats and sweaters which restored the fashion world's interest in knitwear. Missoni is known for sophisticated knitting techniques and an artistic blending of colour.

Muir, Jean 1933–95. Designer. Born London, England. After working at Liberty, where she eventually became a sketcher, Muir joined Jaeger in 1956. In 1962 she began designing a line called Jane & Jane. She set up her own company in 1966. Muir used an exceptionally fine technique to create fluid, timeless clothes in jersey and suede.

Norell, Norman 1900–72. Designer. Born Noblesville, Indiana, USA. From 1922 Norell worked as a costume designer and for the Seventh Avenue firm Charles Armour. In 1928 he joined Hattie Carnegie, where he remained until he founded Traina-Norell with Anthony Traina in 1941. During the 1940s and 1950s Norell made his reputation as one of America's finest designers. He was best known for stylish, elaborate evening wear, especially his sequined sheath dresses. Norell opened his own house in 1960, launching his famous culotte suit in the same year.

Pucci, Emilio (Marchese di Barsento) 1914–85. Designer. Born Naples, Italy. In the mid-1940s, as a member of the Italian Olympic ski team, Pucci was photographed by Toni Frissell for *Harper's Bazaar* wearing ski pants he had designed himself. The magazine then published some of his designs for women's winter clothes which were quickly bought by several New York stores. He founded his own couture house, Emilio, in 1950, producing capri pants and other casual wear. Pucci created prints inspired by medieval heraldic banners – psychedelic designs which are now synonymous with the fashions of the 1960s.

Quant, Mary 1934–. Designer. Born London, England. Quant attended Goldsmiths College of Art in London. In 1955 she worked briefly for the milliner Erik and later that year opened a boutique in Chelsea called 'Bazaar'. Quant was perfectly in tune with the needs of her young, hip clientele. Her inexpensive, classless designs revolutionized dress for the teenage market and created an entirely British look. Items such as mini-skirts, short pinafore dresses and skinny-rib polo-neck sweaters were all popularized by Quant. She also promoted PVC garments and crocheted tops. From 1963 Quant's designs were mass-produced for the US market, where her style was hugely influential.

Rabanne, Paco 1934–. Designer. Born San Sebastian, Spain. After studying architecture at the Ecole des Beaux-Arts in Paris, Rabanne sold designs for plastic jewelry and buttons to Balenciaga, Dior and Givenchy. In 1964 he caused a sensation with the launch of a futuristic plastic dress, the first of many designs to introduce alternative materials. Rabanne opened his own house in 1966, creating garments made of paper, aluminium and chainmail in a process akin to industrial design. He was also inventive in his mixing of leather, fur and knitted wool.

Rhodes, Zandra 1940–. Designer. Born Chatham, England. In 1961 Rhodes attended the Royal College of Art in London. She first sold her designs from her shop in London. In 1968 she founded her own house and in 1969 *Vogue* featured her designs for chiffon scarves, kaftans and dresses with handkerchief points. Taking her handprinted fabrics as the starting point for her clothes, Rhodes became famous for fantastic, floating garments in silk and chiffon.

Saint Laurent, Yves 1936–. Designer. Born Oran, Algeria. Saint Laurent won first prize for a design for a cocktail dress in a competition held by the International Wool Secretariat in 1954. In 1955 he began working for Dior, taking over the house at the age of 21 when Dior died. Saint Laurent attracted controversy with designs such as his 'Trapeze' dress of 1958 and his leather jackets and turtle-neck sweaters of 1960. Though hugely popular, his youthful style did not please Dior's more conventional clientele – he was replaced by Marc Bohan in 1961. Following the establishment of his own house in the same year, he produced a series of innovative designs including the famous 1965 Mondrian dress, thigh-high boots, velvet knickerbockers, see-through blouses and the classic safari jacket. In 1966 Saint Laurent launched his influential 'smoking' jacket and opened a ready-to-wear chain, Rive Gauche. From 1969, when he introduced his own version of the trouser suit, Saint Laurent based many of his designs on masculine jackets and trousers.

Ungaro, Emanuel 1933–. Designer. Born Aix-en-Provence, France, to Italian parents. Ungaro trained in his parents' tailoring firm. He moved to Paris in 1955 and worked for Maison Camps tailors before joining Balenciaga in 1958. In 1962 he began working for Courrèges. Three years later he founded his own house, creating futuristic designs including angular coats, thigh-high boots and metal bras. In 1968 he launched a ready-to-wear line.

Valentino (Valentino Garavani) 1932–. Designer. Born Voghera, Italy. Valentino attended the Accademia Dell'Arte in Milan and the Chambre Syndicale de la Haute Couture in Paris. He worked for Dessès and Laroche in the early 1950s, before opening his own house in Rome in 1959. In 1962 Valentino transferred to Florence, where he was acclaimed for his romantic evening gowns, often with dramatic bows and ruffles. By the mid-1960s he had launched his famous trouser suits for day and evening wear. Valentino was hugely successful with his 1968 White Collection, which included mini-dresses worn with lacy tights and flat shoes. His signature colour is red.

Biographies of 1970s Designers

Armani, Giorgio 1935–. Designer. Born Piacenza, Italy. Armani worked from 1954 to 1960 as a window stylist, and eventually as fashion coordinator, for the Italian department store La Rinascente. From 1960 to 1970 he designed menswear for Cerruti, and from 1970 to 1974 worked freelance for Ungaro, among others. He opened his own company in 1975, creating unstructured, though precisely tailored clothing from fine materials. He was hugely influential during the late 1970s and 1980s with his broad-shouldered, pared-down suits for men and his women's clothes based on masculine garments.

Bates, John 1938–. Designer. Born Ponteland, England. Bates started the company Jean Varon in the early 1960s and soon became known as one of that decade's most audacious designers, producing the briefest of mini-skirts, trouser suits, catsuits and broderie anglaise evening wear. Among his most widely copied designs were the costumes he created for the actress Diana Rigg in the British TV series *The Avengers*. During the 1970s his style became more sophisticated and he had particular success with his extra-long maxi-coats and fluid evening dresses.

Beene, Geoffrey 1927–2004. Designer. Born Haynesville, Louisiana, USA. Beene studied at the Traphagen School of Fashion in New York. In the late 1940s he moved to Paris where he trained at the Académie Julian and at Molyneux. On his return to New York in 1948, he worked for a number of ready-to-wear companies before founding his own firm in 1963. Beene designed graphically striking garments which combine couture quality with the ease of modern sportswear. He showed originality in mixing fabrics and in the use of synthetic materials.

Blass, Bill 1922–2002. Designer. Born Fort Wayne, Indiana, USA. After World War II Blass joined Anne Miller & Co. who merged with Maurice Rentner Ltd in 1959. He became vice president in 1962 and from 1970 the company went under his own name. He was known for his extravagant use of ruffles and lace. Though he often borrowed from the male wardrobe for his sportswear, Blass tailored his suits with a curved silhouette which flattered the female shape.

Bohan, Marc 1926–. Designer. Born Paris, France. Bohan worked freelance for Piguet, Molyneux and Patou, among others, before he was appointed director of Dior's English operations in London in 1958. In 1961 he succeeded Saint Laurent as head designer in Paris. He quickly established a reputation for maintaining the refined, romantic image of Dior while adapting popular, youthful styles to haute couture. He is known for his elegant evening gowns in rich fabrics.

Burrows, Stephen 1943–. Designer. Born Newark, New Jersey, USA. Burrows studied at Philadelphia Museum College of Art and the Fashion Institute of Technology in New York before opening a boutique in 1968. He founded his own firm in 1973 and became famous for clinging, glitzy clothes including highly popular designs such as slinky jersey dresses in bright colours and layered chiffon tops and skirts. Many of Burrows's garments are recognizable by his use of machine-made stitching to produce a crinkled 'lettuce' effect on hemlines.

Cardin, Pierre 1922–. Designer. Born San Biagio di Callalta, near Venice, Italy. Cardin worked for a tailor in Vichy from the age of 17. He moved to Paris in 1944 and found work with Paquin, Schiaparelli and Dior. He opened his own house in 1950. By the 1960s he had developed into an original and influential designer for both men and women. In 1964 he showed his avant-garde 'Space Age' collection and became famous for his catsuits, mini-skirts and bodystockings. In the 1970s he continued to show innovative designs using more supple fabrics, often with sunray pleating; he also won acclaim for his layered chiffon evening wear.

Clark, Ossie 1942–96. Designer. Born Liverpool, England. From 1957 to 1961 Clark attended Manchester College of Art and the Royal College of Art in London. He began designing for the boutique 'Quorum' while still a student and became a full-time designer in 1966. Clark was responsible for some of the most innovative styles of the 1960s and 1970s, including hot-pants, maxi-coats, gypsy-style dresses and short, zipped leather motorcycle jackets with large collars. During the 1970s he was known for long wraparound dresses, often with deep necklines and small waists.

De la Renta, Oscar 1932–. Designer. Born Santo Domingo, Dominican Republic. De la Renta studied at the Academia de San Fernando in Madrid. His first design, a debutante gown for the daughter of the US ambassador to Spain, was featured on the cover of *Life* and led to a job with Balenciaga. After a period at Lanvin and Jane Derby, he founded his own house in 1965. De la Renta is best known for his dramatic evening wear, often extravagantly trimmed. During the 1970s he won acclaim for peasant-style garments.

Galanos, James 1924–. Designer. Born Philadelphia, Pennsylvania, USA. Galanos was apprenticed to Piguet in Paris in 1947, and in 1951 founded his own house, based in Los Angeles. His first show in 1953 brought immediate success. He is known for his high standards of tailoring and cutting and for his use of luxurious fabrics. During the 1960s and 1970s he designed many close-fitting, classically draped evening dresses, often with large sleeves and low-cut backs.

Gaultier, Jean-Paul 1952–. Designer. Born Paris, France. At the age of 17 Gaultier sent sketches to several couture houses and in 1970 was invited to work for Cardin for one year. He then designed for Jacques Esterel and Jean Patou, among others. In 1977 he set up his own company, producing witty, anarchic fashions which fused Parisian glamour with flea-market kitsch and London streetstyles. He has developed a reputation as an innovative designer whose work challenges accepted boundaries of gender.

Gibb, Bill 1943–88. Designer. Born Fraserburgh, Scotland. Gibb studied in London at St Martin's School of Art and the Royal College of Art before joining Baccarat. In 1970 he was named 'Designer of the Year' by British *Vogue* and in 1971 established his own company. He became known for his lavish, romantic evening wear, achieving particular success with diaphanous chiffon dresses and embroidered and appliquéd jersey dresses.

Givenchy, Hubert de 1927–. Designer. Born Beauvais, France. Givenchy worked for Fath, Piguet, Lelong and Schiaparelli before opening his own business in 1952. During the 1950s his young, playful style became more sombre under the influence of Balenciaga. Givenchy was hugely influential, particularly through his designs for Audrey Hepburn in the 1961 film *Breakfast at Tiffany's*. In the 1970s he continued to produce chic, wearable couture.

Halston, Roy 1932–90. Designer. Born Des Moines, Iowa, USA. Halston opened a millinery salon in 1953 in Chicago before moving to New York in 1958 to work for the milliner Lilly Daché and then for Bergdorf Goodman. He set up his own ready-to-wear firm in 1966, gaining a reputation for sexy, glamorous clothes with a slim silhouette. He was one of the most sophisticated and influential designers of the 1970s. Among his most widely copied designs were his ultrasuede shirtwaist dress of 1972 and his bias-cut evening dresses with one shoulder strap.

Kamali, Norma 1945–. Designer. Born New York, USA. Kamali studied fashion illustration at the Fashion Institute of Technology in New York. Between 1967 and 1978 she worked as a freelance designer, opening a boutique with her husband in 1968. In the 1970s she produced extrovert, body-conscious clothes such as hot-pants and gold lamé maillots inspired by streetstyles. By 1978, when she set up the company OMO (On My Own), following her divorce, she was recognized as one of the most innovative designers of the decade.

Kenzo (Kenzo Takada) 1939–. Designer. Born Kyoto, Japan. Kenzo attended the Bunka Gakuin College of Fashion in Tokyo. He moved to Paris in 1964 and sold his designs to Feraud, Rodier and others. In 1970 he opened his Jungle Jap boutique in Paris and achieved immediate success with casual, exuberant designs often made in cotton. He based many of his garments on Japanese traditions of layering fabric around the body. Inspired by ethnic costumes, which he mixes and reinterprets to produce colourful, trendsetting garments, he is also known for mixing prints and experimenting with texture.

Klein, Calvin 1942–. Designer. Born New York, USA. After studying at the New York Fashion Institute of Technology, Klein joined Dan Millstein in 1962 and then worked freelance until 1968 when he set up Calvin Klein Co. He became famous for his sleek, understated suits and sportswear made from natural fabrics. By the late 1970s his designs had become increasingly sophisticated, with broad-shouldered jackets and slim, softly tailored separates. Klein is also known for the hugely successful marketing of his 'designer label' jeans and underwear.

Lagerfeld, Karl 1938–. Designer. Born Hamburg, Germany. At the age of 17 he won first prize for a design for a coat in a competition sponsored by the International Wool Secretariat and was taken on by Balmain. In 1958 he was made art director at Patou. One year later he began working freelance for several design houses, including Chloé, Krizia and Fendi, making a considerable impact on 1970s fashions. His innovations at Fendi included removing the heavy linings in fur coats to make more supple garments and dyeing furs in strong colours. At the ready-to-wear company Chloé he created luxurious, feminine evening wear of the highest quality. In 1983 he became design director of Chanel and was highly successful with his controversial mixing of Chanel's hallmark tweed suits, gilt buttons and chains with modern, streetstyle elements.

Lauren, Ralph (Ralph Lipschitz) 1939–. Designer. Born New York, USA. While studying business at City College in New York, Lauren worked for Bloomingdales, Brooks Brothers and others. Appointed designer for Beau Brummell Neckwear in 1967, he created 'Polo', a line of luxury handmade ties. In 1968 he began designing menswear for the Polo division. Womenswear was added in

1971. In 1972 he launched his own label which became associated with classic, Ivy League-style garments. His 'Prairie' look of 1978, based on fringed leather jackets, full-sleeved cotton blouses and denim skirts worn over white petticoats, was also highly successful. His costumes for Robert Redford in the 1974 film *The Great Gatsby* and his designs for Diane Keaton in *Annie Hall* (1977) were two of the most recognizable styles of the 1970s.

Missoni, Ottavio and Rosita Knitwear designers. Ottavio born 1921 in Dalmatia, Yugoslavia; Rosita born 1931 in Lombardy, Italy. After founding the Missoni company in 1953, the couple produced their first knitwear collection for Rinascente stores in 1954 and launched their own label in 1958. They rose to prominence in the 1960s and 1970s, creating fluid, boldly patterned dresses, coats and sweaters which restored the fashion world's interest in knitwear. Missoni is known for sophisticated knitting techniques and an artistic blending of colour.

Miyake, Issey 1938–. Designer. Born Hiroshima, Japan. Miyake graduated in 1964 from Tama University in Tokyo. In 1965 he moved to Paris to study at the Ecole de la Chambre Syndicale de la Haute Couture. He then worked for Laroche and Givenchy before joining Geoffrey Beene in New York in 1969. He founded the Miyake Design Studio in 1970 and showed his first collection in New York in 1971. An experimental and visionary artist, he created highly original garments, many of which could be draped around the body in different ways. Using traditional Japanese techniques of layering fabric, he explores texture and structure with unusual materials such as moulded plastic and woven bamboo.

Montana, Claude 1949–. Designer. Born Paris, France. Montana began his career selling handmade papier-mâché jewelry decorated with rhinestones in London street-markets. His designs appeared in British *Vogue* and when he returned to Paris in 1972 he worked for MacDouglas and Complice. He founded his own house in 1979. He produces tough, masculine garments often in leather. In the 1970s his designs strongly influenced French ready-to-wear.

Mugler, Thierry 1948–. Designer. Born Strasbourg, France. Mugler joined Gudule boutique in Paris in 1966 as assistant designer. In 1973 he created a collection under the label 'Café de Paris'. He set up his own house in 1974. Strongly influenced by Hollywood glamour and gangster style, he produced clinging, theatrical clothes which can either be highly minimalist or vampy and ornate. In 1977 he was one of the first designers to use padded shoulders, heralding a new shape for the 1980s.

Muir, Jean 1933–95. Designer. Born London, England. After working at Liberty, where she eventually became a sketcher, Muir joined Jaeger in 1956, and in 1962 began designing a line called Jane & Jane. In 1966 she set up her own company, known for fluid, refined, timeless clothes in jersey and suede.

Rhodes, Zandra 1940–. Designer. Born Chatham, England. In 1961 Rhodes attended the Royal College of Art in London. She first sold her garments from her shop in London. In 1968 she founded her own house. Taking her handprinted fabrics as the starting point for her designs, she became famous during the 1970s for fantastic, floating dresses in silk and chiffon, often with handkerchief hems. Her designs feature Art Deco motifs, zigzags and pale, delicate colours. In the late 1970s she revived the crinoline and in 1977 her 'Conceptual Chic' collection brought glamour to Punk styles with garments made from ripped jersey held together with diamanté safety pins.

Rykiel, Sonia 1930–. Designer. Born Paris, France. She began her career by making maternity dresses for herself in 1962. Then she designed for her husband's firm 'Laura' and in 1968 set up her own boutique in Galeries Lafayette in Paris. She helped to revive interest in knitwear by creating subtle outfits from soft wools such as angora. Her clinging sweaters, teamed with versatile skirts and trousers, are shaped to suit a slim figure.

Saint Laurent, Yves 1936–. Designer. Born Oran, Algeria. Saint Laurent won first prize for a design for a cocktail dress in a competition held by the International Wool Secretariat in 1954. In 1955 he began working for Dior, taking over the house at the age of 21 when Dior died. Though hugely popular, his youthful style did not please Dior's more conventional clientele – he was replaced by Marc Bohan in 1961. Following the establishment of his own house in the same year, he produced a series of innovative, sophisticated designs including his influential 'smoking' jacket, see-through blouses and safari jackets. He opened a ready-to-wear chain, Rive Gauche, in 1966. In the 1970s he created many stylish designs based on masculine jackets and trousers which perfectly suited the tastes of cosmopolitan women. His vibrantly coloured evening wear, by contrast, became increasingly romantic and his 1976 collection, showing full skirts, boots, vests and shawls, brought ethnic dressing to haute couture.

Ungaro, Emanuel 1933–. Designer. Born Aix-en-Provence, France. Ungaro trained in his parents' tailoring firm and then moved to Paris in 1955. He worked for Maison Camps tailors until he joined Balenciaga in 1958. In 1962 he moved to Courrèges. Three years later he founded his own house, producing futuristic designs including angular coats, thigh-high boots and metal bras. In the 1970s his clothes became more supple and in the later part of the decade he was innovative in his combining of textured and patterned materials.

Valentino (Valentino Garavani) 1932–. Designer. Born Voghera, Italy. Valentino attended the Accademia Dell'Arte in Milan and the Chambre Syndicale de la Haute Couture in Paris. He worked for Dessès and Laroche in the early 1950s, before opening his own house in Rome in 1959. In 1962 Valentino transferred to Florence, where he was acclaimed for glamorous evening gowns often featuring large bows and ruffles. In the 1970s he designed highly successful day-wear outfits including knife-pleated skirts and long coats worn over trouser suits. He is also associated with the revival of flamboyant, romantic evening dresses in the late 1970s.

Versace, Gianni 1946–97. Designer. Born Calabria, Italy. Versace worked with his dressmaker mother before moving to Milan in 1972, where he worked freelance for Genny, Complice and Callaghan. During the 1970s he developed a reputation for evening wear and for leather-trimmed knitwear for Callaghan. In 1978 he founded his own house, making sensuous, clinging garments often cut on the bias. Drawing on historical references, he created clothes that were bold, sexy and modern.

Biographies of 1980s Designers

Alaïa, Azzedine 1940–. Designer. Born Tunisia. Alaïa studied at the Ecole des Beaux-Arts in Tunis before moving in 1957 to Paris where he worked for Dior, Laroche and Mugler. During the 1970s he designed for private clients, launching his first collection in 1981. A revolutionary design for a black leather tunic brought him international recognition. He sought in his designs to enhance the female silhouette, experimenting with flexible fabrics such as wool, leather and Lycra, to create complex garments that clung to the body like a second skin. He popularized the stretch look and made practical yet sexy use of the zipper.

Armani, Giorgio 1935–. Designer. Born Piacenza, Italy. Armani worked from 1954 to 1960 as a window stylist, and eventually as fashion coordinator, for the Italian department store La Rinascente. He designed menswear for Cerruti from 1970 until 1974, when he turned freelance. He opened his own company in 1975. Known for his simple, precise tailoring and for the uncluttered, minimalist look of his clothes, Armani was particularly influential among working women in the late 1970s and 1980s when he contributed wide shoulders to the 'power suit' popular at that time. By the mid-1980s his designs were sleeker and less pronounced. He created large, loose blazers and supple shorts and culottes, invariably in muted tones.

Beene, Geoffrey 1927–2004. Designer. Born Haynesville, Louisiana, USA. Beene studied at the Traphagen School of Fashion in New York. In the late 1940s he moved to Paris where he trained at the Académie Julian and at Molyneux. On his return to New York in 1948, he worked for a number of ready-to-wear companies before founding his own firm in 1963. A master of cut, Beene combined the quality of couture with the ease of modern sportswear. He is known for blending rich fabrics with less expensive materials.

Blahnik, Manolo 1943–. Shoe designer. Born Santa Cruz, Canary Islands. Blahnik studied literature at the University of Geneva until 1968 when he moved to Paris to study art for a year at the Ecole du Louvre. In 1971 he went to New York where his portfolio aroused the interest of US fashion editors who encouraged him in the production of his first shoe collection that same year. Blahnik moved to London in 1971 and in 1973 opened 'Zapata', his first shop. He combines handcraftsmanship with modern techniques, employing a wide range of materials and vivid colours with equal flair to create ethereal footwear which blends elegance and fantasy.

Body Map Designer label. David Holah born 1958 in London, England; Stevie Stewart born 1958 in London, England. Both designers studied at Middlesex Polytechnic until 1982, when they formed the company Body Map in London. One of the brightest design teams of the 1980s, they produced innovative, witty garments which were loose and layered, predominantly in black, white or cream.

Comme des Garçons See **Kawakubo, Rei**

Conran, Jasper 1959–. Designer. Born London, England. Conran attended Parsons School of Art and Design in New York until 1977, when he worked for a short time as a designer at Fiorucci. He then returned to London and created a womenswear collection for Henri Bendel, the New York department store. In 1977 he worked as a consultant for the British firm Wallis before launching his first collection the following year. His basic style has remained constant – a practical simplicity of design using quality fabrics to produce a comfortable and easy fit.

Ellis, Perry 1940–86. Designer. Born Portsmouth, Virginia, USA. Ellis completed a BA in business studies at the College of William and Mary in Williamsburg, Virginia, and an MA in retailing at New York University, graduating in 1963. He worked until 1967 as a sportswear buyer for Miller & Rhoads department store in Richmond, Virginia, before becoming design director for John Meyer of Norwich, New York, and, in 1974, sportswear designer for the Vera companies, where he was given his own label. He started his own company in 1980. Ellis's clothes had the casual ease of sportswear and captured the essence of the American look. His womenswear was playful yet graceful – smart coats and trousers, often cut on mannish lines.

Galliano, John 1960–. Designer. Born Gibraltar. Galliano trained at St Martin's School of Art in London, graduating in 1984 with a highly acclaimed final-year collection inspired by the French Revolution. Part of a new breed of avant-garde British designers which emerged in the 1980s, he has dedicated himself to pushing fashion forward by learning from the past. His innovative and exciting designs are historically influenced, yet highly contemporary. A diverse mixture of cultures and epochs, materials and colours combine in his clothes to produce an entirely new look.

Gaultier, Jean-Paul 1952–. Designer. Born Paris, France. At the age of 17 Gaultier sent sketches to several couture houses and in 1970 was invited to work for Cardin for one year. He then designed for Jacques Esterel and Jean Patou, among others. In 1977 he set up his own company, producing witty, anarchic fashions which revamped Parisian couture by injecting flea-market kitsch and London streetstyle. He has developed a reputation for challenging accepted gender boundaries.

Gigli, Romeo 1950–. Designer. Born Bologna, Italy. Gigli studied architecture. He challenged the tailored traditions of Italian fashion with his first collection in 1984, a bohemian array of long, languorous dresses in sober colours. Integral to his designs is a classicism that lends a subtlety and balance to each garment. In the 1980s his collections were based on dance clothes – stretch fabrics were shaped to create a body-skimming purity of cut.

Hamnett, Katharine 1948–. Designer. Born Gravesend, England. Hamnett attended St Martin's School of Art in London, graduating in 1969. She worked freelance for European and Japanese firms until she set up her own company in 1979. For early collections she produced functional garments based on traditional workwear. In the 1980s she became famous for her 'Choose Life' T-shirt collection – T-shirts printed with political and environmental slogans. In 1986, she produced a 'power dressing' collection which epitomized eighties style.

Jones, Stephen 1957–. Milliner. Born West Kirby, England. Jones trained at High Wycombe School of Art in Buckinghamshire until 1976 and at St Martin's School of Art in London until 1979. After working briefly at Lachasse, he opened his own business in 1980. His quirky, asymmetric designs reintroduced millinery to the fashion world.

Kamali, Norma 1945–. Designer. Born New York, USA. Kamali studied fashion illustration at the Fashion Institute of Technology in New York. Between 1967 and 1978 she worked as a freelance designer, opening a boutique with her husband in 1968. In the 1970s she produced extrovert, body-conscious clothes such as hot pants, gold lamé maillots and high-cut bikinis – beach fashions that became increasingly popular in the 1980s. In 1978, after her divorce, she set up the company OMO (On My Own) and in 1981 introduced her famous 'sweats', a line in sweatshirt fleece fabric for day wear, including the 'rah-rah skirt', which proved phenomenally successful.

Karan, Donna 1948–. Designer. Born Forest Hills, New York, USA. Karan trained at Parsons School of Design in New York and during her second year worked as a sketcher at Anne Klein where, after graduating, she spent almost a year before moving to Addenda. In 1968 she returned to Anne Klein and in 1969 took over from Klein, becoming co-designer for the company with Louis Dell'Olio. In 1984 she set up her own label, DKNY, which has expanded to produce accessories, beauty products and perfume as well as clothes. From the sportswear that she designed for Anne Klein to the practical stretch fabric bodysuits and bodywraps for which she is known, her aim has been to create sexy and wearable clothes for the modern woman.

Kawakubo, Rei 1942–. Designer. Born Tokyo, Japan. Kawakubo studied literature at Keio University in Tokyo. After graduating in 1964, she worked at Asahi Kasei, a Japanese textile company. In 1966 she turned freelance and introduced the Comme des Garçons label in 1969. She became famous in the late 1970s/early 1980s for her radical redefinition of womenswear. Her androgynous designs, incorporating tears, knots and slashes in unexpected places, deconstructed the conventional female silhouette. Though sombre and sexless, her clothes had a great influence on fashion in the 1980s.

Klein, Calvin 1942–. Designer. Born New York, USA. After studying at the New York Fashion Institute of Technology, Klein joined Dan Millstein in 1962 and then worked freelance until 1968 when he set up Calvin Klein Co. He became famous for his sleek, understated suits and sportswear made from natural fabrics. The late 1970s witnessed the hugely successful marketing of his 'designer label' jeans and in the 1980s his notorious advertisements for men's and women's underwear and for fragrances made him a household name worldwide. He announced his retirement in 2003.

Lacroix, Christian 1951–. Designer. Born Arles, France. Lacroix attended the Sorbonne in Paris where in 1976 he completed a course in museum studies. From 1978 to 1980 he worked with Paulin at Hermès and in 1981 became artistic director at Patou. In 1987 he opened his own couture and ready-to-wear house in Paris. Lacroix creates bold designs: exotic and unusual combinations of luxurious materials and vivid colours, influenced by his frequent forays into museums and markets as well as by the Provence of his childhood. He has reintroduced such fashion staples as the frou-frou petticoat and puffball skirt, and has revitalized couture as a source of inspiration for the ready-to-wear industry.

Lagerfeld, Karl 1938–. Designer. Born Hamburg, Germany. Lagerfeld was employed by Balmain at the age of 17, after winning a design competition sponsored by the International Wool Secretariat. In 1958 he became art director at Patou and one year later began to work freelance for several design houses, including Chloé, Krizia and Fendi. Lagerfeld made a considerable impact on 1970s fashions with his innovative ideas, two of which were to dye furs in vibrant colours and to remove the linings from fur coats, making them more supple and lightweight. At Chloé he became renowned for feminine evening wear of the highest quality. From 1983, as design director of Chanel, he combined the company's hallmark tweed suits and gilt buttons with modern, streetstyle elements to create the characteristic blend of stylishness and impudence that has informed all his work.

Lauren, Ralph (Ralph Lipschitz) 1939–. Designer. Born New York, USA. While studying business at City College in New York, Lauren worked for Bloomingdales and Brooks Brothers, among others. Appointed designer for Beau Brummell Neckwear in 1967, he created 'Polo', a line of luxury handmade ties. In 1968 he began designing menswear for the Polo division. Womenswear was added in 1971. In 1972 he launched his own label, employing high-quality tweeds and fine cotton to create an elegant look redolent of F. Scott Fitzgerald's America. He incorporated other facets of America's past into his 'prairie look' of 1978, based on fringed leather jackets, full-sleeved cotton blouses and denim skirts worn over white petticoats, and into his 'frontier fashion' of the 1980s, with its hooded capes and ruffled blouses. His work is informed by the belief that fashion should be timeless.

Missoni, Ottavio and Rosita Knitwear designers. Ottavio born 1921 in Dalmatia, Yugoslavia; Rosita born 1931 in Lombardy, Italy. After founding the Missoni company in 1953, the couple produced their first knitwear collection for the Rinascente stores in 1954 and launched their own label in 1958. They became well known in the 1970s for their fluid, boldly patterned dresses, coats and sweaters which restored the fashion world's interest in knitwear. Missoni is known for sophisticated knitting techniques and an artistic blending of colour. Both modern and classic, their designs became status symbols in the 1970s and 1980s.

Miyake, Issey 1938–. Designer. Born Hiroshima, Japan. Miyake graduated in 1964 from Tama University in Tokyo. In 1965 he moved to Paris to study at the Ecole de la Chambre Syndicale de la Haute Couture. He then worked for Laroche and Givenchy before joining Geoffrey Beene in New York in 1969. Since showing his first collection in New York in 1971, he has become well known for highly original garments, many of which can be draped around the body in different ways. Using traditional Japanese techniques of layering fabric, he explores texture and structure with

unusual materials such as moulded plastic and woven bamboo. His sculptural designs are timeless.

Montana, Claude 1949–. Designer. Born Paris, France. Montana began his career selling handmade papier-mâché jewelry decorated with rhinestones in London street-markets. His designs appeared in British *Vogue*. When he returned to Paris in 1972 he worked for MacDouglas and Complice, founding his own house in 1979. He produces tough, masculine garments, often in leather. The Montana aesthetic of designing assertive women's clothing without sacrificing the female form contributed to the evolution of the power look of the mid-1980s.

Moschino, Franco 1950–94. Designer. Born Abbiategrasso, Italy. Moschino studied fine art at the Accademia di Belle Arti in Milan from 1967 to 1969, then worked as an illustrator on various magazines. From 1972 to 1977 he was an illustrator for Versace. After designing eleven collections for Cadette, he opened his own company in 1983. Moschino combined basic shapes and traditional methods with irreverent, ironic, often surrealistic imagery to create clothes designed to poke fun at the fashion industry – a black mini-skirt hemmed with plastic fried eggs, for example.

Mugler, Thierry 1948–. Designer. Born Strasbourg, France. In 1966 Mugler joined Gudule boutique in Paris as assistant designer. In 1973 he created a collection under the label 'Café de Paris' and set up his own house in 1974. Strongly influenced by Hollywood glamour as well as science fiction and sexual fetishism, he produced clinging, theatrical clothes which can either be highly minimalist or vampy and ornate. In 1977 he was one of the first designers to use padded shoulders and in the 1980s he employed these, along with tight skirts and armour-like corsetry, to create a look that exuded sexual power.

Ozbek, Rifat 1954–. Designer. Born Istanbul, Turkey. Ozbek moved to England in 1970. He studied architecture at Liverpool University, followed by fashion design at St Martin's School of Art in London, graduating in 1977. In 1978 he worked with Walter Albini for Trell, Milan, and in 1980 became a designer for Monsoon, London. In 1984 he established his own company. In a luxurious combination of ethnicity and London streetstyle, he embellished the classic shapes of Western couture with decorative references to other cultures. He was best known in the mid-1980s for his richly embroidered black cocktail suits and, later in the decade, for his sarong skirts, midriff tops and hipster trousers.

Rabanne, Paco 1934–. Designer. Born

San Sebastian, Spain. Rabanne's mother was chief seamstress at Balenciaga in Spain. His family moved to France during the Spanish Civil War and Rabanne studied architecture at the Ecole des Beaux-Arts, Paris, graduating in 1964. He started his career designing plastic jewelry and buttons for Balenciaga, Dior and Givenchy. In 1965 he applied his experience in plastics to dressmaking and continued to experiment with the use of innovative fabrics. Preferring the title of engineer to that of couturier, he makes dresses out of metal discs, chains, paper – even aluminium. He frequently designs costumes for cinema, theatre and ballet.

Saint Laurent, Yves 1936–. Designer. Born Oran, Algeria. In 1954 Saint Laurent won first prize for a cocktail dress design in a competition held by the International Wool Secretariat. In 1955 he began working for Dior, taking over the house at the age of 21 when Dior died. Though hugely popular, his youthful style did not please Dior's more conventional clientele and in 1961 he was replaced by Marc Bohan. The following year he established his own house and in 1966 introduced his ready-to-wear line, 'Rive Gauche'. Famous for his feminizing of the male wardrobe, he has produced many of the sophisticated and innovative classics of post-war women's style, including his influential 'smoking' jackets, see-through blouses, shirt dresses and safari jackets. His collections in the late 1970s and 1980s, showing full skirts, harem trousers and tunics in vivid colours, brought ethnic dressing to haute couture. He announced his retirement in 2002.

Smith, Paul 1946–. Designer. Born Nottingham, England. Smith started his career at 18, working in a clothing warehouse. In 1970 he opened in Nottingham one of the first shops outside London to stock designer clothing. He then took evening courses and began designing his own clothes. In 1976 he became consultant to an Italian manufacturer and to the International Wool Secretariat, and launched the Paul Smith label later the same year. In 1979 he opened his first London shop. His simple, stylish clothes in offbeat patterns and colours for both men and women are widely popular. In the 1980s he was responsible for the revival of boxer shorts and the Filofax.

Ungaro, Emanuel 1933–. Designer. Born Aix-en-Provence, France. Ungaro trained in his parents' tailoring firm and then moved to Paris in 1955. He worked for Maison Camps until he joined Balenciaga in 1958, and in 1962 he moved to Courrèges. Three years later he founded his own house, producing such futuristic designs as angular coats, thigh-high boots and

metal bras. In the 1970s and 1980s his clothes became more supple. Ungaro often experiments with rich, boldly printed materials and contrasting textures to create majestic, billowing garments influenced by his mentor, Balenciaga.

Versace, Gianni 1946–97. Designer. Born Calabria, Italy. In the early 1970s Versace worked freelance for Genny, Complice and Callaghan. He developed a reputation for evening wear, leatherwear and leather-trimmed knitwear. In 1978 he founded his own company. Versace designed sensuous, clinging garments, often cut on the bias. He explored the use of different textures and patterns, introducing a lightweight aluminium-mesh cloth in 1982. His collections were bold, sexy and modern, and combined classical craftsmanship with innovative experimentation. After his death, his sister, Donatella, took over as designer.

Westwood, Vivienne 1941–. Designer. Born Derbyshire, England. Westwood attended Harrow Art School for one term, leaving to become a teacher. In 1971 she began designing for the shop that she opened in Chelsea with Malcolm McLaren, variously known as 'Let it Rock', 'Too Fast to Live, Too Young to Die', 'Sex', 'Seditionaries' and 'World's End'. In 1981 she presented the 'Pirate' collection, her first London catwalk show, and in 1983 began to show in Paris, gaining a worldwide reputation. The following year her partnership with McLaren came to an end. Anarchic subversion is integral to her work, from the fetishistic 'Bondage' collection inspired by her association with the punk subculture of the 1970s, to the sexually loaded reinvention of the Victorian crinoline in 'Mini-crini', her collection for Spring/Summer 1985. Westwood continually plunders ideas from other cultures, both past and present, and twists them into rebellion.

Yamamoto, Yohji 1943–. Designer. Born Tokyo, Japan. Yamamoto studied law at Keio University. He graduated in 1966, then attended Bunka College of Fashion, Tokyo, until 1969, when he became a freelance designer. He set up his own company in 1972 and in 1977 launched his first collection in Japan. Guided by the Japanese philosophy that irregular forms are beautiful in their lack of artifice, Yamamoto, like his contemporaries Kawakubo and Miyake, rejects the conventional female fashion silhouette, creating sombre, unstructured garments that layer and drape the body. They often have oddly placed flaps and lopsided hems.

Sources for 1920s Fashion

Anderson Black, J., and Madge Garland
 A History of Fashion, 1975

Baynes, Ken, and Kate Baynes, eds
The Shoe Show: British Shoes since 1790, 1979

Blum, Stella
Everyday Clothes of the Twenties, 1981

Boucher, François
A History of Costume in the West, 1965

Bradfield, Nancy
Historical Costumes of England, 1958

Costume in Detail, 1968

Brooke, Iris
A History of English Costume, 1937

Byrde, Penelope
The Male Image: Men's Fashion in Britain 1300–1970, 1979

Carter, Ernestine
The Changing World of Fashion: 1900 to the Present, 1977

Collard, Eileen
Women's Dress in the Twenties, 1981

Contini, Mila
Fashion, 1965

Cunnington, C. Willet
English Women's Clothing in the Present Century, 1952

Cunnington, C. Willet, and Phillis Cunnington
The History of Underclothes, 1951

De Courtais, Georgine
Women's Headdress and Hairstyles, 1973

Dorner, Jane
Fashion in the Twenties and Thirties, 1973

Etherington-Smith, Meredith
Patou, 1983

Ewing, Elizabeth
History of Twentieth Century Fashion, 1974

Dress and Undress: A History of Women's Underwear, 1978
Fur in Dress, 1981

Gallery of English Costume
Weddings, 1976

Ginsburg, Madeleine
Wedding Dress 1740–1970, 1981

The Hat: Trends and Traditions, 1990

Hall-Duncan, Nancy
The History of Fashion Photography, 1979

Hamilton-Hill, Margot, and Peter Bucknell
The Evolution of Fashion, 1066–1930, 1967

Hansen, Henny Harald
Costume Cavalcade, 1956

Howell, Georgina
In Vogue: Six Decades of Fashion, 1975

Jarvis, Anthea
Brides, Wedding Clothes and Customs, 1850–1980, 1983

Langley-Moore, Doris
Fashion through Fashion Plates, 1971

Laver, James
Costume, 1963

A Concise History of Costume, 1969, revised edition 1995

Lee-Potter, Charlie
Sportswear in Vogue since 1910, 1984

Lynam, Ruth, ed.
Paris Fashion: The Great Designers and their Creations, 1972

Martin, Richard, and Harold Koda
Jocks and Nerds: Men's Style in the Twentieth Century, 1989

Mulvagh, Jane
Vogue History of 20th Century Fashion, 1988

O'Hara, Georgina
The Encyclopaedia of Fashion, 1986

Peacock, John
Fashion Sketchbook 1920–1960, 1977

Costume 1066 to the 1990s, 1986

The Chronicle of Western Costume, 1991

20th Century Fashion, 1993

Men's Fashion, 1996

Ridley, Pauline
Introduction, *Fashion Illustration All-Colour Paperback*, 1979

Robinson, Julian
The Fine Art of Fashion: An Illustrated History, 1989

Saint Laurent, Cecil
The History of Ladies' Underwear, 1968

Waugh, Norah
Corsets and Crinolines, 1954

The Cut of Women's Clothes 1600–1930, 1968

Wilcox, R. Turner
The Mode in Costume, 1942

The Dictionary of Costume, 1969

Yarwood, Doreen
English Costume: From the Second Century BC to 1950, 1952

MAGAZINES

L'Art et la mode, 1925–1927

The Bestway Bag and Scarf Book, 1924

The Bestway Magazine, 1922–1925

Fancy Needlework Illustrated, 1920–1928

The Girl's Own Paper and Women's Magazine, 1923–1927

Hutchinson's Magazine, 1926–1928

The Ladies' Field, 1920

The Lady's World, 1920–1929

Woman's Weekly, 1928–1929

DRESSMAKER MAGAZINES

The Haslam System of Dresscutting, 1928–1929

Weldon's Dressmaker, 1921–1925

Weldon's Jumpers, Blouses and Skirts, 1926–1927

WOMEN'S INSTITUTE JOURNALS

Designing and Planning Clothes, 1925

Designing with Foundation Patterns, 1920

Drafting and Pattern Designing, 1924

Draping and Designing with Scissors and Cloth, 1924

Dress Decoration and Ornament, 1925–1926

Tailored Garments, 1922

Underwear and Lingerie, 1921–1923

TRADE JOURNALS

Costume (Journal of the Costume Society)

Good Style and Make, 1920–1921

The T. Eaton Catalogue (Mail Order), 1920

Anderson Black, J., and Madge Garland
A History of Fashion, 1975

Arnold, Janet
Patterns of Fashion 2: English Women's Dresses and their Construction c. 1860–1940, 1966

Baynes, Ken, and Kate Baynes, eds.
The Shoe Show: British Shoes since 1790, 1979

Boucher, François
A History of Costume in the West, 1965

Bradfield, Nancy
Historical Costumes of England, 1958

Costume in Detail, 1968

Brooke, Iris
A History of English Costume, 1937

Byrde, Penelope
The Male Image: Men's Fashion in Britain 1300–1970, 1979

Carter, Ernestine
The Changing World of Fashion: 1900 to the Present, 1977

Contini, Mila
Fashion, 1965

Cunnington, C. Willet, and Phillis Cunnington
The History of Underclothes, 1951

English Women's Clothing in the Present Century, 1952

De Courtais, Georgine
Women's Headdress and Hairstyles, 1973

Dorner, Jane
Fashion in the Twenties and Thirties, 1973

Etherington-Smith, Meredith
Patou, 1983

Ewing, Elizabeth
Dress and Undress: A History of Women's Underwear, 1978

Fur in Dress, 1981

Gallery of English Costume
Weddings, 1976

Ginsburg, Madeleine
Wedding Dress 1740–1970, 1981

The Hat: Trends and Traditions, 1990

Hall-Duncan, Nancy
The History of Fashion Photography, 1979

Hansen, Henny Harald
Costume Cavalcade, 1956

Harrison, Michael
The History of the Hat, 1960

Howell, Georgina
In Vogue: Six Decades of Fashion, 1975

Jarvis, Anthea
Brides, Wedding Clothes and Customs, 1850–1980, 1983

Kelsall, Freda
How We Used to Live: 1936–1953, 1981

La Vine, W. Robert
In a Glamorous Fashion: The Fabulous Years of Hollywood Costume Design, 1981

Langley-Moore, Doris
Fashion through Fashion Plates, 1971

Laver, James
Costume, 1963

A Concise History of Costume, 1969, revised edition 1995

Lee-Potter, Charlie
Sportswear in Vogue since 1910, 1984

Lynam, Ruth, ed.
Paris Fashion: The Great Designers and their Creations, 1972

Martin, Richard, and Harold Koda
All-American: A Sportswear Tradition, 1985

Jocks and Nerds: Men's Style in the Twentieth Century, 1989

Mulvagh, Jane
Vogue History of 20th Century Fashion, 1988

Peacock, John
Fashion Sketchbook 1920–1960, 1977

Costume 1066 to the 1990s, 1986

The Chronicle of Western Costume, 1991

20th Century Fashion, 1993

Men's Fashion, 1996

Robinson, Julian
Fashion in the Thirties, 1978

The Fine Art of Fashion: An Illustrated History, 1989

Saint Laurent, Cecil
The History of Ladies' Underwear, 1968

Spellor, Reggie
'Scoop', What a Picture! Photographs of the Thirties and Forties, 1981

Viera, Mark A.
Hollywood Portraits: Classic Scene Stills 1929–1941, 1988

Wilcox, R. Turner
The Mode in Costume, 1942

Five Centuries of American Costume, 1963

The Dictionary of Costume, 1969

Yarwood, Doreen
English Costume: From the Second Century BC to 1950, 1952

MAGAZINES

Good Housekeeping, 1933, 1934

Leach-Way Fashions, 1931–1933

Modern Weekly, 1931

Sartorial Gazette: The Tailors' Magazine, 1930

To-Day: The New National Weekly, 1938–1939

Vogue, 1933–1937

Weldon's Ladies Journal, 1934–1937

Woman's Own, 1936–1938

Woman's Pictorial, 1939

Woman's Weekly, 1930–1934

Woman's World, 1937

PRACTICAL DRESSMAKING AND KNITTING JOURNALS

Bestway: Men's Knitted Wear, 1936, 1938

Bestway Patterns and Transfers, 1933–1934

Fashions for All, 1933

Home Fashions and Home Fashions Pattern Service, 1930–1934

Leach's Home Dressmaker, 1935

Paton's and Baldwin's Knitting Books, 1930, 1935

Roma's Pattern Book, 1937

Simplicity Pattern Book, 1938

Vogue Pattern Book, 1937, 1938, 1939

TRADE JOURNALS, CATALOGUES, ETC.

Bradley's Catalogue, Summer 1938

Bradley's Catalogue: Sale, Winter 1939

Furs of Distinction, 1934–1935

Laver, James
Beau Brummell Was Right, catalogue published by Moss Bros, 1960s

Lilley and Skinner: Shoe Catalogue, 1935–1936

Pall Mall: Fashions for Ladies, Spring 1938, Autumn 1938, Winter 1939

Perfection in Style and Quality Gentleman's Wear, 1934–1935

Portraying Gentlemen's Clothes of Character, 1933–1934

Tailor's and Outfitter's Diary, 1937

Tailored Wear for Gentlemen, Spring/Summer 1935

When Autumn Comes: Styles for Ladies' Wear, 1933, 1934

Sources for 1940s Fashion

Anderson Black, J., and Madge Garland
A History of Fashion, 1975

Baynes, Ken, and Kate Baynes, eds
The Shoe Show: British Shoes since 1790, 1979

Bradfield, Nancy
Historical Costumes of England, 1958

Brooby-Johansen, R.
Body and Clothes: An Illustrated History of Costume, 1966

Byrde, Penelope
The Male Image: Men's Fashion in Britain 1300–1970, 1979

Carter, Ernestine
The Changing World of Fashion: 1900 to the Present, 1977

Contini, Mila
Fashion, 1965

Cunnington, C. Willet
English Women's Clothing in the Present Century, 1952

Cunnington, C. Willet, and Phillis Cunnington
The History of Underclothes, 1951

De Courtais, Georgine
Women's Headdress and Hairstyles, 1973

De la Haye, Amy
The Cutting Edge: 50 Years of British Fashion 1947–1997, 1997

De Marly, Diana
Fashion for Men: An Illustrated History, 1985

Dorner, Jane
Fashion in the Forties and Fifties, 1974

Ewing, Elizabeth
Dress and Undress: A History of Women's Underwear, 1978

Fur in Dress, 1981

Gallery of English Costume
Weddings, 1976

Ginsburg, Madeleine
Wedding Dress 1740–1970, 1981

The Hat: Trends and Traditions, 1990

Hall-Duncan, Nancy
The History of Fashion Photography, 1979

Hansen, Henny Harald
Costume Cavalcade, 1956

Harrison, Michael
The History of the Hat, 1960

Howell, Georgina
In Vogue: Six Decades of Fashion, 1975

Jarvis, Anthea
Brides, Wedding Clothes and Customs, 1850–1980, 1983

Kennett, Frances
The Collector's Book of Twentieth Century Fashion, 1983

La Vine, W. Robert
In a Glamorous Fashion: The Fabulous Years of Hollywood Costume Design, 1981

Langley-Moore, Doris
Fashion through Fashion Plates, 1971

Latour, Anny
Kings of Fashion, 1958

Laver, James
Costume, 1963

Laver, James, and Amy de la Haye
Costume and Fashion: A Concise History, 1995

Lee-Potter, Charlie
Sportswear in Vogue since 1910, 1984

Lynam, Ruth, ed.
Paris Fashion: The Great Designers and their Creations, 1972

Martin, Richard, and Harold Koda
Jocks and Nerds: Men's Style in the Twentieth Century, 1989

Mulvagh, Jane
Vogue History of 20th Century Fashion, 1988

O'Hara, Georgina
The Encyclopaedia of Fashion, 1986

Peacock, John
Fashion Sketchbook 1920–1960, 1977

Costume 1066 to the 1990s, 1986

The Chronicle of Western Costume, 1991

20th Century Fashion, 1993

Men's Fashion, 1996

Polhemus, Ted
Streetstyle, 1994

Polhemus, Ted, and Lynn Proctor
Fashion and Anti-Fashion: An Anthology of Clothing and Adornment, 1978

Probert, Christina
Lingerie in Vogue since 1910, 1981

Robinson, Julian
Fashion in the Forties, 1976

The Fine Art of Fashion: An Illustrated History, 1989

Saint Laurent, Cecil
The History of Ladies' Underwear, 1968

Simon, Pedro
The Bikini, 1986

Wilcox, R. Turner
The Mode in Costume, 1942

Five Centuries of American Costume, 1963

The Dictionary of Costume, 1969

Yarwood, Doreen
English Costume: From the Second Century BC to 1950, 1952

MAGAZINES AND JOURNALS

Butterick Fashion News, London, 1940–41

Croquis Couture: Série Robes et Ensembles, Créations Eté, Lyons, 1949

Fashion: Lorraine Fashion Studios, New York, 1949

Fashions and Fabrics, London, 1948–1949

Garment Fashion: Coat and Suit Edition, New York, 1945

Glamour, New York, 1948

Harper's Bazaar, London, 1940–1949

Home Fashions, London, 1940–1945

Illustrated, London, 1948

Mademoiselle, New York, 1949

Needlework Illustrated, London, 1941–1946

Les Premiers Dessins, Paris, 1947–1949

Robes Pratiques: Revue Périodique, Paris, 1949

Sartorial Gazette, London, 1940

Stitchcraft, London, 1940–1943

Vogue, London, 1940–1949

Vogue Pattern Book, London, 1940–1943

Weldon Fashion Series, London, 1940–1945

Woman's Weekly, London, 1947–1949

Anderson Black, J., and Madge Garland
A History of Fashion, 1975

Baynes, Ken, and Kate Baynes, eds.
The Shoe Show: British Shoes since 1790, 1979

Boucher, François
A History of Costume in the West, 1965

Bradfield, Nancy
Historical Costumes of England, 1958

British Millinery Magazine
British Millinery Exhibition Catalogue, 1957

Brooke, Iris
A History of English Costume, 1937

Byrde, Penelope
The Male Image: Men's Fashion in Britain 1300–1970, 1979

Carter, Ernestine
The Changing World of Fashion: 1900 to the Present, 1977

Contini, Mila
Fashion, 1965

De Courtais, Georgine
Women's Headdress and Hairstyles, 1973

Dorner, Jane
Fashion in the Forties and Fifties, 1974

Drake, Nicholas
The Fifties in Vogue, 1987

Ewing, Elizabeth
History of Twentieth Century Fashion, 1974

Dress and Undress: A History of Women's Underwear, 1978

Fur in Dress, 1981

Fashion Institute of Technology, New York
All-American: A Sportswear Tradition, 1985

Gallery of English Costume
Weddings, 1976

Ginsburg, Madeleine
Wedding Dress 1740–1970, 1981

The Hat: Trends and Traditions, 1990

Hall-Duncan, Nancy
The History of Fashion Photography, 1979

Howell, Georgina
In Vogue: Six Decades of Fashion, 1975

Jarvis, Anthea
Brides, Wedding Clothes and Customs, 1850–1980, 1983

Kelsall, Freda
How We Used to Live: 1936–1953, 1981

Lee-Potter, Charlie
Sportswear in Vogue since 1910, 1984

Lynam, Ruth, ed.
Paris Fashion: The Great Designers and their Creations, 1972

Mulvagh, Jane
Vogue History of 20th Century Fashion, 1988

O'Hara, Georgina
The Encyclopaedia of Fashion, 1986

Peacock, John
Fashion Sketchbook 1920–1960, 1977

Costume 1066 to the 1990s, 1986

The Chronicle of Western Costume, 1991

20th Century Fashion, 1993

Men's Fashion, 1996

Robinson, Julian
The Fine Art of Fashion: An Illustrated History, 1989

Saint Laurent, Cecil
The History of Ladies' Underwear, 1968

Wilcox, R. Turner
The Dictionary of Costume, 1969

Yarwood, Doreen
English Costume: From the Second Century BC to 1967, 1967

MAGAZINES AND JOURNALS

British Millinery, 1956–1958

Harper's Bazaar (UK), 1950–1959

Harper's Bazaar (US), 1950–1959

Idées Détails Couture, 1953–1956
Officiel de la couleur des textiles de la mode, 1955–1957

Stella, 1955–1958

Les Tailleurs et manteaux de Paris, 1951–1954

Vanity Fair, 1951–1959

Vogue (France), 1950–1959

Vogue (UK), 1950–1959

Vogue (US), 1950–1959

Haslam, Miss G.A.
The System of Dresscutting, 1950, 1952, 1955, 1958

Sources for 1960s Fashion

Anderson Black, J., and Madge Garland
A History of Fashion, 1975

Baynes, Ken, and Kate Baynes, eds
The Shoe Show: British Shoes since 1790, 1979

Byrde, Penelope
The Male Image: Men's Fashion in Britain 1300–1970, 1979

Cardin, Pierre
Pierre Cardin: Past, Present and Future, 1990

Carter, Ernestine
The Changing World of Fashion: 1900 to the Present, 1977

Chenoune, Farid
A History of Men's Fashion, 1993

Clark, Rowena, ed. (from The Costume Institute, The Metropolitan Museum of Art, New York)
Fabulous Fashion: 1907–1967, 1967

De Courtais, Georgine
Women's Headdress and Hairstyles, 1973

De la Haye, Amy, ed.
The Cutting Edge: 50 Years of British Fashion 1947–1997, 1997

De Marly, Diana
Fashion for Men: An Illustrated History, 1985

Ewing, Elizabeth
History of Twentieth Century Fashion, 1974

Dress and Undress: A History of Women's Underwear, 1978

Fur in Dress, 1981

Fashion Institute of Technology, New York
All-American: A Sportswear Tradition, 1985

Gallery of English Costume
Weddings, 1976

Ginsburg, Madeleine
Wedding Dress 1740–1970, 1981

The Hat: Trends and Traditions, 1990

Hall-Duncan, Nancy
The History of Fashion Photography, 1979

Howell, Georgina
In Vogue: Six Decades of Fashion, 1975

Jarvis, Anthea
Brides, Wedding Clothes and Customs, 1850–1980, 1983

Kennett, Frances
The Collector's Book of Twentieth Century Fashion, 1983

La Vine, W. Robert
In a Glamorous Fashion: The Fabulous Years of Hollywood Costume Design, 1981

Langley-Moore, Doris
Fashion Through Fashion Plates 1771–1970, 1971

Lee-Potter, Charlie
Sportswear in Vogue since 1910, 1984

Lynam, Ruth, ed.
Paris Fashion: The Great Designers and their Creations, 1972

Martin, Richard, and Harold Koda
Jocks and Nerds: Men's Style in the Twentieth Century, 1989

Mulvagh, Jane
Vogue History of 20th Century Fashion, 1988

O'Hara, Georgina
The Encyclopaedia of Fashion, 1986

Peacock, John
Costume 1066 to the 1990s, 1986

The Chronicle of Western Costume, 1991

20th Century Fashion, 1993

Men's Fashion, 1996

Probert, Christina
Lingerie in Vogue since 1910, 1981

Saint Laurent, Cecil
The History of Ladies' Underwear, 1968

Simon, Pedro
The Bikini, 1986

Yarwood, Doreen
English Costume: From the Second Century BC to 1967, 1967

MAGAZINES AND JOURNALS

L'Art et la mode, Paris

Cecil Gee, Trade Journals, 1962–1965, Cecil Gee Men's Wear, London

Failsworth Hat and Cap Collection, Trade Journals, 1965–1966, Failsworth Hats (London) Ltd.

Femme Chic: Les Documents officiels de la haute couture de Paris, Paris

Harper's Bazaar, London

Honey, London

Jardin des modes, Paris

Linea Italiana, Milan

Marie France, Paris

L'Officiel de la couture et de la mode de Paris, Paris

Queen, London

Sir, Men's International Fashion Journal, Amsterdam

Vogue, London

Vogue, New York

Vogue, Paris

Vogue Pattern Book, London, New York

Woman's Journal, London

Anderson Black, J., and Madge Garland
A History of Fashion, 1975

Baynes, Ken, and Kate Baynes, eds.
The Shoe Show: British Shoes since 1790, 1979

Cardin, Pierre
Pierre Cardin: Past, Present and Future, 1990

Chenoune, Farid
A History of Men's Fashion, 1993

De Marly, Diana
Fashion for Men: An Illustrated History, 1985

Ewing, Elizabeth
History of Twentieth Century Fashion, 1974

Dress and Undress: A History of Women's Underwear, 1978

Fur in Dress, 1981

Ginsburg, Madeleine
The Hat: Trends and Traditions, 1990

Hall-Duncan, Nancy
The History of Fashion Photography, 1979

Howell, Georgina
In Vogue: Six Decades of Fashion, 1975

Kennett, Frances
The Collector's Book of Twentieth Century Fashion, 1983

La Vine, W. Robert
In a Glamorous Fashion: The Fabulous Years of Hollywood Costume Design, 1981

Lee-Potter, Charlie
Sportswear in Vogue since 1910, 1984

Martin, Richard, and Harold Koda
Jocks and Nerds: Men's Style in the Twentieth Century, 1989

Moke, Johnny, and Jan McVeigh
Mods!, 1979

Mulvagh, Jane
Vogue History of 20th Century Fashion, 1988

O'Hara, Georgina
The Encyclopaedia of Fashion, 1986

Peacock, John
Costume 1066 to the 1990s, 1986

The Chronicle of Western Costume, 1991

20th Century Fashion, 1993

Men's Fashion, 1996

Probert, Christina
Lingerie in Vogue since 1910, 1981

Robinson, Julian
The Fine Art of Fashion: An Illustrated History, 1989

Simon, Pedro
The Bikini, 1986

MAGAZINES

Burda International, Offenburg, Germany

Elle, Paris

Fashion Knits, Paton's Knitwear Magazine, Bradford and London

Fashion Weekly Newspaper, London

Girl About Town, London

G.Q., Gentleman's Quarterly, London

Harper's Bazaar, Milan

Harpers and Queen, London

Moditalia, Florence

19, IPC Magazines Ltd, London

Nova, IPC Magazines Ltd, London

L'Officiel de la couture et de la mode de Paris, Paris

Simplicity Pattern Book, London

Sir, Men's International Fashion Journal, Amsterdam

L'Uomo Vogue, Milan

View, Men's Fashion, London

Vogue, London

Vogue, New York

Vogue, Paris

Vogue Patterns, New York and London

Woman's Journal, London

Sources for 1980s Fashion

Cardin, Pierre
Pierre Cardin: Past, Present and Future, 1990

Carnegy, Vicky
Fashions of a Decade: The 1980s, 1990

Chenoune, Farid
A History of Men's Fashion, 1993

De Courtais, Georgine
Women's Headdress and Hairstyles, 1973

De la Haye, Amy
The Cutting Edge: 50 Years of British Fashion 1947–1997, 1997

De Marly, Diana
Fashion for Men: An Illustrated History, 1985

Ewing, Elizabeth
Fur in Dress, 1981

Ginsburg, Madeleine
The Hat: Trends and Traditions, 1990

Kennett, Frances
The Collector's Book of Twentieth Century Fashion, 1983

Laver, James, and Amy de la Haye
Costume and Fashion: A Concise History, 1995

Lee-Potter, Charlie
Sportswear in Vogue since 1910, 1984

Martin, Richard, and Harold Koda
Jocks and Nerds: Men's Style in the Twentieth Century, 1989

Miyake, Issey
Issey Miyake: Photographs by Irving Penn, 1988

Mulvagh, Jane
Vogue History of 20th Century Fashion, 1988

O'Hara, Georgina
The Encyclopaedia of Fashion, 1986

Peacock, John
Costume 1066 to the 1990s, 1986

The Chronicle of Western Costume, 1991

20th Century Fashion, 1993

Men's Fashion, 1996

Polhemus, Ted
Street Style, 1994

Simon, Pedro
The Bikini, 1986

Ribeiro, Aileen
Dress and Morality, 1986

Robinson, Julian
The Fine Art of Fashion: An Illustrated History, 1989

MAGAZINES

Donna, Milan

Elle, London

For Him, London

G.Q., Gentleman's Quarterly, New York

Harpers & Queen (Harpers & Queen International), London

Harrods Magazine, London 1985–1987

L'Officiel de la couture et de la mode de Paris, Paris

Per Lui, Milan

Sposabella, Milan

L'Uomo Vogue, Milan

Vogue, London

Vogue, New York

Vogue, Paris

Vogue Italia, Milan

Vogue Patterns, London

Vogue Patterns, New York

CATALOGUES

Ciao Sportswear, London, Spring/Summer 1985

Costume Changes: Jewellery Department, 1987

Harrods, Grosvenor Fur Collection, London, 1982–1985

International Menswear Fair Catalogue, 1984

Lingerie Luxury: Lingerie Collection, 1987

Marc O'Polo, London, Spring/Summer 1985

Martinique Club Adventure, London, 1988

Relay: Menswear, Summer 1985

Acknowledgments

I would like to thank Liz Salmon, Assistant Keeper of Arts, Stoke-on-Trent City Museum and Art Gallery, for the use of the museum's archives and for help and assistance with my research.

Thanks are also due to Janet Dunham, of Zero Antique Clothes Shop in Newcastle-under-Lyme, for her kindnesses and help, and for the loan of her many costume magazines.

Lastly, I extend my gratitude to the Yale School of Art and Design, Wrexham, Clwyd, for the use of their facilities.